TRANSLATION, BIOPOLITICS, COLONIAL DIFFERENCE

Other titles in series:

Specters of the West and the Politics of Translation
edited by Naoki Sakai and Yukiko Hanawa
(2000)

"Race" Panic and the Memory of Migration
edited by Meaghan Morris and Brett de Bary
(2001)

Impacts of Modernities
edited by Thomas Lamarre and Kang Nae-hui
(2004)

TRACES
A MULTILINGUAL SERIES OF CULTURAL THEORY AND TRANSLATION

Translation, Biopolitics, Colonial Difference

Edited by
Naoki Sakai and Jon Solomon

HONG KONG UNIVERSITY PRESS

Hong Kong University Press
The University of Hong Kong
Pok Fu Lam Road
Hong Kong
https://hkupress.hku.hk

© Traces, inc. 2006

ISBN 978-962-209-773-5 (Hardback)
ISBN 978-962-209-774-2 (Paperback)

All rights reserved. No portion of this publication may be reproduced or transmitted in any form or by any means, electronic or mechanical, including photocopying, recording, or any information storage or retrieval system, without prior permission in writing from the publisher.

British Library Cataloguing-in-Publication Data
A catalogue record for this book is available from the British Library.

Digitally Printed

Statement of Purpose

Traces, a multilingual book series of cultural theory and translation, calls for comparative cultural theory that is attentive to global traces in the theoretical knowledge produced in specific locations and that explores how theories are themselves constituted in, and transformed by, practical social relations at diverse sites. We eagerly seek theory produced in disparate sites, including that critical work that has often emerged in a hybrid relation to North American or West European "theory" as a result of the colonialism and quasi-colonialism of the past few centuries. We will publish research, exchanges, and commentaries that address a multilingual audience concerned with all the established disciplines of the social sciences and humanities, in addition to such cross-disciplinary fields as cultural studies, feminist and queer studies, critical race theory, or post-colonial studies. At the same time, *Traces* aims to initiate a different circulation of intellectual conversation and debate in the world, a different geopolitical economy of theory and empirical data, and a different idea of theory itself.

Editions of *Traces* are published in Chinese, English, Japanese, and Korean. Each contributor is expected to be fully aware that she or he is writing for and addressing a heterogeneous and multilingual audience: in the manner of a local intellectual under a colonial regime, every contributor is expected to speak with a forked tongue. *Traces* is an international series. Yet the international space that it generates and sustains, and to which contributors as well as readers are invited, is fundamentally different from that of an internationalism based on one major language's subjugation of other minor languages. Indeed, it is hoped that the social space in which we argue and converse will challenge the space of the nation and national language. Constituted in processes of translation, among multiple languages and registers, this social space is actualized in our exchanges and debates, and in debates among authors, commentators, translators, and readers.

Senior Editor
Meaghan MORRIS, Hong Kong

Steering Committee
Brett de BARY, Ithaca*
DING Naifei, Chung-li
GAO Jianping, Beijing*
Yukiko HANAWA, New York*
KANG Nae-Hui, Seoul*
KIM Eun-shil, Seoul
Toshiaki KOBAYASHI, Berlin
KOJIMA Kiyoshi, Tokyo*
J. Victor KOSCHMANN, Ithaca*
Thomas LAMARRE, Ithaca*
Brian MASSUMI, Montréal
Meaghan MORRIS, Hong Kong
Yann MOULIER BOUTANG, Paris
Naoki SAKAI, Ithaca*
UKAI Satoshi, Tokyo
WANG Hui, Beijing
WANG Xiaoming, Shanghai

Editorial Collective
Éric ALLIEZ, Paris
Ien ANG, Sydney
Dipesh CHAKRABARTY, Chicago
Pheng CHEAH, Berkeley
CHIEN Sechin Y. S., Taipei

Leo CHING, Durham
Chungmoo CHOI, Irvine
CHOI Jungwoon, Seoul
Rey CHOW, Providence
Kenneth DEAN, Montréal
FU Daiwie, Hsinchu
Christopher FYNSK, Aberdeen
Johnny GOLDING, London
Elizabeth GROSZ, New York
Michael HARDT, Durham
HUANG Ping, Beijing
KANG Sangjung, Tokyo
John Namjun KIM, Riverside
KIM Soyoung, Seoul
John KRANIAUSKAS, London
LAW Wing Sang, Hong Kong
Oliver MARCHART, Basel
Alberto MOREIRAS, Durham
Antonio NEGRI, Paris
OKA Mari, Osaka
Peter OSBORNE, London
SAKIYAMA Masaki, Kobe
Ulrich J. SCHNEIDER, Wolfenbüttel
Gabriele SCHWAB, Irvine
SHIM Kwang-hyun, Seoul
Jon SOLOMON, Taipei
TOMIYAMA Ichiro, Kyoto
Thongchai WINICHAKUL, Madison
YU Chih-Chung, Hsinchu

Advisory Collective
Benedict ANDERSON, Ithaca
Etienne BALIBAR, Paris
Tani BARLOW, Seattle
Anne BERGER, Ithaca
Nora BIERICH, Berlin
Sandra BUCKLEY, Montréal
CHEN Kuan-Hsing, Hsinchu
CHO Haejoang, Seoul
CHU Wan-wen, Taipei
CHUA Beng Huat, Singapore
Catherine HALL, London
Stuart HALL, London
Harry HAROOTUNIAN, New York
IYOTANI Toshio, Tokyo
Kojin KARATANI, Hyogo
Benjamin LEE, Houston
LEE Chong-Hwa, Tokyo
LIAO Pinghui, Hsinchu
Tessa MORRIS-SUZUKI, Canberra
Timothy MURRAY, Ithaca
Jean-Luc NANCY, Strasbourg
NARITA Ryûichi, Tokyo
James SIEGEL, Ithaca
Gayatri C. SPIVAK, New York
ZHANG Shengyong, Nanjing

[Associate Editors (*) and the other members of the Steering Committee are also members of the Editorial Collective.]

CONTENTS

Statement of Purpose · v

List of Editors · vi

Contributors · xi

Introduction: Addressing the Multitude of Foreigners, Echoing Foucault · 1
    Naoki Sakai and Jon Solomon

PART 1: TRANSLATION AND PHILOSOPHY

Translation as Dissemination: Multilinguality and De-Cathexis · 39
    Morinaka Takaaki
    — translated from Japanese by Lewis Harrington

Translated from the Philosophical: Philosophical · 55
Translatability and the Problem of a Universal Language
    François Laruelle
    — translated from French by Ray Brassier

From a Postcolonial to a Non-Colonial Theory of Translation · 73
    Sathya Rao

Contents

Part 2: Sovereign Police

A Sovereign Game: On Kinji Fukusaku's *Battle Royale* (2001)   97
   Frédéric Neyrat
   — translated from French by Thomas Lamarre

Globalized-In-Security: The Field and the Ban-opticon   109
   Didier Bigo
   — translated from French by Anne McKnight

The Market and the Police: Finance Capital in the Permanent Global War   157
   Brett Neilson

Part 3: A New Imperial Nomos

The Rule of Imperialism and the Global-State in Gestation   175
   Jacques Bidet
   — translated from French by Jon Solomon

Carl Schmitt and War: On *The* Nomos *of the Earth*   211
   Yamada Hiroaki
   — translated from Japanese by Joshua Young

Against the Closure of the World: What Is at Stake in the New "Great Transformation"   235
   Yoshihiko Ichida and Yann Moulier Boutang
   — translated from French by Christine LaMarre

Part 4: The Multitude and the Foreigners

The So-Called/Self-Saying People   251
   Jean-Luc Nancy
   — translated from French by Richard Calichman

Contents

Anthropos and Humanitas: Two Western Concepts of "Human Being" 259
Nishitani Osamu
— *translated from Japanese by Trent Maxey*

Ecocentric Movies: Bisexual and Italian Transculturations in Turn-of-the-Millennium Cinema 275
Serena Anderlini-D'Onofrio

Bodies and Tongues: Alternative Modes of Translation in Francophone African Literature 295
Tobias Warner

A Rift in Empire? The Multitudes in the Face of War 327
Brian Holmes

APPENDIX

Sovereign Police, Global Complicity: Addressing the Multitude of Foreigners 333
Naoki Sakai and Jon Solomon

Submission Guidelines 337

Traces Publishers 339

Contributors

Serena ANDERLINI-D'ONOFRIO is a Professor at the University of Puerto Rico at Mayagüez. Her book *The "Weak" Subject: On Modernity, Eros, and Women's Playwriting* (1998) is a comparative study of women's authorship in the modern theater. Its Italian translation has appeared for Manifesto Libri by the title *Due in una* (2004). Recently, Anderlini-D'Onofrio has guest edited two issues of *The Journal of Bisexuality: Women and Bisexuality: A Global Perspective* (June, 2003); and *Plural Loves: Designs for Bi and Poly Living* (February 2005), both of which are also available as books by Haworth Press. Her memoir, *Eros, A Memoir of Bisexuality and Transculturalism,* will also appear in 2005 with Haworth Press. Her English translation of Luigi Anderlini's poetry collection, *A Lake for the Heart*, will appear with Gradiva Publications also in 2005. Her book of applied cultural theory on the politics of love and the globe's future is in preparation for an academic press. Her other articles include *Diacritics, DisClosure, Literature, Consciousness, and the Arts, Nebula, VIA: Voices in Italian Americana, Theater, Women and Language,* and *Women's Studies International Forum.* She is the co-translator of *In Spite of Plato*, a book of feminist theory by Italian philosopher Adriana Cavarero, for Polity Press, 1995.

Jacques BIDET is Professor Emeritus at the University of Paris X (Nanterre) where he is a director of research in political philosophy. The senior editor of a journal and a book series both titled *Actuel Marx* (Paris: PUF), he is also president of the International Marx Congress, which convened its fourth congress in 2004. Notable among his many works is a trilogy devoted to the theory of capitalist modernity: *Théorie générale, théorie du droit, de l'économie et de la politique (A General*

Theory: a Theory of Law, Economy, and Politics, Paris: PUF, 1999), *Que faire du Capital?* (*What to do with Capital?* Paris: PUF, 2001), and *Explication et reconstruction du Capital* (*Explanation and Reconstruction of Capital*, Paris: PUF, 2004). *Actuel Marx* can be accessed on the web at http://netx.u-paris10.fr/actuelmarx/

Didier BIGO is Professor of International Relations at Sciences-Po, Paris, since 1988, and senior researcher at CERI. He is Director of the Center for Study of Conflict and the editor of the quarterly journal *Cultures & Conflicts* (Paris: L'Harmattan), and also edits once a year in *Alternatives* (Lynne Rienner ed). He has books and articles in the field of sociology of mobilisation and conflict, sociology of police and armies at the European level, and in IR theory, especially critical security studies. He is the scientific coordinator of the FR5 program of the EC Commission ELISE (European Liberty and Security) and the 6PCRD (CHALLENGE) which both deal with the relation between security and liberty and the illiberal practices of the liberal regimes. ELISE can be accessed on the web at http://www.libertysecurity.org

Ray BRASSIER works at the Centre for Research in Modern European Philosophy at the University of Middlesex, London. In addition to numerous English translations of Alain Badiou and François Laruelle, he has published articles on philosophy and non-philosophy, including, 'Behold the Non-Rabbit. Kant, Quine, Laruelle' in *Pli: The Warwick Journal of Philosophy,* Vol. 12, *What is Materialism?* 2001. His unpublished Ph.D. dissertation, *Alien Theory: the Decline of Materialism in the Name of Matter* (2001), can be accessed on the web at http://www.cinestatic.com/trans-mat/Brassier/ALIENTHEORY.pdf. He is currently working on a book about nihilism called *Nihil Unbound: Philosophy in the Light of Extinction.*

Richard F. CALICHMAN is currently an Assistant Professor of Japanese Studies at the City College of New York, CUNY. His publications include *Takeuchi Yoshimi: Displacing the West* (Cornell University East Asia Series, 2004), *What is Modernity?: Writings of Takeuchi Yoshimi* (Columbia University Press, 2005), and *Contemporary Japanese Thought* (Columbia University Press, 2005). He is currently at work editing a volume on wartime Japanese thought and politics.

Contributors

Lewis HARRINGTON is a Ph.D. candidate in the field of East Asian Literature at Cornell University and an adjunct lecturer at the University of Pennsylvania. He is writing a dissertation on wartime Japanese philosophical discourses of production, technology, and subjectivity. He is also translating essays for a Miki Kiyoshi Reader and finishing a translation of Miki's Kôsôryoku no ronri (Logic of Imagination).

Brian HOLMES is an essayist, art critic and activist, based in Paris where he collaborates with the French journal *Multitudes*. He holds a Ph.D. in Romance Languages and Literatures from the University of California at Berkeley and is the author of a collection of essays, *Hieroglyphs of the Future: Art and Politics in a Networked Era* (Zagreb: WHW/Arkzin, 2002). The majority of his work can be accessed at: www.u-tangente.org

Yoshihiko ICHIDA is an Associate Professor of Social Thought at Kobe University in Kobe, Japan. He is well known in Japan for his commentary and translation of Louis Althusser's work. Ichida co-translated Althusser's *Écrits Philosophiques et Politiques I & II* into Japanese (Tokyo: Fujiwsara Shoten, 1993). His own publications include: *Tôsô no shisô* (*The Thought of Battle*, Tokyo: Heibon-sha, 1993) and *Sensô — wâdogeimu, shisô, rekishi, sôzôryoku* (*War — Word Game, Thought, History, Imagination*, Tokyo: Shinyô-sha, 1989). He is a member of the editorial collective for *Multitudes* (Paris: Exils) and has penned numerous articles on political philosophy.

Christine LAMARRE is a freelance translator who lives in Montreal.

Thomas LAMARRE is an Associate Professor at McGill University and author of *Uncovering Heian Japan: An Archaeology of Sensation and Inscription* and *Shadows on the Screen: Tanizaki Jun'ichirô on Cinema and Oriental Aesthetics*.

François LARUELLE, born in 1937, is the founder of "non-philosophy." He has spent his entire career at the University of Paris X (Nanterre), where he is now Professor of Contemporary Philosophy. Former Program Director at the International College of Philosophy, Paris, he has edited numerous book collections and journals. His own corpus of work has been divided into three periods, the most recent of which marks the full-fledged elaboration of his unprecedented and highly innovative project in non-philosophy. Recent publications include: *Théorie de l' étranger: science des hommes, démocratie, et non-pyschanalyse* (*A Theory of the Foreigner: Science of Men, Democracy, and Non-Psychoanalysis,* Paris: Kimé, 1995); *L'Ethique de l'étranger: du crime contre l'humanité* (*The Ethics of the Foreigner: On crimes against humanity,* Paris: Kimé, 2000); *Introduction au non-marxisme* (*Introduction to Non-Marxism,* Paris: Actuel Marx, 2000); and *Le Christ futur: une leçon d'hérésie* (*The Future Christ: A Lesson in Heresy,* Paris: Exils, 2002). The Organization of Non-Philosophy, a network inspired by Laruelle's non-philosophy, can be accessed on the web at: www.onphi.org

Trent MAXEY is completing his Ph.D. at Cornell University and will be Assistant Professor of History and Asian Languages and Civilization at Amherst College. An intellectual historian, his research focuses on the conceptual formation of religion and its intersection with the state-making process in nineteenth-century Japan. He is interested broadly in how the discursive operation of "religion" interacts with colonial and national formations.

Anne McKNIGHT is an assistant professor in the Department of East Asian Studies, McGill University. Her research interests are in Japanese studies and comparative literature, contemporary popular culture and theory, and Japanese moving image media.

MORINAKA Takaaki is a poet and an Associate Professor at Waseda University in Tokyo. His poetic works have been published in his collections *Shisuta Antigone no koyomi no nai haka* (*A Tomb With No Calendar for Sister Antigone,* Tokyo: Shicho-sha, 2001) and *Morinaka Takaaki shishu* (*Collected Poetry of Takaaki Morinaka,* (Tokyo: Shicho-sha, 1999). His publications on poetics and literary theory also include *Sonzai to hai — Celan, soshite Derrida igo* (*Being and Ashes — Celan, and After Derrida,* Kyoto: Jinbun Shoin, 2004), *Datsukôchiku* (*Deconstruction,* Tokyo: Iwanami Shoten, 1999), and *Han-shiteki bunpô* (*Anti-poetic Grammar,* Tokyo: Shicho-sha, 1995). He has translated a number of books from French and German into Japanese, including Jacques Derrida's *Khôra* (Tokyo: Mirai-sha, 2001) and *Le monolinguisme de l'autre* (Tokyo: Iwanami Shoten, 2001).

Contributors

Yann MOULIER BOUTANG, Professor of Economic Sciences at the University of Compiégne and at the Institute of Political Research (IEP), Paris, is at once economist, researcher, essayist, and political militant. Within the framework of the CNRS, he pursues research on the history of labor movements, slavery, wage labor, international migration, cognitive capitalism, and the impact of new technologies on new productive models and social formation. One of the first figures in France to introduce the works of the Italian *Operaismo* movement (e.g. those of Mario Tronti and Antonio Negri), he is currently senior editor of *Multitudes* (Paris: Exils). In addition to numerous collaborative works on political economy, migration, and international law, he is known for *De l'esclavage au salariat, Economie historique du salariat bridé* (*From Slavery to Wage Labor: an Economic History of the Wage-earner*, Paris: PUF, 1998). *Multitudes* can be accessed on the web at: http://multitudes.samizdat.net/

Jean-Luc NANCY, born 1940, is a Professor of Philosophy at University of Marc Bloch, Strasbourg, France, and a visiting professor at Berlin, UC San Diego, UC Irvine, and UC Berkeley. He has published numerous books, many of them translated into numerous languages, including English, Japanese and Chinese. His writings on philosophy, art, political philosophy, and religion have exercised enormous influence upon a generation of intellectuals across the globe. He is perhaps best known for his writings on sovereignty, community, and being-in-common, as well as the philosophical implications of globalization. A collection of his essays addressing the question of "the common" will soon be published in China.

Brett NEILSON is Senior Lecturer in the School of Humanities at the University of Western Sydney, where he is also a member of the Centre for Cultural Research. He is author of *Free Trade in the Bermuda Triangle ... and Other Tales of Counterglobalization* (University of Minnesota Press, 2004). He co-edited an issue of the e-journal *Borderlands* dealing with issues of sovereignty, territoriality and indigenous rights that can be accessed on the web at: http://www.borderlandsejournal.adelaide.edu.au/issues/vol1no2.html

Frédéric NEYRAT is a Program Director at the International College of Philosophy in Paris, where he conducts a seminar entitled "The Image of Capital." This seminar interrogates the notions of world, territory, image, biopolitics, risk, ecology, and so forth. He wrote his dissertation under the guidance of Jean-Luc Nancy. In addition to his *Fantasme de la communauté absolue* (*Phantasm of the Absolute Community*, Paris: L'Harmattan, 2002), he has recently published *L'image hors l'image* (*The Image Outside the Image*, Paris: Leo Scheer, 2003) and *Surexposés* (*Overexposures*, Paris: Leo Scheer, 2005).

NISHITANI Osamu was born at Aichi, Japan in 1950. After studying law at Tokyo University and French literature and philosophy at Tokyo Metropolitan University, he spent two years at University of Paris VIII (doctor course) in France. He taught literature & philosophy at Meiji-Gakuin University, Tokyo, and has been a Professor of Transcultural Studies in the Graduate School at the Tokyo University of Foreign Studies since 2000. He has translated many French authors such as Georges Bataille, Maurice Blanchot, Emmanuel Levinas, Jean-Luc Nancy & Pierre Legendre. Among his numerous books on historical and political philosophy, notable titles include: *Wonderland of Immortality* (1990, new edition 2002), *On the Age of World War* (1992), *Touch the Nocturnal Palpitation, Logics of World War* (1995), *Detachment and Displacement, Essays on a Spiritual Movement of Modernity* (1998), *The Critical phase of Universal History, Montage of Western Historical Vision* (2000), and, *What is the "War on Terror"* (2002).

Sathya RAO holds a PhD in Philosophy from University of Paris X (Nanterre), where he studied under François Laruelle. He is currently a part-time Professor at Concordia University (Department of French Studies), a postdoctoral fellow at Université de Montréal (the Department of Linguistics and Translation), and an associated researcher at the research center "Le soi et l'autre" (Université du Québec à Montréal). He is co-coordinator of the research team "Poexil" (Université de Montréal), and is the author of various articles and the organizer of conferences on subjects dealing with postcolonialism, translation, and African philosophy.

Naoki SAKAI is a Professor who teaches in the departments of Asian Studies and of Comparative Literature at Cornell University, and has published in the fields of comparative literature, comparative intellectual history, translation studies, the studies of racism and nationalism, and the histories of semiotic and literary multitude — speech, writing, corporeal expressions, calligraphic regimes, and

Contributors

ideographic traditions. His publications include: *Translation and Subjectivity* (in English, Japanese and Korean); *Voices of the Past* (in English and Japanese); *Stillbirth of the Japanese* (Japanese & Korean); *Destruction of World History* (with Nishitani Osamu in Japanese, Korean translation forthcoming). He also edited a number of volumes including *Traces* 1 (co-editing with Yukiko Hanawa) and *Deconstruction of Nationality* (with Brett de Bary and Toshio Iyotani). He has led the project of *Traces*, a multilingual series in four languages — Korean, Chinese, English, and Japanese — and served as its founding senior editor (1996–2003).

Jon SOLOMON trained at Cornell University in modern Chinese, Japanese, and French thought, has held postdoctoral fellowships in Japan, Taiwan, and the United States, and is now an Assistant Professor teaching in the Graduate Institute of Futures Studies and the French Department, Tamkang University, Taiwan. Notable among his translations of Chinese, Japanese, English, and French texts is a Chinese translation (Taipei: Laureate Books, 2003) of Jean-Luc Nancy's landmark essay, *La communauté désoeuvrée*. He is working on projects that connect the disciplinary formation of the Human Sciences to a biopolitics of translation and subjectivity in the context of colonial expropriation and violence. His publications cover four languages, including, in English, "The Sovereign Police and Knowledgeable Bodies: Liu Xiaobo's Exilic Critique" in *Positions: East Asia Cultures Critique* Vol. 10, No. 2 (Fall 2002); and "Taiwan Incorporated: A Survey of Biopolitics in the Sovereign Police's East Asian Theater of Operations," in Thomas Lamarre, Kang Nae-hui, eds., *Traces* Vol. 3.

Tobias WARNER, a recent graduate of Cornell University, adapted his BA Honor's thesis into his article in this issue of *Traces*. He has also translated a short story by Cheikh Sow, "Opportunities Abound for Young Girls," which appeared in the 2004 issue of *Two Lines: A Journal of Translation*. He currently lives in Brooklyn, NY, where he is the editor of *Boldtype*, a monthly email book review, and a contributing editor for *Flavorpill*, a weekly email magazine. He will begin graduate study in the fall of 2005.

YAMADA Hiroaki is an Associate Professor who specializes in the Studies of Language Forms and Communications at the Graduate School of General Cultural

Studies at Tokyo University in Tokyo. He studied French literature at Kyoto University, and after finishing his Master's thesis there, he went to France. At University of Paris VIII, he defended a dissertation entitled "Meaning and the Unconscious — Paul Valéry and Psychoanalysis." His publications include: *Gendai gengoron* (*Contemporary Language Studies*) (co-authored with Kenji Tachikawa, Tokyo: Shinyôsha, 1990) and *Santen Kakuho* (*Three Point Support*) (Tokyo: Shinyôsha, 2001)

Joshua YOUNG works on historical theories of theatrical performance, focusing mostly on the early modern period. He wrote his doctoral dissertation in Japanese literature on the nineteenth-century intersection of literary and street culture in the popular, urban theaters of the day, an intersection concerned specifically with the bodily performance of "talk." Young currently works as the project coordinator in the development of an on-line, multilingual, and open-source database and resource center of performing arts materials from around the world.

Introduction:
Addressing the Multitude of Foreigners, Echoing Foucault

Naoki Sakai and Jon Solomon

Since its inception, *Traces* has explicitly sought to provide readers with the elements for a strategic intervention into the neo-colonial distribution of theory and data.[1] Naturally, such a vast project requires multiple interventions, yet what is unique to *Traces*, we think, is the temporal gambit implicit in a multilingual revue. By proposing to provide, simply at the representational level, the same content at the same time to readers in several different language markets, the performative synchronicity created by *Traces* directly intervenes in the field of "linear progress" and "developmental stages" invariably favored by the powerful historical narratives of colonial modernity.

Given the four language-markets in which *Traces* is currently published, it may appear reasonable to surmise that East Asia and North America form the poles around which this synchronicity is spun into action. From the outset, however, *Traces* has taken upon itself the task of opening these poles to a third — variously European, South and Southeast Asian, African, East European, and Latin American — moment. Or to put it more succinctly, *Traces* has never been interested in legitimating its mission in terms of geopolitical regionalism. Accordingly, it is utterly misleading if some of our readers would take this fact alone as evidence of an unwitting reinscription of the very neo-colonial distribution of theory and temporal lag in which *Traces* initially set out to intervene! For this reason, it is essential to invite readers to recall previous moments of intellectual synchronicity in the East Asian historical experience of "theory" precisely because these moments have been palimpsestically written out (on account of the political milieu in which they were conceived). Far from being a call to rekindle the flames of a bygone era when the alternative between "Pan-Asianism vs. Socialism" marked the political choice of several generations before and after World War Two, we would intend, in a very limited fashion, to call attention to the gargantuan difficulty of articulating transnational intellectual work across the temporal schisms essential to the regime of the West-and-the-Rest. Punctual moments of synchronicity such as that seen in Tanabe Hajime's innovative, critical, yet imperialist, reading of *avant garde* European thinkers such as Martin Heidegger (in the early 1930s at a time when many so-called "Western intellectuals" might not yet have even heard the German philosopher's name) have to be understood in the context of a regime of translation and cross-reading, broadly understood, that was selective at best and quite often simply unilateral. Even today, when Tanabe's *tour de force* in "social ontology" remains untranslated,[2] and, more seriously, a professional knowledge of Japanese language is still virtually unheard of among non-ethnic philosophers, the legacy of this moment of synchronicity can only be effectively seen from the perspective of Japanese language — where it is all-too-easily recuperated by a *transnational* regime of culturalism. Among other instances of historical synchronicity buried under the historical weight of the regime of unilateral translation, Cai Yi's writings on image-thought and esthetic theory in the 1950s[3] and Takeuchi Yoshimi's writings on Lu Xun[4] are equally emblematic. To these instances we might add a whole history of translations of Buddhist texts and terms through the matrix of Humanism and the fantasy of a non-Western "other."

If French-inflected Europeanist theory draws our attention in this volume, we insist that it is part of a critical project to turn inside-out the very terms of knowledge with regard to both its positionality and the bodies that move through it. In short, we recognize the incontrovertible value of exposing theory to its "outside" — in this case, specifically the historical difference repressed by the victory of neo-Liberalism at the end of World War Two as well as the promise of international social transformation repressed by the unilateral regime of translation.

It is well known that the poststructuralist "philosophies of difference" made their mark essentially by proposing historically nuanced readings of German philosophy in light of the political cataclysms of the twentieth century. It is widely

Introduction

acknowledged that the U.S. reception of these "philosophies of difference" played a pivotal role, not just in the global dissemination of these theories outside France, but even in the acceptance grudgingly accorded to these thinkers and their theories within France. At the same time, however, the very same Europeanist disciplines in the United States responsible for the English-language dissemination of these theories unwittingly repeated the founding gesture of the philosophy being deconstructed by occasionally claiming it as their own cultural heritage and, even more gravely, by consistently managing it as their own (intellectual) property. East Asians have been readers of so-called "Western" theory for centuries, yet their readings continue to be seen as "external," both politically and epistemically. How can we continue to accept this kind of positionality?

Seen in the context of postwar East Asia, where the U.S. not only enjoyed the only real sovereignty in the region but also presided over a virtual epistemic hegemony determining the contours of legitimate knowledge in and about the region, this historical situation has meant that "theory" in the context of East Asia today is both doubly repressed and doubly intrusive. No wonder why the identification of theory with "the West" *tout court* could be seen, depending upon a logic of predetermined *positions*, as either an anti-Eurocentric gesture of resistance to, or a Eurocentric argument for, the supposed uniqueness of "the West" and "its" theory. Naturally, such gestures are themselves mutually complicit with an economy of hegemonic amnesia and reified collective memory that sustains the referential ubiquity of the West.

Needless to say, the practico-theoretical problematic of German thought, in both its revolutionary and reactionary aspects, was extremely important to both the Pan-Asianism and the Socialism of a previous era; of course, these currents and contexts were utterly delegitimized and, yes, even criminalized, during a series of political and military battles leading to the postwar consolidation of neo-Liberalism and U.S. imperial sovereignty in East Asia. The undercurrents that run among, (a) the absence of critique about postwar Germany, which sat in a minority position relative to the U.S., over the way the U.S.-led occupation instituted a subtle, reciprocal repression of historical difference — not just by emphasizing Economy as the sole source of political legitimacy but also by reifying the very concept of "the West" (by assuming Germany's inalienable cultural position within it as a bastion of defense against Eurasian Communism) — thus eliminating a question that had previously been so obsessive for modern German thought, (b) the postwar Franco-European deconstruction of modern philosophy and its political derivations, (c) the U.S. reception and dissemination into East Asia of these historically-informed "deconstructions" through the circuits of global English against which national imaginaries (including those of both postwar Europe and East Asia) were figured, and (d) the prewar East Asian projects of resistance and theory that aimed — in very complex and often highly compromised ways — precisely at propagating and fracturing, at the same time, the dominance of "the West" and "Western Theory," are even today extremely turbulent and still highly opaque. Here is where it is essential not to stop at re-presenting these past differences, but also to continue on and discover the extent to which contemporary theory itself — inasmuch as it is tethered, through established disciplinary divisions, historical narratives of heritage and a plethora of institutional practices, to specific geopolitical regions like France or the United States — remains inscribed in the relations of domination codified in the global positioning system of macro-spatiality.

The legacy of macro-spatiality (i.e., nations, regions, continents, worlds, etc.) bequeathed to us by the colonial modernity is, it bears repeating, not a faithful rendition of some supposedly transcendental principle (such as the national sovereignty or the uniqueness of the West), but rather a historically specific form of the appropriation of the Common. It combines a structural expropriation of the means of production with a systemic expropriation of place, doubly inscribing the logic of private property into a regime of communal macro-spatiality (typically associated with the nation-State, but also extending, in our perspective, to the biopolitical forms of control such as nationalized language). Inasmuch as *Traces* is committed to a project joining the disparate temporalities of simultaneous translation and theoretical ex-position, it presents an unusual opportunity to intervene in the geopolitical regime of macro-spatial private property codified in the global flows of knowledge. In other words, *Traces* offers a rare, performative chance to reconfigure the relation between knowledge and the Common in a materialist way that does not presuppose the latter as either essence or teleology.

Hence, we would like to preface this volume by way of describing the politics of knowledge and the social relations of production in relation to a global regime of translation that opens onto the problem of the Common. Although this essay is not an introduction in the conventional sense that details the significance of each individual contribution, it does provide an introduction to a unified vision

Introduction

of the Common — as opposed to a unitary "common vision" — that brings these essays together within the context of our *Traces*.

****

Let us take the point of departure from a dialogue between Michel Foucault and Zen monks in Japan that highlights the problematic relation between anthropological and epistemological regions at the heart of Foucault's Occidentalism.[5] Launching a critical evaluation of the Occidentalism of an important thinker who has remained an inspiration throughout much of this volume, we are not concerned aboutdelimiting his work within the fatigued framework of debates over "Western theory" and "non-Western cultures." Quite the opposite, the critique of Occidentalism itself is a theoretical enterprise whose effects must always be seen in relation to the praxis of social relations and the politics of knowledge. This essay will mount a critical intervention into the link between regionality and thought (specifically, the construction of respective "Western" and "Eastern" regions with their corresponding "ways of thought") that constitutes Foucault's dialogic construction of "the West" and "Western thought," and the conjunctural formation of the two as "crisis."

On the occasion of his second trip to Japan in 1978, Michel Foucault paid a visit to Seionji where an ensuing, brief dialogue between Foucault and several Japanese monks[6] was recorded and published in two different versions, Japanese and French. The main points of the dialogue have been excellently summarized in a penetrating — and ultimately disappointing — analysis by François Jullien, a philosopher and sinologue. Foucault's posture in the dialogue appears incredibly naïve, and there is certainly a strong part of his positions — the conventionalized oppositions between East and West that orient his discourse — that would easily fall under a postcolonial critique today. The dialogue itself is painfully aware of this limit, as Foucault identifies Western thought with crisis, and crisis specifically with the historicity of imperialism and its project of universalism.

Unfortunately, there is today, as far as we know, no extant version of this dialogue in its integral form. Neither of the published versions amounts to a simple transcription. We know that Foucault did not speak Japanese, and we assume that his interlocutors, monks, did not speak French. Presumably, the dialogue itself was conducted in *both* French and Japanese, alternately, with the aid of on-site, consecutive translation. In addition, it is highly probable that further refinements in the on-site translation were made in the process of transcription for the published version. In any case, both versions share what they erase: the practice of translation itself.

François Jullien, recently commenting (significantly, also in the form of a dialogue) at length on Foucault's Zen dialogue, finds in it *"everything...*not only the confrontation, as fleeting as it may be, with a thought from outside, but also at the same time the areas of understanding and misunderstanding... ."[7] Outside, failure, *and* everything: while Jullien's astute reading of the dialogue grasps its global significance beyond Foucault, accounting for what would be called, outside France, the postcolonial aspects of Foucault's Occidentalism,[8] Jullien's "everything" implicitly includes, like Foucault, the crucial element of translation, yet misses its significance for the praxis of social relations. Our task here is not to refute Jullien's reading, but rather to follow his lead, adopt the same posture, and tease out of the Foucauldian dialogue *more* of this elusive "everything" — in this case, the social praxis of translation, a point of departure that would ultimately necessitate a radical reformulation of both Foucault's Occidentalism and Jullien's corresponding "outside."

The dialogue counts a total of three instances in which translation is mentioned. These three instances cover what may be considered to be the multiplicity of translational practices and representations: the metaphorical, the spatio-communicational, and the practico-addressive. When Foucault speaks, at the close of the dialogue, of the way in which philosophy has always been "translated" into disastrous political programs, he appeals to a notion of "translation" as a generalized mode of transposition in relations across the social field. "Philosophy" is translated into "politics": translation names the process that would relate two discretely separate spheres or realms of experience. "Translation" in this sense becomes the metaphor of metaphor, the very principle of its own operation. Our question would be to know to what extent a certain determination of philosophy itself has been based on a particular metaphysics of translation-as-meta-metaphor? Is not metaphor itself a "metaphor" for translation? Before we even begin to answer these questions, let us at least observe that they will inevitably extend across different fields of both knowledge and social formation. In effect, we will be asked to attend to the intersections between, on the one hand, the role of national language and disciplinary specialization in the

Introduction

institutional formation of the modern, national-imperial university, and, on the other hand, the division of the world into geopolitical units based on a supplementary relation between sovereignty and civilizational difference.

Leaving aside these more or less acquired Derridean considerations,[9] let us return now to the beginning of the dialogue, where we once again find, in the second question posed by the monks to Foucault, the issue of translation: "I am told," says one monk, "that almost all of your works are translated into Japanese. Do you think that your thoughts are understood enough?"[10] Foucault dodges the very terms of the question by repeating his well-known critique of authorial intention. In Foucault's response, we can also detect a nascent moment in which one reader of the French "original" and another of the Japanese "copy" both implicitly occupy the same position in relation to the socially produced meaning of the text. All readers, including the author, operate within the same scope of (de)legitimation, and the meaning of the text can only be the product of endless re-readings of readings among these variable positions. What both Foucault and his Japanese interlocutor seem to miss, however, is the potentiality that the Japanese translations may well in fact pose questions of "understanding" back to the "original" French text in such a way that it requires us to ask of French readers exactly the same question. Indeed, we must call into question the assumption of immanence in the monk's query that implicitly links French readers to the French text. The fact that one can suture French language to French community does not in itself guarantee the success of communication. This radical exteriority of social relationships to the production of meaning is precisely thaepoint to which we want to draw attention, in our ensuing discussion of translation, with the distinction between *address* and *communication*. Whereas "address" indicates a *social relation* (that between addresser and addressee) that is primarily practical and performative in nature, hence undetermined and still-to-come, "communication" names the imaginary representation of that relation in terms of pronominal identities, informational content, and receptive destinations: who we are supposed to be and what we were supposed to mean. Theories of communication regularly obscure the fact of address in communication, whereupon they are derived from the assumption that supposedly "we" should be able to "communicate" among ourselves if "we" are a linguistic community. To confuse address with communication is thus a classic hallmark of what we call "the regime of homolingual address."[11]

The institution of homolingual address is a form of homosociality[12] based on a model of community abstracted from the notion of communion or fusion, what Jean-Luc Nancy calls "immanentism,"[13] among its members. What is precisely excluded from such homosociality is the fact of "failure" in communication, a "failure" that does not occur simply because of presumed gaps between linguistic communities, but also because, to try to communicate is to expose oneself to exteriority, to a certain exteriority that cannot be reduced to the externality of a referent to a signification.[14]

Jullien's strategy in reading Foucault, which incidentally forms the introduction to his strategy for reading China through the notion of "outside thought," pivots upon a conception of "outside" that is essentially hermeneutic — and arguably quite different, in its idealist spatiality, from the meaning Foucault first ascribed to that phrase.[15] "Chinese" texts in their foreignness allow the insertion of a heterogeneous element into the constitution of "our" everyday, thus allowing "us" a critical distance upon "our" temporality and identity. Certainly, we would not want to underestimate the critical potential inherent in such moves. Nevertheless, at the same moment that hermeneutics reveals the historicity of our position, it can also be used to institute a certain economy that regulates the distribution of the foreign — typically through spatialized representations of separate linguistic spheres. Naturally, in order to delineate an "outside" and locate the foreign within the hermeneutic economy of the anticipated meaning against the horizon of prejudice and tradition,[16] it is imperative to disqualify forms or instances that obscure or simply do not adhere to the boundary between inside and outside. In order for the merger of horizons to take place, each horizon must be first sanitized of the foreign contamination and homogenized, so that the foreign may come only from without. In terms of linguistic activity, translation is precisely one such form to be disqualified, both in its formal and practical aspects, including notably the exceptional position of the translator, the plurality of language forms among the addressee(s), and the figure or regulative idea that substitutes for the impossibility of making the unity of language an object of experience. Forms of address that take such exteriority into account in the very formation of an impossible interiority are what we call "heterolingual forms of address." The social relationships denoted by such forms do not "add up to" anything — they form what can be called a non-aggregate community. "In this respect, you are always confronted, so to speak, with foreigners in your enunciation

Introduction

when your attitude is that of the heterolingual address. Precisely because you wish to communicate with her, him, or them, so the first, and perhaps most fundamental, determination of your addressee, is that of the one who might not comprehend your language, that is, of the foreigner."[17] Clearly, the distinction between homolingual and heterolingual address thus goes far beyond the question of communication as raised by Foucault in terms of authorial intention. Indeed, our work on translation is designed to illustrate that translation names primarily a *social* relationship whose form permeates linguistic activity as a whole, rather than simply comprising a secondary or exceptional situation.

In Jullien's case, it would be quite easy to show that the constitution of the "outside" is based instead upon the confusion and mobility enabled by the ambiguities inherent in the word "Chinese," which becomes a site of immanence that nevertheless transcendentally sutures an immense plethora of different enunciative positions, historical periods, and social identities. Ultimately, this transcendental suturing enables a notion that particular readers immanently "embody" the ideas of a certain corpus of texts on account of their putative linguistico-ethnic identity. In other words, the presupposition that Westerners understand Western texts in a primary, authentic manner — in short, better than non-Westerners. It may be worthwhile to point out, once again, that the most powerful historical form to-date of this hermeneutic notion has certainly been found in the construction of an idealized, Western readership that is posited as someone who identifies with the position continuous with "Western thought"; Western readership is supposedly capable of comprehending "from within the horizon of the Western *prejudice*," the entirety of Western thought from Heraclitus to Erigena, from Leibniz to James, down to Whitehead and Sartre. It is precisely the figure of Western readership that implicitly underlies the Japanese Zen monk's query about Foucault's work in translation. In a move that demonstrates the way in which this figure is always complicit, that is, co-figured, with another figure, Thierry Marchaisse, Jullien's interlocutor, poses exactly the same problem of immanently embodied transcendental understanding, with the terms simply reversed: "If there is one thing that Foucault effectively cannot do," asserts Marchaisse, "it is to understand Zen *as* it is understood by the monks around him." This statement formally is not any different from saying, "If there is one thing the Japanese readers of Foucault cannot do, it is to understand Foucault *as* the French (or the Westerners) do." Significantly, Marchaisse and the Japanese

Zen monk do not ask whether the Zen monks, or the Westerners, themselves understand "things" in the same way amongst each other — much less how "Zen" or the "Foucauldian text" and the sets of heterogeneous practices within each attempt to manage such distinctions. Jullien, in order to explain this difference, or more precisely, in order to capitalize upon this difference as an unassimilable supplement exterior to the expressions of *our* thought, exclaims, "That's the place where it all becomes Chinese."[18]

Hence, it is only the foreign outside "our" tradition that is incomprehensible. In fact, Jullien, before turning to Foucault, begins his dialogue with Marchaisse by theorizing his own personal experience of presenting Chinese philosophy to those for whom it is so unfamiliar, they can only understand it through misrecognition and ignorance. It is an experience of incomprehension so acute, that, he says, "it is extremely difficult for me *to begin* to make myself heard."[19] Of course, "to begin to make oneself heard" is precisely the situation of address that inheres in or precedes[20] — more precisely, we should say "ex-poses" — every instance of communication. Yet, Jullien's entire focus falls exclusively upon the communicational aspect of the situation, upon the effect of misrecognition that address produces upon his auditors (including, differentially, even himself). It is precisely at this point that the instantiation of "we" in address becomes a presupposed site of interior identity in communication. "Now, this is exactly one of the principal difficulties to which my work exposes me: when I try to present it, I do not *at the outset* "meet" anyone, I have no designated partner."[21] In fact, Jullien's difficulty is itself an incredibly fecund clue: identity does not precede communication, but is rather abstracted from it after the instance of enunciation. The fact that there is no "designated partner" is in fact the essential situation of address, in each and every instance, since address does not require the presupposition of relation (codified through designation) to be effective. Yet according to the communicational model of encounter to which Jullien turns, this constitutive indecision is obscured through representations based on the mutual recognition of designated positions. From such a perspective, the situation of "no 'designated partner'" becomes an obstacle. What is being obstructed? Certainly not the form of address itself. Obstruction, were there any, would occur only when the work of address becomes reified into a thing. Hence, the relation of address becomes identified with the interiority of a "given position" designated as Chinese. The spatialization of relationships and their codification through "given

Introduction

designation" is a key feature of communicational representation. Needless to say, this or that designation in particular is not the only one possible; in the case of "Chinese," it is neither the only one that has been used in the past to describe some of the texts in question, and quite probably not the only one that will be invented by future social formations to come. However, when the "given designation" of positions is assumed, or represented, to be prior to the act of address in communication, the positions themselves become effectively identified with a thing that is supposed to be "outside" of the social relations that produce them, rather than the social relations themselves — what Foucault calls, at the end of Zen dialogue (in a moment referring to the new role assigned to intellectuals), "what is going on at the present."[22] If to speak of knowledge at the exclusion of this relation were the only choice left to us, we would surely join Jullien in experiencing the enormous frustration brought upon us by the ineluctable division between "Chinese" and its outside. Yet, Jullien's negative assessment of the actual situation he encounters in the situation of address should not prevent us from recognizing the immense opportunity that awaits us in the midst of his experience. Seen from the perspective of communication-ex-posed-in-address rather than communication-abstracted-from-address, the undesignated partner who might listen to me presents both of us (and others) with the moment at which social relations can occur — precisely because they remain open.

Sadly, the incredible opportunity that lies behind Jullien's frustrated hopes for a designated partner are buried beneath a mountain of specific difference between languages, nations, civilizations, traditions and races. Predictably, both Jullien and Marchaisse repeatedly appeal to a certain "we" that is not only a relation in address, but also a hermeneutic site of sedimented historical experience and the putative totality of a particular language. "We" thus have a long historical experience of encountering "them," from whence "our" experience is immediately communicable among "us"; "their" experience, by contrast, requires translation. Neither Jullien nor Marchaisse problematize their own dialogue in terms of...dialogue — the potential failure of communication that inheres in every linguistic exchange. Hence, as Jullien remarks just shortly before the ineluctable moment when "it all turns into (incomprehensible) Chinese," dialogue becomes an "impossibility." This impossibility, however, is conveniently contained by "Chinese," thereby excluding it from "French." In this series of equivalencies and surprisingly monologic dialogues, Jullien and Marchiasse thus confuse the pronominal invocation "we" with a group of those who are inherently capable of communicating the same information with each other. Such communication is conceived of solely in terms of accurate repetition.

Now of course, Jullien's partner in dialogue, Marchaisse, does not speak or read Chinese, hence Jullien speaks to him also as a translator, a role to which he appeals for shortly after this comment by highlighting the problems of "a dialogue that does not communicate" and leads to Zen "*satori* — which is ordinarily translated," Jullien reminds his auditor, "by '*illumination* ['Enlightenment'].'" It is impossible for us, in the context of a discussion about and inspired by Foucault — the thinker whose work was in large part devoted to redefining the meaning of the Enlightenment — not to dwell upon the possibilities inherent in this (mis)translation. Jullien, for his part, bypasses the opportunity and proceeds directly to the way in which practice, repetition, becomes a technique leading up to the realization of virtuosity. An integral part of Jullien's argument is that *Chinese* thought has always been concerned with a discontinuous process of "laborious maturation" and "instantaneous realization." Centuries before Zen appeared in China, the *Mencius* text had already charted out the essential ground later assumed by Zen. This historical narrative, which is not of Jullien's invention and to which the Japanese monk in dialogue with Foucault also refers ("It seems that most Chinese specialists believe that Zen Buddhism came from China rather than India"), is a typical object *and* product of culturalist hermeneutics: We all know the story according to which "Zen" is presented as an original *sinification* of Indian *dhyana*, and in this way supposedly provides a model for an original and originary *Chinese* mimeticism — an impossibly contradictory formula — that will serve the cultural analytic of promoting particularity through mimetic reference to the universalism of the West. In this way, cultural interiority is posited as being anterior to the introduction of the foreign. In this limited space, we would simply like to draw attention to what this narrative structure excludes: that the conditions of possibility for identifying the subject of sinification may themselves be posterior to an essential hybridity.

Other points on which to argue with Jullien's position would similarly require far more elaboration than we can mount here, but they are certainly worth mentioning. Alternate interpretations of the texts and schools to which Jullien refers are possible. We note that Jullien's reading of the *Mencius* is strikingly similar to the core concern of Cheng-Zhu neo-Confucianism,[23] which itself bears

Introduction

the inscription of an historically-formulated response to Zen. Needless to say, the practice of Zen itself may also include significant resources for undoing the opposition between "laborious maturation" and the pure form of "instantaneous realization." After all, Huineng's appearance (637–713) as Sixth Patriarch of the Zen lineage, his rejection of the gradualist "Northern School," was aimed precisely at this distinction.

Inevitably, notions of labor as repetition bear within themselves implicit theories of language. The contrast drawn between Jullien and our own position explodes here into a full-fledged parting of the ways when we consider how the very same elements deployed by Jullien (repetition, labor, virtuosity, pure form, neo-Confucianism, Zen, cultural difference, exteriority, materiality, and the constitution of national language) can be all present, yet in a radically different configuration. Inversely, once we admit the extent to which disciplines of knowledge based on the unities of national language and national community intrinsically accord importance to translation — only to conceal it through naturalizing representations that effectively spatialize anterior systematicity, we may begin to see how the role of the translator has significant implications for a typical Foucauldian concern: the role of the intellectual in general. In Jullien's case, it is quite clear that his comments about the esoteric impenetrability of "Chinese" parallels the way in which he draws scrutiny upon the inadequacy of the conventional translation of *satori* as "*illumination*" in French — a word that carries connotations of "Enlightenment" much as the standard English translation of *satori* as "Enlightenment." Here, we must remind ourselves that the positing of the untranslatable and the incommensurable is possible only retrospectively, after the enunciation of translation opens up a space of communication and commensurability. The practice of translation itself remains radically heterogeneous to the representation of translation. Such heterogeneity itself sprouts from the fact that the unity of language cannot be an object of experience in the Kantian sense. Yet Jullien's dialogue with Marchaisse consistently returns to the notion of a systematic unity that underlies and separates the respective Chinese and Western language-worlds. Hence, the role of the sinologue-translator, as seen in Jullien's dialogue with Marchaisse, becomes that of an active agent in the regulation and distribution of the heterogeneous/foreign. In other words, what we are given to see is the way in which the transferential desire to see oneself from another's position is actually created *after the process* of translation. The "positions" themselves are not prior to the translational exchange, but are rather constructed out of it, in posterior fashion, by substituting the spatiality of representation for the temporality of praxis. Hence, the desire to recuperate the authentic meaning of *satori*, now corrupted by an inadequate translation entangled by *"illumination,"* is inseparable from the desire for self-referentiality as a means of regulating the hybridity and heterogeneity that precedes delineations of self and other.

An alternate, genealogical approach to the undeniable inadequacy of translation might instead turn the surplus of *"illumination,"* with its modern connotations of "Enlightenment," back onto *satori*, and vice versa — not as a hermeneutic means of discovering who we have become through a process of laborious maturation, the creation of an accumulated historicity called "our tradition," but rather as the initial and perhaps instantaneous ex-posing of who we really have been becoming for quite some time under the migratory regimes unleashed and policed by Capital. At this point in history, the political project of Enlightenment and the spiritual project of *anatman* or selflessness talk to each other, or remain silent, not in an abstract body of knowledge but in the concrete action of knowledgeable bodies.

Significantly, Foucault's otherwise platitudinous call for a "confrontation" between Eastern and Western thought, the means of overcoming the crisis presented by the end of imperialism, is focused on the figure of the philosopher. "This crisis has produced no supreme philosopher who excels in signifying that crisis...There is no philosopher who marks out this period." If the crisis cannot be signified, the reason is certainly because the "crisis" concerns the very possibility of signification, as such, what Jean-Luc Nancy identifies as the problem of "the sense of the world" in an historical age when "meaning," "world," and "being" can no longer be distinguished.[24] Foucault's interest here falls squarely on the *future*: "if philosophy of the future exists, it must be born outside of Europe or equally born in consequence of meetings and impacts between Europe and non-Europe." Foucault, like all of us, does not *know* what the future holds, yet he *senses* its topographic contours. But where would "outside Europe" be in an age when "Europe" is synonymous, as Foucault asserts, with the universal? Clues to this enigma can be pieced together by placing Foucault's interest in the ninth-century monk Rinzai (Linji in Chinese), whom he finds to be a "great Zen philosopher," alongside his experience of Zen. Significantly, Foucault remarks

Introduction

that Rinzai was "neither a translator nor a founder." Hence, we arrive at the third instance of translation mentioned in the Zen dialogue, the one we have called temporal-addressive. In virtually the same breath, Foucault also cites the example of Rinzai to demonstrate that Zen itself is not wholly Japanese, and, by implication, not wholly Chinese, either. In other words, Rinzai, in Foucault's lexicon, stands as a figure for a philosopher who refuses both the tasks of school-building and of translation inasmuch as they both relate to the project of national construction. Are we not faced here, in a nutshell, with the entirety of anthropological difference since it entered the national-imperial university system with Hegel and Humboldt in the nineteenthcentury? Schools of philosophy in the modern period have invariably been typed as national schools; such constructions are intrinsically built upon a specific regime of translation — it is how "national language" comes to be recognized as such — that provides a metaphysical principle for positing an organic alliance between a particular school or style of thought and a specific geographically defined community.[25] Significantly, after Foucault advances his admiration for Rinzai as a radical philosopher, he immediately retreats, as a show of deference to his interlocutor, back to the default position of national institutions of translation: "I read the French translation by Professor Demiéville, who is an excellent French specialist on Buddhism." *French* translations and *French* specialists, to which we must also add *French* philosophers, the universalism of which (and critiques thereof) relies upon a division of labor thoroughly supervised by the regime of homolingual translation. It is in response to this remark that one of the Japanese monks facing Foucault advances the thesis, held by "Chinese specialists," that Zen is thoroughly *Chinese*. With this exchange, the suturing of enunciative positions and communicational totalities is complete, thereby erasing the moment of address. This moment is emblematic of the entire modern regime of translation spanning the difference between colonial and imperial modernities. What is lost is the fact that the generality of address itself, the very capability of address as such, precedes the assignation of enunciative positions. Perhaps this is the reason why Rinzai is especially well-known, within the Zen school, for his practice of striking the befuddled student: striking is to aiming as communication is to address. For, "addressing does not guarantee the message's arrival at the destination. Thus, 'we' as a pronominal invocation in *address* designates a relation, which is performative in nature, independent of whether or not "we" actually communicate the same information."[26]

In the figure of Demiéville, the *French* specialist of *Oriental* thought, we have the typical sort of body favored by the modern disciplines of the Human Sciences: this is the *body of knowledge*, a system of regularized dispersion, precisely the sort of power-knowledge configuration at which Foucault aimed. The study of these figures and their historicity is precisely what Deleuze and Guattari call "noology" — the way in which the "image" or figure of the body of knowledge, as an instance of the State-form in thought, is marked by an historical transition from the philosopher to the sociologist.[27] We are interested here in the way these figures are in fact co-figured with other figures, with the way the idealized Western reader is co-figured with the area studies specialist, and distributed spatially. It is well known that knowledge in the Human Sciences has been deeply intertwined with national sovereignty and language in the modern period. Just as social divisions created by uneven global development have been encoded in very specific and profound ways into the structure of knowledge, both in terms of disciplinary divisions as well as in terms of the legitimate objects, methods, and theses that compose each discipline, so the meanings of these divisions have been further refracted by the crystallization of nationalized language that has governed the production, dissemination, and reception of knowledge — indeed, the very criteria of truth — in the age of the single world. In short, the Human Sciences as they have developed bear within them — structurally, ideologically, linguistically, and philosophically — the presuppositions of "world history" configured through both sovereignty and colonialism.[28]

****

By now it is clear why we had to take our point of departure from an analytic of Foucault's Occidentalism. Not only Foucault himself but also Zen monks and an area specialist commentator, François Jullien, all operate in the regime of co-figuration that inevitably erases the moments of social relation and construes the dialogue exclusively in communication between fixed subject positions ordered by the homolingual address and localized by spatial representation. Supposedly most sensitive to the perils of reified self-hood, the participants of this dialogue nonetheless are content to fashion themselves as national and civilizational subjects. In accordance with their retrospectively constituted identities, they

Introduction

produce a neat configuration of power-knowledge, according to which the West and the Rest, France and Japan, and white and non-white appear to continue to map the world and the disciplinary classification of knowledge.[29]

The metaphysics of translation evinced in Foucault's "Zen dialogue" by the figure of the area studies specialist marries geo-political regions of the globe to disciplinary divisions in the construction of knowledge. Our name for this joint matrix, the recursive admixtures of world and thought, is the *amphibological region*, a name inspired by François Laruelle's non-philosophy.[30] Typical modernist formulations such as German Romanticism, Chinese Confucianism, and American Pragmatism, would all be examples of the amphibological region, as would the personalities populating it, such as *French* specialists of *Oriental* works (or, quite simply, *French* specialists of *French* works in a world system organized around geopolitical divisions of work). In Foucault's Zen dialogue, the amphibological region is at all times present, no moment being clearer than at the closing section of the interview in which Foucault describes Europe both as a definite geographical region and as a universal category of thought through which categories themselves appear. As such, the amphibological region corresponds exactly to what Foucault, in *The Order of Things* (*Les mots et les choses*), calls the "empirico-transcendental doublet"[31] that characterizes the emergence of Man as both subject and object of (self-)knowledge in the modern period. The amphibological region is, thus, precisely, the quintessential bio-political habitat corresponding to Foucault's modern Man.[32]

The philosopher who is neither a school-builder nor a translator is thus the "philosopher" — if that term is still appropriate — who is no longer concerned with regulating the heterogeneity of world and text through the regime of homolingual translation. In the Zen dialogue, Foucault finds a hint of this precisely in the "experience" of Zen, which is for him in this instance, largely concerned with a new set of relationships concerning the body, or again, the body as an exposed site of relationship. Jullien, a reader whose compelling attentiveness is matched only by a propensity to squander the transformative opportunities that lie therein, seizes upon the ineluctable meaning of this experience, particularly as Foucault's account of it stimulates only a response of silence from Zen monk Omori. Yet the depth of Jullien's observations fall short of calling our attention to the potential significance of Foucault's inscription of the body as an alternative to "philosophy" understood as schools of national translation.[33]

Let us echo Foucault's concern for a philosophy of the future, which we might as well call "the dislocation of the West," by outlining a project that aims to develop a comprehensive theory of translation that would simultaneously address both: (a) a notion of democratic translational practice that replaces the sovereignty of "bodies of knowledge" (typically codified as different regions/nations of the world and their corresponding area studies) with the sociality of "knowledgeable bodies"; and (b) a corresponding reorganization of the Human Sciences based upon a democratic notion of humanity as a transcendental multitude of foreigners-without-the-foreign.[34] Here, it is important to note, we are advocating neither the rise or decline of the West nor the universalization or provincialization of it; neither does our project amount to the disowning of heritage from the past. At the demise of the regime of national translation and under the heterolingual address, it would be very obvious that the West cannot be referred to even in the trope of an organic unity that grows or languishes. Ours is to dislodge the West from the racist logic of homosociality and relocate identity in a non-relational form (Me and the Foreigner are identical in-the-last-instance) that would enable the immense diversity of minor politics and syncretic knowledge. Yet, our task of the dislocation of the West is not easy at all.

****

We might as well have titled this volume of *Traces* "Sovereign Police, Global Complicity: a Biopolitics of Translation and Colonial Difference." It will come as no surprise to many that we associate the theme of complicity first and foremost with the role played by the nation-States in their world system as it has been developing over the past four centuries[35]. While the rise of contemporary technologies of "securidentity" certainly trace their roots to techniques of government advanced by the metropolitan imperial nations — what Michel Foucault calls "governmentality" — there is great need to reread that history, like the history of Liberalism itself, through the experience of the populations in the colonies. In this respect, we cannot afford to continue to indulge ourselves in Occidentalism. Just as the canonization of English literature as a colonial measure in British India was "imported" back into England in order to mask an ideology of class,[36] the roots of governmentality will, we can expect, one day be found to lie in the exceptional practices of colonial administration (vis-à-vis the normative

Introduction

position accorded to "civil society" within the framework of imperialism). The United States of America have undoubtedly embarked on a course that can only further aggravate this history. The unilateral violence of U.S. imperial nationalism is certainly a grave threat to people around the globe (including, of course, people in the United States), yet we would deny ourselves the chance of finding a real identity for the multitude of foreigners if we let the explosions of U.S. unilateralism blind us from noticing how the nation-States together codify a profound form of unilateral power (now exemplified by the apparatus of "securidentity") across the social field. The unilateralism inherent in governmentality as such, only apparently less urgent than that currently exercised by the U.S.A., cannot simply be described through the model of coercion, unless we redefine "coercion" to include the competition instituted by the world-systemic form itself. Indeed, the entire problem of "governmentality" begins, for Foucault, in the Liberal critique of state intervention.[37] Behind the humanist faces of national independence, self-determination, resistance to cultural homogenization, rights and law, we must see how the nation-State itself is intrinsically designed as a transcendental form of quasi-permanent unilateralism in which all nation-States are complicit. From this perspective, the challenge ahead of us is to bring the issue of coercion back into a broader analytic that tries to explain why such institutions and states of domination are such an attractive place for foreigners in the first place?

The global analytic of complicity we propose does not mean that we close our eyes to the actual and highly fluid differences of power between the obviously unequal nation-States and the various populations circuiting through them.[38] This is the Foucauldian perspective of biopolitics, which distinguishes states of domination and the techniques of government that institutionalize and sustain those states from the ebb-and-flow of power-and-play in everyday life that Foucault calls strategic relations. The imperative to national subjective formation, the imperative to form a majoritarian project, to appropriate the minority positions in a state of domination sustained by the communicational techniques of a unitary "voice of the people" and an authoritative "body of knowledge"...*this* sort of unilateralism has proven to be far more durable than the national social projects of any single nation.

In order to understand why democratic nations repeatedly move, in a relatively short space of time, in and out of quasi-fascistic political formations, we need to start accounting for the recursive circuits cycling *between* three very different series, or subsets, of the problem. The divisions are well-known; let us simply summarize them here: first, of course, there is the structural or national series (gender difference, labor difference, and linguistico-ethnic difference); then the systemic series (sovereignty, the West-and-the-Rest, and empire); and finally the political economy series (labor, value, and time). The fascinating debates now raging within the fields of sociology and international relations over the role played by the United States in the current conjuncture generally advance their arguments — a kind of moral posturing — by opening up the contingency of elements in one series only to reify elements in another series. They cannot adequately deal — i.e., in relational fashion — with the fluidity of and between the basic categories such as gender, class, ethnicity, race, geographic region, and civilization. This kind of disciplinary short-circuiting is not only a good sign that entirely new categories of analysis aiming at multiple levels are needed, it also serves as an important clue to understanding how fascist formations, be they colonial or imperial, repeatedly arise. Between the three major subsets of the political problem that creates the conditions for fascism lies a hidden, recursive circuit.

In spite of the attention given to the innumerable forms of hybridity and differences that pre-exist in the contemporary circuits of migration, exchange, and cooperative networking, we continue to see a majoritarian consolidation of "culture" as a kind of fossilized artifact. Needless to say, nationalization is not just a process of "reduction" (as it was termed by the nineteenth-century Spanish colonial administration in the Philippines) conducted upon disparate elements of territory, market, and ethnicity; it also retroactively creates knowledge, bodies, and life. The archive, the language, the culture and the history — in short, the modern fetishization of "communicable experience" — are as much sites of primitive accumulation for the construction of majoritarian subjects of domination as are the modes of production and labor for Capital. Would the usage of terms such as "accumulation" and "exchange" thus suggest their meaning be extended to a metaphorical, or perhaps even literary, sense? Evidently not. The benefits of such accumulation (what Jason Read calls "the real subsumption of subjectivity by Capital"[39]) exclusively accrue to actual, authoritative bodies of knowledge. These bodies are the ones that "speak" the unitary language. Such authoritative bodies could be either people or institutions; in either case, they are the forms of relation regularized according to the apparently natural boundaries of "the

Introduction

individual" and its corollary, the collective. So much has already been written about the process of extreme abstraction required to sustain the premise of the "individual," one might think it unnecessary to repeat it here: the real site of metaphorical excess, when it comes to the authoritative body, is actually to be found in abstractions such as the individual speaking subject and the nationalization of her language.

Nothing sustains and typifies the transcendental representations managed by these authorities, these majoritarian bodies of knowledge, more than the tandem notions of the West-as-a-normative-value and of Modernity-as-an-unfinished-project. Taken together, these two axes form a grid of global proportions along which the microgradient of majority/minority relations is continually plotted. Undoubtedly, herein lies the key to a minoritarian analytic and a new interdisciplinary syncretism on a global scale. But can we really assume the consistency and indexical veracity of the map onto which such positions are plotted?

We all know the story of anti-Eurocentrism, according to which the minoritarian critique of Western hegemony in the context of the (post)colonial nation sustains the critical shock to the "Western" majority formation. By transposing it into a local register, the critique of Eurocentrism becomes a good rhetoric for the elite, whose subjectivity is partly formed in their systemic competition with "the West" through the structural (class) accumulation of value by the labor of their social inferiors. Similarly, the majoritarian dispensation of respect for minoritarian difference short-circuits the possibility of recoding relations on a completely different terrain. The dialectical form of this relation is well known: apparently free, the position coded Master suffers from its actual bondage to the labor of the Slave; the position coded Slave, however, dreams of nothing if not the chance of assuming, finally for itself, the magisterial height of the Master — without realizing that the Master position is always already deprived from the very outset of the possibility of being simply for itself. Certainly the first step out of this aporia is to admit that the very split between the two distinct forms of modernity — the imperial modernity and the colonial modernity — is itself the very definition of something like Modernity in general in the constitution of the hierarchical, non-democratic world of Capital. Even in their very opposition, both the colonial modernity and the imperial modernity are bound to a common index, the normative value of the West, the supposed naturalness of which obfuscates a state of domination. This sleight of hand is accomplished, as always, by the form of an exception. Indeed, as deconstruction has never tired of showing, the dialectical subject *of* history excepts itself *from* history (without taking exception *to* history), thereby eliding the continual presence, or "trace," of third-term "exteriorities" (supplements, exclusions, and displacements).

It is precisely because we look at what we are calling, in an inevitable moment of pure jargon, "traces" or "exteriorities" that we avoid falling into the either/or formalisms of signifying chains and political economy. Instead, we want to draw links between exteriority in the sense described above and the notion of externality utilized by economists. "Externality" names any situation in which the action of two parties (be they friends or enemies) to an exchange (verbal, economic, military, etc.) affects, either positively or negatively, a third party not directly participating in the exchange of the other two. Clearly, this notion of externality could also be applied to the position of the translator as it has been described in the modern, homosocial regime of translation. In the intercourse between nation-States, we will want to know who are the "third parties" affected by their complicity? Will these "third parties" be easily recognizable in the same way as the "speaking subjects" and "legal persons" taken to be constitutive of the nation? Evidently, the answer is negative. Just as the border between two physically adjacent countries does not in itself form a positive space, but is the negative condition for the creation of the national interiorities on both sides of the line; we would expect that these "third parties" would also be found in the silent, stuttering and/or interrupted interstices between the talking subjects and authoritative bodies typically supported by the nation-States.

The attempt to "regularize" the status of these interstitial spaces, even when propelled by good intentions, inevitably has profound implications across the social field — including, of course, the speaking subjects provisionally sustained by the nation-State. It is a truism to say that we are living a time when the previous forms of exteriority and externality are in crisis or have collapsed completely, while new forms proliferate. The development of the systemic integration now culminating in "globalization" is one of the most visible effects of this massive reorganization of exteriority. With the implosion of "unexplored" space, the extension of the comity of nations across the face of the globe, the supplement of exteriority known as "civilizational difference" (the economy of spatialized lawlessness that defined the West by separating its competitive rule of law from

Introduction

a non-West available for lawless, infinite violence) has reached a point of crisis. Elements associated with "Western modernity" can now be found in places that have conventionally been excluded from "the West" — often in forms that are more authentic than what is found in the West itself. At the moment when the global expansion of the two universal forms of Capitalism — the commodity and the nation-State — is finally complete, such civilizational distinctions appear, historically for the first time, as what they essentially are: void of any specific content, and thus, absolutely ideological. No longer is there any ground whatsoever to substantiate the distinction between the West and the Rest. Or, to put it differently, it is no longer possible to continue to disavow that the West is floating and dispersing (with the tides of domination); but it is equally important to note that the West is *not* declining. Hence, our project of the dislocation of the West. No wonder we have seen, in the supposed age of the decline of sovereignty, a call by right-wing thinkers to reinstitute the axis of civilizational difference at the heart of global security management. Since the sovereign nation-State system was initially developed, with the Treaty of Westphalia (1648), at the inaugural period of the imperial-colonial era when the world was divided into two realms, one governed by international laws (the West) and one exposed to the discretion of colonial powers (the Rest),[40] it is no wonder that a breakdown in the apparatus of sovereignty would produce shock waves in the lines of civilizational difference, and vice-versa. Civilizational difference has from the very outset performed the role of a necessary supplement required by sovereignty's impossible quotient of interior consistency.

It is crucial to understand that the apparatus of sovereignty does not initially concern the national space, which is primarily structured by the markers of social distinctions such as class, but concerns first and foremost the international space of a world system. Hence, the relative erosion of sovereignty seen in the transnational flows of global cities does not indicate that the system of sovereignty has diminished; it has simply mutated. It is for this reason that the sovereignty of the nation-State seeks its legitimacy in the discrete imposition of exclusionary rules upon migrants entering its territory and in xenophobia.

We are witness to an age when the toxic waste of sovereignty's implosion is leaching into the very ground on which sovereignty was supposedly constructed — the idea of the nation as a form of organic life. Even as the transnational flows of Capital erode the juridico-institutional form of the nation-State, it continues to be progressively consolidated at a biopolitical level.[41] The nation-State has become a complex form of "life support system." While it positively manages the "life" of the population concerned, it also simultaneously exercises fundamental constraints upon the bodies passing through it, inciting some theorists to ask whether the modern nation-State (and sovereignty) ought not to be understood in relation to the political experience of the "camp"?[42] Needless to say, these "life support systems" serve to manage labor — the one commodity that Capital, until now, has been unable to produce — yet in so doing, they also engender the formation of specific kinds of subjectivity.

In order to understand this change, we will have to chart out the new itineraries and new forms of "exteriority" being posited today, against which "life" is supposed to be a natural given. As the connection between *form-of-life* and *form-of-law* begins to completely coincide, "biopower" assumes position as the major political arena. In a series of public lectures in the late seventies on the birth of biopolitics, Foucault distinguishes the biopolitical problematic that emerges in the eighteenth century from the problems of government in the preceding period and understands it as a modification of "pastoral power." The term "sovereign police," first coined by Giorgio Agamben, an astute philosopher of biopolitics, is of course a combination joining the two forms of state reason that preceded the biopolitical project. As a form of juridical discourse on legitimacy, sovereignty was originally theorized as a form of external limitation upon the power of the monarch. As the obverse complement to this external power, the State deployed a police authority that was naturally external to the people who were its object. In both instances, the composition of State power was conceived or enabled through the application of limitations that were extrinsic by design. With the advent of modern theories of political economy in the context of Liberalism, however, a new series of objects and techniques were enabled, the aim of which was to render the principle of governance completely intrinsic and self-contained. This intrinsic principle was that of a maximal–minimal quotient of efficiency (or intensity) extending, eventually, far beyond the classical concerns of labor and Capital to include all aspects of the social and private body. It displaced the previous forms of sovereign law and police state without, however, eliminating them.

Even as Liberalism's seemingly inexorable expansion has freed more and more spaces from the subservience to sovereign power, the productive power of life itself has become more and more the focus of governmental activity such

Introduction

that the forms of sovereignty and police can now be found in a micro-politics of "life." Foucault implicitly warns against optimism (induced, for instance, by the transformation of sovereignty) when he speaks of an "indispensable hypoderm" complementing the face of power. Foucault is certainly not calling for a metaphysics of the deep, of underlying essence here. The entire style he developed, first archaeological and then genealogical, was motivated, as he continually emphasized, not by an interest in "the way things were, " but rather out of concern for "our immediate and concrete actuality."[43] In other words, Foucault was interested in how the praxis of knowing creates not objects of knowledge, but new subjectivities (which might not be simply subjects of knowledge).

Although "the life" is supposed to be given as an inalienable right at an absolute remove from the purchase of sovereign power, it paradoxically has become invested with sovereign forms. Today, nationalized forms of life (notably "culture" and "language") are still proposed as the "hypoderm" of which Foucault spoke, a substratum or accumulation that supposedly underlies or girds the massive variations in the actual forms of life disclosed by the globalization of Capital. What if the "hypoderm" were not the internal well-spring of national culture, but rather the effect of Capital's increasing penetration? In marked contrast to the great triptych of contemporary social analysis, gender-race-and-class, culture and language are completely occult in their hypodermic status. Nothing exemplifies this situation better than the global index of whiteness today. Formerly one of the world's most highly mobile, diasporic populations, the white population around the globe today has entered a period of amazing fixity on the one hand, and of fluidity on the other; a period of fixity in which "white" bodies are regarded as the most stationary and the least capable of transforming themselves; it is however, also a period of fluidity in which whiteness constantly shifts and transforms depending on the conditions of the social formation. But, precisely because of this apparent fluidity, the obsessive insistence upon whiteness and the efforts to naturalize it have never been more prevalent than today, and whiteness is more frequently than before fantasized by the white themselves as immobile fixity — much like that formerly ascribed, by white colonists, to the indigenous. Is this not what the current notion of "homeland security" aims for? Yet how can one not see such "native preserves" as a kind of biopolitical camp into which precarious labor herds itself in the meager hopes of survival?

In order to bring what may be the most compelling and ubiquitous forms of nationalization left today — those concerning "life" — into the realm of a creative minoritarian resistance that does not aim to "take power" through civil war or "balance power" through sovereign complicity, but rather aims for an entirely different form of social organization, we need to begin by charting out the ways in which forms such as "culture" and "language" typical of nationalized "life" have been formed in the crucible that joins the commodity to the national subject. Communication surely is the ideology of Capital, but this alliance rests on a biopolitics. Even as "life" stripped of any qualifications other than "existence" has become the paramount, universal form of the humanitarian rejection of violence, it paradoxically continues to function as a strategic, necessary tool in the unlimited extension of that violent power. Through the category of "life," the sovereign police try to manage, now quite violently, a series of strategic externalities that amount, finally, to the institution of a highly mobile gradient of majoritarian authority all around the globe. This majoritarian authority should undoubtedly be called the "West." Yet in the familiar series of equal signs that describe its tautological movement (e.g., white = male = Christian = european language = white, etc.), the meaning of the "West" in all historical specificity must be measured against an actual constitutive process that reveals it to be, time and again, so highly arbitrary that it is in fact actually void of any specific content. This is why there is no hope for finding any ground to substantiate the difference of the West and the Rest. The only thing it really names, in the end, is what might be called, paraphrasing Hegel, the bad infinity (of a relation ill-conceived).

Global complicity is obviously, thus, first and foremost, a form of bad cooperation, a form through which Capital appropriates the very solidarities and networks that determine its madly rational mutations. For this very reason, it is imperative to stress, from the outset, that we are not the least bit interested in an analytic of complicity that could be used, in the style of a "political correctness" inquisition, to absolve our friends and damn our enemies. Quite the opposite, what we are aiming to problematize here are the specific forms of exteriority and externality inhabiting the widest possible variety of subjective practices. Ultimately, the minoritarian analytic is not at all concerned with codifications and classifications in the order of knowledge. Although these are necessary, and cannot be compromised, their sole purpose is in the constitution of new human subjects.

Introduction

Far too many of the figures proffered today to populations around the globe as the objects of collective dream and desire — or simply as the form of recognition that has become a prerequisite to such dreams — are nothing but rehashed versions of yesterday's imperial identities, many of which exist only as the spectral others of Modernity (i.e., the premodern). This is the form of subjectivity that is really but a state of domination rather than an active participation in the guidance and development of strategic relations. If contemporary sociology thinks of nothing but an analytic of risk, this is surely the indication, as Maurizio Lazzarato points out,[44] of a massive inability to conceive of invention at the level of the subject. It is only when the possibility of creating something new as a form of *becoming* has been denied (or has been itself absorbed into a predetermined set of targets or destinations) that the question of agency becomes reduced to a calculus of loss and gain. Needless to say, the very notion of a "society of risk" thus formulated would necessarily be unable to avoid complete penetration by the apparatus of governmentality.

With this issue of *Traces*, we originally proposed to prospective authors (cf. the call for papers in the appendix) the idea of bringing *translation* squarely into a politically informed discussion about the production of social relations in much the same way that labor has occupied a central place for theorists since Hegel and Marx. The modern regime of translation is a concrete form of "systemic complicity." In other words, it is a globally applicable technique of domination aimed at managing social relationships by forcing them to pass through circuits on the systemic level (such as national sovereignty). In our research on the transnational discursive structure of both Japanese studies and the institution of the Japanese Emperor system,[45] or again in the relation between imperial nationalism and the maintenance of ethnic minorities,[46] we were persuaded that the geography of national sovereignty and civilizational difference indicates an important kind of subjective technology or governmental technique that has, until recently, been thoroughly naturalized by an anthropological discourse of culture. It is only today that we can begin to see how a multiplicity of disciplinary arrangements forming an economy of translation (in place since the colonial era but far outliving colonialism's demise) actually produces differentially coded subjects, typically national ones, whose constitution is interdependent and, at specific intervals, actually complicit in a single, yet extremely hierarchical, state of domination. Our aim was thus to trace a series of genealogies within which "translation" is no longer seen as simply an operation of transfer, relay, and equivalency, but rather assumes a vital historical role akin to that played by labor in the constitution of the social.

Like labor, language is a potentially totalizing category that concerns not just a specific activity but a form of social praxis that produces, or at least binds, the production of the world and the self. Like labor, language could easily be seen as something that is not the exclusive purchase of the individual, but an essential part of humanity in general (without which any notion of "humanity in general" would necessarily presuppose a sort of global "final solution" leading up to "the last man"). Finally, like labor, language appears to call into question the meaning of repetition and singularity.

Our research into the position of the translator within the modern regime of cofigured, nationalized language, shows a precise parallel to the logic of sovereignty itself. Just as Giorgio Agamben has shown how the logic of sovereignty is based on the form of exception (embodied by the figure of the sovereign), the position of the translator has been represented in a similarly exceptional fashion. Our work has turned this relationship inside out, demonstrating that the regularity of the "national language" as a formation in which the (hybrid) position of the translator has been deemed irrelevant is in fact produced only after the subjective encounter of social difference in translation (or in any social situation in which communication might fail). By proposing to look at the formation of national language through the exceptional position of the translator, we have been able to show that it is indeed a systemic, or transnational, technique of domination. This discovery parallels the growing awareness, largely advanced by Yann Moulier Boutang, of the crucial role in Capitalist expansion played by the various forms of slave labor, rather than the regularized forms of wage labor.[47] Hence, at the back of the call for papers for this issue was a proposal to displace the state of domination managed by the dual normalizing technologies of wage labor and nationalized speaking subjects with the inventive subjectivities seen in the exodus from wage labor and national language.

The similarities between the logic of slave labor upon which wage labor secretly rests and the regime of translation upon which national language is secretly built are profound. In both instances the action of a subject (translation or labor) expresses itself in an object (the work) that is thought to define the generic form of human activity itself. As such, both have potentially political implications, yet

Introduction

are most often associated with the pure economy of exchange. How we propose to look at this exchange, of course, determines the space we accord to individual autonomy and agency. Yet, according to an all-too-familiar reification, the creative potential of human activity is admitted in the constructivist account of social formation only to be turned into an objectivized thing, a series of institutions or objective realities that recursively constrain the way subjects actually work, limiting the power of invention to specific disciplinary rules. Just as the Marxian critique of the commodity fetish proposed to remind us that the fruits of labor, now reified, actually bear within them the trace of a social relation (and hence the possibility of creative transformation), we advance the thesis that translation can also be understood as form of social relation requiring similar critique. In effect, translation appears to us as the social relation from which the critique of communication as the ideology of Capital is most directly linked to a politics of life, or again, the politics in which life becomes invested by Capital.

Notes

[1] Cf. *Traces* Prospectus.
[2] This remark may be misunderstood. For example, Tanabe Hajime's *Zange-dô no Tetsugaku* (*Philosophy as Metanoia*, Takeuchi Yoshinori and James W. Heisig trans. with foreward by James W. Heisig (Berkeley & London: University of California Press, 1990) has been translated into English, but it was precisely in the spirit of the civilizational difference, characteristic of the U.S. sovereignty in postwar East Asia (and the postwar Japanese resentment to it), that this work of translation was framed and exercised. It ignores not only Tanabe's previous philosophical work devoted to the cause of Japanese Imperial Nationalism to which *Zange-dô no Tetsugaku* is intimately connected but also to the fact that translation was already an essential element in his philosophical enterprise.
[3] Cf. Peter Button, *Aesthetic Formation and the Image of Modern China: The Philosophical Aesthetics of Cai Yi*, Ph.D. thesis , Cornell University, 2000.
[4] Cf. Takeuchi Yoshimi, tr. & ed. Richard Calichman, *What is Modernity? Writings of Takeuchi Yoshimi* (New York: Columbia University Press, 2004))
[5] Michel Foucault, tr. Christian Polac, "Michel Foucault et le zen: un séjour dans un temple zen," in Michel Foucault, *Dits et Écrits II, 1976–1988* (Paris: Gallimard, 2001), 618–624. English translation: Michel Foucault, tr. Richard Townsend, "Michel Foucault and Zen: a stay in a Zen temple (1978)," in Jeremy R. Carrette, ed., *Religion and Culture/by Michel Foucault* (New York: Routledge, 1999), 110–114. Footnote references to the dialogue will henceforth be marked by *ZD* ("Zen dialogue"), followed by two numbers referring to paginations in the French and English texts, respectively. The Japanese translation was not available to us at the time this text was composed. Parts

of this argument have been published in Chinese as Su Zhean (Jon Solomon), "*Weilai de Zhexue: Lun Fuke de Xifangzhuyi yu Fanyi Wenti* [Philosophy of the Future: Foucault's Occidentalism and the Problem of Translation]," in Huang Jui-chyi, ed., *Zaijian Fuke* [Revisiting Foucault] (Taipei: Sunghui, 2005).

6. Including Omori Sogen; significantly, the others are not named.
7. François Jullien, Thierry Marchaisse, *Penser d'un dehors (la Chine)[Thinking from outside (China)]* (Paris: Seuil, 2000), 17. Abbreviated *JM*.
8. "What is equally curious is that Foucault plays to the hilt here — and indeed throughout his interview — upon the grand oppositions and the grand habitual baggage: world-thought, East-West, etc." *JM*, 18.
9. Cf. the second half of Jacques Derrida, *Du droit à la philosophie* (Paris: Galilée, 1990), tr. Jan Plug et. al., *Eyes of the University* (Stanford: Stanford University, 2004).
10. *ZD*, 619/111.
11. Naoki Sakai, *Translation and Subjectivity: On "Japan" and Cultural Nationalism* (Minneapolis: Minnesota, 1997), 6. Hereafter abbreviated *TS*.
12. Homosociality here refers to the mode of communal solidarity that is obtained by the boundary of distinction. The assumed homogeneity of the inside is no other than an effect of the erection or marking of distinction by which the outside is posited and excluded. Let us take the example of a xenophobic joke: this sort of joke isolates certain foreigners as an object of laughter, and against this object "we," who are distinguished from "them" by virtue of the fact that "we" can laugh at "them," are consolidated as a community. Laughter serves as the act of the marking of distinction, which gathers "us" together. This use of homosociality should not be confused with the well-known one by Eve K. Sedgwick.
13. Jean-Luc Nancy, tr. Peter Conner, et al., *The Inoperative Community* (Minneapolis: Minnesota, 1991), 3. Cf. Su Zhean (Jon Solomon), "*Fanyi de gongtongti, gongtongti de fanyi* [Translation of Community, Community of Translation]" preface to Shang-Luke, Nongxi (Jean-Luc Nancy), tr. Su Zhean (Jon Solomon) *Jiegou Gongtongti* [La Communauté désoeuvrée] (Taipei: Laureate Books, 2003), I–XV.
14. *TS*, 7.
15. Cf. Michel Foucault, "*La pensée du dehors*" in *Critique* 229 (June 1966), pp. 523–546. Tr. Brian Massumi, "The Thought of the Outside" in Paul Rabinow and Nikolas Rose, eds., *The Essential Foucault* (New York, New Press, 2003) 423–441.
16. Cf. Jean-Luc Nancy, "The philosophical requirement of hermeneutics is, thus, one that concerns preliminary faith, that is to say, a precomprehensive anticipation of that very thing which is the question to be comprehended, or the question which comprehension must finally command." *Le partage des voix*, (Paris: Galilée, 1982) p. 17; tr. Gayle Ormiston, Gayle Ormiston and Alan Schrift, eds., *Transforming the Hermeneutic Context* (Albany: SUNY, 1990), 213, translation slightly modified.
17. *TS*, 9.
18. *JM*, 26. The locution is undoubtedly intended as a pun. The phrase "*C'est du chinois*" has a general meaning like the English phrase, "It's all Greek to me", in which the appellation "*chinois*" is to be understood in a general, rather than specific, way referring

Introduction

to incomprehensibility. Obviously, the meaning here cannot be dissociated from Chinese in all its specificity (otherwise the pun itself would not function as such), hence our literal translation.

[19] *JM*, 9. Emphasis in original.
[20] Address "precedes" communication only if we allow that its "coming first" (*pre-*) occurs only by having already given "itself" up (*cedere*). Communication is thus "ex-posed" by address: it is simultaneously revealed and displaced.
[21] *JM*, 14. Emphasis in original.
[22] *ZD*, 624/114.
[23] Refers to the school of interpretation of Confucian texts initiated by the Cheng brothers (Cheng Hao, 1032–1085, and Cheng Yi, 1033–1107) and Zhu Xi (1130–1200).
[24] Cf. Jean-Luc Nancy, *Le Sens du monde* (Paris: Galilée, 1993), 15; tr. Jeffrey Librett, *The Sense of the World* (Minneapolis: Minnesota, 1997), 5: "Consequently, when I say that the end of the world is the end of the *mundus*, this cannot mean that we are confronted merely with the end of a certain 'conception' of the world, and that we would have to go off in search of another one or to restore another one (or the same). It means, rather, that there is no longer any assignable signification of 'world,' or that the 'world' is subtracting itself, bit by bit, from the entire regime of signification available to us…"
[25] Deconstruction largely set the stage for a growing body of work exploring this matrix, what we call "the national institution of translation," particularly in relation to German philosophy. Cf. the pivotal role — unthematized — of translation in Philippe Lacoue-Labarthe's *La Fiction du Politique* (Paris: Christian Bourgois, 1987), tr. Chris Turner, *Heidegger, Art and Politics — the Fiction of the Political* (Cambridge: Basil Blackwell, 1990); the works of Antoine Berman, *L'épreuve de l'étranger* (Paris: Gallimard, 1984), tr. S. Heyvaert, *The Experience of the Foreign — Culture and Translation in Romantic Germany* (Albany: SUNY, 1992); and *La traduction et la lettre ou l'auberge du lointain* (Paris: L'ordre philosophique, 1999); and Sathya Rao, *Philosophies et non-philosophie de la traduction*, thesis submitted to the Department of Philosophy, University of Paris X, Nanterre, March 2003.
[26] *TS*, 4–5.
[27] Gilles Deleuze and Félix Guattari, *Milles Plateaux* (Paris: Éditions de Minuit, 1980), 466; tr. Brian Massumi, *A Thousand Plateaus* (Minneapolis: University of Minnesota, 1987), 376. Brian Holmes's brilliant critique of the "flexible personality" behind Cultural Studies suggests ways in which the figure of the sociologist (previously critiqued by the Frankfurt School notion of "the authoritarian personality") is undergoing historical metamorphosis. Cf. Brian Holmes, "The Flexible Personality — for a new cultural critique" in Brian Holmes, *Hieroglyphs of the Future — art and politics in a networked era* (Paris/Zagreb: What, How and For Whom and arkzin.communications, 2003), 106–137.
[28] Jon Solomon, tr. Frédéric Neyrat and Jerôme Maucourant, "La traduction métaphysicoloniale et les Sciences Humaines: la région amphibologique comme lieu biopolitique [Metaphysicolonial translation and the Human Sciences: the amphibological region as biopolitical site]," *Rue Descartes* No. 48 (Paris: PUF, 2004).

29 Jon Solomon, tr. Brian Holmes, Bérénice Angremy, François Matheron, Charles Wolfe, "L'empire et le régime de la traduction unilatérale," [Empire and the regime of unilateral translation]" in *Multitudes* (Paris: Exils), Numéro 13 (2003), 79–88. Also in Italian as: tr. Federica Matteoni, "Impero e il regime della traduzione unilaterale: un dibattito a Taiwan," in *DeriveApprodi* No. 23 (2003), 155–159.

30 The classic example, in philosophical terms, of an "amphiboly" is, of course, found in the common theoretical premise that secretly joins Materialism to Idealism. Foucault recognized that this amphibological problem would find its apex in the figure of "modern Man," who oscillates between transcendental and empirical positions. While deconstructive philosophy excels at demonstrating the indecidability of the terms, it still cannot explain why the typical formula, "the real = X," always comprises some sort of recursivity between the terms, nor, for that matter, why Science has no need for the Concept. In Laruelle's "non-philosophy" (which holds for us the prospect of being the sort of philosophy-of-the-future for which Foucault calls), amphibological figures such as "the concept of Man" or "the theory of X" are structured by an economy of Decision that invariably relies upon a combination of two-and-a-half or three terms (i. e., the terms of a dyad, such as "theory" and "matter", plus a synthetic term, such as man-the-sociologist, which is the reflection of one or both of the terms of the dyad). The problem of "philosophical Decision" in Laruelle's account covers the entirety of the recursive relation between philosophy and the real in which either empirical forms surreptitiously become the basis for transcendental postulates or transcendental forms are installed as the basis for empirical judgments. Laruelle's non-philosophy is not a form of deconstruction that plays upon undecidability to destabilize metaphysical presuppositions, but is rather a rigorous critique of idealist materialism from the point of view of the non-relational Identity of the Real, which has the specific structure of determination-in-the-last-instance. Cf. François Laruelle, *Principe de Minorité* (Paris: Aubier Montaigne, 1981), part of which has been translated into English: François Laruelle, tr. Ray Brassier, "The Decline of Materialism in the Name of Matter," in *Pli* Vol. 12 (2001), 33–40.

31 Michel Foucault, *Les mots et les choses — une archéologie des sciences* humaines (Paris: Gallimard, 1966), 329; The *Order of Things: An Archeology of the Human Sciences* (New York: Vintage, 1971), 312.

32 Edward Soja's erudite argument for a postmodern geography astutely dilates Foucault's apprehension of the amphibological nature of spatiality, yet Soja's fecund materialist understanding of spatiality still cannot avoid repeating the hermeneutic circle ("As a social product, spatiality is simultaneously the medium and outcome, presupposition and embodiment, of social action and relationship." (Edward Soja, *Postmodern Geographies — the reassertion of space in critical theory* (London: Verso, 1989), 129). No wonder Soja characterizes Foucault's vision of spatiality as "ambivalent." Evidently, the amphibolies discovered by Foucault appear "ambivalent" only when seen from the indecision of philosophy, including its materialist variant. Here, we cannot elaborate an alternative concept of the region that is not based on the traditional amphibological determination, both transcendental and immanent, of "being" + "at" + "there." We are

Introduction

merely concerned with Foucault's inability to open up the problem of amphibological spatiality in relation to the location of the West, evinced in a 1976 interview between Foucault and specialists in the discipline of geography. Cf. "Questions à Michel Foucault sur la géographie," in *Dits et Écrits II* (Paris: Gallimard, 2001) 28–40; tr. Colin Gordon, "Questions on Geography" in C. Gordon, ed., *Power/Knowledge: Selected Interviews and Other Writings 1972–1977* (New York: Pantheon, 1980), 63–77. In this interview, Foucault is confronted by geographers concerned over his general deployment of spatial tropes and metaphors along with a studious avoidance of the terms of geography per se. His interlocutors offer a challenge: "Your domains of reference are alternately Christendom, the Western world, Northern Europe and France, without these spaces of reference ever really being justified or specified" (31/67). Foucault cursorily defends his approach, as Soja points out, by "reassert[ing] the spatiality of power/knowledge" (Soja, *op. cit.*, 20). Here we simply want to show that Foucault's notion of power/knowledge as spatiality must be turned, not, as the geographers imply, towards a new, more precise definition of the location of the West, nor even towards the marvelous, infinite dispersion of locality championed by Soja, but by moving in the direction of a new conception of "totality," such as Foucault seems to have intended for the concept of discourse. Needless to say, this "totality" would need to be defined in a rigorously democratic, non-hierarchical way with the sort of extreme care displayed by Laruelle's concept of determination-in-the-last-instance. Cf. François Laruelle, *Introduction au non-marxisme* (Paris: Actuel Marx, 2000), 39–56.

[33] We would like to advance a formula that would highlight the radical transition implicitly suggested by Foucault's future philosophy: *Whereas philosophy in its most general form as a pretense of knowing the real* (either in terms of a materialist identification of the real with matter or a phenomenological identification of the real with the phenomenon) *produces Bodies of Knowledge that Capitalize upon the amphibological regions of the World* (understood, in philosophical fashion of course, as given), *a non-philosophy of the future begins, without donation or essence, from the identity of the multitude as foreigner.* According to this non-philosophy, "Me and the Foreigner are identical," but this identity is only to be determined "in-the-last-instance" — before which point the two are radically (i.e., unilaterally) distinguished. Cf. François Laruelle, *Théorie des Étrangers* (Paris: Kimé, 1996), 159–169.

[34] The term "foreigner-without-the-foreign" is used to designate an identity that is a donation-without-being-given,"a radically transcendental and therefore rigorously unenvisageable form of exteriority" (Ray Brassier, *Alien Theory: The Decline of Materialism in the Name of Matter*, thesis submitted to the Department of Philosophy, University of Warwick, 2001, 144). Naturally, it has nothing to do with the mediation of a nation-State or the fantasy of a specular unity; other alternative names might include the stranger-without-estrangement, the outsider-without-outside, and/or the alien-without-alienation. Cf. "Vers une science des étrangers? (entretien avec Michael Hardt, propos recueli par Brian Holmes et Jon Solomon)" [Towards a science of foreigners? (interview with Michael Hardt prepared by Jon Solomon and Brian Holmes)], in *Multitudes* (Paris: Exils), No. 14, (2003), 73–80; and Jon Solomon, tr. Erik del Bufalo,

"No-soberanía para las multitudes: Recursos para una Democracia de Extranjeros, a partir de François Laruelle [Non-sovereignty for the multitudes: resources for a Democracy of Foreigners from François Laruelle's Non-Philosophy']" in *Revista Latinoamericana de Estudios Avanzados* (Caracas: Cipost), No. 17 (2001).

[35] Jon Solomon, "Taiwan Incorporated: A survey of biopolitics in the sovereign police's east Asian theater of operations," in Thomas Lamarre, Kang Nae-hui, eds., *Traces: a multilingual series of cultural theory* Vol. 3, (Hong Kong: University of Hong Kong, 2004), 229–254.

[36] Cf. Gauri Viswanathan, *Masks of Conquest*, (New York: Columbia University Press, 1989); and Bernard S. Cohn, *Colonialism and Its Forms of Knowledge* (Princeton: Princeton University Press, 1996).

[37] Cf. Sakai Takeshi, *Jiyûron — 'genzaisei no keifugaku'* [On Freedom — 'the archaeology of the present'] (Tokyo: Seitosha, 2001).

[38] Sakai Naoki, "Hensha atogaki"[Editor's postface], *Soryokusen kara gurobarizeshon e: Gurobarizeshon Sutadizu* [From Total War System to Globalization – Globalization Studies] Vol. 1 Yamanouchi, Yasushi & Sakai, Naoki ed. (Tokyo: Heibonsha, 2003), 319–324; Sakai initially explored the problem of complicity in his analysis of the postwar US –Japan relationship as a complicity between universalism and particularism, "Modernity and Its Critique: The Problem of Universalism and Particularism," The *South Atlantic Quarterly*, Summer 1988,Vol. 87, No. 3.

[39] Jason Read, *The Micro-Politics of Capital: Marx and the Prehistory of the Present* (Albany: SUNY, 2003).

[40] Carl Schmitt advances this argument in G.L. Ulmen, tr., *The Nomos of the Earth* (New York: Telos, 2003). See Part III: The *Jus Publicum Europæum*. The implications of Schmitt's argument for biopolitics have been succinctly argued by Tazaki Hideaki, "*Konjitsu no sei-seiji no naka no nîche* (Nietzsche in Contemporary Biopolitics)" in *Shisô*, No. 919 (Tokyo: Iwanami, 2000).

[41] Two related works in Chinese language come to mind: Luo Gang, ed., *Zhishifenzi luncong* [Intellectual Papers], Vol. 4 "*Diguo, dushi yu xiandaixing*" [Empire, City, and Modernity] (Jiangsu: Jiangsu Renmin, 2005); and Antonia (Yen-ning) Chao, *Daizhe caomao daochulüxing* [On the Road with a Straw Hat] (Taipei: Juliu, 2001).

[42] Cf. Giorgio Agamben, tr. Daniel Heller-Roazen, *Homo Sacer: Sovereign Power and Bare Life* (Stanford: Stanford, 1995); and Zygmunt Bauman, *Modernity and the Holocaust* (Ithaca: Cornell, 2001).

[43] Michel Foucault, *Naissance de la biopolitique — Cours au Collège de France, 1978–79* (Paris: Gallimard/Seul, 2004), 25.

[44] Maurizio Lazzarato, *Les Révolutions du Capitalisme* (Paris: Les empêcheurs de penser en rond, 2004), 256: "The social sciences try to grasp the new situation by defining the society of control as a society of risk. A negative and ambiguous way of saying that the eventual creation of the new is no longer an exception, that the power of the creation of multiplicities is the source of the constitution of the real."

[45] Naoki Sakai, "You Asians," *The South Atlantic Quarterly*, Harry D. Harootunian and Tomiko Yoda, ed., vol. 99, no. 4, Fall 2000:789–818.

Introduction

[46] Sakai Naoki, "*Nihonjin de aru koto*"[On being Japanese] *Shiso*, no. 882, Dec. 1997: 5–48; Naoki Sakai "Subject and Substratum", *Cultural Studies*, vol. 14, no. 3 and 4, 2000: 462–530.
[47] Cf. Yann Moulier Boutang, *De l'esclavage au salariat — Économie historique du salariat bridé* (Paris: Presses Universitaires de France, 1998).

Part 1
Translation and Philosophy

TRANSLATION AS DISSEMINATION:
MULTILINGUALITY AND DE-CATHEXIS

MORINAKA TAKAAKI
— *Translated from Japanese by Lewis E. Harrington*[1]

Situation and Problematic

For whom do various languages exist today? And, in order to express one's own thinking today, what kinds of linguistic abilities are we acquiring, and how are we being compelled to adapt ourselves to various language systems? In other words, what are the conditions that make it possible for us to say "I" and occupy the position of embodied subject–grammatical subject [*shutai-shugo*] today? Just what kind of political–economic–cultural structures lie therein, and in order to express one's singularity within these structures, what kind of path can "I" clear, and what kind of linguistic scenarios can I create? It is precisely these kinds of questions that need to be made visible and be clarified, and especially after "the events of 9/11," they are urgent questions that need to be rethought and elaborated.

"9/11" — it is not simply a cliché to regard this as a symbolic date and a privileged caesura (*césure*) in today's world situation. At present, when it has just been declared "major combat operations in Iraq have ended,"[2] it is necessary for us to reconfirm that we are facing an utterly new situation in world history since the twentieth century. This new situation, first of all, refers to a new politics based upon the return of the "sovereign." According to Carl Schmitt's definition, the "sovereign is he who decides on the exception."[3] As Schmitt emphasizes in his *Political Theology* (first edition, 1922; second edition, 1934), however, "sovereignty" is a "borderline concept," and the "exception" is not an "emergency decree" or "state of siege" in their usual senses.[4] That is, what is posited here is a "total exception" that cannot be grasped through a general norm as expressed by an "ordinary legal prescription"; thus, the "decision" is not based on a general norm.[5] Schmitt states that the sovereign "decides whether there is an extreme emergency as well as what must be done to eliminate it."[6]

The position of "the sovereign" within the legal system is twofold and paradoxical. The sovereign "stands outside the normally valid legal system," and at the same time because he "has the authority to decide whether or not to suspend" even the constitution, he also belongs "within the normally valid legal system."[7] The sovereign is completely ambiguous, and because of this ambiguity is a being that possesses extraordinary and literally extralegal power. Thus as Schmitt legitimately — regardless of his intentions — indicates, it is a matter of course that "all tendencies of modern constitutional development point toward eliminating the sovereign in this sense."[8] The type of being whose "actual mark" is "the authority to suspend valid law" is an other that cannot be subsumed within the modern legal system.[9]

That said, what is the current situation in the United States? At present it is clear that this country has not only presented itself in the guise of a "sovereign" in the Schmittian-sense, but also that it is exercising its power as the sole "sovereign" in today's world. The United States after 9/11, that is, after that event which was the most negative "evaluation" and the strongest backlash against the political–economic–cultural currents that are called "globalization," immediately declared an "exception" that suspended all international laws, and thereafter repeatedly made "decisions" as "the sovereign" within that situation and continued carrying out a war against asymmetrical others whom they have named "terrorists" (or "rogues"). This series of processes ("The battle of Iraq is one victory in a war on terror that began on September the 11th, 2001 — and still goes on"),[10] which progressed as if it were pre-programmed, shows that our age has recalled the Schmittian paradigm and has completely revived it.

What has resulted is an immense crisis — the system of international law that was constructed through the calamities of the two world wars is already a thing of the past for this new empire as the subject of global capitalism; it has no hesitation in declaring its opposition to the many "old" sovereign states of Europe.

Translation as Dissemination

What has resulted is also the new operation of concentration camps — just as the Third Reich of Schmitt's age gave rise to Auschwitz, everyone knows that *this* empire has facilities for interning "terrorists" at its Guantanamo Bay naval base. Moreover, the military–political reorganization of the world through the initiative of the United States is bringing about fundamental change in no small number of countries. For example, even in Japan, the "Anti-Terrorism Special Measures Law" was passed less than a month and half after 9/11 without substantial deliberation; Japan's "Self-Defense Forces" have been enabled to provide "cooperation and assistance activities" in "foreign regions" in concert with the use of armed force by the American military; and, once again, bills related to "military-emergency legislation" [*yûji hôsei*] are being rushed through the National Diet. These are the most clear changes since the 1997 "New Guidelines (=Guidelines for the U.S.–Japan Defense Cooperation)," and it goes without saying that they foreshadow the attempt that will probably take place in the very near future to "revise" Japan's "constitution" itself, in which it is specified that "war as a sovereign right of the nation" is "renounced" "forever."

That said, in this new age — which, to repeat, is a "newness" that erases the lessons from the two world wars — what is happening with language? There exists a highly calculated *realpolitik*, and if one were to refer to the mediation of language and make it an object of analysis after witnessing the thousands and tens of thousands of deaths that have resulted because of this *realpolitik*, it might be regarded as a withdrawal from reality or escape into speculation. However, it is impossible for questions of language in this age to be politically neutral or innocent. This cannot be reduced to a simple media critique. In other words, this does not only mean, for example, the hypothesis that the media = mediation of international news in the age of globalization takes the English language as its standard, and that an explicit or implicit framing probably occurs therein because of it. Today, even theoretical discourse is forming a large-scale circuit of sending and receiving through English, and is expanding even further. And, the selection of language in theory and the setting up of its address is always unavoidably accompanied by political significations. Theory is not sent from any old place and it does not circulate in any old language; and, we must be much more sensitive about the politics of language, in which what is called theory must select a language or oppress or forget a language. Theory that lacks this awareness can even be said to contain a large defect on the basis of this one point. In that case, however, how can we be aware of the politics of language in theoretical discourse, and what kind of discursive mode should we choose? Today, after "9/11" what kind of linguistic apparatus should we prepare?

English-Language Imperialism and the Economy of Languages

It is probably unnecessary to point out that the theoretical discourses of various genres today are not exempt from English-language imperialism [*Eigo teikokushugi*]. The condition for thought today is, in short, that every kind of thought must presuppose that it will be translated into English. Regardless of the region or language in which it is enunciated, to the extent that it attempts to maintain communicability, thought cannot reject being mediated by English. This may already be a global condition, and if so, then the survival of theoretical discourse can even be said to be determined by whether or not it accepts being mediated by English.

This, of course, is an extremely perverted [*tôsaku*] situation. To think that theory can only be communicable through the single language of English is symmetrical to Heidegger having regarded his mother tongue alone as a suitable language for philosophical thinking. Heidegger held up as an historical exemplar the phantasm of a Greek language prior to its being Latinized, and thus having its essence damaged, and asserted that because "of the special inner relationship between the German language and the language and thinking of the Greeks," the French "speak German when they begin to think."[11] This remark reveals the obstinate obsession of this philosopher and the politics derived from it; i.e. the attempt to supplementarily reconstitute an exhausted national identity by fabricating the image of a Greece that has never existed in reality and by repeating the image in the direction of the future by imitating it. It goes without saying that it is possible for any natural language to give rise to "thought" through that language's unique conceptual formation, and that there can be no language that is exclusively privileged with regard to "thought." Likewise, it is a mistake to immediately deduce the concept of "communicability" from the fact that the English language is widely used; it is thus mere fantasy to regard the English language as contributing qualitatively to thought. Hence, theoretical discourse must always take into account precisely the politics of language that makes one think that this kind of situation currently in progress is an inevitable, natural

Translation as Dissemination

process. Nonetheless, it is clear that within today's theoretical discourse there is a power of domination and control that can only be called English-language imperialism. What is the ideology that supports, accelerates, and expands this power?

First, there is the view that recognizes the multiplicity of languages but regards English as being positioned in the dimension of generality that is the common denominator [*kyôyaku*] of that multiplicity. This is, in other words, a view that regards English as a "common language" [*kijiku gengo*] that possesses a value similar to that which "the dollar" possesses in relation to other currencies: by making English function as such a language, this view tries to make it possible to relate all languages to each other. Herein lies a viewpoint derived from economics that tries to express the value of various languages through the single language of English.

This economic viewpoint necessarily presupposes a certain concept of translation, one in which translation is regarded as the transmission [*dentatsu*] of the meaning or signified of discourse. If one takes this view, then concepts within various languages can be exchanged untouched, as it were, transcending the differences of language systems. In short, each language would have a dimension of the "transcendental signified" (Derrida), wherein it is thought that concepts can be mutually transmitted without them undergoing an essential transformation; and if such is the case, then there is no reason to resist theoretical discourse being transferred, from the various languages in the dimension of "particularity" to English in the dimension of "generality." In other words, what is at issue here is efficiency in transmission, economy in translation, or rather translation as economy. Derrida says the following in reference to the "transcendental signified" in "translation":

> In effect, the theme of a transcendental signified took shape within the horizon of an absolutely pure, transparent and unequivocal translatability. In the limits to which it is possible, or at least *appears* possible, translation practices the difference between the signified and the signifier. But if this difference is never pure, no more so is translation, and for the notion of translation we would have to substitute a notion of *transformation*.... We will never have, and in fact have never had, to do with some "transport" of pure signifieds from one language to another, or within one and the same language, that the signifying instrument would leave virgin [*vierge*] and untouched [*inentamé*].[12]

One view would posit a difference between the signified and the signifier, would regard both as if they were substances divisible by one another, and would extract a "pure signified." In this manner "the horizon of...transparent, and unequivocal translatability" would be posited. However, this view is a complete misunderstanding of the essence of language, an extreme reduction of the possibility of language, and it goes without saying that it is a reduction that in certain historical contexts is clearly accompanied by political effects. When the fictitious ideology of a "transcendental signified" operates, the "transformation" of language that ought to occur is evaded; and in our age this fiction makes one feel that the massive friction and resistance that is in fact arising does not exist, and it simultaneously prompts an immense cathexis, from various languages always to the single language of English.

Since this ideology of language and its relation to translation has become so common today, it may have become difficult to be conscious of its political effects. Clearly, however, it has the function of concealing the negative meanings of "globalization." The economic manipulation that the putative "generality" of English is carrying out, that is, the manipulation by which the "particularity" of all languages other than English is suppressed, and the fiction of a "transcendental signified" is made to function, thereby prompting an incessant cathexis toward English, is also a manipulation that with regard to individual languages takes the outward form of exchange among relative values. In other words, it shows the outward form of one idiom (particular language) and another mutually expressing their values. In the age of globalization, however, English is in fact not merely one idiom among many. Instead, English is regarded as the "general form of value" [*Allgemeine Wertform*] able to originate and determine the value of languages. Its "mediating movement" is identical to what Marx discovered within the "universal commodity" of "money":

> Since all other commodities are merely particular equivalents for money, the latter being their universal equivalent, they relate to money as particular commodities relate to the universal commodity.
>
> We have seen that the money-form is merely the reflection thrown upon a single commodity by the relations between all other commodities.... What appears to happen is not that a particular commodity becomes money because all other commodities express their values in it, but, on the contrary, that all other commodities universally [*allgemein*] express their values in a particular commodity because it is money. The mediating movement

vanishes in its own result, leaving no trace behind. Without any initiative on their part, the commodities find their own value-configuration ready to hand, in the form of a physical commodity existing outside but also alongside them.[13]

The English language as "money" has a dual use-value. Alongside its use-value as an idiom, "it acquires a formal use-value, arising out of its specific social function."[14] And when the various languages enter into the "process of exchange" through this mediation, they will find "their own value-configuration" "ready to hand" in the "general form of value" called the English language.

To say the same thing from a slightly different angle, what becomes clear through this formulization is the strange position held by "the national" in the age of globalization. What is problematized through the process of globalization, that is the movement of mediation by the "money" of "English = the dollar," is the operation that seeks to rearticulate the "value" of "the national" in relation to "the global," and to place "the national" within "transparent, and unequivocal translatability." This means that no language can in itself be immediately "national" in this day and age. If a language can be "national," it is only in relation to English as a "global" language, and only to the extent that it expresses its value through the "money" called English.

Translation as Dissemination

If this is the case, what kind of critical practice can one undertake in the face of this kind of linguistic ideology? That is, how can one resist the homogeneous hegemony of a language that behaves as if it were a universal "genus," when in fact it is simply one particular "species"? Exactly what kind of strategy can we use to oppose "this false semblance" becoming "firmly established"?[15]

Here one may envision the possibility of surmounting this situation with a kind of theory of alienation. That is, one might seek to recover the uniqueness or authenticity of one's language that has been alienated within the "general form of value" through the mediation of English. To do so, one might appeal to the naturalness of one's mother tongue as one's cultural–corporeal–affective place of origin, and privilege it as a form of opposition. One might reaffirm the uniqueness and immediacy of one's body, which possesses an unconscious that has been formed by the mother tongue. This would be one choice. In general, it is precisely the libido that has been cathected to the mother tongue that is thought to be the most originary and irreplaceable for the subject, and thus there is a certain persuasiveness to the view that this could become the foundation for resisting the economy of general "exchange" among languages centered around English.

As we have seen, however, today's linguistic situation has made such a choice completely powerless. When one language claims to constitute a dimension of generality that is the common denominator of multiplicity, then to oppositionally privilege particularity, regardless of the manner in which one does so, will not only fail to transform the hegemonic structure, but will conversely strengthen that structure. The essence of today's English-language imperialism is the destruction of all fantasies of unmediatedness-immediacy [*mubaikaisei-chokusetsusei*].

This being the case, we must seek another method for opposing the power of English as a "common language" and its general economic power, without falling into the kind of linguistic patriotism or nationalism that makes appeals to the naturalness of a mother tongue or idiom. Is such a method, however, really possible?

To practice *translation as dissemination* — this is what we might provisionally call this kind of method. The movement of language that Derrida in the course of his readings of the texts of Mallarmé and Sollers named "dissemination" is not evoked here as a literary-esthetic metaphor. On the contrary, this movement indicates a very real linguistic and economic dimension.

What is "dissemination"? Roughly put, it is a movement that dissolves even the units of the "word" (*mot*) or "term" (*terme*) that are formed by the unity of the signifier and signified, and a movement in which letters (*gramme*) and the numerous ideas connected with them metastasize while deviating from the linear organization of discourse. Derrida, for example, draws attention to the very dense and difficult prose of "Gold" (*Or*), which Mallarmé placed at the beginning of his *Divagations*:

> Gold (OR)
>
> ....At the crash of a Bank; vague, mediocre, gray.

> Currency, the terrible precision engine, clean to the conscience, loses even its meaning.
> By the light phantasmagorical [*fantasmagORiques*] sunsets when clouds alone are sinking, with whatever man surrenders up to them of dreams, a treasure [*trésOR*] liquefaction crawls, gleams on the horizon [*hORizon*]: I thereby gain a notion of what sums can be, by the hundreds and beyond, equal to those whose enumeration, in the closing arguments during a trial [*pROces*] involving high finance, leaves one, as far as their existence goes, cold [*fROid*]. The inability of figures, however grandiloquent, to translate, here springs out of a case; one searches, with this hint that, if a number increases [*se majORe*] and backs up, toward the improbable [*l'impRObable*], it inscribes more and more zeros [*zéROs*]: signifying that its total is spiritually equal to nothing, almost.[16]

As one can see, the word = signifier "*or*" (gold) is scattered throughout the whole text, giving rise to a peculiar discontinuous chain of many enclaves. This "*or*," however, is strictly speaking neither a "word" nor a "signifier." "*Or*" takes leave of the union of the signifier/signified, and therefore takes leave of the unity called a word, and weaves together a text from among the terms which originally have no semantic connection or necessary relation, forming deeply interpenetrating new significations. Such is the effect of dissemination. At that moment, "*or*" is not a concealed theme, nor is it even a germ from which the text as a whole germinates. If one speaks of a germ, then it is always already *a divided germ*: "each term is indeed a germ, and each germ a term. The term, the atomic element, engenders by division, grafting, proliferation. It is a seed [*semence*] and not an absolute term.... A term and a germ, a term that disseminates itself, a germ that carries its own term within it. Strengthening its breath with its death. The seed is sealed; the sperm, firm."[17]

Derrida says, "dissemination figures that which *cannot be* the father's."[18] Put differently, dissemination continues to be the movement of a centerless scattering that avoids the scene of "castration," and hence the circulation of signifiers structured by the orientation of the privileged signifier of the "phallus." According to Lacanian psychoanalysis, the phallus as the signifier of the lack of the penis is transcendent and therefore indivisible. Thus, signifiers-letters (*lettres*) that substitute for it are also indivisible. What dissemination problematizes, however, is the singularity of that kind of signifier of lack, and the totality of the linguistic system structured with it as its center ("the lack does not have its place in dissemination").[19] Therefore, dissemination neither presupposes nor posits a symbolic order. Thus the movement of dissemination is equipped with a potentiality that traverses not only one language but multiple language systems, and ultimately problematizes the view of the unity and autonomy of a language system itself. For example, what exactly is being said in the text *"Fors,"* which Derrida wrote for Abraham and Torok's *The Wolf Man's Magic Wand*? From one of Freud's five major cases, Abraham and Torok take up the patient who is called "the Wolf Man" because in his "nightmare" "six or seven white wolves" are represented as sitting on the branches of a "big walnut tree." They regard his dreams as phenomena of translation among multiple languages, and undertake a bold experiment of listening to them in a totally new way. According to this listening, the patient's dreams are multilayered formations that consist of at least the four languages of Russian, German, English and French, and their associations arise from the layering, transcription, and transformation of the "letters" and "sounds" of these multiple languages: "the presence of the wolf is…only associated with the semantic family that certain languages group under the initial sounds *gr, kr, skr.*"[20] The patient's "secret" is in this way both repressed and exposed in dissemination. Abraham and Torok-Derrida call this kind of linguistic activity "cryptonymy" (cryptic encoding):

> Cryptonymy…thus…consist[s] in…picking out from the extended series of allosemes, a term that then (in a second-degree distancing) is translated into a synonym….In fact, the very possibility of the cryptic structure within the divided self, as well as the analysis of the partitions in the intrasymbolic surface, proposes a total rethinking of the concept of *Ichspaltung* [the splitting of the ego]….In the unconscious, this "word" is a "mute word," absolutely heterogeneous to the functioning of other words in other systems. How would one be able to contain, within the opposition between words and things, the trace this "word" constitutes of an event that has never been present?…[It] requires an entirely different graphology, an entirely other topology, an entirely new theory of the symbol.[21]

Translation as dissemination dissolves the linear order of language, organizes a dispersed association of ideas irreducible to a single theme, cuts open the closure of the symbolic order, is in itself meaningless, but nonetheless makes it even possible, through its endless displacements and permutations, to indicate an event that does not belong to the site of presence.

Translation as Dissemination

For these reasons, this kind of movement, if it can completely maintain and develop its principles, should be able to bring about the following number of important consequences as its effect.

First, this movement, which refuses to recognize the fiction of the "transcendental signified" at any level, would view as a priori impossible the resistance-free transfer of concepts in their translation between languages. Conversely, it would view friction and wounding, and hence transformation, as indispensable moments of translation. It is perhaps this kind of direction that Walter Benjamin indicates in his now classic essay "The Task of the Translator." When Benjamin states that the task of the translator lies in "large measure [in] refrain[ing] from wanting to communicate something, from rendering the meaning,"[22] in "integrating many tongues into one true language,"[23] and in "ripening the seed of pure language,"[24] he is fundamentally criticizing the view that regards translation as only a means for the exchange of information. Now it is in fact probably impossible for one to ignore the dimension of "meaning" while translating. What would ensue would be simple confusion or fantasy. However, when Benjamin presents "a theory that strives to find, in a translation, something other than reproduction of meaning,"[25] it is neither abstract speculation nor fantasy that is indicated. The "pure language" that he speaks of is, of course, not a "pure" universal form that sublates the particularity of languages. Rather, what Benjamin demands is the kind of "primary element" [*Ur-Element*][26] in which languages are able, apart from all generality, to encounter each other only in their differences, and to intervene in each other. Such a primary element cannot exist, given its nature. However, it is precisely this primary element, which certainly cannot be given in the mode of presence, that in fact makes possible the translation among various languages, or whose arrival is promised in the translation of languages.

Second, when exposed to this movement, no language can arrogate to itself a generality that is the common denominator of multiplicity, and instead a certain site of universality will emerge, formed from the singularities [*tokuisei*] of languages lacking in generality. At the very least, this movement indicates such a possibility. In this movement, the language that embodies the "general form of value, " that is, the "common language" that expresses the value of various languages as if it were the dollar, loses that function.

On this point, it is deeply significant that what Mallarmé "disseminated" in his textual practice was the word = concept "gold" (*or*), and the fact that this took place precisely in the age of "the gold standard," in which the value of various kinds of money were traced back to gold. In fact, Mallarmé's theory of literature was directed toward the dissolution of money = language as the "general form of value." He writes:

> Language...leads to the same facility and directness as does money [numéraire facile et représentatif.] But, in the Poet's hands, it is turned, above all, to dream and song; and...achieves its full potentiality [virtualité].[27]
>
> [N]o doubt, because of money's incapacity to shine abstractly, the gift occurs, in the writer, of amassing radiant clarity with the words he proffers, such as Truth and Beauty.[28]

The Wager Called De-Cathexis

This movement, however, must further bring about, as its effect, a transformation in the relation between language and libido. Generally, the subject lives while consciously or unconsciously cathecting psychical energy to an idiom. On the one hand, as has already been touched upon, the idiom called the mother tongue probably has an exclusionary [haitateki] importance here. For example, it is generally thought that both the subject's unconscious and its first memories are formed by the mother tongue. It is beyond doubt that the linguistic milieu in the first stage of subject formation called "primary identification" is decisive for the future of the psychical apparatus [appareil psychique]. It is also generally credible that even for those who are bilingual or multilingual, the mother tongue forms the first (or last) corporeal–emotional bond and nucleus. On the other hand, there are also instances where the idiom upon which the cathexis of psychical energy is concentrated is not the mother tongue; which is to say, we are very frequently encouraged to cathect the majority of our psychical energy to the language of the other as the effect of political–economic–cultural choice or coercion. As is clear from what we have already seen, English itself is the privileged object of cathexis today. Urged on by the fantasy of "communication," people entrust their psychical apparatus to English, which is only one among many idioms. It is just as though English were a pole of transference (whether good or bad), and through it the subject could be reunited with the *imago* of the impossible father.

Translation as Dissemination

Nonetheless, when the subject is placed under "translation as dissemination," this kind of relationship between language and libido is decisively transformed. Therein, the libido ceases to cathect exclusively to a specific language, and what might be called a suspended condition of linguistic cathexis emerges. That is, when the subject continues to be in touch with the "potentiality" (Mallarmé) of various languages as an effect of "dissemination," the subject suspends its blind cathexis to the "common language," and at the same time interrupts the cathexis to the "mother tongue," which is believed to be "natural." In a sense, this could be called an *unnatural* condition; for, the subject can neither identify with an assumed generality nor return to the dimension — albeit an imaged one — of primacy = particularity. This condition, when seen from the viewpoint of the political dynamics of the normalization of the subject, could be said to be a kind of "illness." In fact, however, it can be regarded as illness only from the viewpoint of a negative interpretation that forgets language as the experience of irreducible multiplicity and potentiality, that regards language as a substantial unity, and that urges rectification of the flow of libido. This is an attitude of indeterminacy that is certainly difficult to maintain indefinitely. However, it is precisely this difficult attitude that is demanded today, that is the subject's linguistic position demanded by our historical present: being the subject *of* translation, or rather, being *the subject as translation*, in order to remain open, open toward true multiplicity and universality.

Have we made things a little too abstract or schematic? Or have we ended up portraying an ideal distanced from the reality of daily practical linguistic activity? Whatever the case may be, in order to avoid simultaneously both imperialism and nationalism in language, and to critique the politics of the "general form of value," we think it necessary to secure, even if only as an ideal, the possibility of a linguistic apparatus based upon these principles. Today, the "communication" that is spoken of in the age of "globalization" is in many cases simply the belief in an oppressive generality that can never become universality. This kind of counterfeit universality must be destroyed. In order to do so, one must, in each and every situation and instance, leave unresolved the resistance and transformation in translation, and experience its irreducible detour as communication. "Translation as dissemination" can continue to exist as this kind of experience.

All the same, we must renew our questioning. When this kind of "translation as dissemination" is generalized as a principle of communication, what kind of position will one end up taking in relation to one's own language or to the language of others? And at that time, with what name could we possibly call ourselves? The answer is incalculable. However, regardless of who we are, at that moment we might, at the very least, possess the right to question the kind of "humanity" expressed by today's English language in support of the politics of imperial nationalism, and possess the right to seek the abolition of the representation of such a "humanity."

Notes

1. The translator would like to thank Ayako Kano for her help in improving this translation.
2. We would like to specify that this essay was written from 2 May to 5 May 2003.
3. Carl Schmitt, *Political Theology: Four Chapters on the Concept of Sovereignty*, trans. George Schwab (Cambridge, Massachusetts: The MIT Press, 1985), 5.
4. *Ibid.*
5. *Ibid.*, 6.
6. *Ibid.*, 7.
7. *Ibid.*
8. *Ibid.*
9. *Ibid.*, 9.
10. From the presidential remarks of George Bush on 1 May 2003. For the full text see: http://www.whitehouse.gov/news/releases/2003/05/iraq/20030501-15.html.
11. Martin Heidegger, "Der Spiegel Interview with Martin Heidegger" in Gunther Neske and Emil Kettering, eds., *Martin Heidegger and National Socialism: Questions and Answers*, trans. Lisa Harries (New York: Paragon House, 1990), 63. According to Heidegger: "For along with the German language, Greek (in regard to the possibilities of thinking) is at once the most powerful and the most spiritual of languages." Martin Heidegger, *Introduction to Metaphysics*, trans. Gregory Fried and Richard Polt (New Haven: Yale University Press, 2000), 60.
12. Jacques Derrida, *Positions*, trans. Alan Bass (Chicago: University of Chicago Press, 1981), 20.
13. Karl Marx, *Capital: A Critique of Political Economy*, Volume 1, trans. Ben Fowkes (Harmondsworth: Penguin Books, 1976), 184–187. Translation modified.
14. *Ibid.*, 184.
15. *Ibid.*, 187.
16. Stéphane Mallarmé, "Gold" [OR] [1897] trans. Barbara Johnson in her *A World of Difference* (Baltimore: The Johns Hopkins University Press, 1987), 204. For the French original see Stéphane Mallarmé, "OR" in *Igitur Divagations Un coup de dés* (Paris: Gallimard), 295–296.

Translation as Dissemination

17. Jacques Derrida, *Dissemination*, trans. Barbara Johnson (Chicago: University of Chicago Press, 1981), 304, 325.
18. Jacques Derrida, *Positions*, 86. Emphasis in the original.
19. Jacques Derrida, *The Post Card*, trans. Alan Bass (Chicago: University of Chicago Press, 1987), 441.
20. Jacques Derrida, "Fors" in Nicolas Abraham and Maria Torok, *The Wolf Man's Magic Word: A Cryptonymy*, trans. Nicholas Rand (Minneapolis: University of Minnesota Press, 1986), xli.
21. *Ibid.*, xli, xliii-xliv.
22. Walter Benjamin, "The Task of the Translator" translated by Harry Zohn in *Walter Benjamin Selected Writings Volume 1: 1913-1926*, edited by Marcus Bullock and Michael W. Jennings (Cambridge, MA: The Belknap Press of Harvard University Press, 1996), 260. Translation modified.
23. Walter Benjamin, 259.
24. *Ibid.*
25. *Ibid.*
26. *Ibid.*, 260.
27. Stéphane Mallarmé, "Crisis in Poetry," in *Mallarmé: Selected Prose Poems, Essays, and Letters*, trans. Bradford Cook (Baltimore: The Johns Hopkins Press, 1956), 42–43. Translation modified. For an approach to this same theme, but which comes from a very different context, see Jean-Joseph Goux, *The Coiners of Language*, trans. Jennifer Curtiss Gage (Norman, OK: University of Oklahoma Press, 1994).
28. Mallarmé, "Gold," 204.

Translated from the Philosophical: Philosophical Translatability and the Problem of a Universal Language

François Laruelle
—Translated from French by Ray Brassier

Of Philosophy as a Universal Language-Thought or Principle of Sufficient Language

1. By what right does one raise the problem of translation as far as philosophy itself is concerned, within what limits is it possible to reduce philosophy to a language or para-language? Into which other non-natural language can one claim to translate it? These two questions go together here.

We shall answer the first with the following thesis:

Because philosophy and language are mixed together according to the principle of absolute metaphor, it is impossible to treat philosophy as one would treat a "natural" language.

Philosophy and language — or even speech — belong to each other both in fact and by right, and have done so since long before the "linguistic turn", but can one conclude from this that philosophy is not only a matter of language but — albeit in its own fashion —- a discourse for empirical forms of knowledge? Certainly, philosophy's proclaimed deaths and ends allow it to subsist operating as a common tongue stuttered by all disciplines at the end of metaphysical narratives. Was it ever anything other than the discourse of cultures and forms of knowledge, but a unifying discourse, superior to those natural languages which proved too Babelish? If philosophy is a language in a metaphorical sense, still more is it the meta-phor par excellence or the meta-physics which internalizes languages, the universal metaphor-language, but precisely a language which bears within itself the meta-physical structure of meta-phor. It is thus not a mere language or a mere linguistic metaphor of language, which would be absurd and circular, it is a meta-physics of language, and hence of metaphor, a combination of metaphor (as displacement in general of language relative to itself) and of metaphysics. This mixture amplifies one and the other, but renders the situation complex. The latter is impossible to analyze by analytical means — whatever they may be — on pain of vicious circularity. If, at a pinch, the metaphysical can be preliminarily derived from metaphor and from the power of language, this becomes impossible and philosophy irreducible to language and even to a usage of the latter as soon as the metaphysical assumes its sense and scope which is that of being supported and swept away by the *épékeina*-phoric or by the postulation of a Real irreducible to all positing in the mode of the meta — as begins to become clearly perceptible with Plato, and in fact with every philosopher if correctly analyzed. The *épékeina*-phoric is that which is most singular to philosophy, its accomplishment, and that which conditions in return its metaphorical base. Strictly speaking, the essence of philosophy is mixed up with language in such a complex fashion (and on that basis, with this or that particular language), that it is obviously irreducible to a natural language and a linguistic analysis. Irreducible means here that it is not a terminological degeneration or excrescence, a reification or cancerization of language (even if it contains such an aspect of reification on account of its categories and transcendental terms, its governing statements etc.), and by the same token that it is not amenable to logical analysis unless it be one presupposing the prior reduction or amputation of its *épékeina*-phoric sense.

2. The technical concept for philosophy's supposed sufficiency as a universal language or an absolute metaphor, which uses natural languages in order to guarantee itself that surplus value of translatability which the Logos accords itself, is that of transcendental recursiveness.

What about the complexity of this philosophico-linguistic mixture? Philosophy is an activity not of localization but of totalization, in the precise sense of an auto-encompassment, not in the sense of an objectified whole. This auto-encompassment or auto-reference of philosophy is transcendental, which is to say real in a sense that is non-empirical and constitutive of its objects. It thus pertains in all its dimensions and to all its terms, affecting them all and leaving none unperturbed.

A transcendental recursiveness is not comprehensible logically, mathematically or mechanically.

Every analysis and reduction of philosophy to such logico-analytical procedures oscillates between forgetfulness and vicious circularity. Either it presupposes what is in question, that is to say, the possibility of such treatments, thereby "forgetting" its object's original transcendental character. Or it surreptitiously postulates a prior philosophical act granting it the right to carry out such a treatment, failing to see that if philosophy authorizes the latter, it is because it authorizes itself through such a treatment, thereby becoming self-authorizing in a viciously circular fashion.

3. Such logico-analytical treatments will only prove possible by way of methodological precautions and definitions of objects no longer falling within the purview of absolute metaphor but employing a language-thought that is other than philosophical.

If philosophy is absolute metaphor because it is *épékeina*-phoric (real and transcendental), this mixture is undecomposable analytically and non-composable synthetically on the basis of philosophy and language supposed as entities "in-themselves", which would precisely be a particular philosophical thesis. Their reciprocal entanglement forbids a logico-linguistic analytic because every decision of this sort about philosophy is such that it continues to belong to the latter or is itself contaminated by transcendental auto-reference, or else falsifies its object at the very outset, or gratuitously imposes upon it a reduction of its meaning. Philosophico-linguistic hybridization is a law of the World, but it cannot be reproduced as such at the level of its explanation. Yet, philosophy is so complex that all spontaneous logical or logico-empiricist analysis of language, even the understanding of philosophy as a game — of language or a form — of...life remains a transcendentally recursive philosophical enterprise, which merely distends philosophy, reproducing it without explaining it, like an application of absolute metaphor to itself. The hybridization of forms of knowledge is a trivial slogan and the mediocre form of this style of recursiveness. The auto-hybridization of philosophy and language under the auspices of the former is a little less so, but is in reality theoretically sterile. What would be needed for such objects is a procedure close to that of mixing, whilst not repeating it in a circular fashion: that of the modeling of the recursive mixture of philosophy and language. Every attempt at an analytic which would clarify, elucidate or dissipate the confusions of philosophical language (from Kant's, or even Leibniz's, to Wittgenstein's) is only an attempt to purify or purge philosophical hybridization, a temptation which remains eminently...philosophical. There is an anti-philosophical reductionism, which is still governed by philosophy.

This aporia must be extended to encompass every labor of logico-linguistic clarification or even deconstruction undertaken vis a vis philosophy, which would not subordinate the latter to a legitimacy superior to that of philosophy, thereby remaining subject to the latter's transcendental auto-reference. In particular, the linguistic turn inscribes itself within the logic of this philosophical auto-reference, it remains one of the latter's particular modalities, and its innovatory scope should not be overestimated. It provided the last century with work, but has only been a mode of that universal turning which philosophy itself is.

Concluding Thesis
The Principle of Translation or Sufficient Language under whose auspices philosophy presents itself remains a desire and a transcendental illusion. The problem of a universal language of translation (universal rather than communal, general and private like philosophy), above all if it is to constitute a translation of philosophy, must therefore be formulated in terms other than those of philosophical recursiveness but with the latter's help.

Philosophical Translation

4. We call "non-philosophy" that new language, alien to philosophy, into which we wish to translate a given philosophical discourse.

Let's take the expression that we are making into an occasion for translation, the biopolitics of translation. It is a philosophical theory of translation but we are in turn going to translate it into another language of thought which is no longer the philosophical or a system similar to that of Nietzsche and Foucault. In other words, we must apparently invert it and pose the problem of the translation of

Translated from the Philosophical

the biopolitical. Why this new project? Is it a gratuitous play on this expression, or else is it a case of rendering it intelligible and of putting forward its theory, a theory of the formulation of this expression itself? We are not going to explicate it and comment upon it as a simple theoretical object but treat it from the outset as a particular philosophical language (that of Nietzsche and Foucault), which is at the same time a thought, but we are going to subject this language-thought to an exercise in translation into an entirely other language-thought, specially made for translating (and) thinking, for translating-thinking in the same gesture, which is to say performatively, that type of language which the philosophical is. The project is not that of a translatology or of a philosophy of translation, but of the translation of philosophy itself by means of a universal language.

We are thus transferring the problem of translation from the terrain of natural languages to that of philosophy itself. The problem concerns the object before concerning method. Can one extend in this way the concepts of language and translation to philosophy, which presumes to take hold of them? But from this point of view the problem is only para-Leibnizian and does not define an intra-philosophical theory of the translation of concepts by means of the logical or mechanical reduction of notions with a view to constituting a universal dictionary of "thoughts" or an inter-expression of doctrines. It supposes a "non-philosophical" type of universalization of the Leibnizian project and a critique of the supposedly sufficient Translato-logos which philosophy attributes to itself. And an equivalent universalization of the philosophical project, engendered by Foucault, of a bio-politics of translation, other mode of the philosophical Translato-logos. One might say that the non-philosophical project is that concerning which philosophy displays only symptoms — a language which would finally be genuinely universal, endowed with corresponding powers of translation, of alien language and of fiction, and which would stop presupposing or simply desiring that it was all these things as does the Logos.

5. The formula "Translated from the Real" encapsulates philosophy; the formula "Translated from the philosophical according to the Real" encapsulates non-philosophy.

What does the non-philosophical posture signify in terms of the problem of language and translation? Non-philosophy is not only a new theoretical language but an alien language of thought, one which is practiced as the translation of a particular philosophical language or doctrine. Concerning the first point, non-philosophy harbors a non-analytical but certainly not anti-analytical program.

Philosophy posits a Principle of Quasi-universal Translatability, the Principle of Sufficient Translation, which governs translatology from above. But our problem is less that of natural languages than that of the translation of philosophy relative to itself, as well as between itself and its particular systems, and forces us to reconsider translation's relation to its object. The conditions for this translation of philosophy are probably of a non-translatological order and don't fall under the aegis of a philosophy of translation, which is valid for natural languages but not for translation between philosophical systems and between the forms of knowledge they mobilize. A linguistico-transcendental epistemology may settle the first case by way of operations to be carried out on languages and through the discovery of their limiting conditions, but the second uncovers a problem of an entirely other order of generality and other type of complexity, that of the relation of translation to the translated itself. What can translation do when it is examined specifically as translation of philosophy relative to itself or to empirical forms of knowledge, and related to the translatable and the untranslatable? What is it that is translated in non-philosophy as translation if it is not a natural language? Our problem concerns the immanence of translation's relation to its object and its cause and what one is to understand by the "translated", finding out whether the latter issues from a translatable or from an untranslatable which is the cause of translation.

Non-philosophy transforms philosophy with a view to constituting itself into a language of universal translation but at the price of a limitation of the principle of general translatability which is that of philosophy, certain nuances excepted.

It is imperative to thematize translation's philosophical conditions insofar as it is invested as a matter of fact within languages and forms of knowledge, but to do so in a non-philosophical register or to elaborate the theory of these conditions themselves and not only gather them together. More particularly, any philosophy selected postulates explicitly or without knowing it a double principle, that of the universal translatability of languages (with many nuances and obstacles excepted) and of philosophy itself into its systems; and that — symmetrically correllative — of the philosophizability of translation itself. Universal philosophizability and translatability are coupled without preliminary examination

Translated from the Philosophical

in the name of a limitless increase in the communicability and auto-legitimation of philosophy. Even translatability governs translation as its principle, sweeps it up and guides it through epistemological and linguistic obstacles, or across limits that this or that particular system believes it is laying down for translation whereas it is in fact waging war against another equally particular system. A non-philosophy will lay down a limitation for these two principles without requisitioning local "obstacles" or "difficulties," which are always controllable and of a level that is inferior to that which is in question. On the contrary, it will appeal to an instance of the Real as untranslatable and more, as without-translation, as already-translated-without-translation, or as immanence (of) the translated. And secondarily, non-philosophy will invoke the necessity of possessing a spontaneously practiced natural language as the basis for all philosophy, and thereby of a condition which is necessary for philosophy but irreducible, as operative language, to the latter's two principles. The analysis of philosophizability and translatability requires the practice of a natural language that philosophy's idealism claims to sublate, internalize and master, a practice that is positive in the manner in which a science is practiced and one which will help the Real to transform philosophizability and translatability into non-fundamental or non-sufficient forms. This double condition, concerning determination on the one hand, and the material or the object on the other, instantly transforms these philosophical objectives into mere principles, requirements, or desires which will remain ineffectual. The philosophizability of translation, the translatability of philosophy will be obliged to terminate in this particular form, to abandon this presumptuous type of universality and to accept more limited kinds of effective or operational realization, ones providing them at last with objects or obliging them to operate within the limits of experience. And here, in this non-philosophical project, the limits of experience are no longer natural languages but philosophy's relation to its objects and systems, a relation which we shall in turn have to relate to the Real of the last instance and to this reality proper to natural language as practiced and only practiced. The principle of sufficient translatability is equivalent to a program of philosophical foundation that a non-philosophy which would be the unified theory of philosophy or of translatology and of a natural language would come to realize/delimit through its double conditioning, thereby short-circuiting the philosophical sufficiency of translatology without eliminating the latter.

6. The immanence of the Real, which is the already-translated, the Translated-without-translation rather than the untranslatable, implies translation's unilateral or irreversible character, a conception which is obviously challenged by philosophy for whom sufficient translatability means a translation that is possible in every direction, a recursiveness of translation.

Like mathematics, philosophy wants to be a universal interface, an operator of translation between all forms of knowledge, explicitly a general language of thoughts (Leibniz), sometimes even an absolute and not only a logico-mathematical language (Hegel). To be such a language of reality is expressed as "Logos". Philosophical language is thus always a machine endowed with reciprocally convertible or inter-expressive double-faces, the linguistic Turn merely constituting a supplement of convertibility for philosophy and language. Non-philosophy, by way of contrast, constitutes itself as a radical rather than absolute language, according to general conditions of determination which tear it away from philosophy as linguistico-transcendental mixture and, initially mixture of the real and the transcendental. It uses in a secondary fashion methods close to the logico-analytical, without the positivism that the latter acquires when it in turn becomes a philosophy. It cannot be a machine with two-faces, it is the identity of a unilateral duality or a duality with one face but one that has been extracted from the philosophico-linguistic complex. It is the non-logos, certainly not an anti-logos, but one must understand that the Logos is the language-for-the-World. The abandonment of the logico-linguistic style which was part of the twentieth century and its illusions in no way implies a lack of interest for the problem of "language" (which remains in spite of all a gregarious and unitary generality) and above all of languages, but a re-evaluation of their relations to philosophy and their meaning for the subject (of) translation.

That translatology, which is most cautious and sensitive to obstacles and impossibilities of all types, to all the phenomena of alterity, remains in thrall to sufficient translatability. The non-philosophical conception puts translation, under the aegis of its cause and its transcendental essence, out of reach of the obstacles of the source language, but by the same token limits or includes within the concept of translation not only the conditions for its practical feasibility, but even more so those for its effective reality. Insofar as philosophy aspires to be a universal language for regional forms of knowledge, allowing for their reciprocal translation, we do not renounce this objective, but maintain that it can only be attained

Translated from the Philosophical

under non-philosophical conditions. First, it is necessary that philosophy be rendered capable of translating its own systems into one another and to put an end to their mutual incomprehension without putting an end to their differences and in a certain manner to their inexchangeability; thus to raise "philosophy" ['la-philosophie'], which is only a general, historico-institutional master-key, riven with permanent conflicts, to the status of an identity that would be genuinely universal or valid for all of its systems. Because philosophy is inseparable from forms of knowledge, this transformation will also be that of its relation to these forms of knowledge. Non-philosophy is that universal language-thought possessing a univocity that is no longer philosophical in kind but of-the-last-instance, into which systems and forms of knowledge can be translated, but translated into this language prior to and the better to be translated into one another.

We distinguish exchangeability or translation as encompassed within a general element which is necessarily philosophical in kind or convertibility which regulates this exchange, from unilateral translation or translation by inexchangeability. "The equivalent" (either "sought for", or "general"), that favored word of translators and economists, is a nest of questions begging assumptions and paralogisms, and harbours the most archaic of philosophical pretensions. If there is an "equivalent" that is emergent, productive and critical rather than viciously circular and conservative, it is unilateral or of-the-last-instance. As the target-language, non-philosophy, by virtue of its condition of reality and in its possibility, is untranslatable into philosophical language; it is only amenable to translation on account of the material from which it draws its vocabulary and its syntax. If natural languages remain difficult to convert and are translatable only at the cost of accident, incongruity, delay and their seizing up, one may consider philosophy at once as an attempt at smoothing them out and finally translating them, and as an enterprise that is incapable of realizing its goal since it reproduces these difficulties of translation within itself, capitalizing them at least as much as the benefits it accrues from this supplementary power of translation. From this point of view, non-philosophy elaborates and distributes otherwise this decision-of-translation. It limits the process of translation, eliminating — albeit only within the element of translation's cause and possibility — the mixture of its finiteness and its interminability. On the other hand, it ratifies as a rightful or a priori necessity translation's ambivalence as terminable/interminable, but does so by restricting the pertinence of that ambivalence to the presence of the philosophico-linguistic mixture and to its function as a "material". The decision-of-translation still exists within non-philosophy, and is even inextricable from the subject (of) translation, the non-philosopher as existing-subject-translator. But this decision, by way of contrast to the decision of translation from one language into another, is non-decisional of itself. It is determined to be of this type by a cause which has the character of a radical Un-translatable, which is to say, by an identity (of) cause of translation.

The Un-translatable in the radical sense of this word, as distinct from its sense as absolute, is neither translatable nor untranslatable in the sense in which a mixture of these two characteristics would allow. It is the Real as cause-of-the-last-instance. But it would be better to say that the Real is "without-translation" (just as it is "without-analysis"). It is for this reason, which lays low the Principle of Sufficient Translation, that the decision (of) non-philosophical translation of the Logos is carried out according to-the-without-translation-of-the-last-instance, but opens up an infinite translatability, one previously bridled or bounded by the Principle of Sufficient Translation or philosophy's terminable/interminable translatability. In a general fashion one must, here at least, stop trying to proceed deductively from translatability's empirical conditions to its possibility, and from the latter to its reality. It is necessary to invert, and perhaps more than invert, the causality, to proceed from the without-translation and from the language to be translated, the Logos, to the reality of the possibility of translating the Logos itself, its systems and the forms of empirical knowledge mobilized by it.

7. Non-philosophical translation is "non-Euclidean" in spirit.

"Translation" is often used metaphorically in the non-Euclidean style, as a translation of one geometry into another. The inverse is also possible. Translation's bi-univocal logic, even in the shape of a Principle of the best possible translation, of the optimal translation which nevertheless presupposes a field of translations or a curve of possible equivalents for a unique term or statement, loses its pertinence in non-philosophical translation. As cause-by-immanence of translation, the Without-translation suspends the regulated mixture of quasi-infinite unicity and/or multiplicity of equivalents for a unique traductandum. Since it withdraws itself from the operation, it frees a unilateral duality of possibilities. On the one hand the Without-translation excludes all translation, it is more than merely the "impossible" for translation. On the other hand, for any term taken from the Logos (a doctrine, a system, a concept), it renders possible a limitless (unless it be limited by that which is finite in the philosophical material) infinity of non-philosophical translations or equivalents.

Ultimately, unilateral translation implies: (1) that non-philosophy in its essence is not translatable into the language which it translates; a thesis which is philosophically and, doubtless, linguistically incomprehensible; (2) that it is translatable into philosophy from the very restricted viewpoint of its material, which it constitutes for the language of translation; (3) that every system translated from philosophy into non-philosophy ceases to be translatable into another as yet untranslated system, and that it becomes so in another system only if the latter has itself been translated into non-philosophical. Non-philosophy is not an inter-systemic translation, but a translation-in-the-last-instance of systems as identities.

A Universal, Alien, Language of Translation

8. Non-philosophy is specified here as a unified theory of philosophy and language.

Non-philosophy contrasts with the solutions of the linguistic analysis or logic of philosophy as a genuinely universal (rather than common, etc.), and for this reason utterly, alien language, one needing to be learned as a foreign tongue. It does so in the detailed form of a unified Theory of philosophy and language, comprising the following aspects, which are of pragmatics, of theory, of alien language and of fiction. Philosophy corresponds to none of its aims, unless it be by way of symptoms, and still less to its means.

 i. An aspect of pragmatics, a use of philosophy for the benefit of tasks or instances that are other than philosophical or which do not fall under the aegis of transcendental auto-reference, and which are thus immanent in a more radical fashion. Non-philosophy does not have its site in logic and language which are for it merely instruments and materials. It constitutes a new use of philosophy rather than its end. The death or end of philosophy, post-philosophy, etc., presuppose a conception of the latter as auto-encompassing in a manner excluding all possibility of its use. To propose a use of philosophy (la *philosophie*) is necessarily to relinquish its spontaneous practice, just as to program its auto-extinction is to relinquish every use of philosophy other than the intra-philosophical. It is thus more than a change of function and a pragmatism internal to philosophy or a doctrinal position. A pragmatism that has been universalized in accordance with the foundations of non-philosophy, one which is no longer a particular doctrine but instead a postural aspect of the latter, must extend from forms of knowledge to philosophy itself but do so by establishing itself as a democracy of uses and "services". Such a transmutation is possible only if the philosophico-linguistic complex or mixture becomes the material on the basis of which the subject as Stranger, rather than being the former's dispossessed claimant, now constitutes itself with the help of that mixture's occasional participation.

ii. The aspect of a quasi-linguistics destined to substitute itself for that self-consciousness or spontaneous self-reference which predominate in philosophy. Non-philosophy is not a language traced from natural languages or from linguistics, but a language-linguistics. Philosophy must be ushered into the realm of forms of knowledge but without being simply reduced to one of them. Philosophy is not a rigorous theory but an auto-significance, a spontaneous onto-linguistics possessing a self-consciousness or reflexiveness but no self-knowledge. Loquor ergo sum: this amounts to a philosopher's cogito insofar as he/she speaks the Logos, but one through which he/she proves only his/her existence as spoken-speaking subject, and in no way his/her reality as existing-subject-translator or his/her knowledge of the latter. This is the transcendental illusion, or even the hallucination, of the spoken-speaking subject and its sufficiency, the Principle of Sufficient Language. The theory of "philosophical language" has yet to be elaborated for reasons that are not only pragmatic, but first and foremost theoretical.

iii. An aspect of translatology developing the power of translation between forms of knowledge acquired by this unified theory or language; specifically, the concept of "unilateral translation" which transforms its translatological or biopolitical concept and their philosophico-linguistic presuppositions. Philosophy is a particular language precisely insofar as it parcels itself out into doctrines that are semi-private, semi-communal. It is Babel distilled to its ultimate essence, torn from the realm of languages and becoming transcendental. Philosophical Babelism goes hand in hand with philosophy's auto-referentiality and thus tries hard to disguise itself. Non-philosophy is a universal language and thus strictly indivi-dual or, as we will say, indivi-dual in-the-last-instance and consequently likely to treat philosophemes and doctrines, as well as forms of knowledge, as the vocabulary and the grammatical rules which it requires and which constitute its means of expression. It is not a doctrine within philosophy or a system, and from this point of view we will distinguish a universal philosophy — a tautology devoid of effective reality — from the universality of philosophy in the mode of non-philosophy. Or again, a future philosophy, for example a philosophy of the future, and the future of philosophy, which is a thought of the non-philosophical type without necessarily being the latter.

ix. An aspect of alien language, the unified or immanent language being radically universal and thus radically alien, such that empirical forms of knowledge have to learn it in order to communicate in a way which we shall call democratic, not subjugated to communicational capital but using that language in order to liberate itself. Universal translation does not occur between natural languages and ultimately in a reversible way between a source language and a target language, but between all of these, albeit only insofar as they support empirical forms of knowledge, and that universal and thus unilateral language which is non-philosophy. We must learn non-philosophy and make it our own as the most foreign of all languages. More precisely, the subject-speaking-non-philosophical must make philosophy his/her own, use its vocabulary and syntax with a view to manifesting him/herself as that speaking which is most radically foreign to the philosophy-language rather than to natural languages. Radical language-thought does not program the "death" or "end" of the Logos in itself or in something else, but a suspension of the latter's sufficiency as language which is particular-and-total, private-and-recursive. If the Logos is par excellence the speaking-which-speaks, non-philosophy is the language which speaks, from the Real, as Other-than... philosophy, the speaking-subject-Stranger.

x. An aspect of quasi-literary fiction that this unification of philosophy and language takes on. A theory rather than a fiction of universal language but one which is capable of fictional effects; — the idea, which is certainly difficult to put into practice, of a fictioning translation (*traduction fictionnante*) or of a philo-fiction. Philosophy finds itself embarrassed by a terminological viscosity, a semantic motionlessness that prevents it from being fictioning (*fictionnante*) and causes it to confuse a proliferation of concepts doubling themselves specularly in proportion to their scarcity with that fictional power which produces indivi-dual clones as so many dazzling or newly risen stars shining off-shore from philosophy's spiral-nebula.

Procedures

9. The procedure consists in suspending the Principle of Sufficient Language and in modeling that complex object which is absolute metaphor or the Logos under the conditions of-last-instance of the Without-translation.

i. Suspension of the Principle of Sufficient Language, hence of philosophizability and translatability supposed as universal or merely general. A suspension acquired in virtue of the conditions of the problem's initial formulation, which would not have been possible or even envisageable outside the Real in the radical sense of that word. This formulation frees the philosophico-linguistic mixture of its sufficiency relative to the Real or of its sense as Logos. It constitutes philosophy's real content as a supposedly "universal" language or Logos.

ii. This mixture is modeled through the construction of a model combining philosophy's transcendental power and the linguistic power of analysis, in a duality-without-mixture, a duality of the "hybrid" (*mixte*), which is itself the apparent aspect of the duality, this time unilateral, which the mixture forms with the Real. This modeling of the Logos is also acquired in its possibility and legitimacy along with, and at the very outset of, the initial formulation of the problem of a language that would be radical, immanent and universal in-accordance-with the Without-translation. Just as we do not from the outset reduce philosophy to the signifier or to signifying practices, we do not from the outset reduce the Logos to the logico-analytical. The Principle of Sufficient Language is much more powerful and profound than any confusions, logical or otherwise, more powerful than the lack of sense proper to metaphysical statements or even the logocentrism of philosophical speaking. It is not possible to model the Translatologos without using a natural language, which is required in an operational manner as speech and discourse rather than as the object of a linguistics.

The translation of philosophy consists in producing a clone of the latter under the conditions of the without-translation.

Non-philosophy, considered as a thought-language, is the clone of philosophical language. The possibility of the two preceding operations is discovered in reality and in-the-last-instance as production of a clone — language obtained on the basis of the Logos, which does not replicate the latter according to the mode of philosophical auto-reference but exists in an entirely other mode, which is that of being-determined-in-the-last-instance. This language is translated from the philosophical and contains the immanent limits of a philosophisability and translatability whose universality this time is effective.

Translated from Biopolitics

10. Non-philosophy is a translation of the Logos within the strict non-philosophical limits of the Logos.

A "biopolitics of translation" implies so many philosophical presuppositions that it is incorporated, as we have already stated, into our problematic as a particular doctrine, which we must in our turn "translate" into non-philosophical language. But the passage from the biopolitics of translation to the (non-philosophical) translation of biopolitics is apparently only an inversion; for this type of translation is a limitation of the philosophizability and the translatability implied in the expression "biopolitics", and a "realisation" or "effectuation" of the latter precisely within the limits of a non-philosophical experience of the philosophy encapsulated in this expression. It is carried out in the form of a redefinition of life, of the translator subject, of translation, and lastly of the expression's universal scope.

Translated into non-philosophical language-thought, "life" ceases to be intertwined with the operation of translation and determines it without reciprocity.

Nietzsche and Foucault posit a production of life by translation at worst, their reciprocal determination at best. Life is now such, as immanent life which says or names the Real without determining it, that it instead determines translation.

We transform the occasional expression or language-thought (the Logos), "the biopolitics of translation" into another language-thought and we do so on the spot or in an immanent fashion from the point of view of practice, and also from the point of view of that "language-thought" whose immanence renders it indivisible in its terms. A translation that constitutes the theory or explanation for this occasional expression and which, with the same terms and on the basis of their philosophical relations, reveals another experience of life and of translation, in the form of statements endowed with an axiomatic and theorematic aspect. Nothing could be further from a doctrine opposing itself to the preceding one (similarly, a language does not oppose itself to another) or from the description of a previously unnoticed state of affairs. The practice of language-thought is henceforth immanent and only describes objects and acts from within the bounds of an axiomatic apparatus.

Life as lived (of) translation and other first name for the Real is strictly undivided without forming a totality. It would be better to say that the lived of translation is immanent or lived-in-lived and without-the-operation-of-life. Of course, this is the Without-translation or the Without-logos rather than the "Untranslatable", and, as a result, it determines translation and its operations only-in-the-last-instance, assuming them without alienating itself in them, bringing them forth into the new language-thought without relating itself back to them, transforming them into elemental hybrids [mixtes simples] without intertwining itself with them to form those mixtures that philosophers propose to unravel whilst in fact busily retying them all the more indissolubly.

11. The lived (of) translation implies the "dualysis" (the unilateral duality) of the "bio(political)" theme, that of the immanent lived or lived-without-life and of the subject (of) translation.

Such a subject exists and exists only as translator and even only as translation of a language-thought into one which is entirely other, that is to say, it exists as system of operations assumed in-the-last-instance in the mode of a radical lived. There is no already given subject "behind" the operations of non-philosophical translation (reductions, modeling, cloning), the subject constitutes itself or exists within the immanence of cloning as assumption of these operations by the lived. The latter thereby raises or abstracts an existing-subject-translator in which it

Translated from the Philosophical

does not lose itself precisely because it does not alienate itself in it, rendering it instead heteronomous to the source language which, however, it uses as subject.

12. The translator exists for-language or is in-struggle against communicational capital.

The translator thereby changes in function and in status. To exist is to translate the philosophical into the non-philosophical, but translation does not exhaust the lived, which nothing exhausts or which is foreclosed to the very act of translation. If, at a pinch, one can say "I translate therefore I am," it is impossible to proceed deductively from translation to the Real, only to being or life but not to the radical lived. The metaphysical subject is also translated into an existing-subject-translator, which has lost its transcendental illusion, the narcissism or sufficiency generally concomitant with the target-language but which are now for us those of the source-language. But by virtue of this very fact the subject has been constituted-in-the-last-instance as "turned" toward the source or original language, for the benefit of the latter and for its salvation.

What is a translator for if not granting — as if to their very salvation — full meaning to the communication of idioms? One must distinguish two movements belonging to each other but in a relation of unilateral duality. Doubtless, on the one hand, an accumulation of communicational capital which the biopolitics of translation necessarily ensures, the translation of natural languages in general; but also, on the other hand, the de-capitalization, if not of the lived, of the subject's life or existence at least, which is to say, the salvation of what is the language-thought par excellence, the one which turns all other thoughts and languages into language-thoughts the moment it translates them through unilateral translation. The non-philosophical translator has as his/her task to ensure the salvation of the Logos outside its auto-enslavement.

The translating-subject exists-Stranger (*existe-Etranger*) in a relation of struggle with philosophical language, not on account of the latter, but through its lived-without-translation. Being-in-philosophical language (*L'être-à-la-langue philosophique*) is now no more than a material for a translation, which is for the latter or for the-philosophical as world-language. The biopolitics of translation was a concern for language accompanied by a simultaneous or reversible concern for the subject, a discipline producing the being of the subject. But a more radical "subjective" use of the Logos is possible, a pragmatics which bears a therapeutic care or concern only insofar as it transforms it into the salvation saving the world-language from its appearances.

13. Non-philosophy is the non-Adamic language-thought.

Non-philosophy as universal language-thought may appear as an attempt at philosophical and, in this instance, translatological cancellation. Might it be an Adamic language, one which has been revealed to men? Not in the sense of an originary and historically first language. Non-philosophical language supposes that only its material, only the language to be translated is revealed to subjects because it is given to them externally in the shape of philosophy. But the latter is precisely that which must be transformed as existing-subject-translation. Non-philosophical language is first in the sense in which priority is now devoid of the primacy of the Real. It is transcendental rather than empirico-linguistic. In the final analysis, it is more than originary, it is uni-originary through its cause and archi-originary through its transcendental essence, real-in-the-last-instance. Is there a double language? A single stock with numerous species, the philosophical, and a certain regime or pragmatics of this idiom. Language-thoughts are "two" only in the form of a unilateral duality. Ultimately, non-philosophical language is universal in a radical mode. "Universal" languages are either of the creationist or the artificialist type, the former functioning all too well but forgotten, the latter not functioning at all. As for those technological and cobbled-together (*bricolées*) languages, they immediately increase the stockpile of communicational capital and are merely international rather than universal.

FROM A POSTCOLONIAL TO A NON-COLONIAL THEORY OF TRANSLATION

SATHYA RAO

A Postcolonial Reading of Some Contemporary Theories of Translation

As A. Berman has remarkably demonstrated in his critique of the ethnocentric practice of translation (Berman 1999) and T. Niranjana in her analysis of the subverted use of translation made by the British colonial authority (Niranjana 1992) as well, translation and power are intimately linked. Just as a given theory of translation implies a specific political and philosophical system, a political theory produces its own *praxis* of translation. According to these two thinkers, the dualist model of translation, which distinguishes an original from a copy, seems to be particularly suited to the political and philosophical system of colonization. For the former, this model is the direct inheritance of the Platonist caesura between the non-sensible or meaning and the sensible or letter, which is supposedly unworthy of consideration (Berman 1986: 64). Generalized in the West, the Platonist model of translation was particularly popular during the period of French classicism, at which time it was known as "*Les belles infidèles*" and later on was vigorously criticized by the German romanticists (Goethe, Novalis, and Schleiermacher among others). In essence, this posture consists of systematically curbing the strangeness of the original work by "acclimatizing" it (semantically and/or syntactically) to the host culture and/or language, seeking to translate no more than a biased impression of strangeness and reducing the process of translation to a mere literary adaptation or *pastiche*. For the latter, translation relies on the philosophical preconception of a "transparent" and "unmediated" reality setting itself up as the original and ignoring therefore the cases of multiplicity and otherness. As a colonial instrument of domination, translation puts into practice Hegelian dialectics in such a way that the colonized (e.g., Indian subjects) were deprived of all history and maintained in a state of inferiority from which the only way out was to internalize (sometimes unconsciously) the colonizer's original spirit. As S. Bassnett clearly points out:

> [...] Europe was regarded as the great Original, the starting point, and the colonies were therefore copies, or 'translations' of Europe, which they were supposed to duplicate. Moreover being copies, translations were evaluated as less than originals, and the myth of the translation as something that diminished the greater original established itself. It is important also to remember that the language of 'loss' has featured so strongly in many comments on translation (They rarely consider that there might also be a process of gain). The notion of the colony as a copy or translation of the great Original inevitably involves a value judgement that ranks the translation in a lesser position in the literary hierarchy. The colony, by this definition, is therefore less than a colonizer, its original. (Bassnett 1999: 4)

Whereas the colonialist model of translation is based upon the discriminative or "asymmetric" relationship between the original and the copy, the colonizer and the colonized, the meaning and the letter, its postcolonial counterpart seeks to consider the point of view of the periphery. Unlike colonial totalitarianism, which extends its domination abstractly, the postcolonial perspective has an acute awareness of its spatial and temporal locations. Within this context, the difficulty of escaping from the colonial authority turns into that of grasping the unity of postcolonialism which involves, according to one of its most famous exegetes, "multiple activities with a range of different priorities and positions" and therefore cannot be understood within a "uniform theoretical framework given that it is in part characterised by a refusal of totalising framework" (Young 2001: 64). Based upon the same idea of multiplicity, postcolonial theories of translation succeed in freeing themselves from the colonial discrimination between the original and the copy. To this end, such theories incorporate a specific element of ambivalence, *différance*, indeterminacy, etc., which will upset the colonial order. Broadly

From a Postcolonial to a Non-colonial Theory of Translation

speaking, this disturbing factor has a double effect: on the one hand it threatens the original's authority by pointing out its "constructional" defect, on the other hand, it aggravates to a certain extent the otherness of the margin. In Tsenay Serequeberhan's words, "what seemed to be clear and unambiguous has become obscure and opaque" (Serequeberhan 1994: 16). This structural ambiguity constitutes the material for an unprecedented "Non-colonial" theory of translation whose principles will be defined thanks to the works of the French philosopher François Laruelle.

Even though they belong to the "mainstream" history of philosophy and linguistics, the theories of translation set out by G. Mounin, W. V. O. Quine and H. Meschonnic can be subjected to a "postcolonial translation." All these theories have indeed, in one way or another, criticized the dualism of the "metaphysicolonial" tradition (language/world, analytic/synthetic truths, signifier/signified) and put forward a unified conception of translation as well as ethics based upon the principles of "Dialectics," "Indeterminacy," and "Continuity." By using this neologism, we seek to avoid any (meta-)segregationist distinction between the discriminatory argument of colonial rationale as defined by the postcolonialist discourse, and the most classical metaphysics as denounced by Mounin, Quine and Meschonnic. Given that they all shake the foundations of the traditional edifice of the dualist theory of translation and put forward an ethical conception of the Other, these developments contribute, each in its own particular way, to the postcolonialist war of emancipation.

Shaped by the colonial rationale, the traditional critique considers Mounin's theory of translation within the framework of the epistemological discrimination between poetry and science, semantics and syntax, world and language (Ladmiral 1994: 106). Far subtler than its counterpart, the postcolonial reading will favor continuity by laying the emphasis on Mounin's critique of translation as an interlinguistic "conversion" of transcendent contents (Mounin 1963: 42–43) as well as on his dialectical theory of translation. The French linguist's critique relies not only on his refusal of an ontology of substance reinforced by his attachment to Humboldt's hypothesis of heterogeneity between cultural and linguistic systems, but also on his strong rejection of solipsism. It is indeed the externalization from "idealistic consciousness" (Mounin 1975: 199) originating from the "phenomenologist thesis" (Mounin 1976: 27), supported by such tragic thinkers as S. Kierkegaard and M. Blanchot, that allows the positioning, or rather the evaluation, of inter-linguistic difference on an objective basis: the Bloomfieldian situation. Moreover, this dynamic of externalization relies on Mounin's use of the Weinreichian idea of "zone of contact" (Weinreich 1953: 1). Interpreted empirically, this notion gives an objective and measurable content (Mounin 1963: 3–4) not only to the relationship between world and language, but also to the latter's inner structural complexity. From this empirical point of view, the double reef of an epistemological-ontological divide and of a synchronic monologue (as implied by Whorf's thesis according to the French linguist) is thus circumvented. In fact, language extricates itself from the idealistic illusion as it goes back dialectically to the "concreteness" (Mounin 1975: 9) of the world, and so becomes objectively determinable through the processes of diachrony, ethnographical enquiry, and scientific examination.

Before examining the ethical philosophy induced by Mounin's linguistic theory, it is important to stress two other points. Firstly, the empirical return described above leads to a re-evaluation of the metaphysical notion of the Untranslatable, which then becomes empirically quantifiable (Mounin 1963: 273–274). Secondly, the process of translation must not be reduced to its sole phenomenological practice, just as the theoretical question of its possibility must not be considered as a mere truism. As reformulated by Mounin, translation questions the internal unity of the structural field of linguistics from the outside (i.e., from the objective account of its "oblivion") rather than from the inside (i.e., from the perspective of the "prejudicial objection"). The elements of Mounin's ethics are to be found conjointly in his literary works and in his linguistic speculations. Rooted in the (Humboldtian) ground of regional differences, this ethics simultaneously pre-empts the possibility of an inter-linguistic communication-translation (invalidated by the phenomenological thesis), the poetic "promise" (Mounin 1975: 208) made implicitly by language to translate the most intimate thoughts, and the perspective of a scientifically (and not ideally) unified theory of linguistics (Mounin 1975). Furthermore, it is this same ethical return to the reality of facts that leads Mounin to dismiss the idealistic discourse on "Négritude," Black art or pre-logical mentality in order to return to the Black man's "actuality" (Mounin 1948: 297), that is to say his concrete humanity. Ironically, Mounin's ethics opens out onto a teleological horizon of communion

From a Postcolonial to a Non-colonial Theory of Translation

remarkable at the same time for its extreme generosity and for its unitary design. Initially discarded, philosophical idealism returns with Mounin's use of "linguistic universals" (Mounin 1963) and his colonial perspective, shared by A. Martinet, of a "global language" (Mounin 1963: 219–220) used exclusively for the circulation of information between equally developed countries. Even though it arms itself with the empirical means to criticize and even to measure the idealistic hallucination in terms of "regions," "structures," or "situations," the French linguist's ethics of communion does not abandon its totalitarian and altogether quite paradoxical scheme: counting the uncountable. The only difference between it and the colonial arithmetic being that Mounin's postcolonial statistics are not unhistorical and metaphysical (everything is universally identical and reciprocally convertible), but always in touch with current reality and (scientific) progress (Mounin 1963: 7–8, 12, 39, 163, 140, 220–221).

Like the works of Mounin, those of Quine are similarly subjected to a colonial reading, which means bringing the philosopher tautologically back to his own dogmatic or arbitrary decision (Hintikka 1969: 63, 71–72, Davidson 1984: 189). In a more charitable way, a postcolonial re-reading will endeavor to soften contradictions through the process of a quasi-idealistic *Aufhebung* (Gochet 1978: 207) for instance, or that of natural evolution (Laugier 1992). The guiding line as well as the limit of such an interpretation is that it is inevitably caught up within the web of the indeterminacy thesis. Aware then of its own arbitrariness, the postcolonial or immanent interpretations will emphasize the Quinian critique against the analytic/synthetic dualism and consider the philosopher's attempt to formulate a non-dualist theory of translation.

Quine's famous critique leads to the condemnation of the "copy theory" (Quine 1969: 27), that is to say the idealistic conception of meaning in the image of Frege's Platonist semantics as well as its mentalist counterparts, such as Russell's psychological semantics. Included in the natural sciences, Quine's behaviorist theory of meaning implies a theory of translation also modeled on inductive enquiry. The originality of this theory is that by refusing the trivial paradigm of a bi-univocal translation, it is bound to assume a state of indeterminacy caused conjointly by the absence of a fact of matter about linguistic meaning (ontological level) and the plurality of equivalent analytical hypothesis for one single "chunk" of reality (epistemological level). It is essential to understand that Quine's theory of radical translation takes place neither on the edge of the analytical divide nor on that of the synthetic reconstruction, but in the "middle" (Quine 1960: 5) or in the "slack" (Quine 1976: 255) between the center and the periphery, the theory and the practice, the identity and the difference. In other words, such a theory is neither a tautological practice of meaning (Bouveresse 1971: 115) nor another traditional empiricist theory of the given (Gibson 1988). The driving force of the Quinian activity of translation is the epistemo-logical chiasmus of "reciprocal containment" (Quine 1969: 83). In other words, translating science, language, or theory amounts to including it on an immanent ontological plane. This theory of translation relies on the following three premises: (1) there is something like an immanent ontological "point of view," which is the internalized (and certainly not the empirical or ordinary) representation of science or language; (2) there is a peculiar reflexivity between this point of view and what it is supposed to represent so that the processes of "naturalisation" of science or "regimentation" of language end up resolving their unity from the inside rather than from the outside, i.e., from the perspective of an epistemological foundationalism (Quine 1969: 83–84) or that of a logical reductionism (Quine 1960:158–161); (3) there is a certain contingency or *finitude* inherent in the activity of translation insofar as it takes place in "the middle of "our ontological reality.

Inspired by N. Wilson's well-known "principle of charity", Quine's ethics of translation must also be situated within the scheme of reciprocal containment. From this perspective, this ethics exhibits a triple characteristic. Firstly, it sweeps away the myth of a transcendent or idealistic translator by reminding him of his immanent and therefore restricted position. Secondly, it acknowledges pragmatically, rather than conventionally or empirically, the (rational) proximity between the linguist and the native through the immanent use of the principle of charity. Closer in this respect to B. Malinowski than to L. Levy-Bruhl's thesis of "pre-logical mentality," Quine assumes, admittedly for the sake of procedure, that the native language preserves logical laws (Quine 1960: 58). Thirdly, this ethics tolerates, to a certain extent, diversity not to say imagination especially in the formulation of "analytical hypothesis" (Quine 1960: 70). However, as we have seen in the case of G. Mounin's theory of translation, Quine's theory softens the metaphysicolonial dualism instead of escaping from it. In the first place, the philosopher's "realist" translation does not concern the original's

From a Postcolonial to a Non-colonial Theory of Translation

identity (science, language, theory), but rather its inner ontological representation. "Realism" expresses here both the difficulty and the overt *intention* of such a theory to capture science's identity as it is supposed to be. In the second place, the translator's decision is unconsciously constrained by the evidence of empiricism (which is too deeply confused with that of science) and by his own linguistic habits (which are "projected" onto the native's universe). Thus, it is significant, firstly that Quine's "enlightened" epistemology does not advocate a "change in subject matter" (Quine 1973: 3), but rather carries on founding empiricism in the (epistemological) proximity of science and, secondly that the logician excludes occasionally, for the sake of (methodological) pragmatism, the "blind," the "insane," as well as the "deviant" logics from his naturalized community (Quine 1969: 88). Finally, the Quinian theory of translation is ontologically embedded in its own contingency, as it is partly dependent on the arbitrary and revisable inductions of the translator, on the progress of science and, eventually, on the passage of time:

> Our boat stays afloat because at each alteration we keep the bulk of it intact as a going concern. Our words continue to make passable sense because of continuity of change of theory: we warp usage gradually enough to avoid rupture. (Quine 1960: 4)

By diverting suspicion of totalitarianism from its own enterprise onto the works of Meschonnic, the colonial reading has made his work out to be something like a neo-Hegelian attempt to achieve the unity of knowledge (Meschonnic 1981: 17). Traditionally condemned for its inter-disciplinary wanderings, and also for its undoubted taste for controversy, Meschonnic's "poetics" (*poétique*) has rarely been interpreted from the postcolonial perspective of its continuity. Such an interpretation will emphasize the "poetician's" critique of the metaphysicolonial "dualism of the sign" (*dualisme du signe*), and his singular effort to transcend this dualism in order to formulate a non dualist or "rhythmic" theory of language applicable to the fields of translation and ethics.

The struggle against the sign's "millennial domination" in general and against its subversion of the activity of translation in particular is surely one of the priorities of Meschonnic's poetics. Speaking from the conjoint perspective of Saussure's concept of "linguistic value" and Benveniste's theory of enunciation, the poetician denounces the seizure of language by the dualist logic of the sign insofar as it leads to the ontological distinction between the "fullness" of things and the "emptiness" of words, the latter being considered as mere "substitutes" for the former (Meschonnic 1975: 20). Operating within the theological nostalgia of the "sacred union," such a logic synthesizes either an instrumentalist or an anti-instrumentalist conception of language. The former reduces language to a technological means of action and implies the existence of a transcendent reality ignoring the historic and linguistic actuality. The latter, in the ghostly image of the Heideggerian notion of poetical "mystery" (*Geheimnis*), abstracts language from its referential use, and endows it with an over-aesthetic and even negative function. Far from being antagonistic, these are two sides of the same scheme of domination, which pretends to restrict its semiotic absolutism by invoking a "fake" minority or periphery (Meschonnic 1999: 191). It is in this context of complicity between the signifier and the signified, that the poetic treatment of translation should be set. In fact, all of Meschonnic's efforts are directed towards the liberation of the activity of translation from the dualism of the sign and its various avatars. In the case of translation, this imperialism obliges, in a schizophrenic way, one to choose between the perspective of meaning, signifier, theory, and "*langue-cible*," and that of signified, form, practice, and "*langue-source*." Whereas the former leads to "literary disaster" as it gives no proper consideration to stylistic dimension, the latter produces a "conceptual stasis" (Meschonnic 1999: 23) insofar as it neglects the contents of the message to the sole benefit of its idealized form. According to Meschonnic, the "hermeneutical" or "generalized" (Meschonnic 1978: 220) model of translation, as established by F. Schleiermacher in the 19th century and implemented by M. Heidegger, M. Serres, and G. Steiner (Meschonnic 1999: 15), constitutes the main danger for the integrity of translation. Finding its extension in the latest phenomenology, this deviant model of translation can be characterized by: (1) the general confusion between the notions of understanding, interpreting, communicating, translating, and even speaking language, which are all subsumed under an undifferentiated and "pan-semiotic" theory of language; (2) the production of an ahistorical conception of meaning cut off from the living actuality of enunciation and assimilated either to the full evidence of things or to their nostalgic and silent absence in the case of phenomenology. With respect to the Heideggerian theory of translation, this nostalgia takes the form of attempting to hear back the forgotten truth of the *etymon*; (3) the externalization of the activity of translation in the impersonal form of the sign or, on the contrary, the

From a Postcolonial to a Non-colonial Theory of Translation

internalization of this activity within the consciousness of the translator who therefore arbitrarily imposes his own choices, intentions, and *vouloir-dire* upon the inner economy of the "system-text."

Meschonnic's anti-dualist theory of translation falls within a unified or "poetic" conception of meaning, language, and knowledge, which means that it cannot be considered merely as a regional elaboration. Based upon the interchangeable concepts of "value," "continuity," "rhythm," or "*signifiance*," this theory succeeds in holding together the opposites (signifier/signifier, meaning/form, original/translation, text/context, etc.), within the "un-idealised" or rather "de-hegelianized" (Meschonnic 1975: 510) process of contradiction. Continuously related and without hierarchical relationship, these antagonistic terms form the immanent unity of poetical enunciation and translation. Instead of being located inside the translator's almighty subjectivity or submitted to an inhibitory idea of the original, the activity of translation is the process of "decentering" (*décentrement*) the original text, that is to say its re-formulation not only in another language but also through the translator's poetic enunciation or "spontaneous philosophy of language" (Meschonnic 1999: 80). From the ethical perspective of rhythm, the translation is considered as a purely *relational* activity taking place within the contingency of history and consisting of the "renewal (*renouvellement*) constantly on the way of identity by alterity" (Meschonnic 1999:190). Such an alterity is not the artificial correlate of the universalism of the sign, it is what Saussure called the "radically arbitrary" (*radicalement arbitraire*), which historically reveals the possibility of poetical "adventure":

> The sign only know difference, correlative to universality. The museum of antiracist struggle and decolonization, is aware of these notions, which have failed like the sign over the poem. We were all the same. Now we are all different. Both statements are equally worthless. But alterity – rhythm is the Other of sign, the 'Jew' of sign – displays that it is through alterity that difference occurs. (Meschonnic 1995: 156)

Although it introduces a requirement of democracy within the traditional theories of language and translation insofar as it replaces dualisms by enunciative continuity, Meschonnic's poetics (of translating) is faced with a major problem. It is unable to fix or contain its own continuity without running the risk of self-totalization:

> One does not pretend to hold something, to stop something. But only through this movement, in passing, situating and situating oneself. A more fleeting ambition than that of understanding. Which would mean grasping and being grasped. We are all Apollinaire's wandering Jew who was reading while walking. Pretending to do something else would be presumptuous. (Meschonnic 1975: 401)

For this structural reason, the process of continuity is for Meschonnic's poetics (of translating) as much an anti-Hegelian strategy of expansion as a matter of survival.

In the light of the previous analysis, a "Non-Colonial" Theory of translation (NCT) will have to avoid two major obstacles: (1) restricting colonial discrimination to the weak and contextual extension given by the current postcolonial discourse and (2) being caught up in the continuity of postcolonial anti-dualism. From the unprecedented perspective of the NCT, the colonial cut (now generalized as the "metaphysicolonial" cut) should be considered as a totalitarian system defined by its claims to self-importance and self-translatability. Furthermore, this system ultimately and universally sets itself up as the original, and tolerates a periphery (i.e., a deficient Platonic copy) insofar as it contributes to a reinforcement of its authority. From the same perspective, the postcolonial continuity of translation should no longer be thought of as a means of overcoming the metaphysicolonial divide. On the contrary, it designates the various mechanisms which limit the pretension of the original, thus making its violence more tolerable. These mechanisms are of two complementary types: the *transcendent* and the *immanent aggravations* of the original. In the first case, the original is identified with the unreachable Other or Unconscious, which is literally "remembered" (Berman), "aimed at" (Benjamin), or "listened to" (Heidegger) through translation. In the second case, the original is struck by an internal alteration, which obliges it to "grow" (Benjamin), to "continue" (Meschonnic), or to "evolve" (Quine) through the living and material process of translation.

The Invention of a Non-colonial Theory of Translation: Untranslating Homi Bhabha's Postcolonial Theory of Translation

Most postcolonial theories of translation, not to say all, reject the dualist model of translation. Although this rejection takes various forms, it is unanimously

From a Postcolonial to a Non-colonial Theory of Translation

directed against the dualist rationale of translation which is characterized, in essence, by the three following features: (1) the hypostasis of the original; (2) the exclusion of the periphery; (3) the practice of translation as a mere repetition (of the original). From the postcolonial perspective, the condemnation of the colonial theories of translation is as much a constitutive moment as a trivial procedure. Insofar as this condemnation is universally shared by postcolonial theories of translation, it cannot be mobilized to distinguish one critical assessment from another. In other words, postcolonial theories are, more or less, equalized in the light of their common and undifferentiated critiques of colonial translation's rationale. Another way to consider the postcolonial critiques against the dualist model of translation would be, on the contrary, to emphasize their critical specificities. In this perspective, a given postcolonial theory of translation would be regarded as a singular attempt to sever all ties with the totalitarian claims of colonial translation. As a result, there would be as many postcolonial critiques of the dualist model of translation as postcolonial theories of translation. Therefore the difficulty of stating a particular critique of colonial translation evolves into that of grasping the irreducible diversity of postcolonial critical accounts implied by R. Young's pluralistic statement. Is it possible to get out from the alternative between a unitary or a relativistic account of colonial translation? The answer to this question is closely linked to the assumed relationship between colonialism and postcolonialism, which reflects, in turn, that between original and copy. Instead of claiming that these (couples of) terms are either absolutely identical or incommensurable, one possibility would be to assume that they are dialectically related, and, thus, translatable the one into the other.

There is indeed a structural connivance or translatability, pointed out more or less clearly by several postcolonial thinkers (Fanon 1986, Said 1978, Bhabha 1994), between colonizer and colonized, colonialism and postcolonialism, original and copy. This complicity can be formulated as follows: by giving a differentiated and critical account of colonial authority, postcolonialism simultaneously smashes into pieces colonialism's monolithic shell and re-activates its strategies of domination. The colonial ogre's appetite is indeed directly proportional to postcolonial (lack of) imagination, just as colonialism can only fantasize the figures of otherness from the biased perspective of its authority. Both the Orientalist vision of the colonizer and the colonized's monolithic representation of the West merge as stereotypes. In essence, postcolonial performances of translation can be characterized as follows: (1) the deconstruction of the colonial original's authority or totality on the basis of its supposed structural incompleteness, indeterminacy, failure, etc.; (2) the generalization of this defect through the ideal and/or material process of translation colluded with the proliferation of (postcolonial) difference within the enclosure of the original; (3) the practice of translation not as a repetition, but rather as a "quasi-transcendental" (Derrida 1987: 220) relationship continually activated by its inner failure and/or "supplement." No wonder then that the postcolonial theories (of translation) are systematically battling against the ambivalence or self-translatability of their particular position. Caught within the restless movement of ambivalence, translation is condemned to spin itself out so that it becomes the imperfect metaphor of its own process. Displaced, continued, and even deported, translation ends up losing its identity to become not only its own quasi-transcendental metaphor, but also one signifier among others of a new and ever fashionable ideology according to which economics, history, and literature are to be construed from the perspective of flux, migration, and metaphor. This ambiguity leads surreptitiously to another question: what is the nature of the alleged complicity between postcolonial and poststructuralist theories (of translation)? To what extent are they continuously translatable one into the other? If this complicity can be traced back to the fact that "the 'high European theory' of structuralism and poststructuralism is of broadly non-European origin" (Young 2001: 68), it appears, on second thought, to be highly problematic. Firstly, the connivance with postcolonialism conceals and thereby betrays the Jewish dominant characteristic of poststructuralism by assuming (often subconsciously) its "particular" universality. Secondly, it generalizes the (structural) "equivocation" (*équivoque*) between postcolonialism and poststructuralism (and more generally postmodernism), so that they become inter-translatable and ultimately indistinguishable. Thirdly, as a consequence of the following statements, postcolonial theories miss practically as well as theoretically the real diversity of postcolonial identities, which can be reduced neither to the Jewish dominant *ethos* nor to a structural equivocation (i.e., defect and/or supplement) without stable identity. Just as the ambiguous history of collaboration between poststructuralism and postcolonialism needs to be untangled, the sporadic struggles for resistance (e.g., against the universalism of Derridean deconstruction)

From a Postcolonial to a Non-colonial Theory of Translation

led by thinkers such as W. D. Mignolo (Mignolo 2000), A. Khatibi (Khatibi 1983) and even Bhabha need to be assessed objectively.

Whereas postcolonial theories (of translation) are constantly threatening to abuse the power of their own enunciation (Young 1990: 156, Fludernik 1998: 46), a NCT will have to be able to avoid all authoritarian gestures. In this perspective, François Laruelle's[1] "generalized deconstruction" of the "Philosophies of difference" (Laruelle 1987) may yet prove to be definitive. Not only does this unjustly neglected analysis furnish us with the means for immobilizing the process of translation's "(self-)metaphorisation" once and for all; it also provides an unprecedented point of view from which to re-consider translation. According to the French philosopher, the philosophies of difference — under which banner he gathers the enterprises of Nietzsche, Hegel, Heidegger, and Deleuze — in general and Derrida's deconstruction — informing most postcolonial theories of translation (Bassnett 1999, Niranjana 1992, Bhabha 1994) — in particular are vitiated by a structural imperfection. While pretending to deconstruct and/or overcome the *logos* of metaphysics, they remain under its domination and even reinforce its logocentrism. Located at the margins of metaphysics and resorting to a quasi-religious experience of the Other, the philosophies of difference never really put a foot outside the metaphysical ground nor elucidate the identity of Otherness. In the best of cases, they simultaneously expand the empire of logocentrism (which becomes able to rule from the margins) and accentuate the feeling of indeterminacy (which renders the margins ever more unreachable) simultaneously. Undermining the whole history of philosophy from Heraclitus's archaic continuity to Derrida's fashionable *différance*, this paradoxical scheme constitutes the "syntax" of philosophical language. Laruelle's greatest achievement consists precisely in discovering a point of view immanent enough to avoid being enmeshed within the fluidity of difference yet sharp enough to distinguish unequivocally between difference as object and its differential movement. Strictly speaking, this peculiar point of view designated by the term "vision-in-One" (*vision-en-Un*) must be differentiated from its "source" also characterized as "the One" (*l'Un*) or "the Real" (*le Réel*). Whereas the latter is radically indifferent *vis-à-vis* the philosophical because it is "immanence and not thinkable on the terrain of transcendence (ekstasis, scission, nothingness, objectivation, alterity, alienation, *meta* or *epekeina*)" (Laruelle 1999: 141); the former does "require that philosophy (which provides a usage for language and of thought) be given. (...) It is the taking into account not of philosophy in general, or as supposedly in-itself, but of philosophy's autonomy, now released from the grip of its hallucinatory absolute form and indexing its specific reality and structural consistency as 'philosophical Decision'" (Laruelle 1999: 143). By considering philosophy unilaterally through the vision-in-One, the French philosopher manages not only to get out from its hermeneutical circle (i.e., the confusion between the object and the vision of the object), but also to materialize its hybrid yet invariant structure: the "Philosophical Decision" (*Décision philosophique*). More precisely, the philosophical/colonial Decision describes philosophy's hallucinatory pretension to give itself as the Real, thereby gaining an "absolute autonomy" as well as a complete control over the other disciplines. In Laruelle's words,

> Philosophy is self-reflection, self-consciousness; it thinks, or in the best of cases, feels that it thinks when it thinks, this is its *cogito*, an immanence limited to self-reflection or to self-affection. It is a practice of thought, or a feeling and an affect. Philosophy thereby manifests through this nothing more than its own *existence* and does not demonstrate that it is the Real to which it lays claim, nor that it knows itself as this *pretension*. Implicit in its existence is a transcendental hallucination of the Real, and in philosophical 'self-knowledge', a transcendental illusion. (Laruelle 1999: 139)

Within this unprecedented context, Derrida's deconstructive enterprise turns out to be a programmed philosophical attempt to overcome the untranslatability between the Being and the Other. Derridean philosophical decision does indeed paradoxically combine an ideal and a literal side, a Greek and a Jewish component — "Jewgreek is Greekjew" writes Derrida quoting James Joyce's *Ulysses* (Derrida 1967: 228). But instead of considering this ambiguity naively (or perhaps literally) in terms of its effects — as expressed by phrasal locutions such as "neither ... nor ..." (*ni ... ni ... à la fois*), "both ... and ..." (*tantôt ... tantôt ...*) — Laruelle questions its contradictory inner unity from the perspective of the vision-in-One. In so doing, the author comes to the conclusion that "It (deconstruction) consists of an amphiboly of two incompatible experiences of the signifier; an amphiboly enforced through the vague generality of perception as a blind spot which, like an untranslatable or an undeconstructible (*indéconstructible*) element, falls outside deconstruction since it remains part and parcel of it" (Laruelle 1989: 197). In other words, the unity of deconstruction ultimately relies on its own incapacity

From a Postcolonial to a Non-colonial Theory of Translation

to elucidate or rather deconstruct the identity of the sign. For this reason, Derrida continuously falls victim (*pharmakon*) to deconstruction's hallucinatory self-perception. More fundamentally, "what announces itself in the omnipresent motif of Difference, *Differenz* or *Austrag* (Heidegger), *Différance* (Derrida)," goes on Laruelle, "is the attempt to bring the philosophical decision to its point of dislocation or maximal dehiscense but in such a way as not suppress it, maintaining instead as a de-scission. Heidegger and Derrida experiment with a new type of 'catastrophe' or 'discontinuity', but they remain constrained by the strophic movement or transcendence of a Turning point (*Kehre*, Heidegger)" (Laruelle 1989: 191).

François Laruelle's "non-philosophy" can be mobilized not only to criticize most postcolonial theories (of translation) insofar as they are directly indebted to Derrida's *différance* (and to philosophy in general), but also to help formulate the principles of an NCT. As one of the most innovative postcolonial theories, Homi Bhabha's entreprise is the perfect occasion to activate the vision-in-One's power of translation. Although they both seem to share more or less similar objectives (critique of philosophical and/or colonial authority, refusal of any discriminating dualisms, and search for a performative alternative to repetition), Laruelle's non-philosophy and Bhabha's postcolonial theory differ fundamentally. There is no better context in terms of which to assess this difference than to compare their respective theories of translation. First of all, it is important to insist upon the fact that translation is neither a local application of postcolonial theory nor its universal or self-referential paradigm. Like Bhabha's postcolonial entreprise in its globality, translation is subjected to ambivalence such that it becomes, as we shall see, both the disjunctive and renewed site of the entire theory's metaphorical re-enunciation. Similarly, the postcolonial thinker's reference to Derrida's work is ambivalent; as becomes apparent when we compare the two different versions — translations of the same article "The Other question" published in *Out there: Marginalization and Contemporary Cultures* (1990) and in *The Location of Culture* (1994). In the interval between these two versions, the well-targeted critique against Derrida's anti-Western use of Otherness: "The place of otherness is fixed in the west as a subversion of western metaphysics and is finally appropriated by the west as its limit-text, anti-west." (Bhabha 1990: 73). has become mainly allusive: "What does need to be questioned, however, is the mode of representation of otherness." (Bhabha 1994: 68). This change of emphasis can only be explained by being resituated within the framework of the ambivalence between "pedagogy" and "performance" used in "DissemiNation" (Bhabha 1994). In fact Bhabha's translation of Derrida operates the displacement from a pedagogical reading of *différance*, which finds itself pushed back to the formal limits of its (anti-)western authority, to a performative interpretation carried out from the location of the postcolonial thinker's assumed "foreignness." As Bhabha makes clear in the opening sentence of "DissemiNation": "The title of this chapter — DissemiNation — *owes* something to the wit and wisdom of Jacques Derrida, but something more to my own experience of migration (my emphasis)" (Bhabha 1994: 139). In other words, Bhabha re-enunciates or "addresses" Derrida's self-referenced *différance* with the "supplement" (*supplément*) of his own positive difference, which is no more (self-)critical. Significantly enough, Bhabha's supplementary re-enunciation of Derrida's position receives a palpable consistency in relation to the question of translation:

> Unlike Derrida and de Man, I am less interested in the metonymic fragmentation of the 'original'. I am more engaged with the 'foreign element' that reveals the interstitial; insists in the textile superfluity of folds and wrinkles; and becomes the 'unstable element of linkage', the indeterminate temporality of the in-between, that has to be engaged in creating the conditions through which 'newness comes into the world'. (Bhabha 1994: 227)

However, by idealizing the "foreign element" for the sake of performance, Bhabha tends to underestimate the importance of the translational "debt" (*la dette, die Aufgabe*) he "owes" to Derrida and Benjamin.

In "How Newness enters the World. Postmodern space, postcolonial times and the trials of cultural translation" (Bhabha 1994), the author redefines translation thus:

> Translation is the performative nature of cultural communication. It is language in *actu* (enunciation, positionality) rather than language *in situ* (énoncé, propositionality). And the sign of translation continually tells, or 'tolls' the different times and spaces between cultural authority and its performative practices. The 'time' of translation consists in that *movement* of meaning, the principle and practice of a communication that, in the words of de Man 'puts the original in motion to decanonise it, giving it the movement of fragmentation, a wandering of errance, a kind of permanent exile. (Bhabha 1994: 228)

From a Postcolonial to a Non-colonial Theory of Translation

By positing a "Third Space" in between the original and the copy, Bhabha breaks into pieces the mimetic system of their co-determination. The former loses its transcendant appeal and encounters the perspective of its own spatial and temporal contingency. And the latter no longer reassures the original as to its self-reflexive and fantasmatical effect. Bhabha's PostColonial Translation (PCT) opens up a "space of hybridity" wherein the original gives place to a multiplicity of incommensurable cultural locations and translation discloses an unprecedented possibility of "newness." More precisely, postcolonial translation is neither the repetition of the same original authority nor the relativist equalization of different linguistic communities. It is the performative process of "negotiating" time and space within the disjunction; or, in other words, the "rearticulation" of the Same from the differential (and no more objectified) perspective of the Other's radical arbitrariness and untranslatability. Bhabha's "newness" or "foreigness" consists in relocating the performance of translation within the future tense of enunciation and the spatial experience of displacement. Thus PCT combines in an ambivalent manner a process of disjunction (which interrupts the mimetic connivance between the original and the copy) and a performance of re-enunciation or "revaluation" (which offers to the copy its full autonomy as a postcolonial and creative subject). As a circulating metaphor/metonymy in Bhabha's disrupted works, translation colludes with the political process of "transcultural negotiation" between disjunctive sites, that is to say the acceptation and regulation of "the differential structure of the moment of intervention without rushing to produce a unity of the social antagonism or contradiction" (Bhabha 1994: 25).

Even though they apparently share the same critique of the metaphysicolonial discrimination between the original and the copy as well as the same desire to raise translation from the rank of a mere repetition to that of a real performance, NCT and PCT rely on very different principles.

Firstly, whereas NCT considers the original as a radical immanence indifferent to the (colonial) world and therefore untranslatable into it, PCT continues to reflect the original colonial authority *at the limits* of its own *finitude* or contingency. Mimicry is the evidence that the colonial authority is still (re)active at its borders. Instead of exorcising colonialism's self-sufficiency completely, Bhabha saves it *in extremis* in the guise of a chaotic background of minorities, locations, and narratives. These are as many ghostly remnants of the colonial-national past and metaphysics. Shorn of transcendence, the non-colonial original or "without-translation" remains unequivocally undisturbed or foreclosed to the (margins of) colonial world's claims which is itself reduced, from the radically external perspective of the vision-in-One, to a contingent or "non-sufficient" occasion. In other words, there is no borderline inter-translatability between the without-translation and the colonial world. The without-translation is the non-hybrid identity or translation of Bhabha's unstable "Third space": it unilaterally performs the disjunction between the *faktum* of the colonial world and its hallucinatory self-sufficiency. In so doing, it unveils the ambiguous structure of the colonial/philosophical Decision of translation without participating in it (as a continuum of displacement, for example). In the case of PCT, this hallucination — perceptible as the mimicry of the Real — consists in discovering "newness" or "foreignness," rather than mere compromise, in the point of disruption between the present and the past, the signified and the signifier, the original and copy.

Secondly, contrary to PCT, NCT endows translation with a transcendental or radically foreign (*étrangère*) identity or agency in such a way that its performance gets out of the hermeneutic circle, be it that of colonial repetition or that of postcolonial rearticulation. Embedded in its ontological ambivalence, PCT is never really autonomous *vis-à-vis* the original whose effects it helps to "supplement" and "estrange." Figuring "folds," "wrinkles," "time-lags," and phrasal "interruptions" (hyphens and points) in the spatio-temporal course of the textual stuff, Bhabha's displacements keep being performed on the basis of the colonial material. Although this material's unity is diffracted beforehand, it continues to be relatively (re)active. But as a *radically* foreign performance, NCT is not a mere "rearticulation," "revaluation," "reversal," or "re-enunciation" of the original. It is said, to paraphrase Laruelle's words, of the Without-translation, but said concerning the colonial material whose autonomy and reality are now taken into account or introduced (Laruelle 1999: 145). There is indeed no material and/or ideal inter-translatability between the without-translation and the transcendental agent of translation: the latter cannot retroactively disturb or translate (*a fortiori* at its borders) the former, be it in the form of its material "fold," its monstruous estrangement through diffraction or its idealist-Nietzschean re-enunciation. The transcendental agent of NCT has a *consistent* identity which is the non-hybrid translation of Bhabha's PCT synthetic (identity through material ductility) and analytic (alterity through formal diffraction) *a priori*. To put it another

From a Postcolonial to a Non-colonial Theory of Translation

way, the transcendental agent of translation is the stable translation of the postcolonial border whose unified identity is extracted from the without-translation according to what Laruelle calls the mechanism of "Determination-in-the-last-instance".

Thirdly, whereas the PCT achieves an ambivalent move of dis(re)placement (i.e., the ambivalent conjunction of displacement and rearticulation), NCT succeeds in giving a consistent unity to the process of translation thanks to the pattern of "unilateral duality" characterized by the French philosopher thus:

> This duality is not one which has two sides: the Real does not constitute a side, only non-philosophy or philosophy's relative does so. It is no longer a bifacial or bilateral apparatus like the philosophical one, but one that is *unifacial* or *unilateral*. A duality which is an identity which is not a synthesis: this is the very structure of Determination-in-the-last-instance. (Laruelle 1999: 143)

Performed then as a unilateral duality, NCT extracts from the without-translation the transcendental identity or translation of the colonial world. This translation is specified occasionally through the colonial material which is now deprived of its hallucinatory self-sufficiency. Contrary to the PCT, the without-translation is radically indifferent to (or untranslatable in terms of) the colonial world, rather than being haunted by its marginal and ghostly remnants. Moreover, the transcendental agent of translation does not operate through a process of (self-) dis(re)placements. It is given a *radically* (rather than a *relatively-absolutely*) disjunctive identity which cannot be displaced, mediated or translated (in)between its own terms, mediation and/or limits. In a word, far from displacing the original towards the limits of its untranslatability, the transcendental identity of translation is so consistently autonomous that it cannot affect materially (e.g., through germination, evolution, folding, etc.) and/or ideally (e.g., through remembrance, oblivion, renewal, etc.) the without-translation backward. The transcendental identity of translation does not displace (itself) onto the scattered sites of the former colonial unity, it performs without ambivalence the indifference of the without-translation *vis-à-vis* the colonial self-sufficiency and gives to every occasion of translation (including its own) the extent of a contingent location outside the colonial discriminative ontotopology (totality/localities, centre/periphery, fundamental/particular).

Colonial translation	Postcolonial translation (PCT)	Non-colonial translation (NCT)
Original	Third space	Without-translation
Copy	Hybrid	Transcendental identity ("translation-in-one")
Repetition, representation	Performative re-enunciation from a particular location	Performative enunciation of the Without-translation
Homogeneous space hierarchically structured	Heterogeneous space: fragmentation, folding, diffraction	Non-homogeneous or chaotic space without unifying textual-ontological plane nor colonial fragments
Continuous time teleologically oriented	Discontinous time: interruption, time-lag, exile	Non-continuous or transcendental time without historical-ontological succession nor colonial remnants

Bibliography

Bassnett, Susan and Trivedi, Harish (eds.). *Post-colonial Translation. Theory and Practice.* London and New York: Routledge, 1999

Berman, Antoine. "L'essence platonicienne de la traduction." In *Revue d'esthétique* (12), pp. 63–73, 1986.

Berman, Antoine. *La traduction et la lettre ou l'auberge du lointain.* Paris: L'ordre philosophique, 1999.

Bhabha, Homi. "The Other Question: Difference, Discrimination and the Discourse of Colonialism." In Ferguson, R., Gever, M., Minh-ha, T., and West. C. (eds.), *Out There: Marginalization and Contemporary Cultures.* Cambridge and London: The MIT Press, pp. 71–87, 1990.

Bhabha, Homi. *The Location of Culture.* London: Routledge, 1994.

Bouveresse, Jacques. *La parole malheureuse. De l'alchimie linguistique à la grammaire philosophique.* Paris: Les éditions de Minuit, 1971.

Brassier, Ray. "Behold the non-rabbit: Kant, Quine, Laruelle." In *PLI: The Warwick Journal of Philosophy*, vol.12; What is Materialism?. Conventry: University of Warwick, pp. 50–82, 2001.

Davidson, Donald. *Inquiries into Truth and Interpretation.* Oxford: Oxford University Press, 1984.

Derrida, Jacques. *L'écriture et la différence.* Paris: édition du Seuil, 1967.

Derrida, Jacques. *Psyché.* Paris: Galilée, 1987.

From a Postcolonial to a Non-colonial Theory of Translation

Fanon, Frantz. *Black Skin, White Mask*. London: Pluto, 1986.
Fludernik, Monika. "The Constitution of Hybridity: Postcolonial Interventions." In *Hybridity and Postcolonialism. Twentieth Century Indian Literature*. Tübingen: Stauffenburg Verlag, 1998.
Gibson, Roger. *Enlightened Empiricism, An Examination of W.V. Quine's Theory of Knowledge*. Tampa: University Press of Florida, 1988.
Gochet, Paul. *Quine en perspective*. Paris: Flammarion, 1978.
Hintikka, Jaako and Davidson, Donald (eds.). *Words and Objections, Essays on the Work of W.V.O. Quine*. Dordrecht-Hollande: Reidel, 1969.
Khatibi, Abdelkebir. *Maghreb pluriel*. Paris: Denoel, 1983.
Ladmiral, Jean-René. *Traduire: théorèmes pour la traduction*. Paris: Gallimard, 1994.
Laruelle, François. *Les philosophies de la différence. Introduction critique*. Paris: PUF, 1987.
Laruelle, François. *Philosophie et non-philosophie*. Bruxelles: Pierre Mardaga éditeur, 1989.
Laruelle, François. "A Summary of Non-Philosophy" (translated by R. Brassier). In *PLI: The Warwick Journal of Philosophy*, vol. 9: Philosophies of Nature. Coventry: University of Warwick, pp.138–148, 1999.
Laruelle, François. "Identity and Event" (translated by R. Brassier). In *PLI: The Warwick Journal of Philosophy*, vol. 10: Philosophy and Science. Coventry: University of Warwick, pp. 174–189, 2000.
Laruelle, François. "The Decline of Materialism in the Name of Matter" (translated by R. Brassier). In *PLI: The Warwick Journal of Philosophy*, vol.12: What is materialism?. Coventry: University of Warwick, pp. 33–40, 2001.
Laugier, Sandra. *L'anthropologie logique de Quine. L'apprentissage de l'obvie*. Paris: Vrin, 1992.
Meschonnic, Henri. *Le Signe et le Poème*. Paris: Gallimard, 1975.
Meschonnic, Henri. *Poésie sans réponse. Poétique V*. Paris: Gallimard, 1978.
Meschonnic Henri and Ladmiral Jean-René. "Poétique de la traduction…/ Théorèmes pour … la traduction." In *Langue française* (51), pp. 3–18, 1981.
Meschonnic, Henri. *Politique du rythme, politique du sujet*. Paris: Verdier, 1995
Meschonnic, Henri. *Poétique du traduire*. Paris: Verdier, 1999.
Mignolo, Walter D. *Local Histories Global Designs*. Princeton: Princeton University Press, 2000.
Mounin, Georges. "Premières réponses à l'enquête sur le Mythe du Nègre." In *Présence Africaine* (2), pp.195–198, 1948.
Mounin, Georges. *Les problèmes théoriques de la traduction*. Paris: Gallimard, 1963.
Mounin, Georges. *La communication poétique*. Paris: Gallimard, 1969.
Mounin, Georges. *Linguistique et philosophie*. Paris: PUF, 1975.
Niranjana, Tejaswini. *Siting Translation. History, Post-structuralism, and the colonial context*. Berkeley: University of California Press, 1992.
Mounin, Georges. *Linguistique et traduction*. Bruxelles: Dessart et Mardaga, 1976.
Quine, Willard Van Orman. *Word and Object*. Cambridge: The MIT Press, 1960.

Quine, Willard Van Orman. *Ontological Relativity and Other Essays.* New York and London: Columbia University Press, 1969.

Quine, Willard Van Orman. *The Roots of Reference.* La Salle: Open Court, 1973.

Quine, Willard Van Orman. *The Ways of Paradox and Other Essays.* Cambridge: Harvard University Press, 1976.

Quine, Willard Van Orman. *From a Logical Point of* View. Cambridge: Harvard University Press, 1980.

Quine, Willard Van Orman. *Theories and Things.* Cambridge: Harvard University Press, 1981.

Rao, Sathya. "*La traduction aux mains de la philosophie: théorie d'une manipulation.*" In *Post Scriptum.org*, No 3, Autumn 2003.

Said, Edward. *Orientalism.* London: Routledge and Kegan Paul, 1978.

Serequeberhan, Tsenay. *The Hermeneutics of African Philosophy. Horizon and Discourse.* New York and London: Routledge, 1994.

Weinreich, Uriel. *Languages in Contact.* New York: Publication of the Linguistic Circle of New York, 1953.

Young, Robert. *White Mythologies. Writing History and the West.* London: Routledge, 1990.

Young, Robert. *Postcolonialism. An Historical Introduction.* London: Blackwell, 2001.

NOTE

For an introduction to F. Laruelle's "non-philosophy", cf., *A Summary of Non-Philosophy* (Laruelle 1999) and Ray Brassier's remarkable commentary "Behold the non-rabbit: Kant, Quine, Laruelle" (Brassier 2001).

PART 2
SOVEREIGN POLICE

A SOVEREIGN GAME:
ON KINJI FUKASAKU'S *BATTLE ROYALE* (2001)

FRÉDÉRIC NEYRAT
— *Translated from French by Thomas Lamarre*

In a Japan in economic collapse, with record rates of unemployment, over 800,000 youths opt to desert the now useless sites of learning. The terrified authorities promulgate a law, "Battle Royale," which is liable to "reform" the education system: the students of a randomly selected class sent off to an island, where they must kill each other off; there can be only one winner.

1

Desertion always comes first. At any beginning, for anything to begin, a hole or void always comes to light. Power is deathly afraid of the void, for the void evokes an unpleasant memory, that of its own origin — the groundless ground at the origin of Power. Power knows that desertion is always a disidentification, a "de-being" or ontological disaster (*désêtre*), in which the subjection that Power masterminds may falter.

It's far more serious when youth deserts — those who have not yet had the time to experience the virtues of the States' Ideological Apparatuses. Youth in the desert, youth in de-being, is violence in its pure form. But of what kind of violence, and purity, are at stake?

Frédéric Neyrat

Youth became a political problem when it became a subject as such, not an incomplete adult or a future adult, but a present adolescent demanding the present: here, now, all; yes, but all at once. Capitalism did indeed invest this psychic interstice in the process of subjectivation, finding it exactly identical things to wear, eat and entertain , creating the Teen, a diminutive for a diminished subject, one that met the demands of the generalized will-to-consume characteristic of our era. And it is precisely from this point that Capital must be considered today: the productive system finds its origin and its limit in the general mobilization of bodies, affects, souls, and earthly resources available for consumption (always adapted, yet again transformed, already replaced — destroyed and recomposed); The "Age of Access" as the American economist Jeremy Rifkin has called it.[1] The Teen of Capital — the *Teenytal* — is thus at once the economic solution to the political problem of carrying out the subjections necessary to maintain the State; and to all that remains of their sovereignty.

Yet the Teen of Capital did not come first: all began with a form of genealogical disjunction, with a new break in the vertical flow of transmission: the horizontal demand for immediate consumption was, to begin with, the sign of a rejection of mediation, of all forms of representation. The year 1968 symbolizes this break in France and for other countries. It would certainly be important to compare, and to distinguish between, the multiple forms of this break: it begins rather earlier in Japan, from the 1960s at least (with struggles led by the national student league (*Zengakuren*)). We nonetheless assume as follows, as hypotheses: (1) the imperative to consume, which marks the "new face of being" (Heidegger), affects the whole of the globalized world; (2) this imperative was not simply imposed from above but was only able to take root by meeting with a desire that rose to meet it, only to drag it lower than it ever wished (as with subversive reappropriations or consumer riots like those in Harlem in 1954 or Los Angeles in 1992) or by meeting with one that preceded it; (3) adolescence, as a time of carnal composition and subjective recomposition, is the support adequate to such desire. A serious inquiry would look for the ways in which, in each country, it so happened that mediations were called in question. In those instances in which this break was not able to follow through, one might well imagine that the imperative to consume was imposed not by calling mediations into question but by disavowing them. The desertion of the sites of learning imagined by Kinji Fukasaku in his film re-opens this rejection, this refusal, and reawakens the specter of a dangerous disconnection.

A Sovereign Game

Still, there is nothing revolutionary about these youths who abandon the schools. The fear they inspire comes simply from the fact that their desertion unmasks a void that their continued presence served only to mask: the void of Japanese institutions incapable of achieving the very goals that bring them to life. What causes fear is the void, the very void of Japanese society. This is the very principle of violence.

We say: the very principle of violence. It is really not a matter of political violence, in the sense of a violence that has justice, equality, or liberty as its ends, where this end itself would be subjectivized. Rather this is an instance of violence at the very core of the political — *mystical violence that goes to the non-political heart of the political* — that lays bare its groundless ground.[2] The place that the students leave empty is analogous to the place that Power must take care to occupy to take its stand. Whether they wish it or not, whether they know it or not, those who thus make the void are squarely in the position of Claimants. That's what Power knows. The void is a bad memory, since it recalls the violence that Power had to carry out to establish the base for its Right. And the Right is a second violence, liable to be just, that takes shape through the inclusion of a first violence that is itself without justice.[3]

2

It is for this reason that the "reform" of the education system promulgated by Japanese Power implies an extreme outburst of violence, violence without limits. The class drawn at random is taken hostage. A classroom has been reconstituted on the desert island to which they have been led (which desertification may recall the school desertion). The one who directs the operations is their former professor, surrounded by soldiers, who from now on will assure that Order reigns, with knifes and bombs if necessary. Nothing short of this murderous use of violence will bring the students to accept the rules imposed on them.

The violence of Power appears as the expression of an alleged "reform," and we learn that the parents of the students know what's up on the desert island. "Battle Royale" thus falls within the domain of the law, as an expression of the general will. Yet the will at work is only a will to death — a violence without limits responding to that which has put back into play the very origin of the *passage to the limit* at the heart of Right. From then on, the violence expressed by the law is the first violence, the violence before the law, and no longer the second violence.

The violence of the "reform," however, has at stake an even greater violence, since the rules are as follows: the students must kill one another, they have three days to do it, at the end of which only one of them may survive; if more than one remains, all the survivors will die. What is put in place is nothing more or less than an Auto-Extermination Camp, which seems to materialize the political axiom of Giorgio Agamben: the Camp is the "new *nomos* of modernity."[4] But this is a very particular sort of camp, one that is not at all reducible to what could be done in the Nazi Camps: the Camp in *Battle Royale* has incorporated the norms of biopolitical and hyper-spectacular Capitalism: competition on the one hand, whose end is literally to produce survivors (or "bare life," to evoke Agamben's term); but also the massive presence of mass media. The students are apprised of the rules not by their professor, who is there to impose order, but by a video: a totally congenial hostess presents the rules to them in the fashion of a TV game show.

Still this is not at all a parody of game shows, nor is this a film that would decry mass media, as this has already been done; it is a matter of showing the very real extension of the Camps into mass media, which, from the end of 20th century, produces "games" in which "voluntarily" imprisoned individuals must seduce one other, or battle one another, or survive in extreme conditions, and so forth. The students in *Battle Royale* are thus exposed to their daily reality, which blows up in their face with the greatest cruelty; when blood really and truly begins to flow. What is exposed is the coupling of military force with the System of Control put in place by media in-formation.

The problem — *the problem for Power* — is that one never knows how these individuals subjectivize the events they undergo. Many reactions appear inside the Auto-Extermination Camp. Some refuse the rules by committing suicide; they thus escape the game but by submitting to it fundamentally. Others agree to "participate," battling and killing one another. Still others try to create a pocket of peace within a universe where violence reigns, as if to recreate a more familiar, more human environment. Bad solution: to create true borders where they do not exist, demands an instituting force, and not the simply private use of a territorial appropriation. These will die very rapidly, submerged by a wave of murder.

A Sovereign Game

How to resist? Three individuals will try to move against Power, pirating the computer system, fabricating a bomb. A classic way of resisting (one of them takes his "activist" parent as a model); and yet another useless response: they literally do not weigh enough, and are killed not by Power but by those who participate in its "rules."

Two peculiar individuals remain, who, unlike the others who are armed to the teeth, have for self-defense only a lid for shield and a pair of binoculars. Two individuals in flight, in pursuit of another kind of desertion within the island itself. They know that they have no protection, and cannot come up with any, but flee from the rules that determine the space in which they are nonetheless confined. There is a sort of naiveté, or unconditional purity, about these two. And that may be what will save them.

3

Battle Royale breaks into three basic times, which appear to follow one another in a very dialectical fashion. First time: *Desertion*. Second time: the violent response of power, which does its work of negation as will to auto-extermination — the time of the *Camp*. The third time, which leads out of the Camp through fundamental violence, is murder, followed by *Flight*.

The two survivors have a very peculiar subjective position indeed. Their purity draws them out of the violence of the Camp — there where the most unjust violence flows, their non-violence overflows. Still, resolution comes about through the murder of their professor who entraps them: as they leave the Camp, they take up weapons, with only this as their watchword, as their password: "Class." This is no longer the same desertion as the first one: it is now subjectivized, and follows from the flight that they achieved in the Camp (a flight from the "rules" of the "game"). What has happened?

Power commits a major error in its auto-exterminatory anticipation: violence imposed where a mystic violence is in play will ultimately have as its effect a form of rebellious subjectivation, potentially more dangerous than the a-subjective desertion that it wished to eradicate.[5] In effect, the Flight of the two students bears with it all their experience, which is nothing other than a *sovereign experience*. Theirs is the *sovereignty of non-acting* precisely where an integral violence acts — the sovereignty of an unactualized force. Then [comes] the passage through murder, which is nothing but the sovereignty of Evil in the sense theorized so aptly by Bataille (and which he called *transgression*). Then [there is] the Flight of two freedmen, entered clandestinely.

All of this may appear quite exaggerated, or extremely trivial... What miserable sovereignty! Sovereignty of the outlaw! Yet let us recall that the law of a government that institutes "Battle Royale" is a law emptied of all justice. Flight is no more outside the law than it is within the law, because the state of permanent exception rules, in which force and law, "exclusion and inclusion, exterior and interior, *bios* and *zoe*, law and fact, enter into a zone of irreducible indifferentiation."[6]

This may be a sovereignty-in-waiting, this sovereignty of which the two freedmen are bearers, that which remains when the political has failed and reduced itself to the Camp and Control. [It is a] sovereignty of transition that takes on "mystical" violence when this violence no longer manages to cover its tracks in legal justice. Miserable sovereignty — for miserable times.

4

But how sure are we that this resolution adds up dialectically? Something seems to trouble this pure logic: the intervention of the professor. Suddenly, in a theatrical finale, he appears as the story's engineer, as the one who knows everything from the start, and the one who has pulled every string. It is he who forces the students to murder, by defying them with a pistol that turns out to be nothing but a squirt gun; it is thus he who forces them to escape. Can one speak of an authentic emancipation?

The story is quite a bit more complicated: there is the girl who had not deserted (a scene shows her coming to attend class, entering an empty room, where only the professor is present; she thinks she has the schedule wrong). From the start of the "game," apparently, the professor wished to save her. Kitano himself plays the professor, who goes by the name Kitano. Kitano reigns over the bloodbath — Kitano, whom we also know to be a painter in real life, exhibits at the end of the film a painting in which the girl student remains in all her Glory, unscathed. Kitano, the character, who wishes to save the only being who has not deserted

A Sovereign Game

— but not to save her from the game: *he asks her to commit suicide with him*, threatening her with his harmless gun. She is presented with two solutions: either she accepts double suicide, thus completing the work of auto-extermination insofar as she kills one more person. Or she refuses this offer and assumes herself exposed to death, which doesn't turn out to be the case. Here everything becomes infinitely twisted and inverted. A moment of vacillation, *which comes from the very status of Kitano*: at once in the film as actor, and outside the film as a real person. There is certainly nothing original about this cinematic procedure; but there is something novel and unexpected about the way that it is inscribed in the overall apparatus of the film and of the era that the film expresses. *Status of generalized indifferentiation*: inside/outside the law, real/imaginary, etc....

As always, the resolution involves the intervention of a third party: here there is the student (a friend of the girl) who murders the professor, thus fulfilling the last words of his father, who, upon killing himself, left him this message (this legacy) — "Courage" — the film's first password. After the murder, the girl student will be able to undertake a Flight that will not have been preceded by any desertion. And what if that was in fact the deepest wish of professor Kitano? In the very end, does he not wish to compensate for her non-desertion, or otherwise to force her into Flight? Is it a question of completing the game, or of thwarting it? That is undecidable: both possibilities can be envisioned.

Or maybe both should be abandoned, both left to cancel out. Because we go astray in wishing to penetrate the mystery of Kitano's desire. This mystery is that of game itself, of another game that is not (or not simply) the "game" of "Battle Royale." In the classroom to which they have been led, one of the students asks, "Question: why have invented this game?"

Kitano replies: "It's your fault. You make fun of adults. And why not. It's your right. But don't forget: life itself is a game."

There's the game and the Game. The game of reform, and another Game in which that game is immersed. Kitano is not the master of this other Game. When we look at the finale scene of murder, it has an aura of farce about it, or rather of Comedy: we think Kitano is dead; he gets up, as if nothing were wrong, to answer the telephone, to chew out his daughter, to blow the phone to pieces with his gun (now a real gun), as in the most caricatured of Westerns; he then dies suddenly, collapsing like a puppet. Thus the invisible wires that support that puppeteer are revealed, under the control of some unknown, cosmic scene.

Frédéric Neyrat

There's the game and the Game: that in which one can impose rules, and that which is imposed on any Master whatsoever. A "Game of life," that wages much more than political sovereignty can contain. When such a will to limitless capture — this excess — tempts Power, it is limitless violence that is expressed. Greek tragedy in the news. Before this excess of power only one possibility remains: reference to some "non-written" right capable of countering the law in effect. But, as those commentators who have drawn inspiration from Höderlin's rather odd translation of Sophocles's tragedy have aptly shown, the nocturnal right claimed by Antigone ultimately cannot be attributed to any god; there is no divine guarantor capable of judging the excess of Creon: as Lacan says, Antigone's act of rebellion expresses only her "pure desire;" it is a decisive act inscribed in a Game over which no Master holds sway.[7]

Yet Antigone represents not the pure heroic exception but the very essence of all subjective singularity. Antigone's "pure desire" is that of a child, of any child whatsoever. The first scene of the film shows the arrival of one of the winners of the "game" — a girl, a pre-teen with a doll in her arms. And we think: the game has gone so far that it now touches all youth. *They are killing children.* But it is also possible to imagine that youth will reply to the fundamental violence done to it, that youth will find it necessary to make itself a *Rebellious Subject* in order to defend itself within a world falling to pieces, in which fathers and teachers kill themselves with might and main.

The journalist is surprised: "she smiles." We see the face of the young girl intermittently, eclipsed with camera flashes. These eclipses are the cinematographic indices of an event, of a subjectivation that always implies the passage of negativity and emptiness at the heart of the subject; traces or evidences of a *burden* proper to the representation of all radical experience. The smile of the child is sovereign.

> Time is a child at play, it is the kingdom of a child. (Heraclitus)

Post-scriptum: What the Future Reserves for Us

Quite frankly, I saw *Battle Royale* as a thoroughly uninventive film in cinematic terms. It might be dubbed a B-film, with some striking scenes here and there. But what characterizes this type of film is precisely its ability to function as a veritable

A Sovereign Game

apparatus of capture: in tune with the world, with the flow of media images and new modalities of power, *Battle Royale* is not directly or audaciously opposed to the era, but simply indicates a possible "line of flight" (to borrow from Deleuze). It is in this respect that a cinema that some will deem "minor" will sometimes be — and only sometimes — richer and more fruitful than so-called "auteur" cinema (although undoubtedly this distinction itself should be thoroughly revised).

The relation of philosophy to the aesthetic in general (and to cinema in particular) is exceedingly problematic: can I be sure not to have "forced" this film, not to have made it say something it doesn't show? It seems to me essential to look at this question in the affirmative: our era requires some forcing — in order not to nurture those miserable sovereignties in flight from new systems of control and from unrestrained powers. Thus I used *Battle Royale* as a pretext, a pretext to think *to the utmost* what may not actually be in the film. Thinking to the utmost is to affirm the forces of an era without any assurance that they will follow through. This is undoubtedly dialectical, all promise and anticipation — but *for anticipation itself*, without object, much as Derrida speaks of a "messianic without Messiah."[8] An anticipation that would have as its function to take on something, to take on something in writing; at the very least. In this instance: let youth make itself a Rebellious Subject!

What must be affirmed is precisely "let youth make itself." To say that youth is already there, already rebellious, would be to say too much — to hallucinate. To say that youth is not there, would be presumptuous. To say that youth might be there commits very little. To say "let youth makes itself" returns it not only to *its* possible but also enjoins this possible to be there on behalf of a speech that cries out. There's truly a lack of exclamations today, of *active participation in what might be*. For it isn't possible to separate what we promise of glory, sovereignty and joy, from what it supposed to be "reality," a "reality" not even returned to its void but to its full necessity; a rickety and false conception, which does not let time be, which fixes the present, tacking it to statistical tables. Promise, however, is *what the future reserves for us*, precisely what we do not master. But let it not be said that the absence of mastery must result in forfeiting all creative imaginary! This creative imaginary, we speak of it *in reserve*.

The *reserve* is what Heidegger aptly theorized under the name of the "non-disclosed," which is not a sort of pocket of being outside being, but being as a power-of-not (*puissance de ne pas*); in sum the contrary of Power, if one thus names the Political Sovereignty expunged of all retreat, of all reserve, of all limit. The power-of-not might be called potential, but it is a potentiality without end, without completion. A potentiality that is infinite in the sense that it knows that it cannot come to completion, yet finite because it does not await a final incarnation. The power-of-not can thus become Justice, and just political action, if it knows what nocturnal ballast it must bear in becoming just. Without definitive and assured ground, potential Justice is without guarantee; this is why it *can* withhold itself.

When the political lacks this reserve, it falls unilaterally back on singularities — artists, politicians, whomever. Flight, Desertion, Exodus are the stages proper to this process of singularization, of which we wished to show some possible realizations in our account of Kinji Fukasaku's film. It seems to us that its youth, as all youth, bears something that touches precisely on what the future *reserves* for us. Youth is entirely in tune with processes of subjection, with the state of institutions, juridical norms and systems of control. We would need to continue our inquiry: what place does the globalized world leave to youth when what reign are commercial relations, production formatting, the imperative to consume, and the "virtual" anticipation characteristic of the world of the cultural industry? This place will have to be occupied by Subjects, or by Constructions of which Subjects will only be the salient moments.

In this respect, we see only a simple tautology in the expression "rebellious subject": to be subject is inevitably to appropriate that which is given to us in the form of a selection, a negation, a death-to-self, which brings into play the question of transmission and the possibility of successive life proper to any being capable of death and speech. Rebellion is consequently not something directly political, but something introduced in the dimension of the Game with a capital G, the Game that weighs down that game which amuses or exterminates — the two being able to intertwine, as we've seen.

The Game thus has everything to do with childhood. It is perhaps this childhood that the *Teenytal* must bring forth in itself, this initial Sovereign Game that is the *reserve* of all establishing of rules. It is certainly "non-written," and the appeal to it in the last instance invites us to rethink the space that the tragedy of Antigone still symbolizes for us, with her supreme act. At the heart of tragedy resides a non-knowledge, a domain to which no earthly power lays claim, a

A Sovereign Game

nocturnal share that is the object of a disavowal. It is Oedipus who thinks, wrongly, to have solved the riddle of the Sphinx, it is Creon who inverts the order of life and death — but it is likewise Antigone who, as Hegel writes, "did not pass the test of daylight," who is not able to break out of her status of heroic exception. Against a Hegelian movement of reconciliation that he found too sound, Bataille would again bring to the surface a form of negativity that utterly exceeds all forms of synthesis: "The greatest danger is the forgetfulness of the dismal underground, which the birth of awakened men ruptures. The greatest danger is that men who cease to wander in obscurity of sleep and Mother-Tragedy end up submitting to useful labour."[9] But another kind of danger lies in wait for negativity when it becomes insomniac: to sink body and soul into the Mother-Tragedy... To make the "rupture" in Societies of Control and "virtual realities" matter, it is no longer enough to oppose the shadow share to the law of daylight — because the latter has become blinding. We must elevate the shadow share to the level of the Game, to that of Comedy informed by tragedy. It is no longer so much a matter of burrowing into the underground of the "labyrinth" (another of Bataille's terms) in order to tap the Negative, as it is to make the Negative pass between the Game and game in order to mark their difference. It is thus not a matter of revoking Tragedy, but of finding a mode of positioning that breathes life into its truth for something profoundly revolutionary. This may be the "will to chance" of which Bataille spoke: let all be carried away, put in play, *even the rupture of being* that a simple laugh inscribes in the register of sovereign refusals.

Revolution: is it really the adequate term to speak of this *anticipatory burden* that promises here and now, this burden that refuses to unburden itself in the manner of Power when it anticipates, outside itself, the object of its potential reversal. What community is possible for this ontologically riddled revolution? This is the one that must be affirmed here and now. Right away. There's nothing to fear: *to draw from its reserve, to draw from it with sovereign power, only serves to expose the shadow share to the friendship of daylight, harmlessly.* A daylight protected from its electronic double.

Notes

[1] Jeremy Rifkin, *L'âge de l'accès — la révolution de la nouvelle économie* (Paris, La découverte, 2000).

² See Jacques Derrida's *Force de loi* (Paris: Galilée, 1994), particularly his interpretation of Walter Benjamin's essay, "Critique of violence" (in *Essais* vol. 1, Collection Folio [Paris: Gallimar, 2000]), from which this essay drew much of its inspiration.

³ We should introduce greater complexity into our schema, but, simply put, this "without justice" is one that is not a justice or a "second" reason in the sense of one that would be anticipated; anticipation that integrates the timeless time of the ungrounded, the fictive chronology of what-will-have-been-necessary-for (establishing the base for a Right).

⁴ Giorgio Agamben, *Homo Sacer 1. Le pouvoir souverain et la vie nue*, Paris, Seuil, 1997.

⁵ This error is not in the least foreign to the workings of the dialectic: the dialectic implies such a passage through error, because it is this very passage that draws from a being what one believed it was, and what it was *not yet*. A passage that is manifest in *Phenomenology of Spirit*: *Absolute Spirit* is incarnated among beings whose communication is always established on the model of a dialogue of the deaf. It would suffice to note, for instance, the degree to which Antigone and Creon do not understand one another, the degree to which the dialectical synthesis of the law "publicly in force under the sun" (Creon) with "non-written" laws (Antigone) comes about by way of a third position — a philosophical decision.

⁶ Agamben, *Homo Sacer*, 17.

⁷ For Hoderlin's strange and luminous translation, see *L'Antigone de Sophocle*, trad. P. Lacoue-Labarthe (Paris: Christian Bourgois, 1978), 53. For Jacques Lacan's commentary, see *L'éthique de la psychanalyse* (Paris: Seuil, 1986), 323–375. The reader might also consult my analysis in *Fantasme de la communauté absolue* (Paris: L'Harmattan, 2002), 133–144.

⁸ Jacques Derrida, *Spectres de Marx* (Paris: Galilée, 1993).

⁹ Georges Bataille, *Oeuvrescomplètes* (Paris, Gallimard, 1970), I: 494.

GLOBALIZED-IN-SECURITY:
THE FIELD AND THE BAN-OPTICON

DIDIER BIGO
— Translated from French by Anne McKnight

Introduction

The discourses that the United States and its closest allies have put forth asserting the necessity to globalize security have taken on an unprecedented intensity and reach.[1] They justify themselves by propagating the idea of a global "in-security," attributed to the development of threats of mass destruction, thought to derive from terrorist or other criminal organizations and the governments that support them. This globalization is supposed to make national borders effectively obsolete, and to oblige other actors in the international arena to collaborate. At the same time, it makes obsolete the conventional distinction between one constellation of war, defense, international order and strategy, and another constellation of crime, internal security, public order, and police investigations. Exacerbating this tendency yet further is the fact that since September 11, there has been ongoing frenzied speculation throughout the western political world and among its security "experts" on how the relations between defense and internal security should be aligned in the new context of global in-security.

In my opinion, it is this "field" of unease management professionals which lies at the heart of the transformations explored in this issue of *Traces*. This emergent field of the unease management explains, on the one hand, the formation of police networks at the global level, the policie-arization of military functions of combat, and on the other hand, the transformation, the criminalization, and the juridification of the notion of war. Moreover, this field of unease management also accounts for how a form of ban-opticon *dispositif* is established in relation to this state of unease. This form of governmentality of unease is characterized by three criteria: practices of exceptionalism, acts of profiling and containing foreigners, and a normative imperative of mobility.

Given these terms, is it still possible to speak of a "global complicity" and a drift towards a new "fascism"? Does there, in practice, exist a single strategy that unifies different groups of professionals — whether they be agents of the police, the military, or the intelligence services — that seek to change the existing regime, curtail civil liberties, and put all individuals under its control and surveillance? Did Orwell's *1984*, in fact, prefigure 2004? In the following argument, I will develop the two instruments of analysis mentioned above: the field of professionals of unease management and, the ban-opticon. My analysis will show that we are far from a global complicity as a unified strategy but that the combination of unease and ban-opticon creates, as effects of anonymous struggles, a globalization of domination.

The Trans-Nationalization of In-Security: The Place of the In-Security Professionals in the Governmentality of Unease Beyond the State

In the approach to (in)securitization processes that I propose here, it will be important to avoid the reigning tendency (the doxa) of the field. This commonly involves attributing a coherent set of beliefs to the professionals involved in the field, an approach I avoid in order not to gratuitously unify their divergent interests, by analyzing them wrongly as willing allies or accomplices. On the contrary, it is important to differentiate clearly between various parties' standpoints on how to prioritize threats that may include terrorism, war, organized crime, and what is called migratory invasion or reverse colonization, while at the same time marking the correlation between various *métiers*, which may include professions of urban policing, criminal policing, anti-terrorist policing, customs, immigration control, intelligence, counter-espionage, information technologies, long-distance systems of surveillance and detection of human activities, maintenance of order, re-establishment of order, pacification, protection, urban combat, and psychological action. These *métiers* do not share the same logic of experience or practice, and do not converge neatly into a single function under the rubric of security. Rather, they are both heterogeneous and in competition with each other. As we will see, this is true, even if the differentiations mapped out by the near-mythical idea of the national impervious state-controlled border tends to disappear, given the effects of trans-nationalization. Three key events are taking place, now that it has taken several centuries for these *métiers* to differentiate in the first place: a de-differentiation of professional activities as a result of this configuration; a growth in struggles to re-define the systems that classify the social and cultural struggles as security threats; and a practical redefinition of systems of knowledge and know-how that connect the public and private security agencies who claim to possess a "truth" founded on numerical data and statistics, applied to the cases of persons who feel the effects of the in-securitization, living in a state of unease. Such professional managers of unease then claim, through the "authority of the statistics," that they have the capacity to class and prioritize the threats, to determine what exactly constitutes security. Here, this concept is reduced to the correlation between war, crime, and migration, and does not include (the loss of employment, car accidents, good health itself abruptly made in-secure as social benefits are dismantled) all elements which are considered, on the contrary, as normal risks. Finally, this "authority" of the statistics and the routine of collecting them with their technologies and categories, allows such professionals to establish a "field" of security in which they recognize themselves as mutually competent, but at the same time find themselves in competition with each other for the monopoly of the legitimate knowledge *on* what constitutes a legitimate unease, a "real" risk.

Within the production of this regime of truth and the battle to establish the "legitimate" causes of fear, of unease, of doubt and uncertainty, the in-security professionals have the strategy to overstep national boundaries and form corporatist professional alliances to reinforce the credibility of their assertions and to win the internal struggles in their respective national fields.[2] The professionals of these organizations, in particular the intelligence services, draw resources of knowledge and symbolic power from this trans-nationalization. Eventually, these resources may give them the means to openly critique the politicians and political strategies of their own respective countries. This explains how, as we have seen, when the President of the United States invokes a threat, he is only credible as long as he has not been contradicted by the intelligence community. If his claim turns out to be unfounded, then the credibility of his refusal to reveal sources for his statement, purportedly based on reasons of national security, is put in grave doubt.[3] In the event of professionals of politics and in-security professionals clashing directly, keeping this sort of knowledge secret is no longer considered as proof of a hidden truth accessible only to the politicians. On the contrary, it casts doubt on the possibility that they might even *have* access to this truth, and can create a belief inside the population than politicians' truth is what could very well be a misrepresentation or an outright falsity. (An obvious case is the one concerning the weapons of mass destruction in Iraq, and in particular, the weapons' ties to Al Qaeda.) Thus, often, the only thing left for the politicians to do is to play the card of charisma to make their opinion more convincing. They must then bank on an inflated level of public confidence and demand that the electorate maintain an almost quasi-religious belief in their judgment, while citizens' groups grow still more skeptical over the information to which they *do* have access.[4]

The notion of State, as conceived by international relations theory, cannot adapt to the result of these tensions created by trans-national bureaucratic links between police, intelligence agencies, and the military. Contrary to what is claimed by the mainstream of cynical-realist writers on international relations, once these differentiated bureaucracies, with their respective positions, exist, it becomes impossible to return to a national interest, or assume a nationalist convergence of interests allowing all parties to rally around a single government. On the contrary, these differentiated bureaucracies are actually forged in the crucible of international networks, and they autonomize different political sectors expressly for the purpose of ensuring that they exceed the domain of professional politicians. This tendency is particularly acute in the European arena, which has conventionally organized itself primarily under the space of the national. For the past thirty years in Europe, new organizations have emerged, by which I mean networks and informal groups that transcend national frontiers and localize the spaces of political decision-making.[5]

Only sociological work on the trans-nationalization of police and military bureaucracies has been able to show that it is no longer tenable to maintain the classical notion of the State. This demise is particularly evident in the privatized segments of these sectors, including professionals of the management of unease, and actors whose *métier* involves risk assessment and accompanying issues of insurance coverage.[6] These sociological works identify a transversal field of processes of (in)securitization, whereby a certain number of professionals from public institutions with domains internal to the nation — such as police — or external to the nation — such as the military and private enterprises selling protection or technologies of control and surveillance — occupy the dominant positions. By maintaining these positions, they exclude alternative discourses and make resistance posed by non-professionals quite impossible. The field is thus established between these "professionals," with specific "rules of the game," and rules that presuppose a particular mode of socialization or habitus. This *habitus* is inherited from the respective professional trajectories and social positions, but is not strongly defined along the lines of national borders.

In very simple terms, we can no longer distinguish between an internal order, reigning thanks to the police by holding the monopoly on legitimate power, and an anarchic international order which is maintained by an equilibrium of national powers vis-à-vis the armies and diplomatic alliances. In effect, the State is no longer the double-faced Janus god, familiar to us from antiquity. Cast into doubt is the relevance of seeing a rigid separation between internal and external scenes that is so fundamental for the school of Raymond Aron realism. The logics of state administrations are completely scrambled. The status of State territoriality is under discussion, as well as the State capacities of territorial surveillance and control over that same territory. Even beyond these questions of the State capacity of survey and control, the equivalence between society, nation, and state is symbolically cast into doubt. Those who govern can no longer rely on the rhetorics of sovereignty, citizenship, and State reason with the same performativity. Politicians' ability to manage is thrown into question, as is the correspondence between their beliefs and actual situations. This form of political crisis suggests that the State could be out of date, no longer relevant, and that it is, in fact, more appropriately seen in the realm of ritual. The suspicion, initially applied to politicians in the former Communist regimes, has in fact become a general property of all political discourse. Domination has been de-coupled from the State territorial form and its traditional political classes. This means that domination is not less powerful, but it now takes on new forms: the trans-nationalization of bureaucracies of surveillance and control, shifts in systems of accountability between businesses and politicians regarding the definition of work and the forms its redistribution should take, and new trans-national lifestyles and professional cultures. But as they encounter the trans-national, these forms only add to the untenability of the territorial state as it was classically defined by Hobbes and Max Weber, and this encounter can, in fact, undermine the bases of legitimacy that the traditional political classes cannot yet effectively abandon.[7] In parallel to the ascent of a corporate-based world, this trans-nationalization has thus impacted the entire ensemble of bureaucracies and agents who make up the State, once it is admitted that the State is no longer a unitary actor. This trans-nationalization has not simply affected private entities, NGOs and protest movements; it has primarily affected actors commonly considered as public entities. The trans-nationalization of bureaucracies has created a socialization and a set of differentiated professional interests that takes priority over national solidarities.

The Field of Professionals in the Management of Unease — The Stakes of Knowledge

Given that this field of professionals has long been in existence, it is surprising that it has never become the subject of analysis. Why has this blind spot persisted when this field plays such a central role in relations of domination? This is no doubt due in great part to the common perception of the military and police as the obedient executors and zealous servants of the State, a discourse found equally in the internal discourse of these professionals and in the critical discourse on the repressive State apparatus. Moreover, the make-up of disciplinary knowledges in the social sciences — in particular the insistence that political science only concerns domestic issues and the international relations, is completely autonomous from domestic issues — has obscured the relations taking place through the whole ensemble of professionals. The disciplines have tended to divide the field into two entirely exclusive social universes, envisioned as the world of police and the world of the military. This has the effect of devaluing in one single blow all the "intermediary" institutions such as military police, border guards, and Customs agents. The structuring of academic knowledge has blocked analysis by reproducing the mapping of state borders onto organization divisions. The result is that separate bounded entities are created — an internal and external domain, divided according to the former being ruled according to the social contract and a monopoly on violence, opposed to the latter's antithetically anarchic international system and a Hobbesian horizon expanded to an international level supposing the possibility of war between each state and the others. A corresponding division is maintained between the police and systems of national justice, seen as belonging to the internal domain, and the military and diplomacy considered as external to this domain.

The simple fact of describing police actions across borders, as we have done earlier in our book [note 8], disturbs the categories of traditional understanding that depend on the radical separation between the inside and the outside.[8] Descriptions of military activities within a domestic context, or the surveillance of the Internet by intelligence agencies, and the developments incriminal justice at the international level have the same effect.[9] Rob Walker has shown elsewhere how this inside/outside opposition both serves as the limit of the political imagination, and the source of its coherence.[10] As Ethan Nadelmann underscores in the preface of his pioneering analysis of DEA agents who conduct work outside of the US: "This book represents the first significant engagement of two scholarly disciplines — US foreign policy and criminal justice — that have had remarkably little to do with one another. The vast majority of criminal justice scholars have extended their attentions no further than their nations' borders... Among students of US foreign policy,... almost no one has paid much attention to issues of crime and law enforcement...".[11]

Now other works including mine have advanced a step further — some would say a step too far — by reconsidering the lines that have been traditionally drawn as the legitimate borders of academic knowledge. We have been particularly concerned to advance a political sociology of international relations that reintroduces international phenomena, by making them normal and banal social facts on a daily basis. When we break down the dichotomy between knowledge of the inside and the outside, the border between the police world and the military world is demonstrated to be more permeable. We can thus take account of all the intermediary agencies such as polices with military status, border guards, customs agents, or immigration agents, to better understand the links these agents make among themselves, and how the effects of their positions have implications on their respective narratives. Furthermore, breaking down this dichotomy allows us to understand how a semantic continuum is constructed, situating the struggle against terrorism at one end and the reception of refugees at the other end of the continuum. The "deconstruction" of the boundaries between different disciplines of knowledge has allowed a coherent field of analysis to emerge, a configuration having its own rules and its own coherence — the field of professionals of the management of unease. The field becomes intelligible where previously one saw only marginal subjects confined by disciplines that mutually ignored one another and constructed themselves in opposition to one another, or at best in the intersection between different areas. Such new fields of intelligibility include police working beyond borders, international justice condemning military crimes, and the construction of the image of the enemy within by intelligence services, such that their profiling applies to certain groups of foreigners resident within a country itself.

With our theory of the field of the unease management professionals, we can thus cross the habitual line traced by the social sciences between internal and external, between a problem couched in terms of defense and problems of the police, and between problems of national security and the problem of public order. This hypothesis indeed reunites the military as well as the police and all the other professionals of management of threats in its own terms of figuration (in the words of Norbert Elias) or *habitus* (to use the term of Pierre Bourdieu).

After having hesitated across the span of several articles on how precisely to state this hypothesis — interpenetration between sectors, merging of different social universes... — I now prefer to speak in terms of de-differentiation of the questions of internal and external security.[12] This de-differentiation of internal and external security allows us, in effect, to recall the socially and historically constructed character of the process of differentiation, in terms of the socio-genesis of the Western State as outlined by Norbert Elias or Charles Tilly. It also allows us to think the field of security as a field crossing the internal and external, a new generative space of struggle between security professionals that produces common interests, an identical program of truth, and new knowledges.

To comprehend this field, as it establishes itself within a trans-national space of the management of unease in societies of risk, it is necessary to perform a genealogy of the field, to note the similarities that are consistent throughout the space, and to establish what is significant about the differences, which are as much professional as geographic. One benefit of this approach is to show how police cooperation is linked to the questions of border control, immigration, the fight on terrorism, relations with armed forces, and trans-Atlantic relations; we could even include the relations between public and private management of security under this aspect of police coercion. The idea is to refuse to create an ivory-tower academic problem by considering the organizations called national police as self-contained objects determining what defines the police today. These days, doing police work constitutes less and less a national question, and consists less and less of an activity restricted to public organizations known by the official names of national police forces.[13]

Policing in Networks, Policing at a Distance

The activities of policing have become *vastly* more extensive. Police activities are formed of connections between different institutions, and function in networks. Their formation also occurs as they take on a large new spectrum of activities, and project it well beyond national borders. These geographic implementations of networks deterritorialize police activities in terms of mission and institutions and now include the judiciary itself, with the implementation of Eurojust inside Europol. These "policing" activities, in particular those devoted to surveillance and maintenance of public order, now take place at a distance, beyond national borders, as for example, with detective experts of hooligans in international football matches, or for antiglobalization protest and demonstrations. But it *also* occurs beyond traditional police activities and reaches foreign affairs. The bypassing of borders through the policing of internal security also occurs through the dispatch of internal security advisors abroad, in the consulates who issue visas to permit people to enter the Schengen zone. It affects the airline companies who, instead of police, are delegated the task of verifying passports and hire private security guards and train their personnel to these tasks of control. It even transforms the role of the militaries in their tasks of peace consolidation and reconstruction, as they now are asked to oversee also potential organized crime activities which could affect internal security, and finally, it creates links with the intelligence agencies by sharing some of the same databases. All these activities participate in what is called the "debriefings of internal security abroad" where surveillance projects itself on spaces, states, and persons judged as a danger and a threat to national security and public order.

This tendency to operate beyond national borders occurs not only through the activities linked to the Schengen system of surveillance and the actions in that frame of each member state's liaison officer, but also exceeds the actual borders of the European Union when it creates demands on EU candidate countries, such as those placed on the ten new member countries to be added to the EU in 2004, or when it extends to the EU's "circle of friends," by conditioning economic aid to the permission to have police and immigration activities inside each of these countries.

At the same time, these police activities are themselves undergoing a redefinition whose effect is to enlarge the spectrum in a particular way. It would be patently misguiding to assume that these activities are primarily oriented toward crime or anti-terrorist actions despite rhetoric. The principal activity rather consists of keeping the poorest foreigners at a distance, through controlling the flux of mobile populations. Fifteen years of intensive rhetoric have created the belief that poverty, crime and mobile populations are inextricably linked, but the correlation between crime, foreignness and poverty is altogether false.[14]

The term of "internal security," now used to designate security at the European level, is a gauge of these two new kinds of reach. On the one hand, reach is geographic, with the dimension of European (and trans-Atlantic?) cooperation; on the other, the reach derives from the role and duties of the various agencies affected by security. The geographic reach, and the redefinition of spheres of competence it implies, have been the object of numerous commentaries. But the actual extent of the changes that have taken place at the everyday level, have been miscalculated due to the belief in the discourse of the suspension of controls inside the EU and their localization at the external border of EU, which supposedly creates freedom of circulation for all inside the EU. In fact, we must realize that controls have been delocalized and modernized, but they have in no way been done away with: controls continue both inside, an aleatory mode at the external border, and even outside. Both in-security professionals and politicians have remained silent on this issue of how activities linked to the control of the transnational flow of persons have extended their reach and are now fortified by adding to the definition of security these tasks on top of the traditional tasks of combating crime. The effect of that extension of the definition of internal security at the European level is that it puts wildly disparate phenomena on the same continuum — the fight on terrorism, drugs, organized crime, cross-border

Globalized-In-Security

criminality, illegal immigration — and moreover controls the transnational movement of persons, whether this be in the form of migrants, asylum-seekers, other border-crossers — and even more broadly the control of any citizen who does not correspond to the *a priori* social image that one holds of his national identity (e.g. the children of first-generation immigrants, minority groups...). Control is thus enlarged beyond the parameters of conventional crime control measures and police of the foreigners, by including also control of persons living in zones labeled "at risk" (e.g. the *banlieues* — popular suburbs, or declining city centers) and put under surveillance because they correspond to a type of identity or behavior supposed to derive from these predispositions of risk.

This new reach of activities enables a new, more individualized logic of surveillance. Its new reach privileges the Ministers of the Interior and the Ministers of Justice, insofar as these ministers in particular have realized how to combine the new logics of surveillance at the level of European police collaboration through the form of a network of relations between functionaries that permits them to understand the situation beyond national borders. This enables a body of expertise on extra-territorial matters, permitting us to see ministers in charge of internal security internationalized. This reach happens in the same way as it does for customs and takes place to the detriment of the social ministers (minister of labor, etc.) or specialized ministers (European affairs, etc.). And this reach goes so far as to impinge upon the domains of the Minister of the Interior and the ministers oriented toward international affairs — foreign affairs and defense. The ministers of the interior then take on initiatives addressing foreign political matters insofar as they may say that it is to prevent repercussions on internal security matters.

Several works have recently drawn our attention to ways in which national police systems are structured in differentiated networks, and draw on international resources according to their respective professional specialties, including drug trafficking, terrorism, maintenance of order, and hooliganism. This differentiation of specialty means that the police, therefore, do not form a single unique and homogenous network. We would be better served by thinking of an "archipelago of policing," or a mosaic that holds together the national police, military police, customs, immigration, consulates, and even intelligence services and the military, in the way, for instance, that international police in the Balkans currently operate. These archipelagos are structured beyond their "common" activities, along lines of cultural identification (e.g. French, British, German, or Northern and Southern

European, etc.); *métier* (e.g. police, police with military status, customs agents); organization level (e.g. national, local, municipal); mission (e.g. intelligence, border control, criminal police); knowledge (perceptions of threats, and of a hierarchy of adversaries); and technological innovation (computer system, electronic surveillance, police liaison officers who are key in the management and exchange of information between agencies).

For quite some time, the field of in-security has been structured through transnational exchanges of information, and through the routinization of processes dealing with intelligence information. It would be naive to view this phenomenon as a simple effect of globalization. The national police have been networked ever since they were created as institutions. As opposed to the judiciary and criminal police, the prerogative of the intelligence police has always been conducted irrespective of territorial boundary, and has focused on people's identities, whether real or fictional, regardless of their origin or place of dwelling. Since the end of the nineteenth century, police collaboration has been quite active against "subversives." But there is no doubt that the idea of Europeanization has caused relations to deepen beyond the former capabilities of Interpol since the end of the 1970s, with the creation of the Berne and Trevi clubs. The ideas of free movement and border control appear in full force at the European level in the nineteen-eighties. The legal categories of border, sovereignty and policing have been compromised by five main transformations: the distinction between the internal and external borders of the EU; the creation of international detention zones in airports to immediately send back foreigners who do not have the right papers to enter into the Schengen area; the attempt to impose the term of "economic refugee" and to redefine who is a refugee, with the consequence of narrowing the door to people seeking the right to asylum; the use of the term "immigrant" instead of the term "foreigner," with the effect to include some national citizen inside the scope of the suspected foreigners; and the relativization of the term of foreigner opposed to national in the interest of strengthening the distinction between community member and Third Country Nationals as non-members.

But, due to the inability to entrench and maintain borders as advocated by the rhetoric of security, each organization, each country, individually or in collaboration with others, tries to displace the locus of control upstream to block and deter the will to travel in the country of origin, and to displace the burden of controlling movement and crime back onto other police.[15]

Globalized-In-Security

These changes have caused a profound disjunction between the discourse on European internal security and the practices actually carried out. The external borders are indeed sometimes arbitrary places, but in no instance do they represent an effective electronic security barrier. Land borders are very easily breached, and often the police allow candidates to enter, and proceed, as long as it is clear that they have no intention of remaining in the territory of the country conducting immigration control. In fact, the border controls internal to Europe are not actually dismantled as it was promised by the rhetoric of free movement and its checks and balances. Control is privatized, downloaded onto the airline companies and the airports who, in turn, subcontract the job to private security companies.[16] Control is also sometimes maintained, but simply displaced geographically by a matter of kilometers. And certainly it is true that by far the greatest measure of control is exercised through the visas and the controls in the consulates of passengers' country of origin. The articulation of the SIS and visa allocation structure practices of control, guide the tactical decisions in the war on fraud concerning false documents, and influence the process of making in-duplicable documents using technologies other than finger-printing, such as numeric photographies, facial or retinal scanning and other biometric techniques. These technologies, permitting the police to survey and punish beyond borders via the collaboration between security agencies, are multiplying, a tendency which polarizes the *métier* of policing. In general, two types of policing become apparent within the parameters of the national police institution: the first utilizes personnel who are unqualified or minimally qualified but are present and visible at the local level as an auxiliary to the municipality, the prefecture, or other police; the second type takes an opposite approach by employing a few people who are highly qualified, and in close contact with other security agencies and agencies of social control, whose two chief characteristics are discretion and distance.[17] In what they call an osmotic relationship between high-ranking spheres of government and private strategic actors, these individuals take it as their mission to prevent crime by acting upon conditions in a pro-active way, anticipating where crime might occur, and who might generate it. Their job then consists of making prospective analyses departing imaginatively from certain points, such that they become reflecting point of the ensemble of societal transformations. These professionals believe that they are more professional and competent than the others, and their ambition is to assemble cells of openly available information, social-scientific data, and the techniques of police intelligence operations. This dream of a common and consensual epistemic community haunts the imaginary of these professionals who conduct societal transformations at a distance — a geographic and temporal distance piloted by the logic of anticipation. This perspective places them in a virtual space from which they may oversee everything, all the while being so discreet that they themselves are no longer seen. We also no longer see those who actually carry out the actions of the imaginary — the large numbers of police, judges and prison guards. Population management operates less like a rooted practice of herding than a nomadic practice that follows the seasonal migration of populations who are created as the effect of such proactive logics.

Surveillance at a distance means working to control the ingoing and outgoing movement of populations. It occurs through "lock," and through mechanisms of exclusion such as visas, controls put in place by the airline companies, deportations and readmissions. It impacts not only freedom of movement, but also creates carceral spaces, though they may not normally be categorized as such (detention centers and international airport detention areas, called in France and Greece "waiting zones").[18] Because its de-localized policing function is downloaded to the consulates located in the traveler's country of origin, this mode of control is much less visible than police working on the front lines of border control. Refusal to issue a visa becomes the first weapon of the police, and as such it becomes the place of greatest arbitrariness in terms of decision-making. Police practice is directed at the surveillance of foreigners or poor ethnic minorities and extends its reach beyond its prior limits of criminal investigation, through pro-active actions that enable the police to pinpoint groups "predisposed to criminality" according to sociological knowledge. The diagram of the guilty changes: it no longer derives from supposed criminality, but supposed "undesirability." Prisons that confine the guilty are less significant in this *dispositif* than the new carceral spaces such as holding areas that reproduce the same carceral conditions as prisons, but without the legal judgment of guilt. The relaxation of surveillance on the majority of individuals seen as too heavy, too totalizing, benefits the global harvest of information and the targeting of the most mobile groups: the diasporas, migrants, and if the argument holds, tourists.

I have applied the notion of "field" to these professionals engaged in internal security to describe the institutional archipelagos within which they work, whether privatized or public. In the name of security, these professionals manage technologies of control and surveillance whose goal is to tell us who and what should inspire unease, as opposed to what is inevitable.

Field and Networks

As I analyzed in my book *Police in Networks, the European Experiment*, as well as in several articles, a field should be defined in terms of four dimensions: first, the field as a field of force, or a magnetic field, a field of attraction that polarizes around the specific stakes of the agents involved; second, the field as a field of struggle, or a battle-field, that is able to understand the "colonizing" activities of various agents, the defensive retreats of others, and the various kinds of tactical algorithms that organize bureaucratic struggles; third, the field as field of domination vis-à-vis another field, the field as a positioning inside a larger political and social space permitting the possibility of statements making truth claims on the basis of knowledge and know-how; and fourth, the field as a transversal field, whose own trajectory reconfigures social universes that were formerly autonomous and shifts the borders of these former realms to include them totally or partially in the new field. Exemplifying this in the case of security is a shift that reconfigures certain police and military *métiers* as well as the intermediary *métiers* that follow upon the de-differentiation of internal and external through the practices of violence and technologies of identification and surveillance.

If we are to attempt a preliminary definition of the field of in-security professionals, or more generally of the management of unease, we would begin by saying that the field depends less on the real possibility of exerting force as in the classical sociological accounts of Hobbes or Weber, where the field would be defined purely as a function of coercion. It rather depends on the capacity of the agents to produce statements on unease and present solutions to facilitate managing unease. It also depends on the capacity of people and techniques to conduct their research into this unfolding body of statements at a routine level, to develop correlations, profiles, and classify those that are necessary to identify and place under surveillance (see graphics in the appendix). Unease can raise fears, risks, and the perception of non-intentional threats. But, at the same time, agencies use their analytical capabilities to anthropomorphize danger, and construct a vision of the enemy, sometimes causing, whether intentionally or not, a social polarization that extends or restructures political alliances. The process of (in)securization rests, then, on the routine abilities of agents to "manage and control life," in Foucault's words, across the concrete material conditions that they put in place.

1) The field as a field of forces

If the field of in-security functions as a field of forces exerting their pressures on the agents who engaged in it, it is because it compounds with a certain homogeneity found in these agents' bureaucratic interests, their similar ways of defining the potential enemy, and the similarities in the way they gather knowledge on this enemy through diverse technologies and routines. It tends to homogenize these agents' ways of looking into a limited array of anthropomorphized types, to define a "focalization" shared by all who draw on the field.[19] To understand the positions and discourses that situate these agents, it is necessary to correlate them with their professional socialization and their positions of authority, in terms of their roles as spokesmen of "legitimate" institutions within the field of in-security professionals or the management of unease.

2) The field as a field of struggles

A field of forces, the in-security field also functions as a field of struggles within which the agents situate themselves, with the resources and the differentiated goals that structure their positions. In this sense, the field of in-security is a "field of struggles to conserve or transform the configuration of the field's own forces".[20] If such struggles occur between these actors, if these competitions take place, it is because they, in fact, do have the same interests, the same sense of the game and recognize the same specific stakes. But in order to avoid stereotypes, it is necessary not to assume an automatic correspondence between positions and certain types of discourses. The stakes within these small groups can be affected by such dynamics as interpersonal behaviors or multipositioning strategies. Moreover, the analysis of the differences between positions should not let us forget that the tactics of bureaucratic "colonization" do not advance step by step and locally by incremental enlargement, they may jump to other activities (for example from threat of terrorism to natural catastrophes in the name of speed and discipline). Such is the case even if it is necessary to pragmatically believe in

Globalized-In-Security

the proximity of these activities by building semantic bridges inside the continuum of risks, threats and in-security .[21] The fundamental thing is that any action undertaken by one agent to shift the economy of forces in its favor has repercussions on the whole ensemble of other actors. These struggles are fundamental to understand the internal economy of the field and the processes of formation and reach that characterize it.

In the specific case of the field of in-security, the "field" is determined by the struggles between police, intermediaries and military agencies about the boundaries and definition of the term "security," and around the prioritization of the different threats, as well as the definition of what is not a threat but only a risk or even an opportunity. The central question relevant to defining security is thus to know who is authorized or to whom is delegated the symbolic power to designate exactly what the threats are. In this respect, it is impossible to evaluate the meaning of threats by judging exclusively on the manifest basis of statements themselves. We must qualify this by paying attention to who is in the position of enunciation, and to the positions of authority of the enunciators themselves, keeping in mind their personal, political and institutional interests within the field. It is no doubt too early to definitively define the centrifugal forces that compel the police and military to share the same interests, the same rules, and the same vision of what is at stake (i.e. what are the emerging threats). Despite the current state of the field, one could imagine centripetal forces that would work to cause the field of in-security to diverge again along the boundary of internal and external activities, or even break it apart in different arrangements, while maintaining the same categories (for instance, a division according to technologies). If the transformations of conflicts did not have a direct and determining impact on the field of security, the chance of a revival of the military threat from Russia, or China, however remote, could immediately be interpreted as extremely dangerous, and could reintroduce a cleavage which would bring back an earlier police/military division of labor, impairing the tendency to share resources. But in fact, the extension of so-called humanitarian missions or the maintenance of order in the non-Western countries threatens to accelerate the effects of the field by merging even more policing, intelligence and military activities. September 11 has clearly played a role in producing a convergence between positions taken on internal and international security. But this convergence has also re-valorized military efforts and has legitimized the fact that the "war" on terrorism should no longer be conducted under the aegis of the police. Above all, it has underscored how the effects of the field were propagated in both directions of enlargement mentioned to include new geographies (transatlantic, new alliances and revival of a different NATO) and the will to mobilise and extend to all professionals of the unease management, the role of "antiterrorist" surveillance.[22]

3) The field as field of domination

The field of in-security also functions as a field of domination in relation to other social fields, including sometimes the field of the professionals of politics. It tends to monopolize the power to define the "legitimately recognized threats" (global organized crime, global terrorism, war on terror...). This is to say that the agents of the field fight for the authority to impose their definition of who and what inspires fear. In the competition between the field of the professionals of politics and the field of the professionals of in-security, indeterminate spaces exist where each agent is "obliged to negotiate," and where "collusive transactions" operate in the strong sense of the term.[23] The field, as I have just described it, essentially encompasses not only the public bureaucracies, but also includes private bureaucracies, businesses, political intermediaries, and associations who work to "develop a security-oriented mindset" in the public sphere. Our understanding of these private actors is still incomplete, but there is more and more convincing work available that helps us comprehend the complex links between these entities and the public bureaucracies.[24] The field of security exercises its "force" or "capacity of attraction" by its power to impose on other agents through the belief that the insiders of the field as "experts" possess the supplementary knowledge and secrets that only professionals may have. This belief is reaffirmed through everyday routine work and technologies, as well as "exchange and sharing of information," as a certain approach to social change, to risk, threats and enemies, which is constantly invoked and reconfirmed. The field of in-security is thus in the heart of the field of power as a bureaucratic field composed of experts having the capacity to claim that they know better than others, even if others are the professionals of politics, including the head of states. In this field, the agents, be they governmental or non-governmental agencies, enter into struggles with the goal of settling a specific sphere of practices, (operations that may consist of classing, sorting, filtering, excluding, profiling, or enclosing) through the various institutions of laws, rules, norms, and the daily routine knowledge of what rules and resolutions of such "settlement" are permitted or forbidden. Even if national professionals of politics still play a key role in structuring security issues, because of their daily involvement in settling security practices, the agencies and bureaus that comprise the world of security are arguably the sole agents able to assert, with some success rate, their definition of what inspires unease. While it is certainly true that all these agencies have an interest in maintaining the terms that political actors use to label and frame the issues, they overlay and invest these definitions with their own significances and practices. In this respect, the ongoing conflicts between agencies work in conjunction with the struggle that each agency undertakes to be recognized by politicians who still retain the power to abolish or reform them (i.e. the homeland security restructuring the bureaucratic balance of power between FBI, CIA, State Department, Defense Department, Pentagon, border guards…). This struggle also occurs in conjunction with the struggle to exclude other actors (churches, human rights organizations, Red Cross, alternative medias) by disqualifying their points of view on the definition of threats and on the the public policies aiming to prevent the threats.

The following eight effects of the field of security allow us to identify the field's domination effects: first, the systems of representation belonging to agents who previously did not share these systems converge, due to their shared interest in entering into the struggle to define and prioritize "emerging threats"; second, professionals in the field of in-security place all global social transformation that affects society and to which politicians are unable to respond under the rubric of threat, whose ultimate consequence is defining an enemy. And this convergence occurs even if the immediate experience of the agents has led them to privilege their own roles, their own specific missions for which they entered into competition to begin with (global organized crime versus global terrorism); third, security agencies recognize from a practical point of view that any standpoint, even those of different nations or professions, can stabilize or de-stabilize the whole body of relations that the agency maintains with others. Thus each agency integrates this practical recognition within its strategies, certain security agencies that formerly appeared as marginal to the worlds of the police and the military now modify their images and appear, whether rightly or wrongly, to be at the core of the *dispositifs* of surveillance and control — agencies such as customs, immigration, national guard, police with military status; fifth, professionals of politics favor a differentiated allocation of missions and budgets that benefits these "intermediary" agencies and relativizes the authority of more traditional agencies; sixth, contacts and international networks in the economy of national or regional budget struggles become necessary; seventh, knowledge and know-how in the management of unease have a determining influence on how practices of violence are resolved; and eighth, such management takes place at a distance through technologies targeted to this use.

4) The field of in-security as a transversal field

The problem is not therefore to follow a fixist conception of borders that we would imagine laid down once and for all, but to adopt a dynamic conception of borders where borders are themselves on the move. In such an approach, the main stake is to state precisely what such a dynamic conception would consist of. Borders are the "concretization" of power struggles in a specific space which is often materialised in a territory. Michel Foucher's formula goes beyond the exclusive frame of the national border to coin the concept of social borders where space is not directly correlated with a uni-dimensional vision of the territory.[25] Borders are indeed sometimes institutions existing in the material world, such as the physical borders of states, or borders adjudicated by the juridical relation that regulates the differentiation between the inside and the outside. But sometimes their property of fluidity is more important than the material existence of the border, if the field is in formation and is not sufficiently established to make the costs of entry prohibitive. The materialization of the borders by law or by professional norms is thus often lagging behind the reality of the borders of a field structured by the struggle relations and the attraction relations. Materialization of borders legitimates and consecrates a particular moment when it was in the interest of all actors to negotiate in the precise way that resulted. This temporal gap signifies that it is extremely difficult to empirically trace the borders of the field by examining it solely from the point of view of its institutional characteristics, as they inevitably retrace a moment that is actually anterior to the relations of force that caused that moment to materialize.

The "transversality of the field" is a term that allows us to mark off the space beyond national borders that characterizes the relations between agents (essentially public) of the field, without presupposing the existence of another higher level of enclosure (such as the EU, the idea of Europe in a broader sense,

Globalized-In-Security

or the western world).[26] The notion of transversality allows us to integrate the idea of "glocality" introduced by Japanese management companies to brand the same products with different advertisements coined for local people and that James Rosenau popularized to show that many phenomena connect the global and the local. Glocality and transversality allow us to understand that the field of in-security is deployed at a level that is neither reducible to the national political field, nor to a level between two nations, or even to the European level. The State, here, is not the space of convertibility, or "universal currency," for different modes of social capital. Bourdieu, here, is wrong and was not careful enough to distinguish the transnational and transversal characters of the globalization process. Beyond the State, the notion of the transversal field of in-security allows us to analyze a space that is indeed social and political, but that transcends the division of internal/external or national/international imposed by the territorial state of mind. This social space or this field of in-security, is empirically constructed as a result of the differentiated positions of different security agencies (national police, local police, Customs, border control services, intelligence agencies, armies, etc.) in different European countries (the centrality of the French police, the diversity of the English police, German federalism, in the near future Polish specific traditions etc.). So, it is effectively defined not just by the place that these agencies occupy as national players, but also by the trans-national networks of relations that they have formed in a space larger than their proper spaces, a space whose cyclical defining property is its tendency to enlarge itself incessantly due to its refusal to recognize boundaries, whether they are geographic or cultural.[27]

For these reasons, when describing and analyzing the field of in-security, it is not sufficient to merely reconstruct the practical knowledge of the respective actors by means of interviews, or merely inventory of the agencies that make up this know-how. Because in doing so, the governing assumptions of this method are that by merely adding the bureaucratic and political actors of the the EU member states — supposedly "natural" partners for these relations — we have a "logical frame." This frame is, in fact, given by the fact that nation-states are naturalized as the arena where all in-security relations are negotiated, and where the effects of in-security have to be understood by examining the interactions of these member nations states, judging their resemblance and differences to the other member nations states, following the criterion of a national "culture" or national "specificity." Our method consists, instead, of describing the relations that derive from practices (of surveillance, of control, etc) and not from "supposedly national cultures." These practices that derive their agency from being embedded in (or transversal to) various organizations and institutions, whose space is yet to be determined through professional métiers and networks, are inscribed into a social space beyond the boundaries of the cultures of national States. The field then creates forms of collaboration and competition whose space is yet to be established between agencies previously little in contact with one another (armies, intelligence agencies, military police, border control, Customs, judiciary police, civil security, the justice system). This compels the police to move part of their operations beyond state borders and to remain there (see UN policing missions, Kosovo or even now Afghanistan). Similarly, the field compels the military to become more and more interested in what occurs within national borders (see phone taping, monitoring of transborders activities inside, and now detention of "enemy aliens" inside). It is even more compelling for the agencies (intelligence services, police with military status, or customs and immigration offices) that mediate between these two realms by obliging them to re-structure their missions along the line of the so-called new global threat (which itself varies in time: global organized crime, failed states or now war on terror). The field's effect introduces new systems of interaction between the agencies by re-structuring their boundaries concerning missions, laying the ground for eventual budgetary competition, and playing with their roles within the overall function of coercion, or more precisely, the management of threats. It compels the privatization of certain forms of in-security (above all, over individuals, but also over local or community matters and sometimes going as far as the privatization of military activities), and compels public agencies to focus on the forms of in-security that stretch between the internal and external domains. It may change, on rare occasions, the overall sense of priorities. It makes the police world privilege organized crime and terrorism over prevention or community policing, and makes the military world allocate more public discourses and sometimes resources to the so-called "transversal threats" and their prevention (i.e. terrorism, organized crime, with the development of biometrics, huge data bases of surveillance, change in airports, traditional war, state building, and reconstruction of democracy) than to the (previous) questions of deterrence and proliferation. The contemporary field of in-security at the European level can then be described as a certain universe producing a specific knowledge, confronting social agents existing at different

Globalized-In-Security

institutional positions. In this field we find "representatives" of security issues not only among the territorially-based agents we would expect, such as police, or "gendarmes" as police with military status, customs agents, high-ranking functionaries of the ministries of the Interior, of Foreign Affairs or Defense departments; we also find politicians who specialize in these issues. Military strategists join this field and enter into struggles modifying the complex economy of relations between the previous agencies of "internal" security (police, police with military status, Customs, immigration, and asylum services), however tangentially. The new reach of the military correlates with a general tendency to place strategic emphasis on internal security while becoming disinterested in more classically defence-related questions. These in-security professionals have traditionally come from the realms of police, customs, and gendarmes, but more recently have tended to come from new fields: the ranks of lawyers, diplomats, military officials, and managers of companies working in the production of materials used by these administrations, politicians specializing in defence-related issues, members of associations related to these *milieux*, and last but not least, academics who specialize in security studies.[28] Thus the agents of the field of in-security, despite their apparent diversity, can be defined as professionals of the management of threat or unease, producers of power-knowledge on the couplet of security/insecurity.

But what is essential is not to exhaustively name these agents, but to discern and analyze what holds these different constituent parts together, what makes them enter into competition for a set of stakes that they had never previously recognized when they were indifferent to each other. This is why my research dealt with the practices and relations between four previously unconnected conceptual worlds — internal security, external security, war and conflict, and crime and delinquency — in the attempt to think the relations between the police and the army, crime and war, upperworlds and underworlds, agencies responsible for surveillance and their targets and technologies. Here, it is necessary to tie together earlier works on these issues to show how the narrative space of the agents I have just discussed vis-à-vis threats is re-translated, first, into a space of social positions by the intermediary of their particular social and institutional positions or *habitus*, and via a transversal *dispositif* that connects their practices. But what is immediately at stake here is to understand how practical effects of the field enter into operation.

To speak of a field such as the field of in-security requires that we go beyond inventorying the agencies that one suspects of participating in the "function" of coercion. It requires that we immediately interrogate the characteristics, limits, and effects of the field. Empirically, it is necessary to describe the effects of the field by giving examples and showing how they act, whether this occurs in terms of "polarization," "differentiation," "fold," "involution," or even "hollowing-out".[29] We need indeed to set the constraints and opportunities that the field gives to the agents — effects which are visible — and to understand their less visible relations both inside and outside the field. These field effects will trace the limits of the field in rough contours — limits that are never given, but depend on the particular (con)figuration of a given moment of a struggle within the field, and this specific field and other fields — and will determine the effects of domination between the fields concerning truth of contested norms (i.e. truth about the weapons of mass destruction and the competition between the professionals of politics and professionals of in-security for the "last word").

The Ban-Opticon Dispositif

The set of the field's effects I mentioned above does not derive only from the processes and relations between the agents of the field. It is also the result of their relations with other fields. These relations are formed by the *dispositifs* that cross between institutions, and are not reducible to the logics of these institutions, or even to the *habitus* of their agents, in Bourdieu's sense of the term.

Michel Foucault speaks of the *dispositif* of sexuality and the *dispositif* of the prison.[30] We know quite well that his thinking on the prison was inspired by Jeremy Bentham's image of the panopticon, due to the fact that it simultaneously stood for architecture, discourse, field of rationality and strategic project, at the same time as it embodied the will to scientific knowledge. Discussions about Foucault's use of Bentham generally draw attention to two points: first, criticisms on Foucault's partial reading of Bentham; second they remind us that the actual number of prisons actually constructed on Bentham's model was quite small, as well as the fact that the prison changed function during the classical period, as in the case of the institution of galley slaves, when they were not on ships. But, to answer to this criticism, what is central to acknowledge, is that the *dispositif* is

Globalized-In-Security

not manifested in a single institution of the prison. It is, rather, transversal. It requires heterogeneity, diversity. It is not the prison's function as an enclosed punitive space that is crucial, but rather the fact that the prison concentrates in one specific space the mechanisms of control and surveillance that are scattered throughout society in institutions such as factories, barracks, and schools....In Foucault's work, the panopticon is useful because it allows us to comprehend not only the prison, as it does in Bentham, but serves as a way of understanding how society functions at large.

If the in-security program undertaken by some agents is, without a doubt, a *programmatic* strategy of an escalating generalized surveillance to a level that is both as globalized and as individualized as possible, it is not at all the *diagram* of the effects of power and resistance (see diagram p. 142). If the panoptic *dispositif* exists in the Foucauldian sense, it is in a fragmented and heterogeneous way, and there is no centralized manifestation of it, quite contrary to the various claims of US imperial domination that have been promulgated since September 11. If its effects persist, the sense of empire to which it is subject corresponds more to Hardt and Negri's use of the term Empire, in which the various political processes of state coalitions, maneuvres of large corporations, and the effects of polling that empiricize the "unease" of mass destruction converge towards the strengthening of the informatic and biometric as modes of surveillance that focus on the trans-border movements of individuals. This diagram is not a *panopticon* transposed to a global level; it is what we call a *ban-opticon* — combining the term "ban" of Jean-Luc Nancy as refigured by Giorgio Agamben and Foucault's "panopticon".[31] This formulation of the ban-opticon allows us to understand how a network of heterogeneous and transversal practices function and make sense as an in-security at the trans-national level. It allows us to analyze the collection of heterogeneous bodies of discourses (on threats, immigration, enemy within, fifth column, radical muslims and good muslims, exclusion and integration…), of institutions (public agencies, governments, international organizations, NGOs…), of architectural structures (detention centers, waiting zones and Schengen traffic lanes in airports, integrated video camera networks in some cities, electronic networks outfitted with security and video-surveillance capacities), of laws (on terrorism, organized crime, immigration, clandestine labor, asylum seekers, reform of penal codes for acceleration of justice procedures, and diminution of the rights for defendants), and of administrative measures (regulation

Didier Bigo

of the "*sans papiers,*" negotiated agreements between government agencies vis-à-vis policies of deportation/repatriation, "common" aeroplanes hired specially for deportation with costs shared by different national polices…). It allows us to understand that the surveillance of everyone is not on the current agenda, but that the surveillance of a small number of people who are trapped into the imperative of mobility while the majority is normalized, is definitely the main tendency of policing in the global age.

I would like to sketch out, here, three dimensions of this ban-opticon, to convey how control and surveillance of certain minority groups takes place at a distance. This surveillance of the minority profiled as "unwelcome" is, in my opinion, the strategic function of the diagram; function opposed to the surveillance of the entire population (or the "Pan-"), which is only the dream of a few agents of power, even if the rhetoric after September 11 is along a "total" information (see the Pentagon's Total Information Awareness Program).

The ban-opticon is then characterized by the exceptionalism of power (rules of emergency and their tendency to become permanent), by the way it excludes certain specific groups in the name of their future potential behavior (profiling), and by the way it normalizes the non-excluded through its production of normative imperatives, the most important of which is free movement (the so-called four freedoms of circulation of the EU: concerning goods, capital, information, services and persons).

This ban-opticon is deployed at a level that supersedes the nation-state, and which forces governments to strengthen their collaboration in more or less globalized spaces, both physical and virtual, sometimes global or Westernized, and still more frequently Europeanized. The effects of power and resistance are thus no longer contained by the political matrix of the relation between State and society. They exceed the frame of representations inscribed within the nation-state, disconnect the direct relations between state and individuals inside, and between the external of the nation-state in its relation with other states, as a different universe.

1) *Exceptionalism as indefinite suspension of norms*
To speak of, the exceptionalism of power refers to the relation of juridical production of "special" laws and its symbolic effects of legitimation (emergency, exception, derogatory, administrative, routines issued from old special

legislation…), as well as to how the "dominated" of a specific time and place are socialized by their rulers to believe that they are deciding what kind of dominating powers are acceptable. This relation, as we know, is far from being stable and far from being given once and for all. The distinction between governor and governed is an effect at the macro level of molecular relations of power (and resistance). Liberalism has tried to legitimate its own domination through the idea of the separation of powers by which power is supposed to limit itself, particularly in the dimension of checks and balances, with the effect that the population actively consents finally to be accomplices of its own domination and rely on "justice" and lawyers for its "freedom." Framed in that way, Liberalism is the contrary of Exceptionalism. Liberalism is seen as the opposite of a "sovereign" or "reason of the state" thinking. But between the definitions of Exceptionalism as suspension of law or break in normality, there is room for other visions of Exceptionalism that combine exception both with liberalism and with the *dispositif* of technologies of control and surveillance which is routinized. Exception works hand in hand with Liberalism and gives the key to understanding its normal functioning, as soon as we avoid seeing exception as a matter of special laws only.

Nevertheless, one of the first questions of the present is about the status of these special laws and the exceptional powers they enable. It does not seem that they "suspend every law," they just derogate from normalized legislations, some of which are special laws that we have become habituated to living with. But they install in the heart of our present time the idea that we are living in a "permanent state of emergency" or in a permanent state of exception. Does their mere existence not reconfigure the existence of routinized norms? Is it the norm that defines the exception or the exception that defines the norm? Giorgio Agamben, strongly influenced by Carl Schmitt, invokes the possibility that exercising sovereignty means not only the possibility of being at the same time within the juridical order but also, at the same moment, outside of it, given the possibility that sovereign power can proclaim a state of exception (*Ausnahme*), thereby suspending the validity of its own juridical order.[32] The exception is then more interesting than the norm since it defines the limit that permits the establishment of interiority, which is to say, to "enclose the outside," as Blanchot writes . This process of interiorization allows sovereignty or exception to delimit both the space and the object to which it applies. But for this to take place it is necessary for the sovereign to "overhang" this space, to exteriorize itself, in order to delimit the limits of inclusion. The paradox thus resembles Escher's famous ink-drawn hands as they draw one another. In thinking the contingency of the line drawn, it is necessary to think not only in terms of inside and outside, but in terms of the meta-level that allows the contingency of the drawing of the border between inside and outside. This is what one could call an overlapping hierarchy, or the effect of auto-organization where the institutor and the instituted of the line are mutually constitutive. The topological figure that represents this co-production of the institution where the instituted not only depend on the institutor, but where this institutor is itself instituted by its instituted, is the same figure as the one which allows us to understand the objective indetermination of the borders and which makes the differentiation between internal and external an intersubjective difference — the figure of the Möbius ribbon or stip.[33] This figure suggests a topology that blocks the traced line of a circle from simply cutting the sacred off from the profane, internal from external, institutor from instituted. It is no longer possible for the border to be made objective, forever given and intelligible simply because it is inscribed in space and time. The border depends on the look given by the observer and his position, and his judgment on what is internal or external will vary according to this position, in the same way as his view of what he institutes, or what is instituted upon him. From that point of view on what a border is, the relation of exception is but one of the sovereign relations of exclusion, it is a relation of exclusion that engenders the sense of norm and juridical order in suspending — for a certain time — an object of the juridical order, and which is different from a simple relation of spatial interdiction that would fabricate an outside by enclosing it in a circle.

It is this "suspension" of juridical categories and the possibility of inventing new ones at the same time in order to fill the "hole ," that creates *uncertainty* and doubt. Uncertainty from which power can profit in practice, to destabilize the "old" categories and by redefining them (i.e. concept of war, of prisoner of war, of asylum seeker...), against their previous juridical meaning, in shifting their relations by an infusion of new "category" (i.e. enemy combatant). Thus as long as the US government continues to invoke the difference between the war on terrorism and the war on what concerns the rules applied to prisoners of war, it plays an extreme form of exceptionalism that suspends juridical order and reconfigures it by putting in place new categories that must be defined and that occupy a space previously filled by another concept. This process persists as long as it continues to redefine the pact of protection, in refusing to apply it to foreigners living on its own soil, as it historically did with Japanese internees during the Second World War, or when it power asserts itself beyond its own proper territory by "executing terrorists " in Yemen by sending missiles, while presenting this action as an international police operation and an executive decision of justice. This particular form of exceptionalism that one can designate as illiberal practices at the heart of liberalism seems to us to be one of the contemporary features of the ban-opticon.

2) *Exclusion and pro-active governmentality*

The ban-opticon's second defining trait is its ability to construct categories of excluded people connected to the management of life. The ban is a limit condition of the political relation.[34] As one of our informants from an intelligence agency explained, "if the media and judicial policy exaggerate the phenomenon in order to reassure good citizens and deter the others, they are in effect operating at the level of tactics, which can be modulated according to public opinion. In contrast, what is strategic, is to collect information on the part of a society who no longer lives under the same rules with the same norms as the mainstream." Far from the spotlight, targeting the "abnormals," a re-fashioning of policing and surveillance is taking place, enabled to enlarge its scope by the use of intensive technologies of biometrics and shared databases. There, beyond the simulacrum of a politics of proximity designed to reassure the good citizens, and the zero tolerance designed to deter the rest, the knowledge upon the "others," which is by far the most significant resource in the management of masses and crowds, is acquired. By mixing files from the public realm — social security, taxes — and the private realm — insurance, credit bureaus, supermarkets — with police dossiers, it is possible to classify and sort among the elements to formulate what and who must be surveyed. According to these police and criminal "experts," these processes keep the repressive machine from getting jammed, at the same time they allow it to avoid conveying a negative image that could invoke a sense of oppression barely being held at bay.

The goal of the normalization and management of societal risks should not be seen purely as a police responsibility, they said. Its distribution across the whole assembly of systems that manage risk should be recognized — insurance, societies of private investigators, retail superstores, and public welfare institutions. This program of risk management and normalization is based on the ideals of rational choice, and on using the proactive techniques of management to anticipate individuals' movements. It is spread throughout society and encourages people to collaborate, as in the cases of local security contracts, collaborations between police and educators, and, for instance, the case of Italy, where converging visions of neighborhood committees, of municipal authorities and police, combine to put the blame on immigrants. The basic units conducting proactive analysis will not be limited to the police, but will vary and sometimes include the military and customs officials, and will be linked to insurance, social and credit organizations, schools, prefectures, tax organizations and social security organizations, consulates and criminologists, provided that they are action-oriented.

All this effort to collect information and proliferate data that is now technologically possible has but one goal, to substitute the logic of proactivity for the two other logics: repression and prevention .[35] The pure repressive logic inevitably intervenes too late and is directed at the individual, the policemen are the firemen of crime; the other is a preventive structural logic diminishing the roots of violence that, according to the police, is no more effective than a smokescreen, or a reform impossible to implement without also changing political or economic regimes. The logic of proactivity aims *to act before* an infraction is committed, by collecting information oriented toward repressive action, and anticipating the behavior of dangerous individuals or groups. Prevention is therefore always invested with a virtual coercive dimension. The game is no longer the commission of an act itself, but the "signal" that an infraction might possibly be committed by an individual or a group who potentially represents a risk. The priority now is no longer on sanctions, but on regulation. The issue is less about condemning an individual than about deterring others, but it consists above all of managing movement, flux, and managing groups of people in advance, analyzing their potential future, in order to normalize them.

3) *Normalization and the imperative of free movement*
In contemporary society, normalization occurs primarily through the imperative of free movement of people, in particular in the European Union (or Schengen) space (which is different from the North American space of NAFTA in that it

explicitly recognizes this imperative), and through the combination of three elements: a connection between speed and movement, the right to movement, and the freedom to move on a global scale. It is this normalization that Zygmunt Bauman refers to when he invokes the new logics of exclusion between those who are free to circulate and those who are trapped in the local. In effect, as he alerts us in his book "*Globalization: the Human Consequences,*" globalization can be analyzed as a spatio-temporal compression that modifies the modes in which people come and go.[36]

But in contrast to Bauman's claim, we need to distinguish more precisely between movement and being free, and see how a metonymy becomes established through this fusion of circulation/liberty to both diminish the notion of liberty, and provoke disequilibrium between the notions of security and liberty. Zygmunt Bauman seems to believe himself in the liberty of the richest, and proposes more mobility for the poorest, seeing neither how this normative imperative of mobility imposes itself, nor the *dispositif* that makes mobility desirable. He sees the repressive dimension of the *dispositif only for the poor*, but seems to neglect its considerable normative and productive dimensions, where the two are completely indissociable. Power is not only repressive. It induces and produces modes of behavior. The discourses on free movement are central. They normalize the majority and permit surveillance to concentrate on a minority.

Conclusion

In conclusion, this *dispositif* whose strategic function is the control and the surveillance of a certain selected group of people exempted from the majority and, which hinges on the field of professionals of the management of unease, is effectively composed as a dispositif of discourses — narratives of police, military, customs, and judicial institutions on free movement, the terrorist threat, transnational organized crime; discourses on the links between these phenomena and im-migration, minorities, and now asylum-seekers — of specific architectural facilities — such as centers for separating out foreigners, detention zones within international airports, retention centers for deporting persons who entered a territory illegally, intake centers for refugees, asylum centers such as Sangatte, where prisoners waiting administrative action are consigned — by regulatory decisions (such as those determining access for lawyers or detainees' parents to places that in practice invalidate the right to free access) or by administrative measures (both arbitrary and humanitarian in inspiration, like the fact of having put people in detention zones in Roissy Charles de Gaulle in a kennel nearby held by the "gendarmes" for their dogs, for them to be fewer in number in the overcrowded rooms of the hotel in which they are primarily detained); and finally, "scientific" discourses on the reasons behind migration and asylum, statements on their relation to the individualization and trans-nationalization of violence, and philosophical and moral propositions on illegal migrants, false refugees, or the young children of immigrant parents.

This *dispositif* is no longer the panopticon described by Bentham. It is a ban-opticon. It depends no longer on immobilizing bodies under the analytic gaze of the watcher, but on profiles that signify differences, on exceptionalism with respect to norms, and on the rapidity with which one "evacuates." The *dispositif* of this new surveillance takes another form, recalling technologies of information technology and virtual reality. This *dispositif* appears like a virtual montage (morphing) of all the positions of individuals in the process of flux. From an initial image (the immigrant, the ghetto youth) to a final image (terrorist, drug-runner), all the steps of transformation are re-constituted virtually. In this respect, this *dispositif* channels flows instead of dissecting bodies. Like the panopticon *dispositif*, this banopticon *dispositif* of morphing produces a knowledge, and produces statements on threats and on security that reinforce the belief in a capacity to decrypt, even prior to the individual himself, what its trajectories, its itineraries will be. This *dispositif* depends on the control of movement more than the control of stocks in a territory. It depends on "monitoring the future" as in Philip K. Dick's novel "Minority Report" more than the surveillance of the present in accordance to the official past. It is a management at a distance in space and time of the "abnormals." As previously people had been assigned places of residence, they are now placed in "waiting zones" and assigned identities not even lived as such. A skin color, an accent, an attitude and one is slotted, extracted from the unmarked masses, and evacuated if necessary. Policing is thus an affair of the margin, of clean-up, and needs concern itself only minimally with "norms." These new logics of control and surveillance are not necessarily much more effective, more rational. The advantage for the unmarked masses is that they have the impression of being free, to the benefit of the institution, and since control only bears on a few, it is more economical. Only the control of crime is less effective than before as a consequence of these *a priori*. Its sphere of application remains fragile and subject to resistance.

There is no doubt that we must come back to a more detailed research to the connection between the practices of security professionals and the systems of justification of their activities, as we reflect on how procedures of truth-claims are formulated, and how the centers of their production are localized, questions from which academics are by no means excluded. It is also important to understand the relations between trans-nationalization, globalization of in-security agencies' practices and those of their "targets" to put them in relation with — in as much as one can — the specific process of Europeanization. This process is conducted more or less in the different political arenas by systems of justification of construction and priority of unease, which correspond to each national and professional culture, but out of which emerges the necessity of an organization like Europol to act as a kind of "stock exchange of threats, fears and uneases" and of their management. This institutionalization creating in return a transfiguration of the threats by giving them the quality to be "global" and then "more dangerous." It is finally necessary to reconnect questions of the constituting of a space of liberty, security and justice with questions of the construction of a society beyond its status as a national state, posing the problem of how its identity is mapped out, and to understand how the convergence of uneases circling around the figure of the poor extra-communitarian migrant speaks volumes about how liberalism operates in a society of risk. In effect, as Foucault reminds us, "if we agree to see in liberalism a new art of governing and governing each other — not a new economic or juridical doctrine — if it really amounts to a technique of governmentality that aims to consume liberties, and by virtue of this, manage and organize them, then the conditions of possibility for acceding to liberty depend on manipulating the interests that engage the security strategies destined to ward off the dangers inherent to the manufacture of liberty, where the constraints, controls, mechanisms or surveillance that play themselves out in disciplinary techniques charged with investing themselves in the behavior of individuals ... from that point on the idea that living dangerously must be considered as the very currency of liberalism."[37]

SPACE OF INSTITUTIONAL POSITIONS / GRAPHS

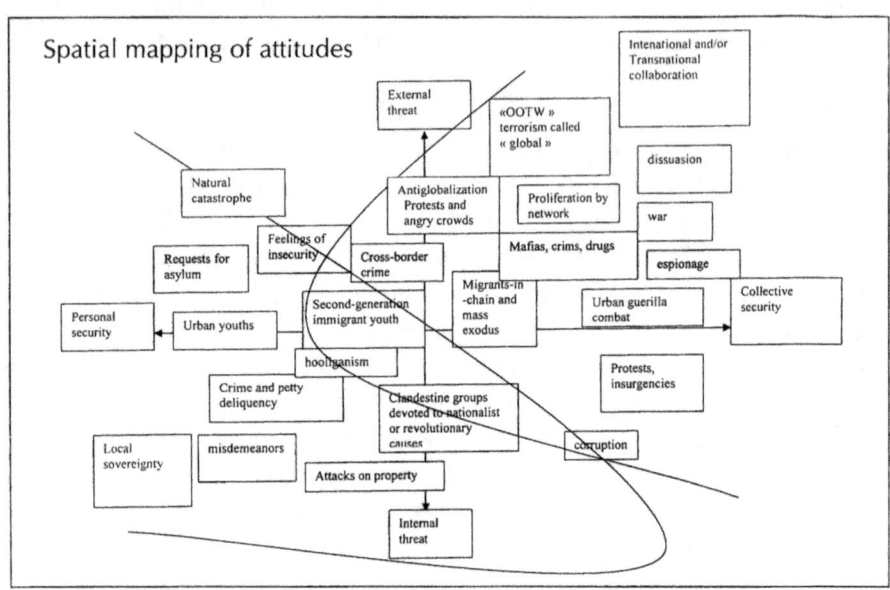

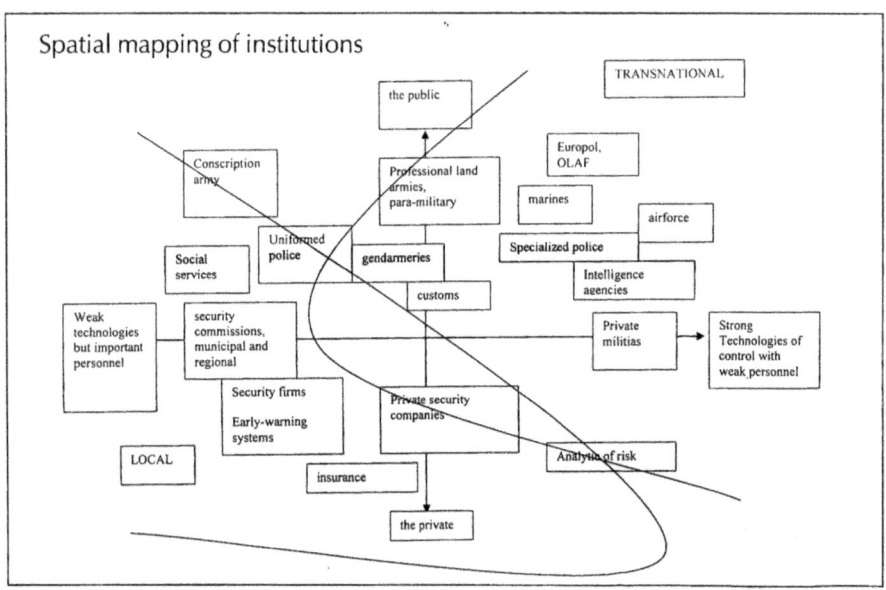

Bibliography

Agamben, Giorgio. *Homo Sacer : Sovereign Power and Bare Life, Meridian*. Stanford, Calif.: Stanford University Press, 1998.

———. *Means without End: Notes on Politics, Theory out of Bounds. Vol. 20*. Minneapolis: University of Minnesota Press, 2000.

Allison, Graham T. and Philip Zelikow. *Essence of Decision: Explaining the Cuban Missile Crisis*. 2nd ed. New York: Longman, 1999.

Anderson, Malcolm. *Frontiers, Territory and State Formation in the Modern World*. London: Polity Press, 1997.

———. "Les Frontieres: Un Debat Contemporain (Frontiers: A Contemporary Debate)." *Cultures et Conflits* 26–27 (1999): 15–34.

Anderson, Malcolm, Monica Den Boer, Peter Cullen, William Gilmore, Charles Raab, and Neil Walker. *Policing the European Union, Clarendon Studies in Criminology*: Oxford University Press, 1996.

Balibar, Etienne. *L'europe, L'amérique, La Guerre: Réfexion Sur La Médiation Européenne*. Paris: la découverte, 2002.

Bauman, Zygmunt. *Freedom, Concepts in Social Thought*. Minneapolis: University of Minnesota Press, 1988.

———. *Globalization: The Human Consequences, European Perspectives*. New York: Columbia University Press, 1998.

———. "On Globalization: Or Globalization for Some, Localization for Some Others." *Thesis Eleven* 54 (1999): 37–49.

———. *Thinking Sociologically*. Oxford, OX, UK; Cambridge, MA, USA: Blackwell, 1990.

Bigo, Didier. "Circuler, Enfermer, Éloigner. Zones D'attente Et Centres De Rétention Des Démocraties Occidentales." *Cultures & Conflits*, 23, automne, Paris, L'harmattan. (1996): 192.

———. "Europe Passoire Et Europe Fortresse, La Sécuritisation/Humanitarisation De L'immigration." In *Immigration Et Racisme En Europe*, edited by Andrea Rea and Laura Balbo. Bruxelles: Editions complexe, 1998.

———. "Frontières Et Sécurité Dans L'union Européenne: Les Illusions Du Contrôle Migratoire." *Culture et Conflits*.

———. "L'europe De La Sécurité Intérieure: Penser Autrement La Sécurité." In *Entre Union Et Nations: L'etat En Europe*, edited by Anne Marie Le Gloannec, 296. Paris: Presse de Sciences Po, 1998.

———. "The Moebius Ribbon of Internal and External Security." In *Identities, Borders, Orders*, edited by Mathias Albert, David Jacobson and Yosef Lapid, 91–116. Minneapolis: University of Minnesota Press, 2001.

———. *Polices En Réseaux: L'expérience Européenne*. Paris: Presses de la Fondation nationale des sciences politiques, 1996.

———. "Sécurité Et Immigration." *Cultures and Conflits* (1998): 7–202.

———. "Sécurité Et Immigration: Vers Une Gouvernementalité Par L'inquiétude ?" *Cultures & Conflits* (1998): 13–38.

———. "Security and Immigration: Towards a Governmentality of Unease." *Alternatives/ Culture & Conflits* (2002).
———. "Security, Borders, and the State." *Border Regions in Functional Transition*, edited by James Scott and Allan Sweedler, 63–79. Berlin: Institute for Regional Studies, 1996.
———. "Vers Une Europe Des Polices? (Towards a European Policing Policy?)." *Revue francaise d'Administration publique* 91 (2000): 471–82.
———. "When Two Becomes One: Internal and External Securitizations in Europe." In *International Relations Theory and the Politics of European Integration*, edited by M. Kelstrup and M. C. Williams. London: Routledge, 2000.
———, ed. *L'europe Des Polices Et De La Sécurité Intérieure*. Bruxelles: Complexe, 1992.
Bigo, Didier and Institut des hautes études de la sécurité intérieure. *Polices Post-Communistes; Une Transformation Inachevée?, Les Cahiers De La Sécurité Intérieure, No 41.* Paris: IHESI, 2000.
Bourdieu, Pierre and Loic J. D. Wacquant. *Réponses: Pour Une Anthropologie Réflexive.* Paris: Seuil, 1992.
Butterwegge, C. "Mass Media, Immigrants, and Racism in Germany. A Contribution to an Ongoing Debate." *Communications* 1996, 203–20.
Caporaso, James A. *The Elusive State: International and Comparative Perspectives.* Newbury Park, CA: Sage Publications, 1989.
Dal Lago, Alessandro. *Non-Persone: L'esclusione Dei Migranti in Una Società Globale, Interzone.* Milano: Feltrinelli, 1999.
Deflem, Mathieu. "Bureaucratization and Social Control: Historical Foundations of International Police Cooperation."*Law and Society Review*, no. 34.3 (2000): 739–78.
Deleule, Didier and Francesco Paolo Adorno. " L Héritage Intellectuel De Foucault." *Cités* 2/2000 (2000): 95–107.
Dobry, Michel. *Sociologie Des Crises Politiques.* Paris: Presses de la FNSP, 1992.
Falk, Richard A, Lester Edwin J. Ruiz, and R. B. J. Walker. *Reframing the International: Law, Culture, Politics.* New York: Routledge, 2002.
Foucault, Michel, Graham Burchell, Colin Gordon, and Peter Miller. *The Foucault Effect: Studies in Governmentality: With Two Lectures by and an Interview with Michel Foucault.* Chicago: University of Chicago Press, 1991.
Foucault, Michel, and Colin Gordon. *Power/Knowledge: Selected Interviews and Other Writings, 1972–1977.* Hassocks, England: Harvester Press, 1980.
Foucher, Michel. *Fronts Et Frontières. Un Tour Du Monde Géopolitique.* 2nd ed. Paris: Fayard, 1991.
Girard, René. *La Violence Et Le Sacré.* Paris: Grasset, c1972.
Girard, René and James G. Williams. *The Girard Reader.* New York: Crossroad, 1996.
Guiraudon, Virginie. "De-Nationalizing Control: Analysing State Responses to Constraints on Migration Control." In *" Controlling a New Migration World,"* edited by Joppke Christian Guiraudon Virginie, 256p. London: Routledge, 2001.
———. "Les Compagnies De Transport Dans Le Contrôle Migratoire À Distance." In *De Tampere À Seville, Bilan De La Sécurité Européenne*, edited by Bigo Didier Guild Elspeth, 124–47. Paris: L'Harmattan, 2002.

Guiraudon, Virginie and Gallya Lahav. "A Reappraisal of the State Sovereignty Debate. The Case of Migration Control." *Comparative Political Studies* 33, no. 2 (2000): 163–95.

Hammar, Tomas. *Democracy and the Nation State: Aliens, Denizens and Citizens in a World of International Migration, Research in Ethnic Relations Series*: Ashgate, 1990.

———. "Dual Citizenship and Political Integration." *International Migration Review* 19 (1985): 438–50.

Huysmans, Jef. "Migrants as a Security Problem: Dangers of Securitizing Societal Issues." In *Migration and European Integration. The Dynamics of Inclusion and Exclusion*, edited by R. Miles and D. Thränhardt, 53–72. London: Pinter, 1995.

Kleinman, Mark. *A European Welfare State?: European Union Social Policy in Context*. Houndmills, Basingstoke, Hampshire; New York: Palgrave, 2002.

Lahav, Gallya. "Immigration and the State: The Devolution and Privatization of Immigration Control in the Eu." *Journal of Ethnic and Migration Studies* 1998, 675–94.

Miles, Robert, and Dietrich Thranhardt. *Migration and European Integration: The Dynamics of Inclusion and Exclusion*: Pinter, 1995.

Monjardet, Dominique. *Ce Que Fait La Police: Sociologie De La Force Publique*. Paris: Éditions la découverte, 1996.

Nadelmann, Ethan A. *Cops across Borders: The Internationalization of U.S. Criminal Law Enforcement*. University Park, PA: Pennsylvania State University Press, 1993.

Neocleous, Mark. *The Fabrication of Social Order: A Critical Theory of Police Power*. Edited by VA Sterling. London: Pluto Press, 2000.

Nogala, Detlef. "Policing across a Dimorphous Border: Challenge and Innovation at the French-German Border." *European journal of crime, criminal law and criminal justice* 9, no. 2 (2001): 130–43.

Ocqueteau, Frederic. "L'etat Francais Face Au Commerce De La Securite (the French State and the Security Industry)." *L'Annee sociologique* 40 (1991): 97–124.

Palidda, S. "La Criminalisation Des Migrants." *Actes de la recherche en sciences sociales* 1999, 39–49.

Scott, James C. *Domination and the Arts of Resistance: Hidden Transcripts*. New Haven: Yale University Press, 1990.

Sheptycki, J. W. E. *In Search of Transnational Policing: Towards a Sociology of Global Policing, Advances in Criminology*. Aldershot, England; Burlington, VT: Ashgate, 2002.

Sheptycki, James W. E., ed. *Issues in Transnational Policing*. London: Routledge, 2000.

Strange, Susan. *The Retreat of the State: The Diffusion of Power in the World Economy, Cambridge Studies in International Relations* 49. New York: Cambridge University Press, 1996.

Tournier, P. "La Délinquance Des Étrangers En France — Analyse Des Statistiques Pénales." In *Délit D'immigration, Cost A2 Migrations*, edited by S. Palidda, 133–62: Commission Européenne, 1997.

Tsoukala, Anastasia. "Looking at Migrants as Enemies." In *Controlling Frontiers: Free Movement into and within Europe*, edited by Didier Bigo and Elspeth Guild, 182–204. London: Ashgate, 2004.

Wacquant, L. "Des 'Ennemis Commodes'." *Actes de la recherche en sciences sociales,* no. 129 (1999): 63–67.
Walker, Neil. *Sovereignty in Transition.* Oxford: Hart, 2002.
Walker, R. B. J. *Inside/Outside: International Relations as Political Theory, Cambridge Studies in International Relations; 24.* Cambridge, England; New York: Cambridge University Press, 1993.
———. *One World, Many Worlds: Struggles for a Just World Peace, Explorations in Peace and Justice.* Boulder, Colo.: L. Rienner Publishers; London, England: Zed Books, 1988.
Walker, R. B. J. and Saul H. Mendlovitz. *Contending Sovereignties: Redefining Political Community.* Boulder, Colo.: L. Rienner Publishers, 1990.

Notes

[1] McCarthyism was a purely American phenomenon; the generalization of permanent state of emergency measures was restricted to Northern Ireland only and did not affect British society. But these two logics are now developing at the level of world geography, and they are deepening to "ideally" reach and include all individuals.

[2] To cite merely one example, the French MTS (governmentality of domestic intelligence and counter-espionage equivalent to the British MI5) attempted to prove its force against the DGSE (in charge of foreign intelligence, equivalent of the British MI6) regarding information on terrorist groups in the Maghreb, to put into place an exchange of services between agents working in the war on terrorism and those working on counter-espionage. This happened to give it knowledge and capacities to act upon the exterior, in ways that it was limited from acting on the interior. The result was to establish links between Tunisian, Moroccan, Algerian and Syrian intelligence services who were opposed to the racial-national/culturalist profiling undertaken by the French agencies with which they were collaborating. The DST conducted surveillance of members of government opposition from these countries currently resident in France, which rumors even suggested led to possible assassination attempts. In compensation, the MTS acquired more accurate information than the DGSE, and used this transnational network to reinforce its own internal position. The rivalries between the FBI, DEA and CIA are also well known in this respect. Such intra-national rivalries have impacted oppositional politics abroad, as in the case of Afghanistan and clandestine organizations such as Al Qaeda in the 1990s.

[3] See the statement of the former CIA Director George Tenet on February 11, 2003. Testifying in front of Congress, he contradicted what George Bush's television claim of the previous day in Cincinnatti regarding information on the existence of weapons of mass destruction in Iraq.

[4] In my opinion, this dynamic of the field is a more effective explanation than the theories that stress the "fundamentalist" influence of religious sects, the "messianic" behaviors of Western national leaders such as Tony Blair, George Bush, José Aznar or Sylvio Berlusconi.

5. Among the first to note this link, Susan Strange has situated it in two contexts: the political economies of managing credit and even industrial production, and the politics of knowledge. However, she did not extend her claim to security, thinking that in the security sector if nowhere else, by virtue of sovereignty political professionals were still in the position of making decisions. And if she concurred, along with others, that non-elected banking professionals made decisions in lieu of political professionals, she nonetheless refused to believe that the same was true of the military and the police, whose professional connections she did not see, and which she persisted in imagining as subordinate to national politicians. See Strange, Susan, *The Retreat of the State: The Diffusion of Power in the World Economy,* Cambridge Studies in International Relations, vol. 49 (Cambridge; New York: Cambridge University Press, 1996).
6. Anderson, Malcolm, *Policing the World: Interpol and the Politics of International Police Co-Operation* (Oxford, England; New York: Clarendon Press; Oxford University Press, 1989); Anderson, Malcolm, Monica den Boer, Peter Cullen, William Gilmore, Charles Raab and Neil Walker, *Policing the European Union* (Clarendon Studies in Criminology: Oxford University Press, 1996); Bigo, Didier, *Polices en Réseaux: L'experience Européenne* (Paris: Presses Sciences Po, 1996); Bigo, Didier, "Liaison officers in Europe, new actors in the European security field", p 67–100, in *Issues in Transnational Policing,* ed. Sheptycki, Bigo, Brodeur, Gregory, Johnston, Manning (Routledge, 2000, 247 p.); Nogala, Detlef, "Le marché privé de la sécurité, analyse d'une évolution internationale," *Cahiers de la sécurité intérieure* 24.2(1996):65–87; Deflem Mathieu, "Bureaucratization and Social Control: Historical Foundations of International Police Cooperation," *Law and Society Review*, 34.3 (2000); and Neocleous, Mark, *The Fabrication of Social Order: A Critical Theory of Police Power,* London; Sterling, VA: Pluto Press, 2000.
7. See Anderson, Malcolm, *Frontiers: Territory and State Formation in the Modern World.* Cambridge: Polity Press, 1996; Didier Bigo, "Security, Borders, and the State," in *Border Regions in Functional Transition,* ed. James Scott and Alan Sweedler (Berlin: Institute for Regional Studies, 1996 p 63–79); and Walker, Neil, "European Integration and European Policing," *Policing across National Boundaries,* ed. Malcolm Anderson and Monica den Boer (London; New York: Pinter Publishers, 1994).
8. Bigo, Didier, *Police in Networks, op. cit.*
9. These studies were conducted by the team of the Center on Conflicts and the ELISE network. See http://www.conflits.org.
10. Rob Walker's reading on this point in *Inside/Outside* is particularly important because it reminds us of the extent to which the analytical grid differentiating between inside and outside that our analyses snap to so "intuitively" is the product of the thought of the State, the logic of academic disciplines, and the symbolic practices and profits established by this differentiation. He shows that a different conception of politics in terms of flux and field allows us to bring together categories of practice that had been otherwise assigned to a space of inside or outside, to the detriment of analysis, and allows us to differentiate these practices otherwise. My analysis is strongly indebted to this work. See Walker, R. B. J., *Inside/Outside: International Relations as Political Theory,* (Cambridge: Cambridge University Press, 1993).

[11] See Nadelmann, Ethan A., *Cops across Borders: The Internationalization of U.S. Criminal Law Enforcement* (University Park, PA: Pennsylvania State University Press, 1993). For a more detailed and critical examination, see Bigo, Didier, "Compte Rendu de L'ouvrage de Nadelmann Par Didier Bigo », *Revue française de science politique* 3(1995):167–173.

[12] In other contexts I have explored interpenetration between the respective sectors that overlap across various social universes, the loss of the reference marks and the borders of the actors, blurring of identities. See "Internal and External Security(ies): The Möbius Ribbon," in *Identities, Borders, Orders: Rethinking International Relations Theory*, ed. Mathias Albert, David Jacobson and Yosef Lapid (Minneapolis: University of Minnesota Press, 2001, 206 p.).

[13] Due to space constraints, I will not list the practical collaborations between different police forces at the European level. Many previous works have done this; my priority is rather to suggest how understanding the methodological and theoretical implications of collaboration among European police can benefit our analysis.

[14] See Tournier, P., "La délinquance des étrangers en France — analyse des statistiques pénales", in S. Palidda (dir.), *Délit d'immigration*, COST A2 Migrations, Commission Européenne, Bruxelles, 1997, pp. 133–162 ; Tsoukala, Anastasia, "Looking at migrants as enemies", in *Controlling Frontiers: Free Movement into and within Europe*, ed. Didier Bigo and Elspeth Guild (Ashgate, 2004, p 182–204); Wacquant, L., "Des ennemis commodes", *Actes de la recherche en sciences sociales* 129 (1999): 63–67; and Dal Lago, A., *Non-Persone: L'esclusione dei migranti in una società globale* (Milano: Feltrinelli, 1999).

[15] Bigo, Didier, "Europe Passoire et Europe Fortresse, La Sécuritisation/Humanitarisation de L'immigration," in *Immigration Et Racisme En Europe*, ed. Andrea Rea (Bruxelles: Editions complexe, 1998).

[16] See Lahave, Gallya, "Immigration and the State: The Devolution and Provision of Immigration Control in the EU." *Journal of Ethnic and Migration Studies* 24.4 (1998): 675–94; Guiraudon, Virginie "De-nationalizing control: analysing state responses to constraints on migration control" in Virginie Guiraudon and Christian Joppke, *Controlling a new migration world* (London, Routledge, 2001, 256 p.); Guiraudon, Virginie, "Les compagnies de transport dans le contrôle migratoire à distance", in Didier Bigo and Elspeth Guild, "De Tampere à Seville: bilan de la sécurité européenne", *Cultures & Conflits* 45(Printemps 2002):124–147.

[17] I am indebted to Laurent Bonelli for drawing my attention to how these two types of control are polarized, which once we realize, effectively renders it impossible to see the national police as a unique, stand-alone métier. See Monjardet, Dominique, *Ce Que Fait La Police: Sociologie de La Force Publique*, (Paris: Éditions la découverte, 1996).

[18] See the special issue of *Cultures & Conflits*, "Circuler, enfermer, éloigner: Zones d'attente et centres de rétention des démocraties occidentales," *Cultures & Conflits* 23(Automne 1996), Paris, L'Harmattan. See http://www.conflits.org for all the issues of the journal.

[19] For instance, if the immigrant tends to exist as the common adversary of the police, military, and politicians, this is not because he is designated such by global consensual. This seeming convergence is actually the effect of different modes of insecurity converge to make him intelligible as a subject of security (for the police, crime, terrorism, drugs; for the military, subversion, grey zones, the press; economically through unemployment; demographic through the birth rate and the fear of racial-ethnic mixing…). The discourse on assimilation becomes itself a line of security insofar as it is concerned with integrating people and not developing them, in the interest of precluding future opposition. This change in immigration is not simply a change in perception, discourse or public policy. Above all it derives from concrete practices, in transformations of practical knowledge (savoir-faire) and technologies. If we want to analyze such transformations in knowledge, we need first to re-link them to actual practices, rather turning first to the second-order rationalizations that agents retroactively read into their practices. In other words, to we need to observe face-to-face relations where the impact of technologies actually used counts more than the representations, perceptions, and discourse that agents attribute to their respective roles. See Dal Lago, *Non-Persone: L'esclusione dei migranti in una società globale* (Feltrinelli, Milano, 1999); Palidda, Salvatore, *Polizia Postmoderna: Etnografia Del Nuovo Controllo Sociale* (Milano: Feltrinelli, 2000); Palidda S, «La construction sociale de la déviance et de la criminalité parmi les immigrés: Le cas italien», in Palidda S. (dir.), *Délit d'immigration*, COST A2 Migrations, Commission Européenne (Bruxelles, 1997, pp. 231–266); de Butterwegge, C., "Mass Media, Immigrants and Racism in Germany. A Contribution to an Ongoing Debate", *Communications* 2(1996):203–220; Tsoukala, Anastasia, "Le contrôle de l'immigration en Grèce dans les années quatre-vingt-dix", *Cultures & Conflits* 26/27(1997):pp.51–72; Huysmans, Jef, "Migrants as a security problem: dangers of securitizing societal issues", in *Migration and* European *Integration : The Dynamics of Inclusion and Exclusion*, ed. R. Miles, D. Thränhardt (London : Pinter, 1995, pp. 53–72); Wacquant, Loic, "Des ennemis commodes", *Actes de la recherche en sciences sociales*, 129(1999): 63–67; Heisler, Martin O., *The transnational nexus of security and migration*, to be published; and Bigo, Didier, "Security and immigration, toward a critique of the of Unease", in *Alternatives*, ed. Lynne Riener, vol. 27 supplement (Feb 2002, pp. 63–92).
[20] See Bourdieu, Pierre and Loic J. D. Wacquant, *Réponses: Pour Une Anthropologie Réflexive,* (Paris: Seuil, 1992, p. 78).
[21] We could here also cite the work of Graham Allison on the second and third models, as well as Bourdieu's sociological work. Allison's work is a more detailed analysis of the mechanisms of struggle and allows a better comprehension of the fluidity of subject positions. See Allison, Graham T. and Zelikow, Philip, *Essence of Decision: Explaining the Cuban Missile Crisis* (2nd ed, New York: Longman, 1999). In particular, see the competitions that take place around fluid borders and the open-ended missions that characterize the colonizing activities of the agencies.
[22] To give an example at the European level, as struggles are exacerbated at the national level, that puts pressure on international contacts to triumph nationally. In order to

understand the Europeanization of this phenomenon and its impact, we need research on alliances beyond national borders to promote a certain conception or style of police within these borders exerts force on the more aggregate process of Europeanization. The French national police, and most particularly its services involved in anti-terrorist combat, have been able to use Europeanization as an opportunity to reinforce their power and for certain sub-directorates the possibility of freeing themselves from the classical domains of counter-espionage. The connections are passed from central service to central service with an attempt to be the sole interlocutor of the foreign. On the other hand, the late arrivals of the gendarmes have formed connections at the local level, thereby profiting from their manpower at the borders, and have played the card of the trans-border, working with the police of the *landers* themselves opposed to the BKA (Bundeskriminalamt, German Federal Criminal Police Office) working with French police. The historicity of this context is important. Contrary to what a quick reading of Allison suggests, these struggles are not maintained in perpetuity by an economy of personal desires or because they a re structurally inherent to bureaucracies, but by the dynamic relation that emerges from their reciprocal trajectories and knowledges, practical knowledge and technologies that they employ. The dynamic of struggles takes on the particular configuration of the field that tends to recompose the process of (in)securitization by reconciling the military agencies and police and thus the modification of their relative distance. The necessary thing is to persuade politicians that struggle over budgets, mission, and legitimacy are the most fruitful areas for managing transnational threats. The trajectories of the agencies are determining factors here, in particular those that form new networks of formerly unconnected agencies. This is the case with the gendarmeries that bridge the police and military worlds, or the magistrates who connect the police and judiciary worlds, or alternatively, the case of customs agents in the war on drugs who create bridges between the police and the various economic imperatives that privilege the free circulation of goods. The interests of these intermediary agencies in linking these two sorts of universes are opposed to the interests of the most traditional agencies and in the interior of those who have everything to lose, such as those devoted to deterrence in the military and the public security police within the police. Thus the position of the actors, and still more their trajectories, tends to determine the positions they adopt, the types of discursive registers that they will use, and the kinds of rhetoric they mobilize for their fight, making them effectively blind to their actual similarities and common interests.

23 On the idea of the collusive transaction, see Dobry, Michel, *Sociologie Des Crises Politiques* (Paris: Presses de la FNSP, 1992). At the national level, the French police in Algeria was subject to these transactions. At the European level, the conflict between the Council and the Commission in the frame of the third pillar (Justice and Home Affairs pillar of the European Union) also reflect on occasion these conflicts. For the moment, this approach of relations between the different fields is not sufficiently analyzed. Pierre Bourdieu's research on a rate of conversion of capital via a field of the state are scarcely convincing, and are confined by their dependence on thinking the nation-state. Michel Dobry's work is without doubt the most pertinent, and appropriate

for analyzing these transnational dynamics of domination, but it would be necessary to take the analysis beyond its current domain of multi-sectorial mobilization. Both these analyses contribute to our analysis by showing how untenable is the image of politics conducted by national governments in opposition to one another under a European umbrella. This sort of analysis forces us to question the autonomy of the most powerful actors in the field of security who are political actors in the same sense as the bankers analyzed by Susan Strange. Her analysis, in turn, provokes us to reflect on the limited capacities of the plan of security defined as the local and undertaken by professional politicians.

[24] See Ocqueteau, F., "Polices privées, sécurité privée", *Déviance et Société* 3(1988): 72–99 ; Nogala, Detlef, "Le marché privé de la sécurité, analyse d'une évolution internationale", *Cahiers de la sécurité intérieure* 24(1996):34–67.

[25] See Foucher, Michel, *Fronts Et Frontières: Un Tour Du Monde Géopolitique* (Paris: Fayard, 1991).

[26] On the relations between the structure of the EU and its "stateness," see Caporaso, James A., *The Elusive State: International and Comparative Perspectives* (Newbury Park, CA: Sage Publications, 1989) and Kleinman, Mark, *A European Welfare State? European Union Social Policy in Context* (New York: Palgrave, 2002). Conventionally, each time the border is re-thought it is conceived at another level, as a more global entity, enclosing space. In contrast to this, we propose to think of the transversal nature of the border as a state of non-closure, like the topology of the Möbius strip. See Bigo, Didier in Albert, Jacobson and Lapid, *op. cit*, See also Balibar, Etienne, *L'europe, L'amérique, La guerre: Réflexions sur la médiation européenne* (Paris: Éditions la découverte, 2003).

[27] It is not a question of a series of autonomous, rational fields, but a field in which, for example, the strategic decisions of the BKA have an impact on the German institutions of the BGS, but also impact on the French PJ or the Italian DIA by a series of mediations such as those we have described. See Bigo, Didier, "Sécurité intérieure, implications pour la défense", Rapport établi pour la DAS, French Ministry of Defense (Mai 1998, 207 p.).

[28] Here I acknowledge the critique of Ole Waever and Barry Buzan. They have argued that the field of security as I had defined it in *Polices en réseaux* was too limited and placed too much stress on the relations between essentially bureaucratic agencies, and that created a "fixed point." And thus, they argued, it was necessary to depart from the semantic network created by points of reference explicitly citing security and extends in the analysis to include private actors.

[29] The dynamic of the field of security tends to constantly enlarge itself, but it is of course possible that it diminishes. It is possible to de-securitize. One problem that results thus is that of "holes", which that creates in space or the "differences in pressure" that the undertow of these structures creates. Space is not homogenous to the borders of the field. This is true in terms of the activities as it is in geographic terms. Rather than resembling a sphere, the field resembles the topology of a French *gruyère*. I owe this idea to the intervention of John Crowley at the military school of Saint Cyr Coetquidan

on the forms of contemporary security, and the English terminology itself to Jon Solomon. This topology of the hole or *gruyère* should be connected to the idea of the Möbius strip.

30 The idea of transversal field or network has to be connected to the notion of dispositif of Foucault. See *Le jeu de Michel Foucault* (revue Ornicar n°10, Juillet 1977, repris dans *Dits et Ecrits*, tome III, p. 299) and translated by Alain Grosrichard as "The Confession of the Flesh," in *Power/Knowledge: Selected Interviews and Other Writings, 1972–1977*, ed. Colin Gordon (New York: Harvester Press, 1980, pp. 194–5). Here, Foucault explains his notion of a dispositif: "What I'm trying to pick out with this term is, firstly, a thoroughly heterogeneous ensemble consisting of discourses, institutions, architectural forms, regulatory decisions, laws, administrative measures, scientific statements, philosophical and moral propositions — in short, the said as much as the unsaid. Such are the elements of that apparatus [dispositif]. The apparatus itself is the system of relations that can be established between these elements. Secondly, what I am trying to identify in this apparatus is precisely the nature of the connection that can exist between these heterogeneous elements. Thus, a particular discourse can figure at one time as the program of an institution, and at another it can function as a means of justifying or masking a practice which itself remains silent, or as a secondary re-interpretation of this practice, opening out for it a new field of rationality. In short, between these elements, discursive or non-discursive, there is a sort of interplay of shifts of position and modifications of function which can also vary very widely. Thirdly, I understand by the term 'apparatus' a sort of — shall we say — formation which has as its major function at a given historical moment that of responding to an urgent need. The apparatus thus has a dominant strategic function…there is a first moment which is the prevalence influence of a strategic objective. Next, the apparatus as such is constructed and enabled to continue in existence insofar as it is the site of a double process. On the one hand, there is a process of functional overdetermination…[o]n the other hand, there is a perpetual process of strategic elaboration." I refuse here the translation of dispositif as apparatus to avoid an "althusserisation of Foucault".

31 This term of *Ban*, which comes from Old German, both signifies the exclusion enacted by the community, and serves as the insignia of sovereignty. It's what is excluded from sovereignty on high as exception to the rule and what is excluded from below as discrimination, rejection, repulsion, and banishment. René Girard has already called our attention to this twinning effect of the absolute sovereign introduced by the ban. Giorgio Agamben has developed the "ban" at great length in his analysis of *homo sacer* but he has continued to insist on the dimension of sovereignty and less on exclusion and even less on normalization.

32 Agamben, Giorgio. *Homo Sacer: Sovereign Power and Bare Life* (Stanford, Calif.: Stanford University Press, 1998, p.15).

33 See Bigo, Didier, "When Two Become One: Internal and External Securitizations in Europe", in *International Relations Theory and the Politics of European Integration: Power, Security, and Community*, ed. Morten Kelstrup and Michael C. Williams (London; New York: Routledge, 2000, pp. 171–205).

Globalized-In-Security

34 Agamben suggests that we replace the Marxist schism between man and citizen with a distinction between naked life and multiple forms of life abstractly recodified in juridico-social identities (the elector, the employee, the journalist, etc.). He suggests rethinking politics from the point of view of the experience of the concentration camps, re-linking the two opposing sides of sovereign power and the bio-political, the fact of adjudicating death and the fact of directing life, which Foucault had opposed. He reckons that contemporary power is founded on the disassociation of forms of life and on the will to restore man to his naked life (isolated from his codified form) in radicalizing the exclusion by sovereign exceptionalism. But this thesis departing from a limit situation exaggerates the capabilities of power and confuses its programmatic dream with the diagram of forces (and resistances). Forms of life are constantly in the process of re-emerging, even in the most desperate of cases. Forms of resistance always exist, as hidden transcripts that mock power even where it seems to apply itself in a unilateral manner. James Scott has shown the resistance of slaves, and one could demonstrate ongoing resistance on the part of refugees against the will to make them nothing but docile bodies struggling to protect themselves. See Scott, James C., *Domination and the Arts of Resistance: Hidden Transcripts* (New Haven: Yale University Press, 1990). Their individual will, despite their denudement, cannot be reduced to the will of the States, even in spite of these governmental pressures. Examples in the waiting zones, and in detention centers show how the administration is led astray, flummoxed, trapped by its capacities of declining multiple identities. Refugees are only denizens in the eyes of governments and of professional managers of unease, but in their own eyes they are citizens of multiple states or citizens of the world. See Hammar, Tomas, *European Immigration Policy: A Comparative Study* (Cambridge; New York: Cambridge University Press, 1985). The ability to resist, including resistance taking place in a space like a prison or a camp, leads professionals to try to avoid these situations and to manage from a location "upstream" which is not simply anterior in space, but in prior in time. The film *Minority Report*, where the police are able to intervene even before the crime is committed by an anticipatory knowledge of the future, is the dream of this proactive police. (Philip K. Dick's *Minority Report* is more subtle than the film, and poses a ferocious critique to this police vision. The film dilutes this force of critique somewhat.)

35 To give but one example of technologies operative at the European level, we see multiple databases put in place to permit the profiling of risks associated with certain individuals. Concerning crime, other than the already aging Interpol database, the Siren system facilitates the rapid circulation of judiciary documents and the exchange of information. Since the Amsterdam Treaty and the Tampere meeting, justice follows in step with other security agencies, and does the same thing at a distance via networks. The Sirene network, which passes information on criminal procedures and decisions between states, puts in place magistrates of liaison...The creation of Eurojust and the forgetting of *corpus juris* provoke disequilibrium between the level of judges of instruction and judges of accusation that are able to draw on EU resources, and a defense that is confined within a national frame and has no access to this information But this point is considered secondary to the cause of speed and efficiency.

The Schengen information system manages individual dossiers, and functions as a file preventing illegal migrants from returning to the EU. It is not very effective at managing criminality. In fact, Schengen constantly enlarges its sphere of application under the obligation of uniform visas that acts like a norm not only in the EU but at the level of GATT. In the same way, the exceptional possibilities of identity control in border zones up to twenty kilometers from the border generalizes itself in all countries, even in countries where the concept of legitimate suspicion envelops controls very strictly. It is hardly even contested by the police authorities in question that Schengen institutes an immigration police and that is its priority, even though only five years ago there was a great resistance to using it, and there was no focus on the relation between crime and disappeared persons. This link that the SIS puts in place between criminal files and foreigners' files with respect to foreigners reaffirms the suspicion against them and focuses the attention on small acts of delinquency or illegality while making police and customs infractions primary in importance.

Certainly these techniques reinforce each other and overlap information bases, but scarcely facilitate the elaboration of profiles. In fact, under Schengen, more sophisticated databases have the goal of analyzing groups that pose a risk, as opposed to keeping their movements under surveillance.

The recently adopted database Eurodac will contain digital fingerprints of asylum-seekers, as well as an explication of the motives they have given, and the reasons for which they have been refused. The task is to prevent multiple applications, but also to spot the stereotypical narratives of asylum-seekers. In parallel with Eurodac, a securitized net is being developed to address FADO (false and authentic documents) that will function on the basis of information exchange concerning false documents. The idea is to invert current practice and place the burden of proof on the person submitting the document. In northern Europe, the American company Printrack International is pushing its services that enable tracking and automatic identification of people crossing borders, whether by cards with digitalized fingerprints in ports and airports, or retinal imprints. The goal is to control identities in the most invisible manner possible, due to the fact that this society of individuals does not like to be affected or slowed down when controlled, but as long as they do not register the act of control, they do not protest. One can therefore think of generalizing the system in the future in airports. At present, the link between card and credit and information is under research; it will be the same cards containing such information, some of which will be readable only by the police, and not the card-holder.

Profiling done for Europol files tends to make surveillance more refined and precise, rather than extending its general reach. Europol registers people who are capable of following through on their potential to commit a crime. As distinct from the Interpol databases whose entries are dependent on criminals who are effectively fugitive from justice, the Europol files contain sought-after criminals, suspects who have not yet entered the system of juridical inquiry, lists of possible informants, possible witnesses who might testify about their neighbor or colleague, victims or persons susceptible of being victims. Here it amounts to reconstructing individual or social trajectories, marking

Globalized-In-Security

territories or borders between populations at risk and others, of analyzing and deciding who is dangerous. Here we are at the heart of pro-active logic.

[36] "Globalization divides as much as it unites; it divides as it unites — the causes of division being identical with those which promote the uniformity of the globe. Alongside the emerging planetary dimensions of business, finance, trade and information flow, a 'localizing,' space-fixing process is set in motion. Between them, the two closely interconnected processes sharply differentiate the existential conditions of entire populations and of various segments of each one of the populations. What appears as globalization for some means localizing for others; signaling a new freedom for some, upon many others it descends as an uninvited and cruel fate. Mobility climbs to the rank of the uppermost among the coveted values — and the freedom to move, perpetually a scarce and unevenly distributed commodity, fast becomes the main stratifying factor of our late modern or postmodern times.

All of us are, willy-nilly, by design or default, on the move...some of us become fully and truly 'global; some are fixed in their 'locality'—a predicament neither pleasurable nor endurable in the world where 'globals' set the tone and compose the rules of the life-game.

Being local in a globalized world is a sign of social deprivation and degradation. The discomforts of localized existence are compounded by the fact that with public spaces removed beyond the reaches of localized life, localities are losing their meaning-generating and meaning-negotiating capacity and are increasingly dependent on sense-giving and interpreting actions which they do not control — so much for the communitarianist dreams/consolations of the globalized intellectuals.

An integral part of the globalizing processes is progressive spatial segregation, separation and exclusion." Bauman, Zygmunt, *Globalization: The Human Consequences* (New York: Columbia University Press, 1998, p 2–3).

[37] Interview with Didier Deleule and Francesco Paolo Adorno, "L'héritage intellectuel de Foucault", in *Cités* 2(2000):95–107.

THE MARKET AND THE POLICE:
FINANCE CAPITAL IN THE PERMANENT GLOBAL WAR

BRETT NEILSON

One of the more deplorable aspects of the recent installment of "permanent global war" in Iraq was the constant media banter on the reaction of financial markets. The parading of instant experts, who at once performed the roles of military and financial analyst, seemed almost too consciously to distract from that which the embedded reportage could not show but also could not conceal: the death and terrorization of real bodies. Wall Street bets on quick war, unexpected resistance slows growth, military gains cheer Asian markets, buyers show restraint as ground attack begins — the headlines lauded the market as at once the privileged register of global public sentiment and the moral arbiter of war, albeit one that could turn with the flicker of a sound byte. But within this particular loop of complicity, which seemed temporarily to align networks of state violence, finance, and communication, there were deeper tensions at work, tensions that the "permanent global war" on all its fronts seeks to rebalance and reorganize.

It is no secret that the global financial system, as it evolved in the decades following the first shocks to the Fordist economy in the 1970s, emerged as the symbol and reality of a new order of sovereignty. Decentered, networked, and predicated on circulation and mixture, the world market served not only to override the boundaries of nation-states, but also to construct a new paradigm of hierarchy and command that took hold in all the zones and regions where the old imperialisms had once flourished. For thinkers such as Appadurai, Sassen, Jameson, Latham, and Lee and LiPuma, there exists no more powerful marker of a paradigm shift in the global economic and political orders than this unification of the world market, which paradoxically operates through diversity and diversification.[1] The daily circulation of trillions of dollars, the flight of finance capital from the productive geography of material labor, the objectification, calculation, and distribution of risk by means of formal quantitative operations, the tightening of the relation between technology and exchange, the increasing asymmetries in knowledge and control of the economic forces affecting societies — all suggest a striving toward totality, the creation of a cosmopolitan culture of unimpeded financial circulation that is somehow unimaginable from the perspectives of the citizen-state or the national public sphere. How then to understand the daily hedges, the indexed fluctuations that hitched themselves to information gleaned about a war that seemed precisely to occur at the behest of a new imperial nationalism, a sovereign police action that heeded not so much the logic of the market (by which any object, regardless of location, can be valued and ordered) as the logic of strategy (by which spatially fixed resources, subject to calculation and command in the aggregate, are brought under control by statist elites who simultaneously propagate home front fantasies of security and terror)?

At stake is neither the subordination of the logic of the market to that of strategy nor vice versa. Even if prior to and during the war there emerged future markets trading on the likelihood that the Iraqi regime would endure until a certain point in time, the relation of market-based transactions to the machinations of material and information warfare cannot be reduced to the probabilistic calculations of speculators.[2] Equally, the motives for war cannot be entirely separated from economic factors, whether those identified by the popular slogan "No blood for oil" or those outlined by the more complex arguments that view the conflict as part of the ongoing battle between the dollar and the euro for dominance in world currency markets.[3] In the interplay between market and strategy, circulation and geopolitics, war emerges at once as a mediating and disruptive factor. No longer is it possible to affirm Clausewitz's famous description of war as the continuation of politics by other means. Far from being an attempt to realize an end that could not be achieved by political means, the campaign in Iraq had the overt goal of obtaining something that was already being accomplished through the contingencies of international politics — the

The Market and the Police

disarmament of the Hussein regime. And these same political machinations, at least as played out in the U.N. Security Council, worked precisely to counter the deployment of military force. In this instance, war functioned precisely to subordinate politics, or to reverse Clausewitz's formula, politics became the continuation of war by other means. As opposed to the 1991 Gulf War, where the justification for attack was provided by international law, or the 1999 police action over Kosovo, which sought a moral legitimation, the 2003 assault on Iraq was perpetrated in the absence of any prior extenuating circumstance. This was precisely a pre-emptive war, an action that sought justification in its effects rather than its precedents, in a reorganization of international order by which the invasion itself would appear just.

But the question of justice and, in this case, the severing of the right to justice from the right to peace, cannot be equated with the motives for war.[4] If, as Giorgio Agamben has argued, this deployment of force against right produces a state of emergency that has become the norm for democratic states in the twenty-first century, the question of what is perpetrated in this space of exception remains open.[5] Certainly one can point to the attacks upon the liberty of subjects in the advanced capitalist countries, the collapsing of internal police and external military powers, the fusing of terror and security in a mutually justifying cycle of violence, the increasing stringency of border control and associated restriction of labor mobility, the attempt to reverse the new economy-high technology crash through massive expenditure in the arms and security industries, and the geopolitical maneuvering for the control of centralized energy resources. But when it comes to identifying any one of these as the primary motive for the invasion, confusion becomes as rife as the inconsistencies in the rhetoric of the leaders who seek to justify war. The goals of warfare have become blurred due to the pursuit of a variety of agendas. And not always can these agendas be reduced to the rationality of economy. In the new politics of security, fantasy itself plays a key role. Recent polls indicate that a majority of Americans, up to 60 and 70 percent in some samples, believe that Saddam Hussein was behind the September 2001 attacks on New York and Washington. Similarly, only 17 percent could affirm that Iraqi nationals were not among the hijackers who perpetrated these same attacks. But this is not simply a matter of misinformation or media control. A mere clarification of facts would be insufficient to counter the complex operations of ideology involved in these fantasies. At stake is what Slavoj Žižek calls the "will-to-ignorance," an intense desire not-to-know that operates not only at the affective but also the cognitive level.[6] In analyzing the political meaning of this ignorance, it is necessary to examine precisely the appeal of this refusal-to-know, the comfort of separating oneself from disturbing acts of state by which existing privileges are maintained. Only in this way is it possible to derive an adequate account of why the official justifications for war — disarmament, human rights, regime change — receive willing audience, when they are clearly outweighed by covert (and deniable) motivations and goals.

The displacement of the United Nations, the opening of political cleavages within the E.U., the geopolitical play for resources, the subtraction of liberty from subjects in the capitalist democracies, the defense of the U.S. dollar — all of these are hidden motivations for war. But they are refracted through a variety of institutional and social contexts, such that it is difficult to arrange them in any plausible order or attribute them to a coherent state actor. As is well known, most contemporary wars no longer take the classical form of conflict between sovereign states, involving rather non-state actors such as separatist groups, international organizations, or transnational terrorist networks. An under-commented aspect of the campaign in Iraq involves the attempt to re-contain the conflict within the older interstate model, an effort that arguably reflects the difficulties of fighting decentered organizations such as Abu Sayyaf, al Qaeda, or Jemaah Islamiah. The lack of tangible or admissible progress in the so-called "war against terrorism" necessitates an attack against an enemy that can surely and demonstrably be vanquished — a nation-state. But this return to interstate warfare is in turn undermined by the presence of irregular (or non-state) Iraqi forces and the resort to tactics such as suicide bombing, which are immediately classified as illegal and barbaric as opposed to the civilized advance of coalition troops. Even the force of this rhetoric, however, cannot conceal the fact that there is no single or coherent motivation for the invasion/occupation. Not only do the coalition forces comprise troops from various states (the United States, Britain, Australia, Poland) that all pursue different interests, but within any one of these states, different groups and agencies push different envelopes (witness the conflicts between the U.S. State Department and the Pentagon). These differences are in turn overlaid by the increasing tensions between neoliberal economic agendas that aim to make the world a smooth space for the circulation of capital and nationalist security agendas that seek to re-establish state borders at the command of the

The Market and the Police

sovereign police. While it is true that security presupposes liberal ideology and globalization, seeking to intervene in ongoing transnational processes rather than to isolate or close off territories, it is also the case that capitalism does not simply tend toward the market. As Yann Moulier-Boutang explains, capitalism acts as an "avatar and controller of liberation... a mechanism of control that, at certain moments, uses the canals of the market."[7] At stake in the currently unfolding reorganization of relations between capital and security, the market and the police, is something more than a simple dynamic of deterritorialization/reterritorialization by which the state mediates the collective interests of capital. Rather there exists an evolving tension between two mutually implicated forms or aspects of control: those that subsume the social *bios* to the general equivalence of money (through quantifiable, commensurable relations) and those that search for an outside or absolute place in which to ground the value of money (today the sphere of war).

Not surprisingly these tensions between finance capital and security have become most pronounced in the United States, the world's only remaining superpower and principal economic hegemon (in competition with the E.U.). Among the hallmarks of the George W. Bush administration have been the move toward greater unilateralism in foreign policy, the Rumsfeld-led revolution in military affairs, the promotion of industrial — at the expense of finance capital, and the swing toward economic protectionism in sectors such as the steel industry (despite support for neoliberal economic agendas in the face of protests at international meetings such as the 2001 G8 summit in Genova). As Stanley Aronowitz explains, these tendencies, which were already underway by the time of September 11, have incurred the enmity of finance capital and the foreign policy establishment. Aronowitz observes: "as the nationalist and right-wing character of this administration comes to the surface, the foreign policy establishment (which has been internationalist for more than a half-century), the leaders of financial corporations, and the members of both political parties who have hewed their line have started to worry that this administration is attempting to shift power decisively by, among other tactics, winning over the beleaguered but still substantial fractions of industrial capital and integrating some ailing industrial unions into a new coalition with the social right."[8] One effect of this rift between finance capital and the nationalist war machine has been to sever portions of industrial labor from the alliance they struck with the alternative globalization movement that first expressed itself in Seattle in December 1999.

Having rallied industrial capital (and parts of industrial labor) around projects such as oil drilling in Alaska and the promotion of traditional energy economies (such as coal burning), the neo-conservative security elite finds itself in increasing variance with the leaders of finance capital, who, along with the foreign policy establishment, remain tied to the internationalism embodied by institutions such as the World Bank and the United Nations. Moreover, the incorporation of significant sectors of the U.S. working population into a post-September 11 patriotism, reinforced and perpetuated by new forms of complicity between government and the media, aids and abets this rapid advance of security agendas, within and despite the financialization of everyday life that remains the legacy of the Clinton era new economy.

While most marked in the U.S., these tensions are also manifest in Europe, where alliances between social movements and industrial labor have only strengthened over recent years. Particularly in the wealthy Western European states (or so-called Old Europe), there has emerged a sense that a French–German headed, finance capital-backed assertion of autonomy in the face of U.S. hegemony might create the space for an alternative power bloc given to civil rights and social democracy. But the flipside of this fantasy is a politics of anti-Americanism that clearly fails to incorporate all European nations (witness Spain and Italy as well as Eastern European countries like Poland and Bulgaria that to date remain outside the E.U.). Even in the case of Germany and France, where opposition to the Iraq war has enjoyed official sanction, this anti-Americanism serves only to obscure the continued participation of the state in securitarian and neo-imperialist agendas. Witness France, where conservative President Jacques Chirac has nullified all internal resistance to his politics by invoking an inveterate French anti-Americanism (which does not necessarily entail anti-imperialism or anti-capitalism and encompasses both the extreme left and right), while simultaneously pursuing neo-imperial adventures in Africa (particularly oil rich Congo-Brassaville). If one effect of the Iraq war has been the appearance of irreconcilable political differences within the European Union, a result by no means secondary for the U.S. administration, this should not license an analysis that opposes the brutality of U.S. unilateralism to the virtues of the European approach. By contrast, it is necessary to take stock of Europe's failure to stop the war, to recognize that even if the official opposition grew out of the wrong motives, it emerged alongside (and against) a vast transnational resistance movement that

The Market and the Police

will surely express itself again as the war insinuates itself in other contexts (North Korea, Israel/Palestine, Syria?). To reduce the pro-/anti-war divide to a competition between Europe and the United States is not only to seriously banalize its effects on the Middle East and the wider remaking of international order, but also to ignore the transnational reach of the anti-war movement, which (whatever its political limits or ethical motivations) operated within the borders of the U.S. and its Anglosphere allies, the U.K. and Australia. Europe, as much as the United States, is torn asunder by the evolving tensions between finance capital and the security politics, its economic strength suffering as a result of the internal political divisions emerging from the war. In this sense, there is no longer any America or Europe, just relatively positioned links within the global constitution of Empire.[9]

For many commentators, the U.S.-led military assault upon Iraq was a clear instance of imperial nationalism that disproves the celebrated thesis of Antonio Negri and Michael Hardt regarding the passage to a non-national globally constituted Empire.[10] Indeed, in the protracted lead-up to the war, Negri himself described the escalation of nationalist security politics in the United States as an "imperialist backlash," an argument since elaborated by Hardt, who has suggested that the rise of U.S. unilateralism can be understood as a kind of *coup d'état*, the historical repetition of Louis Bonaparte's reactionary seizure of power in nineteenth-century France, or the eighteenth Brumaire of George W. Bush.[11] Such parallels have an undeniable evocative power, but they do not necessarily license the claim that the Iraq conflict and the current global mission of the U.S. government repeat the old European imperialist projects. Negri's assertion that Bush's unilateralism is "linked to old structures of power, old methods of command, and a monocratic and substantialist conception of sovereignty" has been rethought by Hardt, who warns that "the old imperialisms do not help us understand what is central in our current situation." In both cases, however, there is an attempt to salvage the earlier argument of *Empire* by which the emergent forms of global command represent a definite positive advance over classical nation-state imperialism. Whether one understands the present situation as an "imperialist backlash" or a *coup d'état* makes little difference, what remains constant is a progressive, almost linear model of historical transformation, which makes it appear as if the Empire that emerged during the Clinton-dot.com years is the only Empire possible. Tracing, as they do in *Empire*, the origins of the current global order back to U.S. President Woodrow Wilson's efforts to institute a world government of peace, Hardt and Negri must subsequently backpedal to account for the advent of "permanent global war," as if it were a moment of reaction, an opportunistic seizure of power, or more simply a "backlash." But the model of global constitution they present in the seminal chapter of *Empire* entitled "Mixed Constitution" is much more flexible than this and perfectly adequate to account for current global conflicts.[12]

Reflecting Polybius's division of the Roman Empire into three forms of "good power" — monarchy, aristocracy, and democracy — the model of mixed (or more properly hybrid) constitution delineates a three-tiered order of global command. At the top of the pyramid sits the United States, which, as the world's only superpower, performs the monarchic role of controlling the world monopoly of force, regulating the primary global monetary instruments, and exercising cultural and biopolitical hegemony. Although the U.S. can act by itself, it prefers to act in collaboration with others, and thus a small group of wealthy states (bound together in organs such as the G8 or the Paris and London Clubs) play a secondary role in this wielding of monarchical power. The second tier of global command (or aristocracy) comprises the networks that transnational corporations have extended throughout the world market as well as the more general set of sovereign nation-states that filter the flows of global circulation and exercise discipline over their populations. Finally, the third and broadest tier of the pyramid (democracy) consists of groups that represent popular interests in the global power arrangement: the United Nations and the organs of global civil society, including the media, religious institutions, and non-government organizations (NGOs). This three-tier model of governance differs from the constitutionalism of the modern state insofar as its elements are not organized in an equilibrium of separate bodies, regulated by an elaborate system of checks and balances (like the executive, judiciary, and representative branches of modern liberal governments). Rather there is a marked hybridization of these governmental functions, leading to a fundamental disequilibrium among the existing agents of power. Global monarchical force rules over the unity of the world market, and thus its functions inextricably merge with those of the aristocracy, conditioning and overseeing the formation of complex circuits of production and circulation. The operations of democracy, in turn, fuse with these hybridized forms of monarchy and aristocracy, as the instruments and dynamics of social cooperation (the primary source of surplus labor in the post-Fordist economy) must be constitutionally

The Market and the Police

formalized to ensure their containment in networks of control. The result is a global system that can accommodate strong tensions and pass through various phases of equilibrium and disequilibrium. The current machinations of "permanent global war" can be understood as just such a passage through disequilibrium, a series of displacements or readjustments that attest not a moment of reaction or "backlash" but an ongoing reorganization of global power through a generalized production of fear.

Hardt's description of this readjustment as *un golpe nell'Impero*, the usurpation of power by unilateral monarchical forces and corresponding subordination of multilateral aristocratic elements, provides one way of understanding the current transformations of Empire. But the rhetorical advantage he gains by remembering Marx's essay on Louis Bonaparte — the articulation of an optimism that sides with neither party in this palace *coup* — is earned at the price of a certain schematism. The equation of monarchy with unilateralism and aristocracy with multilateralism robs the earlier model developed in *Empire* of one of its strongest elements — the emphasis on the hybridization of the various forms of global power. Hardt's contention that Bush the son's "Second Empire" seeks to separate the United States from all other world powers and render international collaboration unnecessary certainly accords the current situation of global *realpolitik*, but what is left out of the equation is the way in which the emerging discord between monarchy and aristocracy tears the United States itself apart, preventing it from becoming a "normal" state. In the original model of mixed constitution, the monarchy was certainly not coextensive with the United States encompassing also that group of wealthy nation-states (such as France and Germany) with which the U.S. preferred to act in consonance. Similarly, the aristocracy could not be identified solely with multilateral powers — the E.U., the U.N., and so forth — but comprised primarily the transnational networks of the world market as well as a series of lesser nation-states (outside monarchical institutions like the G8) subordinated to the circulation of global capital. This raises a number of problems with the interpretation of the present global fall-out of the U.S. with the U.N. and Europe as a simple discord between monarchic and aristocratic (unilateral and multilateral) powers.

First, the current world situation is more complex than the thesis of *coup d'état* implies, involving a fracturing of powers within the internal levels of the monarchy (the United States over the other G8 powers, particularly those who opposed the so-called "coalition of the willing") as well as an attempt to subordinate (when they cannot be coerced into cooperation) the institutions of global representative democracy and civil society: the United Nations, NGOs, media organizations, and so forth. Second, the role of the world market and other institutions of global capitalism (transnational corporations, the World Trade Organization, the World Bank, the International Monetary Fund, etc.) remains unspecified in the model of *golpe nell'Impero*. This obscures another level of complicity, as these aristocratic institutions administer the neoliberal hegemony that U.S. militarism seeks to perpetuate but that also undermines the interests of crude U.S. economic nationalism (witness the prevarications of the Bush administration on free trade — the lip service paid to neoliberal orthodoxy but erection of protectionist barriers on the home front). And finally, the containment of the *coup* argument within the discourses of international relations (unilateralism versus multilateralism) assumes the primacy of nation-states as actors in the "permanent global war" and thus papers over the effects of the current reorganization of Empire *within and across states* (as opposed to between them). As a result, the thesis of *golpe nell'Impero* provides little analytical grip with which to interrogate the way in which these readjustments of global command intersect that plane of subjectivity that refuses the equation of humanity with stateness, the restless and productive body of the multitude.

To track the role of the multitude in the currently unfolding struggle of capital and security, the market and the police, it is necessary to place the "permanent global war" in the context of more general capitalist transformations, particularly those associated with the dot.gone crash of April 2000. This market bust punctuated a period of cyber-driven, post-Fordist economic expansion in which the sovereign institutions of global neoliberalism (the World Bank, IMF, WTO, etc.) consolidated their power and practices of financial trading trickled down to become part of everyday life (through Internet brokerage and pension funds in the advanced capitalist countries and micro-credit schemes in the poorer parts of the world).[13] Marked by the production of increasing disparities in the global divisions of wealth and labor, the speculative bubble of the dot.com boom was driven by autoreferential market operations, which is to say that the market functioned as a sphere in which what mattered was not the belief of the individual investor but what the individual investor believed that other investors believed. In other words, economic rationality manifested itself in the work of gossip,

The Market and the Police

linguistic exchange, or cognitive labor. As Christian Marazzi argues, what was at stake was a financialization of the *general intellect*, a process of capture by which the productive capacities of the multitude were transformed into the measurable dispositions of a population of consumers.[14] But this attempt to convert linguistic labor-power into added shareholder's value was not altogether successful. The crisis of the new economy arose from the multitude's refusal of these devices of financial capture or command. Particularly in the new technology sector, where the production of (immaterial) goods through linguistic cooperation created the greatest added value, there emerged a tension between the interests of workers and managers and those of shareholding investors. The percentage of profits returned to workers and managers in this sector was some 73 percent (counting stock options as salary expenses) as opposed to the 20 percent of profits returned to workers and managers in the top 35 companies listed on Wall Street over the same period.[15] While managers certainly pocketed a fair share of these earnings (part of the crony capitalism that would come to the surface with the Enron crisis), this siphoning of profits toward the workers themselves revealed the incapacity of market-driven finance capitalism (the model of shareholder's value) to control the productive-cooperative activity of the *general intellect*. In this sense, the new economy crash and the subsequent crisis of shareholder's value (that continues to this day) signaled the resistance of the multitude to mechanisms of financial capture.

> The problem of the new economy was that the linguistic labor contained in the goods produced coincided with the linguistic labor that capital had to continually extract to ensure its economic growth. This coincidence was nothing other than "bare life put to work" to reproduce the body (or the productive capacity/faculty) of the multitude. The extraction of (surplus) value became blocked when it confronted the impossibility of restraining the bare life of linguistic labor-power, when the *passion* of creative/innovative labor (typical, in its absolute ambiguity, of cognitive work in the new economy) rebelled in hatred against this same work or simply in indifference to a way of life lacking in sense…The economic-financial crisis of the new economy reveals the resistance of the multitude against its transformation into public opinion, against the abstraction of its body that is necessary for the normal functioning of the financialized global economy. It is the multitude, as the precondition of globalization, which throws into crisis the functioning of finance on a global scale. In a certain sense, one can say that the crisis reveals the existence of a sovereignty of the multitude that is stronger that the sovereignty of the imperial or global state.[16]

It is in this same demand for liberty on the part of the multitude that the conditions for "permanent global war" take root. Far from being simply a matter of a palace *coup*, the conspiratorial conceit of a Cheney-led shadow government against the global aristocracy, the war manifests itself as an attack upon the liberty and passion of the multitude. In this sense, it predates September 11 and even the earliest signs of Bush unilateralism (the refusals to sign up to the Kyoto protocol or the International Criminal Court), finding its genesis in the heady neoliberalism that emerged with the fall of the Berlin Wall. If, as many have argued, the new security politics involves a direct attack upon democratic rights and freedoms, it is only the most overt (and justifiable) of a wider series of war operations that don't necessarily obey the logic of geopolitics or military strategy.[17]

In their influential book *Unrestricted Warfare*, Chinese air force senior colonels Qiao Liang and Wang Xiansui describe the current tendency for war to become ever more generalized — that is, for war to be conducted not only through military but also through non-military means.[18] Their list of forms of non-military warfare, which proliferate alongside military actions other than war (that is, missions carried out by armed forces when there is no state of war) is extensive: financial warfare, diplomatic warfare, trade warfare, intelligence warfare, resources warfare, ecological warfare, psychological warfare, economic aid warfare, space warfare, tactical warfare, regulatory warfare, electronic warfare, smuggling warfare, sanction warfare, guerilla warfare, drug warfare, media warfare, terrorist warfare, ideological warfare, and virtual warfare (deterrence). In any given campaign, these methods of operation can be combined with each other to form a new kind of operation. Thus the campaign against bin Laden combines national terrorist warfare, intelligence warfare, financial warfare, network warfare, and regulatory warfare. Or the Iraq campaign combines conventional military warfare with, diplomatic warfare, sanction warfare, media warfare, psychological warfare, intelligence warfare, and so on. Of the new forms of non-military warfare, financial warfare plays a primary role, having "now officially come to war's center stage."[19] The Chinese colonels cite the Asian economic crisis of 1997 (which they attribute to the "terrorist" actions of George Soros) and Lee Teng-hui's subsequent devaluation of the New Taiwan dollar (to launch an attack on the Hong Kong dollar and Hong Kong "red-chip stocks" — companies listed on the Hong Kong stock exchange but controlled by Mainland interests). But whatever the machinations of non-military warfare, the overall trend in this generalization of

The Market and the Police

conflict is for war operations to become ever more linked to the forms of everyday life.

> What must be made clear is that the new concept of weapons is in the process of creating weapons that are closely linked to the lives of the common people. Let us assume the first thing we say is: The appearance of new-concept weapons will definitely elevate future warfare to a level which is hard for the common people — or even military men — to imagine. Then the second thing we have to say should be: The new concept of weapons will cause ordinary people and military men alike to be greatly astonished at the fact that commonplace things that are close to them can also become weapons with which to engage in war. We believe that some morning people will awake to discover with surprise that quite a few gentle and kind things have begun to have offensive and lethal characteristics.[20]

It is the *commonality* of the new forms of non-military warfare that the Chinese colonels emphasize — the possibilities for designing new methods of lethal (and non-lethal) combat that take root in the cognitive processes of communication, knowledge-production, and linguistic cooperation. As Marazzi explains, the fundamental principles of this new warfare raise the same problem as that generated by the crisis of sovereignty in financial globalization: "The fact that anything can be used as a weapon, the *whatever-ness* of the new weapons, is the same thing as the productive potentiality of the *general intellect* — both arise from the sphere of potentiality, from the web of capacities that underlie pre-individual realities, both take root in bare life and the productive power of linguistic (communicational-relational) technologies, and both are disseminated in global society."[21] Just as the money-form itself is at once the artificial register of human commonality and a mechanism of command, so these new forms of warfare unfold "in a gray zone where devices of non-military warfare coexist with a multiplicity of desires for liberty."[22] In other words, the "permanent global war" perpetuates itself on the flesh of the multitude, flourishing (much like the new economy) in the communicational-linguistic intelligence of cognitive labor, but at the same time, decimating and fragmenting the unified global space in which this commonality inheres.[23]

Seen through the kaleidoscopic vision of the multitude, the currently evolving tensions of finance capital and security, the market and the police, are precisely a register of global complicity. These conflicts are internal to Empire and, while they spell havoc for the world's political and financial elites, who rearrange their loyalties under the competing (and contradictory) signs of capital and sovereignty, they have devastating effects upon the productive plane of the *general intellect*. The figure of *golpe nell'Impero* captures something of this complicity, of the elitist and non-democratic nature of these dissonances, but it does not register the perils faced by the multitude as it lives the transition from the society of control to the society of digitized security. These dangers will remain buried and unapparent as long as we understand the current reorganization of world order as a showdown between the U.S. and Europe, monarchy and aristocracy, or unilateralism and multilateralism. Certainly, the U.S. administration has chosen to sideline international institutions and organizations, and this has alienated the doyens of finance capital and foreign policy both within and across its borders. But there is something more at stake in the "permanent global war" than the mere assertion of U.S. imperialist nationalism. Just as money itself is at once a particular good and the general equivalent of all goods, so United States sovereignty is at once a particular sovereignty and the general equivalent of all sovereignties in the globalized world. The current fractures between the market and the police must be understood in this light, since only by tracing their complicity in the networks of Empire might their dual operations within and against the body of the multitude be apprehended.

Notes

[1] Arjun Appadurai. 1996. *Modernity at Large: Cultural Dimensions of Globalization.* Minneapolis: University of Minnesota Press; Saskia Sassen. 1996. *Losing Control: Sovereignty in an Age of Globalization.* New York: Columbia University Press; Frederic Jameson. 1997. 'Culture and Finance Capital." *Critical Inquiry* 24: 246–265; Robert Latham. 2000. "Social Sovereignty." *Theory, Culture and Society* 17: 1–18; Benjamin Lee *and* Edward LiPuma. 2002. "Cultures of Circulation: The Imaginations of Modernity. " *Public Culture* 14: 191–213.

[2] During the war the Irish firm Tradesports ran an electronic futures market on the likelihood that the Iraqi regime would last until the end of the month. They are currently running futures on the capture of Hussein, the capture of bin Laden, and the discovery of weapons of mass destruction in Iraq. See http://sportstrading.com (30 April 2003).

[3] On the dollars versus euros theory of the war see Geoffrey Heard. 2003. "It's not about Oil or Iraq. It's about the US and Europe Going Head-to-Head on World Economic Dominance." http://www.scoop.co.nz/mason/stories/HL0303/S00182.htm (30 April 2003). For a rebuttal see George Caffentzis. 2003. "A Note on the Euro Explanation of

the War." http://www.infoshop.org/inews/stories.php?story=03/04/19/9846210 (30 April 2003).

4. On the separation of the right to peace from the right to justice in the context of the Iraq war, see the contribution of Antonio Negri to the public forum "Disobbedienza e guerra globale" held at the Instituto di Architettura, Venezia, on 2 April 2003. Available at http://www.globalradio.it/articles.php?lng=it&pg=1112 (30 April 2003).

5. For Giorgio Agamben on the permanent state of emergency and the Iraq war see "Une guerre contre l'Europe." *Le Figaro* (7 April 2003) and "Der Gewahrsam. Ausnahmzustand als Weltordnung." *FrankfuterAllgemeine Zeitung* (19 April 2003).

6. On the poll results and the "will to ignorance" see Doug Henwood's interview with Slavoj Žižek on radio WBAI, New York City, 17 April 2003. Available at http://www/leftbusinessobserver.com/Radio (30 April 2003).

7. Yann Moulier-Boutang. 1999. "L'art de la fugue." *Vacarme*. May 1999. English translation "The Art of Flight: An Interview with Stany Grelet" available at http://slash.autonomedia.org/print.pl?sid+03/02/07/1350202 (30 April 2003).

8. Stanley Aronowitz. 2003. "Global Capital and its Opponents." In Stanley Aronowitz and Heather Gautney, eds. *Implicating Empire: Globalization and Resistance in the 21st-Century World Order*. New York: Basic Books. 179–195.

9. On the (internal) disarticulation of Europe and America see Franco Berardi (Bifo). "internazionale futura umanità." *rekombinant*. 6 March 2003. http://www.rekombinant.org/article.php?sid=2012 (30 April 2003). For a response highlighting developments in the U.S., see McKenzie Wark. "The Untied States." <nettime> 11 March 2003. http://amsterdam.nettime.org/Lists-Archives/nettime-I-0303/msg00050.html (30 April 2003).

10. Michael Hardt *and* Antonio Negri. 2000. Empire. Cambridge, Mass.: Harvard University Press. Arguments claiming that war disproves the Empire thesis are too numerous to list, but for a recent example see Luigi Cavallaro. "Lo Stato dell'ordine imperiale." *Il manifesto* (22 April 2003): 13. For a similar argument in the context of the Afghanistan war see Timothy Brennan. 2003. "The Empire's New Clothes." *Critical Inquiry* 29: 337–365.

11. Antonio Negri. 2002. "Il backlash imperialista sull'Impero. Intervista con Ida Dominijanni." *Il manifesto* September 14; Michael Hardt. 2003. "Il 18 Brumaio di George W. Bush." *Global Magazine* 1 (March): 4–5.

12. For further comments on the model of "mixed constitution" and the progressive historical narrative of *Empire* see Sandro Mezzadra and Brett Neilson (2003) "*Né qui, né altrove*: Migration, detention, desertion. A dialogue." *borderlands ejournal* 2 http://www.borderlandsjournal.adelaide.edu.au/vol2no1_2003/mezzadra_neilson.html (30 April 2003).

13. On the financialization of everyday life in the 1990s, see Randy Martin. 2003. "Geography Financialized." In Stanley Aronowitz and Heather Gautney, eds. *Implicating Empire: Globalization and Resistance in the 21st-Century World Order*. New York: Basic Books. 211–228.

14. Christian Marazzi. 2002. "Denaro e Guerra." In Andrea Fumagalli, Christian Marazzi and Adelino Zanini. *La moneta nell'Impero*. Verona: ombre corte. 41–98.

[15] The figures, which date from June 2000, are from John Plender. 2003. *From Going off the Rails: Global Capital and the Crisis of Legitimacy*. New York: John Wiley & Sons. Quoted in Christian Marazzi. 2003. "La borsa valori del nuovo ordine imperiale." *Il manifesto*. 14 March.

[16] Marazzi. "Denaro e Guerra" 76–77. My translation.

[17] On the war as an attack on liberty see most prominently Gore Vidal. 2001. *La fine della libertà. Verso un nuovo totalitarismo?* Roma: Fazi Editore.

[18] Qiao Liang and Wang Xiangsui. 1999. *Unrestricted Warfare*. Beijing: PLA Literature and Arts Publishing House.

[19] *Ibid.* 51.

[20] *Ibid.* 26.

[21] Marazzi. "Denaro e Guerra." 61. My translation.

[22] *Ibid.* 61. My translation.

[23] A striking example of the way in which the war machine dwells in the intelligence of the multitude can be found in an influential work of military think-tank strategy from the RAND Corporation (National Defense Research Institute): John Arquilla and David Ronfeldt. 2002. *Swarming and the Future of Conflict*. Santa Monica: RAND Corporation. In developing a new doctrine of "battleswarm" based on the information networking of small armed units, Arquilla and Ronfeldt state that they are adapting for U.S. military use tactics most recently deployed by the Zapatistas in Mexico and anti-capitalist protesters in Seattle 1999.

PART 3

A NEW IMPERIAL NOMOS

The Rule of Imperialism and the Global-State in Gestation

Jacques Bidet
— *Translated from French by Jon Solomon*

Although the global State does not yet exist, its manifestations are nonetheless with us already. Like the obverse image of a dead star, whose light we receive long after its disappearance, we are already, one way or another, under the influence of this global State even though it has not yet been born.

I am not here to tell you about the "lucky star," or the "good news." Instead, I want to show what is emerging "under our nose," as it were, within the field of imperialism, in symbiosis yet contradiction to it.

Nor have I come to preach in favor of a "good government" for the world, or to advance a "utopia," even a realistic one. What we are dealing with here first of all is the "State," not "government" or "governance." And this concept of the State is not to be understood either as a social State, nor a State of rights, but as *a State of class*. More precisely, for a long time, in a quasi-imperceptible but already significant fashion, something analogous to the nation-State has been figuring itself out under our nose under the guise of a global-State, marking the end of an historical period.[1]

This reflection, falling within the framework of a shared project, is inscribed within essential work on the world system (with its multi-national articulation of centers/peripheries), on the neo-liberal order and its most spectacular and worrisome development today: the imperial expansion of the most powerful of all the central countries. Hence, I have not neglected any of the paradigms that organize the collective thinking of the world citizen movement. I have not lost sight of either *nation-States*, the vitality of which, as we shall see, continues to grow, nor of the constitution of *continental Groups* that seem almost self-sufficient (EU, NAFTA, etc.), and may be expected to compartmentalize the planet for a long time to come, nor especially the *imperialism*, which, in the form of a triad (USA, Europe, Japan) deeply structures the world space. The thesis I would advance does not avoid these obvious statements, nor contradict these major facts, facts with which some may be tempted to refute the thesis, but about which I will show a dialectical relation to the "global-State" tendency over the long term. This analysis, in order to be complete, should consider the social life of the globe as a whole. I will not consider here the cultural, scientific and ecological aspects of the problem, in order to focus on the economic and juridico-political ones.

The theme of "imperialism" must remain central. Imperialism means the "system of the world" — centers/peripheries— understood as a process. What can be designated as an "empire" when we say, for example, the "American Empire" is a specific phenomenon that takes place within the "world system." The world system, however, is not itself an "empire." This is why the theme of "Empire," in vogue today, should not be allowed to mask the theme of imperialism. To the former, I will thus only add a short statement, which concerns the very long term. This short statement is nevertheless already of great importance for the elaboration of a thought about collective action, without which there would be no living-together: for the elaboration of a "politics of humanity." I simply do not pretend that it would be appropriate to work for the construction of some untenable global-State. I want rather to be able to recognize how a state authority of class can historically appear, behind our backs, on a global-scale, as well as the relation it bears to imperialism and the struggles of class and people waged against it.

What Does it Mean to have a "State" (in Gestation) on the Global Scale?

Between the terms *imperialism* and *global State*, there is obviously a contradiction arising from the different conceptual configurations. Lenin's greatness was to put imperialism at the core of his analysis, and to conceive of revolutionary process,

The Rule of Imperialism and the Global-State in Gestation

in the age of capitalism, articulated not only around the rift of class, as the socialist movement since *The Manifesto* had held, but also along the rift of center/periphery, with its incomparable violence and global potential for emancipation. Such was made clear, in particular, at the *Congress of Peoples of the Orient* in Baku, 1920. Third-worldist theoreticians of the 1960s and 70s, such as Samir Amin, Immanuel Wallerstein and others, have, with Braudel, widened the long-term perspective, highlighting the fact that *from its origin* capitalism has exactly defined itself through a particular class *structure* tending to affect each of the entities (proto-States followed by nation-States) in a whole that developed out of Europe, according to a model that eventually generalized itself as well as, at the same time and in equal measure, through the *system* shaped by these entities, through their interrelationships, through a system of centers/peripheries in hierarchical domination or, in other words, through imperialism. *Capitalism is at the same time structure (of class) and system (of the world)*: the relationships between individuals are, in modern times, mediated by relations (structural) of class within the nation-State as well as by (systemic) imperialist relations between nations, increasingly intertwined within each. But these are two kinds of relation that must not be confused: imperialism has neither the form nor, hence, the functional mode, of a global State. The label *"state imperialism"* thus seems to represent a contradiction in terms, the first suggesting a *structural* form (class structure of a given social formation), the second suggesting a *systemic* meaning (world system). Hence, the analysis must be extended.

We need, in effect, to confront a *triple epistemological obstacle*.

1. The first one is related to the State in its manifest form, the one in which it declares itself as a *State of law*. The modern State *supposedly* unites beings declared free, equal and rational (*a declaration*). And it declares that these conditions are realized in the forms of the State of law (*a disavowal*). That this declaration amounts to a disavowal is a point to which we will return shortly. But, in the modern State, to the extent it emerges as such, all persons are *supposedly* born of a common will, which must, through the constitutional process, prove itself as such (albeit largely illusory). It is in this sense that an authority recognized as legitimate, *supposedly* established by all, exists. In fact, nothing of the sort exists in the world System: on a global scale, there is no declaration of a common power, of a supreme authority, equally established by all. Neither is there to be found a rule accepted by all, except

that of "custom," the traits of which are not easily identifiable. The modern States, as we know, do not recognize any putative authority above themselves, except that conceded in the form of treaties, from which they can eventually withdraw. And the ones who dominate the others ostentatiously recognize such power only as independents. This is why the idea of "state imperialism" seems unacceptable.

2. Another reason to exclude the idea of a *global*-State, paradoxically shared by defenders of opposing viewpoints, can be found in the supposedly close relation between the State and the *social State*. From the liberal standpoint, when the social State is destroyed, the State itself comes, it is thought, to an end and the individual is freed from the State. From the standpoint of the "social" critics of liberalism, one assumes that any truly modern State is essentially "social," with variation only in terms of degree. Opposing perspectives thus converge: since there is no global *social* State, a global State is thus impossible. The confusion resides, once again, in the concept of the State itself. Here, the strength of liberal ideology lends its formidable weight to the formation of its ostensible critique. By pretending to abolish "the State," liberalism imposes a *State of class*, which Marx aimed to eradicate. It says "less State" when it creates more of a State *of class*, more constraints and more statist violence *of class*. The essence of the liberal State is to proceed veiled as a non-State, because it is a State-of-class, invisible as such, hidden under the supposed natural-rationality of the economic exchange, of interindividual contractuality, the social bond *par excellence* of "civil society," from which we would need only to lift the barriers, the barriers to human emancipation.

3. Herein lies, in effect, the true theoretical difficulty. It inheres in that the notion of the State, considered at the global level, does not correspond to either the familiar empirical forms of the social State, nor only to the idea of a State of law. This difficulty concerns first of all the *State of class*, the State hidden by disavowal, real yet veiled nevertheless by the "state apparatus" — the whole of the institutions of domination and compromise, the decisive site of class struggle. The problem, in effect, amounts to the fact that the *State of class is "invisible."* It is invisible inasmuch as social classes are. The classes are of course *perceivable*, perpetually reemerging, in an unexpected and brutal fashion, across the landscape. Through social struggle, a conceptual critique

The Rule of Imperialism and the Global-State in Gestation

takes shape, elaborated by social and historical analysis, that finds expression in quotidian demands and eventually even in media discourse. But, just like the relation of human labor under the fetishism of the commodity, the classes are *seen without being seen*. They are not seen for what they are, the central rift in an historically determined form of society, from which its contradictions and its movements could be understood, but are rather taken to be the inevitable return of the eternal (and natural) division between the high and low parts of society. And the *national* State relation that subsumes them is also not perceived for what it is, a relation of class. The reason for this is that it presents itself *in practice* (in the strong sense of its performative effectiveness, beyond the violence that consoles it if need be) *as juridical discourse*, of which no one could pretend to be ignorant nor have the power to defy. Juridical discourse, a product of class struggle all the same, does not recognize any class, only individuals. It does not recognize thus any state apparatus of class, but only supposedly common institutions, framing all of our interactions, individual or associative. Only a "critique of economy" (as Marx proposed) and of culture, only a critical sociology, thus, can make class appear, and thus the power of class, which exerts itself through public as well as *private* institutions (scholastic, mediatized, financial, etc.) as the power of the State of class. This is how "stateness," in its tendency towards the state form, should be understood. We will use the term in order to show that it is emerging, far away on the horizon, on a global scale: like a *global stateness (étaticité mondiale) of class* — which remains, nevertheless, in a dialectic relation to a "stateness" of law.

We now begin to understand the thesis advanced here: the State that we want to talk about is not a "State of law" or a "Social State," but a "State of class," tool for imperialism, but within the condition of a potential contradiction that depends on the dialectical relations between power and law. We live in a time of "ultimodernity," the culmination of modern capitalism, hence the emergence of the "modern State" as it appeared under the pluralist form of the States composing the world system, but figured this time as a global-State that invariably elaborates itself on a global-scale on the horizon of the *longue durée* (the long term). This does not mean the end of imperialism, but rather its paroxysm in a nascent stateness of class. An infinitely weak State, perhaps, the comprehension of which nevertheless requires a strong concept of the State.

Jacques Bidet

For the sake of clarity, it may be necessary to say a word here about the conceptual constellation, an echo of which may be found in the theme proposed to the authors contributing to the present volume that I have introduced into Marxist discourse, especially from my work *Théorie générale*,[2] which pursues an itinerary according to the series of terms: "metastructure/structure/system/global stateness/social practices and tendencies."

The pair structure/system can be understood, as we saw earlier, according to the usual meaning (well explained by I. Wallerstein among others) of the relation between "class structure" and "world system," where "structure" refers to the (abstract) form that is common to various nation-States, and "system" is the (concrete) historico-geographical form of the entirety of these nation-States. I have created the neologism *metastructure* to designate the presupposition of freedom-equality-rationality inherent in the modern structure of class declaration and disavowal. Yet it is an idea I did not invent, because it is really Marx, who has shown that the capitalist structure of class can be understood analytically only as the "inversion" of this metastructure: the capitalist relations of class can only be conceived as a transformation, *Verwandlung*, that is structural, i.e., always already effective, of a relation universally declared to be exchangist within a relation of exploitation (see *Capital,* Book I: we go from Section 1, the metastructural level, to Section 3, the structural level, only through Section 2, devoted to this "transformation" of the relations of market equality into their opposite). Marx shows that the more "concrete" moment of (the modern) structure (of class) can only be exposed from a more "abstract" (or "meta-") moment of the socio-political commodity relation, that "comes back as its opposite." Thus he proposes an economico-political, i.e., dialectical, concept. The antagonistic social practices, which can only be understood through structural conditions and contradictions, refer continuously to this metastructure, which they continuously throw into question, revolutionizing its contents.

I have, for my part, tried to show that this metastructure — not the real but the referential foundation of modernity — cannot be adequately conceived (as Marx tried) in the sole form of the commodity relation, but only in the relation between the two poles of the interindividual and the central, according to its two faces, the one (economic) of the market and the organization, the other (juridico-political) of the contractuality between each of us and among all. This "polar" metastructural duality that concerns on the one hand rational "understanding"

The Rule of Imperialism and the Global-State in Gestation

(with all the possible combinations between market and organization) and on the other hand, political "reason" (with its antagonistic, mutual implication of the freedom allowed to each individual and that allowed to everyone as a whole to reach accord) controls, I believe, the complexity of these inversions within the capitalist structure of class, and thus the State of class as well. This pair, metastructure/structure, provides the key to the "world system" and to its virtual overcoming by a global-State. But I cannot develop here the entire theory. It will suffice to emphasize that "metastructure" is not to be understood as a "superstructure" (which traditionally refers to political institutions). One should be careful to note that the notion of the State (or stateness), which refers now to metastructural order (declaration-disavowal) and now again to structural order, aims at the dialectical relation between these two orders.

Global versus International Economic Institutions

The Imperialist Globalization of the Economy

Nothing could be less simple than to articulate the ensemble of real determinants in this historical mutation named "globalization." I do not seek to provide new information, but rather aspire to understand the facts, in their most general significance, uncovered by Marxist-inspired economy, as it is expressed today, notably among the forums of the "Global Citizenship Movement."

I will assume that this phenomenon is to be apprehended based on the *social* development of productive forces, i.e., not on an abstract evolutionary tendency ascribed to technological progress, but rather in the reciprocal relation (albeit following temporalities that remain incompatible) between forms of production and forms of society. It is in the determined relations of production, specific to a determined stage of capitalism, from fordism to postfordism, that the productive forces seen at work today have been developed; these same productive forces, however, throw into question the very social relations and the institutions within which they are framed. Hence we find overlapping relations among the sociocultural, the juridico-political, and the technological. The companies that succeed, during this technological and systemic phase (in the sense of "world system" still given to this term here), are the ones that are able to establish themselves across the planet, ordering their many components, from extraction to production, marketing, management, finance, according to the sites of optimal profit unless the company decides to anchor itself in an entirely sedentary posture in a zone chosen for its inherent synergy. These companies are the ones that know how to take advantage of the new conditions of production: the mandatory "organization" of the productive process on a greater scale with intrinsically more complex modes of knowledge; the increasingly "immaterial" aspect of products; the immediacy of information; the lower costs of transport...all this allows for computers to deterritorialize the process governing the division of labor, the predetermination and control of tasks, and even the act of production. These companies are the ones that acquire the greatest capacity to colonize the institutions of the centers and to control the corrupt ones in the peripheries as well. It is within such conditions that financial capital is capable of directing the course of neo-liberalism.

Economic globalization appears to be a dominant phenomenon. It could be argued, of course, that trade takes place principally within the grand zones of the "triad." Nevertheless, globalization dominates in the sense that world trade has progressively ceased to be "international," i.e., conducted between companies of different nations, in order to become the business of the "transnationals" (to the tune of 2/3 of the total already). Controlling the hard kernel of world production (the first 200 companies have already secured a quarter of this production), these companies assure the dominance of universal rules destined to insure the disappearance of every import barrier, to hand over all wealth and activity to the appropriation of the market, and to put an end to the economic prerogatives (very unequal, it is true) of the nation on its own territory.

The thesis presented here is that under the specific emblem, unequal and asymmetrical, of the erasure of all borders, *imperialism* (economic, cultural, political and military) *broods a nascent global stateness*. This development foretells, on the horizon of the *longue durée*, the advent of a global-State — about which, we might add that nothing shows its vocation is to replace the extant nation-States (and continental-States) under the guise of an "absolute State."

A Global Legality, Put into Operation by the Apparatus of the Global-State

It can be persuasively argued, I believe, that the formal conditions of the State appear, at the global level, with a *territory*, the planet, a *population*, humanity, and a *law* in force, marked by the power of capital imposing itself under the phenomenal form of the "law of the market." We will return to the characteristics of this territory, delimited but infinite, and of this population, which globalization divides more than unites. Let us start with the power of the law, the essential of which is that it not only present itself as natural, but also exercises itself as the power of class.

The *private aspect* of organizations that arbitrate commercial relations of an international order does not mean that they do not depend on a state function, in the sense of a State of class. On the scale of the nation-State, the dominant classes already rely upon an ensemble of private or autonomous institutions — scholastic, media, jurisdictional (chambers of commerce), monetary (national banks), etc. — able to secure their power, the "autonomy" of which consists in falling outside collective democratic management. The same is true, on an international scale, of institutions of arbitration such as the international Chambers of Commerce, which initiate the *lex mercatoria*, and whose power is measured by their ability to enforce, even indirectly, penalties upon offenders identified by these institutions. Until now, it has been assumed that that this concrete legality, continuously re-elaborated by the agents of the international market, could not contradict national codes. Instead, such legality was ostensibly constituted as a form of rationality, which different, private domestic laws could appropriate. In case of necessity, its decisions were always confirmed by national tribunals. In reality, however, these confirmations, up to the moment in which they become superfluous, have served rather to consecrate these private bodies as the foundation of law — a function of class power projected on the scale of global statist space that is established on the basis of the "law," supposedly natural, of the market, imposing itself rationally, and hence, juridically.

We know the extent to which "international" institutions, such as the IMF, have long moved in this direction, suspending any kind of "financial aid" in the absence of the liquidation of public services and the end of autonomous economic policy. We also know that with the WTO a new step has been taken with the elaboration of a program for the universal privatization of material and intellectual activities, under the ultimate arbitration of the Dispute Settlement Body (DSB), now accorded the power to impose economic constraints upon the recalcitrant, i.e., the monopoly of ultimate legitimate constraint. This might be seen as the first outline of the inauguration of a global state law. It might also equally be said that this is a non-law, effectively outside of any kind of citizen control, yet in force nevertheless. The novelty of the situation consists in the fact that it is no longer simply a question of arbitration since the procedure culminates in the possibility of appeal before a Permanent Committee of seven experts appointed every four years whose decisions, accepted by the DSB, become effective under penalty of sanction. That this committee is under the preponderant influence of the most powerful such that traditional beef cannot stand its ground against hormonal beef does not stop it from functioning as a quasi-jurisdictional, global state body. The capitalist State offers the proof of its existence by virtue of the fact that it operates through institutions, centrally-established, that are capable, via reference to a legality considered common (the market: norms of appropriation at the same time as exchange) of insuring an effective arbitration among capitalist groups, tied to unequal relations of force, but in the form of a compromise that demands the sharing of a certain class power in common. This is what is imperceptibly emerging on the global scale.

GATS: An Indefinite Process of Statification

The most important aspect is the ostensible indefiniteness of the process devoted to unlimited development. The essential point of the WTO is in effect its capacity to *declare* that nothing in the global economy escapes its purview. Covering the whole of international commercial accords, it declares itself competent in every domain, with the official objective of abolishing tariff barriers and the opening of every activity to the global market. It thus arrogates to itself a general prerogative not only over commerce, but also over the global process of production in all its forms, including services and knowledge, that are inscribed in the commercial order. Admission to the WTO is, in principle, global, concerning the whole of existing commercial agreements without restriction. It is not that States are formally constrained to open to the market all their fields of production. They are only strongly encouraged to do so by the threat of measures of retaliation that the most powerful are capable of mounting against them. Above all, the engagements they make by successive steps, often through partially relinquishing aspects of sovereignty already given to continental blocs (NAFTA, EU), have an irreversible character, thus abandoning their power to a superior, global level.

The GATS (General Agreement on Trade in Services) pushes this mechanism to the limits. The declared objective is the abolition of "non-tariff" import barriers, especially the ones created by state communities in order to insure in a non-

The Rule of Imperialism and the Global-State in Gestation

commercial way certain essential forms of production such as education, transport, information, research and health care. "Services,", in the broadest sense, can encompass up to 2/3 of the GDP of developed countries: distribution, finance, culture, environment, communication, tourism, sports, and innumerable professional services (in reality, products and services are closely intertwined: products are transported, distributed, sold, repaired, rented, etc. These are not, thus, solely public services, but all kinds of activities that have the quality of being subjected to an entire set of regulations (financing, people status, etc.), themselves the result of social struggles and political compromises at all levels of public life.

The extension of these accords to services would concern not only new sectors but in fact all human activities, now transformed into economy and understood as a market relation. Within this framework, public services are called upon to be understood as companies on the market. It is not that States are forbidden to produce services through fiscal measures, but rather that these services must remain inscribed in a relation of strict competition with the capitalist market, which has powerful ways of imposing its criteria, in terms of objectives, quality standards, professionalism, monetary and social guarantees, etc. Any nationalization becomes an infraction. Any subvention is already subversive. Any form of labor is considered to be production for the market, a source of profit.

The market is by nature supposed to inherently substitute itself for any other kind of social coordination. I subscribe to an opposing thesis, in the name of a form of institutionalism inspired by Marx, one that I cannot fully explain here. This perspective notably includes two closely related points: (1) There are two diametrically antagonistic forms of rational economic coordination on the social scale, namely, the market and the organization (I leave aside the fact that they form, separately and combined, the modern factors of class, as this point is not the subject of this paper); (2) These two poles of rationality (*Verstand*) correspond to the two poles of possible rationality (*Vernunft*) in modernity, specifically the poles of interindividual and central contract, the relation between the two being the foundation of the properly modern juridical order. A social order founded solely on one pole (either organization or the market — or, equally: either a supposed contractuality between individuals or a supposed central contractuality) might lead to the extinction of law, because it cannot constitute any "contractual" forms and it cannot be the result of any possible agreements. It is in this sense that I have proposed to qualify as a "State without law" that which is proclaimed, in the neoliberal perspective, as a "law without State." The social horizon created in this manner can be qualified as "totalitarian": we pretend to create everything through the market much like, in the Soviet system, one formerly tried to do it through the plan. The political pathologies that result from this situation may be different, but are ultimately of the same intensity.

A Global (Not Just International) State Legislation of Property

The Agreement for the Rights of Intellectual Property (TRIPs, 1995), driven by a universal practice of piracy and substituting for previous accords, has two characteristics.[3] On the one hand, it appears like an increasingly irreversible and restrictive process, but in an asymmetric manner. It certainly does not suggest a rigorously defined legislation but rather minimum standards that the members promise to inscribe in their legislative texts. On the other hand, it appears to be inscribed much more within the framework of the WTO rather than the UN, the specialized administration of which (WIPO) only plays a marginal role of technical assistance to underdeveloped countries needing to "update" their legislation. It is thus a process of global statification with a strong imperialist character, under the wing of an international "body of experts," the competency of which resides in the ability to place all specific legislation in conformity with a law coming from above. We have here a significant process in the institutionalization of a "global language" that is juridical, economic, social, and political. The universal translation machine is in place. The aspect of a *global* stateness, under the guise of an "international" agreement is marked by the fact that the same legality enters into force universally. The *asymmetric* aspect is to be found in the fact that the richest States, if they do not abide by the law, can choose to pay a simple fine. Such was the situation in the only case related to copyrights having come before the DSB: the United States preferred to pay instead of making its legislation, concerning the issue at hand, conform to the standards called for. This ability to escape international law does not exactly lead us back to the logic of the international, but to the fact that the most powerful have greater means to escape state laws, be they national or global.

The Rule of Imperialism and the Global-State in Gestation

The Relation between Imperialism and Global Statification

We should resituate consideration of all of these phenomena and many others, like the legislation on digital rights (which allows charging a fee for access to information) and e-commerce, which diminishes the regal powers of control and of taxation, within the context of the tendency toward deterritorialization related to the development of information.

It is through these processes, of a global-statist character (arising from the global-State), that imperialism gains in power. The destruction of every tissue of national solidarity does not create an undifferentiated globality, but a (nascent) "unequalizing" global statification. Criteria thus impose themselves, norms that are those of the companies from the most powerful States: what kind of qualifications should medical personnel and teachers be required to have, and under what kind of control? What long term obligations towards a given territory will be ascribed to transport and courier companies? Etc....These kinds of agreements are negotiated in secret between representatives of the powers that have interest in these kinds of commitments within the context of bureaucratic complexity that poor countries obviously cannot master. These activities, public or framed within a national scale, do not enter a neutral global market, but a market *organized* on foundations dictated by the most powerful transnationals and their States, which thoroughly penetrate the space of the peripheries. Capital thus develops its potential to work for capital: to quickly take hold of the most immediately profitable sectors of the economy without any thought to general development or sustainable equilibrium.

Globalization, as it now operates, should thus be considered as imperialism. This term, left to Marxism like a dog-bone — to the extent that it is not recuperated by a euphemistic usage, notably in terms of "empire", is actually the most appropriate. The pretended abolition of frontiers is, in fact, an asymmetrical phenomenon (just as the "systemic" configuration of capitalism has been since its conception), much as the opposition between the free circulation of capital and the assignation of labor power residing in the periphery shows us. As we know, not all frontiers have been destroyed. Those of the North remain very powerful. Certain entities from the ex-Third-World, such as China or India, manifest the capacity for resistance and relative autonomy. The dominant aspect, however, is the growing control of transnational companies across the greater part of the planet. Their roots in the country, or in the "continent," of origin is emblematic of their imperialism: behind these companies, States fight in international and regional institutions to promote them, in order that everything be opened to the market, services in particular — the conquest of which the most powerful transnationals, which have the greatest capacity to manipulate the rules in their favor, are the most well-prepared. Capital can, from now on, hunt for labor power wherever it is found, there where it is the cheapest, there where it is the most exploitable, there where it is the most weakened by oppressive regimes.

We can thus see that there is no contradiction, only conjunction, between the element of global statification, according to which a market *ostensibly* more and more open has been established, under a law formally the same for all and subsumed under properly global bodies, and the dynamic of imperialism that maintains itself in a specific fashion by virtue of the fact that the central States dominate in effect and instrumentalize these rules and bodies. Globalization constitutes a decisive factor in the continentalization of humanity, in the articulation of the system in a triad that shares control.

The exponent of exploitation, i.e., structure/system, through which *structural* domination (that is to say, domination defined by a class structure within national space) comes to be multiplied by *systemic* (imperialist) domination evidence of which is found in all that weighs upon immigrant labor power, from income fragility to "double punishment" (which allows host nations to send immigrants leaving prison back to their country of origin) — finds its ultimate version in the *exponential series of structure/system/Structure,* according to which imperial domination (system) strengthens itself through the formal abandonment of national prerogatives in favor of a globalized statist form (Structure) in the exercise of power. "Structure" in this sense qualifies the World State (in gestation) not as a system, but as a structure, a megastructure, one might say, but not a metastructure (although it still bears a relation to its own metastructure, of course). The Global Structure, as a class structure, is a milieu of class exploitation, in addition to (or multiplication of) exploitation within the nation-State (structure) and the world system.

The Rule of Imperialism and the Global-State in Gestation

Global versus International Political Institutions

If the *economic* globalization, which deprives nation-States, at least some of them, of some of their prerogatives, is usually acknowledged as an indisputable fact, the existence of *juridical* globality is less evident, since there is officially only a group of sovereign nations, who, by tying themselves juridically together through agreements upon which they may renege constitute an "international," not "global," law. A "global" law could only exist to the strict extent to which the capacity to declare the law and put it into practice would have been *irreversibly* conceded to supranational bodies in possession of authority and the power to that effect.[4] We have broached this question on the basis of economic considerations. Now, we need to understand it from the more general perspective of the law. Does a law of a "global State" character exist? And, if so, what are its relations to the "systemic" order (centers/peripheries) named imperialism?

"Global" Law as Institution, Declaration, and Performance
Paradoxically, the source of a "global" law, in the very weak sense stated above, is close to, it seems, a *new* "international law" since 1945, following the defeat of nazism. Not only was the UN created as an institution to which all States would potentially be called to adhere, but this universal affiliation, effectively performative in its own right, established an effective obligation. Henceforth, it would be inconceivable for any State to leave this collective organization, whose measures are ostensibly equally valid for all nations and, through them, for all people.

The first principle of the UN Charter is, however, that each State is sovereign, not only in relation to one another, but also in relation to the community of States — a feature that seems immediately to cancel any constraining authority, the UN executive power being exercised only in the form of "resolutions." The fact remains that these stop within the framework of a sort of constitution for the UN, contained in its Charter, which determines the conditions under which these recommendations, declaratory or mandatory, are taken. In this, there is a mechanism for political power, to which every State ostensibly abides. And thus, legitimate power is at stake.

In this manner, a global body of declaration was formed. It was recognized as such and endowed by this fact with a certain authority, that of declaring a universal law, a shared order of law common to all. As Marcelo Kohen perfectly sums up: "through fundamental principles of international juridical order, this law constructed the prohibition against the use or threat of force, the peaceful regulation of conflicts, the right of a people to occupy itself with its own affairs, the respect of the fundamental rights of the person, and the responsibility of international cooperation. It gave a new meaning to sovereign equality, to the respect of territorial integrity, to the importance of non-interference, and to good faith in international relations."[5] We know that certain UN resolutions have exercised an unquestionable influence upon the spirit of this new law. We can refer, for example, to the Declaration Pertaining to the Independence of Nations and Colonial Peoples (December 14, 1960). We would further need to cite the Charter for the Economic Rights and Responsibilities of States,[6] adopted on 12 December 1974 by the UN General Assembly, which guaranteed States the right to nationalize, etc.

It would appear however that this right, formerly marked by a coalition of the Third World, has since fallen into oblivion — notably because of the new balance of power following the fall of the USSR. This situation is illustrated, as we have seen, by the expansion of the WTO. The trend is more generally toward a return to old law as effective norm. At the same time, the workings of the International Court of Justice and the International Criminal Court remain highly problematic on account of the purely contractual foundation of these institutions, favorable to the interests of the predominant States. And the most powerful State, not to speak of it exclusively, refuses to ratify the treaties most indispensable to the achievement of the objectives ostensibly aimed at by the Charter: agreements on the measures to be taken against global warming, for biodiversity, arms control (anti-personnel landmines, chemical weapons), etc. Hence, we have the notion that the today's UN is in regression and historically condemned to remain a marginal body.

"Global" Law as Agent of Global-Statist Imperialism
We could think that the UN is weak because the only modicum of effective power ascribed to it is that which can be exercised in its own name, and because, furthermore, the UN is easily manipulated by its most powerful members. I would offer an opposing thesis: there where one is tempted to see a sign of the weakness of global law is in fact the point of its very efficacy. There is no, or very little,

The Rule of Imperialism and the Global-State in Gestation

"structural" capacity for constraint upon the power exercised through "global" law. But from this *structural* "weakness" (in the sense of the global-State structure) proceeds the specificity of the "law effect" unleashed by the UN, which creates in fact an increase of systemic power (for the good of the systemic center).

Convincing evidence of this point can be found simply by looking at the procedure essential to the institution. UN resolutions, which state the law without having on their own the capacity to put them into practice, are in fact applied only where they are supported by the power of the strongest. The prominence of the Central States within the heart of the "global Statist" body named the Security Council strengthens their properly *systemic* power: the right of veto outlines the narrow limits of what can become the object for a common decision. Such prominence is fed by the legitimacy that the juridical mechanism of the UN confers upon the only resolutions acceptable to those powers or the allies they protect, and from the monopoly they retain to put this law into action. This is what recently occurred when the Council gave itself an *a priori* capacity to repress "international terrorism," at the same time it allowed a wide latitude to the great powers to lead, for their own benefit, this fight. Such law thus actually enters into real force, but in an arbitrarily differentiated fashion (under the aspect of interference) and without any chance of central appeal by the ones directly involved. Already, in national States of class, "whether one is powerful or in need," the odds of being prosecuted are highly variable. Here not only the function of the police, but also that of justice is handed over to the mercenaries concerned. But as anti-democratic as it may be, this is still "the law," the mother of every right, which has decided it so.

In brief, this "international" law, in reality "global" at the same time, considered at this level, is not as soft as it seems. Through it, the legitimacy of a truly *global-Statist* jurisdiction is being mobilized by the legitimation of imperialist interests. The UN is thus not only a powerless "chamber for grievances to be heard." As the principle of an actual power that the "systemic" center can mobilize for its own interests, the former increases the power of the latter, accentuating the asymmetry of *inter*-national relations. But it can only perform this service by virtue of its quality as a *supra*-national factor. The increase in efficacy brought about by it cannot be deduced from the system's form, which, as it does not suppose a common will, cannot in itself produce law. Global Statist law cannot be mobilized, for the good of the system's Centers, unless it is in a certain sense exterior to it, like the universal and the particular.

Jacques Bidet

The only ones who could consider the UN as a "weak" entity are those who would think that recognized global legitimacy is not a decisive support for imperialist companies, for their immediate success, and for their long term plans. Yet this is exactly what was demonstrated by the arm-wrestling conducted between the US and the UN, from January to February 2003, for the grouping of potential allies and the conquest of global public opinion. In the global-State, just as in the national State of class, the most powerful know that it is better to act within a legal state framework, and are ready to go through the trouble and spend all the money necessary in order to manipulate the electorate and public opinion.

The Ultimodern Dialectic of Force and Law
By underlining how the United States "manipulates the UN," we still have not said everything. What is clear in this "instrumental" recourse is the need felt by the power of certain particulars to be legitimated by a universal instance of law, from which they remain ostensibly autonomous. According to a well-known paradox, one that Bourdieu mobilized to illustrate the relationship between the prince and the intellectual, but which has a broader significance, power finds support in the law only in so far as it can provide the public with some proof of its autonomy. Concerning this relative autonomy, we would need to add that it is not to be found only in the social position of the intellectual: it is insured only through an ensemble of power relations within the social multitude, relations tied to the metastructural/structural State form through practice and collective struggles. The question of this rising global Stateness should thus be always considered based on the contradictory dialectical relation between its *structural* reality, according to which a "global" relation of class is deployed that insures, approves, and exacerbates imperialist relations, and its *metastructural* reality-fiction (but not fictional), according to which a global citizenship, and thus a global city, becomes a common claim, in fact always filled with ambiguities (structural and systemic), and for which it is urgent to elaborate a critical response.

The conditions, apparently conjunctural, for the emergence of a (weak) global state authority may appear to have disappeared. The signal for this change was given after 1945 by the obvious danger of disasters within humanity and by the obvious impossibility that the colonial system of formal inequality between nations and non-nations could contain the rage of enslaved peoples. A universal common will would at least have to impose the conditions for the recognition of some of

The Rule of Imperialism and the Global-State in Gestation

modernity's pretensions: national autonomy and peaceful coexistence. The (asymmetric) gradual disappearance of borders, the withering away of dominated States within the international "neoliberal order," and the disappearance of the dangers related to the split between the two antagonistic blocs might seem to have stolen away from this universal common will every reason and means for self-affirmation. Some have thus concluded that the UN is but a form of juridical window-dressing (effectively assured by the power of the "military alliances" around the United States, that is to say by war), serving the formalities of peace for either the good of a "global civil society" according to some, or for imperialism according to others. There is on the contrary, it seems to me, every reason to believe in the situation emerging after the war that there is an irreversible aspect that endures and grows under different forms, simply occulted by the neoliberal order. The fantasy of total power has reactivated the "colonial illusion" of total control over dominated peoples, the illusion of a peaceful and obedient end to history. This irreversible aspect can be seen in and read from various and contradictory angles and levels of analysis: a tendency inherent in the relations of production spanning across borders, and thus an impossibility, in the absence of a recognized legitimate central authority, to insure collective security, the ecological equilibrium, the determination of what is mine and what is yours, in brief, the necessity for a "regulation" of global "rules." But how can rules and laws legitimize themselves other than by emanating from citizens? In brief, the irreversible here needs to be read as an aspect of the statist structural dynamic of global class, and also, successively in opposition, as the "ultimate" moment of the promise-exigency that I call "metastructural" (and of its far-reaching shadow, the denegation) — that is to say, always in the ambiguity of the dialectical relationship between the two terms.

The Global State Would Only Know (Now Only Knows) Civil Wars

In terms of collective security, the major signal comes not only from the terrorist attack on Manhattan, but also from the anthrax episode — an event of "domestic" origin in the end that has revealed the potential omnipresence of weapons of mass destruction available for civil war within a globalized state space. Within the horizon of the global-State, mass violence has taken a new turn: it has become privatized. It has ceased to be simply an external threat, brandished by one State against another, to become a danger in the Hobbesian sense, against which we can fight, according to a classical demonstration, only by conferring the monopoly of legitimate violence upon a single, common body — that is to say, to a state institution, global this time (here, the condition elaborated by Rousseau, according to which peace only exists if the monarch is the citizen, defines the political challenge in its ultimate form). That the dangers with which we are faced in a global-state space are of a private and civil nature is an idea that can be verified by the fact that the firepower of terrorism per se is not to be found among the underground in the Afghan mountains, but first and foremost in the global financial mafia, able to be mobilized for nomadic actions anywhere in the world, and especially in those centers where the most effective weapons and the most significant targets are concentrated. The national "sanctuaries," transitory supports soon to be useless, are only the systemic "links" in a process which is also "macro-structural," that is to say, relying on a statist relationship of class on the global scale which affirms itself by the imposition of the common law of capital, designated as the law of the market.

Conservative thought, in this regard, emphasizes that security can no longer be accessed on the level of a single nation, and it calls for an anti-terrorist coalition. Such thinking would be right if the neoliberal control over the southern hemisphere were not the key factor in this violence; and if terrorism was by nature a promoter of political blocs. Towers have fallen, and the poor have danced, here and there at least. But there is no reason to think that these perverse signs, which move the masses in different ways, are of a unifying nature. They do not form any kind of "camp of nations," oppressed and redeemed. They have rather revealed a violence — suffered, resented, and vengeful — that no coalition for security could contain, but that can only kill itself in the occult and factional strategy of terrorism. In return, this violence_ that generates a primitive form of violence, both systemic and of class, which grabs all wealth, all production, all lands, all community, all human destiny to manage them according to the rule of profit, would only be able to transform itself into a collective power through the solidarity of an anti-class, anti-systemic struggle on a global scale.

The Global State Would Have (Now Has) a Police Force, Not an Army

The military superiority of the United States seems to make it all-powerful. This advantage is, however, in relation to the other big powers, only of an indirect nature, since the confrontation with them occurs solely on an economic level.

The Rule of Imperialism and the Global-State in Gestation

But it does allow the United States large control over the theaters of the South, where all conflicts, it seems, will be resolved for the benefit of the side that calls in America, which itself expects to get an economic and political foothold in return. But the political outcome of such intervention remains far from certain, as it relies upon an increase in power that can only be brought about by a minimum of legitimacy — precisely what is missing.

The United States takes the UN, of course, for a ride. In the Gulf War, the US still needed and could force UN approval because of its ability to blackmail some partners in the Security Council. In the Kosovo war, the UN having been notched down in importance, the US simply bypassed it, pragmatically comforted if not juridically legitimized by the coalition of their immediately concerned allies, thereby crossing the line between legal and moral foundations. In Afghanistan, they obtained a benediction from it, to which they could, given the drama at the time, give the most improbable and extensive interpretation, declaring themselves an entitlement to chase down an enemy designated as global. Yet it remains to be seen if they have the ability to leave behind them an order to their liking. The fact that military supremacy does not assure political domination, and that only the UN can "finalize" such operations, is highly symbolic—that is to say, it goes well beyond the question of the formal powers of the UN. It shows that the "systemic" form has ceased to be exclusively predominant, and that a relation of power, which relies on the increasing impossibility of governing the human multitudes through simple imperialist force, is also a factor in this tendency toward a global stateness.

It is for this reason that imperial war must henceforth take on the traits of a police operation. The GIs are ostensibly legitimate only as presumed policemen of the global order. It is on account of this claim that it seems legitimate for them to deploy the capacity to kill without being killed, holding the privilege to be the armed hand of God-on-earth, the name given by Hobbes to the modern State. The global chief of police, the position arrogated for itself by the No. 1 of the systemic complex — cannot behave like that of the global State. He must cede to this God, which occurs in this instance under the form of the UN — a very small god, miniscule yet the only one that can *officially* preside over the creation of a specific republic, under the attentive constitutional gaze of the entire world. There could not be a supposed global police without a global State.

The notion of "enemy" would have almost disappeared. The surgical and aseptic armed operation that targets only the pathological abscess occurs within the very interior of our common borders. It intervenes in the name of public law, in the name of our resolutions, in the name of the contempt in which such outlaws hold them. But the realization of these global-statist resolutions is put in place by a coalition of "allies" which, as such, are facing "enemies." These enemies are in turn subjected to the rigors of police intervention, which is not accountable to international agreements regarding war (treatment prisoners, etc.)

All this — global Stateness, so-called police — would be only pure fiction if it were possible today, in the twenty-first century, to intervene in the name of the superiority of the West, that is to say, in the name of a pre-modern juridical ideology (which had been active for a long time in the system, at a time when it had already become obsolete with the emergence of the nation-State structure): in the name of the natural rights of the superior over the inferior, in the name of a "manifest destiny" of the best (*aristoi*) and brightest, which is to enlighten, to civilize and to govern the others. This discourse of imperialism was possible behind closed doors, within the confines of national opinion, closed and full of itself. It remains, of course, like background music today. But now, George W. Bush does not have a choice: he also needs to explain himself, to speak eye-to-eye, ostensibly among equals, to every citizen of the world. To him comes the impossible task of convincing us that the infinitely weak pose a danger to all. And, if he does not succeed, if he cannot, through blackmail or threats, rally enough States to each cause, if in the end he has to wage war without the forms of supposed legitimacy, or in forms that are formally legitimate but against manifest public opinion, he knows that the price to pay will be heavier still, and the victory more uncertain in the long term.

Global State and Remarkable Nations
The workings of the UN are thus essentially contradictory. The declaration, inscribed in the UN Charter, concerning the equal rights of States cannot be held as meaningless. Yet the reason for this cannot be found in some moral strength and the proclamations to that effect, but in the fact that it is not easy to dissolve States, even the weakest, in the "universal market," and this because there has

The Rule of Imperialism and the Global-State in Gestation

never been a "civil society" without an organization of an important part of social life that has been achieved in some manner by consent (which does not necessarily mean democratic), *outside of the market*. And, in a broader sense, without a nation — the repository for the sacred in common existence. Nations do not disappear in the market, into supposed international civil society, like sugar in water. There is today not only a *resistance* to the fact of the State, but, in every country of the world, an extreme *densification* of national existence. This situation, which is invisible at the Center, is perfectly clear as soon as we adopt the perspective of the multitudes. People never cease to see their destiny as being taken away from the customary, local, particular, familial, and clannish order, in order to be constituted according to an ever tighter network of laws, obligations, risks, security, perspectives, liberties, and constraints, which are related to the densification of national laws and regulations. Thus, paradoxically, while market barriers are lowered, the statist space grows denser. Hence, all the power and all the violence, the phenomenon of national decomposition/recomposition, the local wars of language, of religion, of petroleum and of diamonds, in which the groups implicated see at stake (in the machine of the multinationals destroying them) their most intimate and tangible interests.

But henceforth, there is no longer any particular State beyond the seal of superior sacrament given by the strict sense of the term "international community," the community of nations establishing supranational authorities. Under the guise of imperialism, this creates a kind of dialectic between, on the one hand, the recognition "in spite of everything" of the sovereignty of States — as unilaterally minimal as possible, to be sure—as the pacifying principle necessary for economic "investment," and, on the other hand, the fact that this recognition can only refer to a supposed will that is universally common. We are thus brought back to the modern question of civil society and the State, but this time in an ultimate version where the modern game of the nation-State is played out under the guise of the global-State. "Ultimodernity" would be, I propose, the appropriate term. It marks the essence of the question of the State, which immediately brings forth the one of the citizen. Hence, we may better understand why universal citizenship appears today like an idea pertaining to struggle and the future.

Jacques Bidet

Terms and Concepts Suggested by Our Time

This analysis leads to a critique of some current terms. For example, the "international community," which is meaningful only in the precise sense of the community of States inasmuch as it acts through the institutions and rules recognized by all, that of the Nations "United." There is no "community" with some legitimate authority except to the extent the "union" of these nations represents a constitutional fact (as limited as it may be) in the modern sense of the term, referring to the supposed accord given by each individual to the State to which he or she belongs. There would be little to say about this expression if it were not constantly used in the media (including the most "educated" part of the press[7]) to identify by virtue of a universal legitimacy the most diverse "systemic" organizations, i.e., everything from the IMF, which ostensibly brings "aid to the international community," to NATO, which targets its "interventions" in the name of peace and security (as can do any coalition of "allies" working for a good cause). This expression works like the most innocently "reactionary" of ideological covers, designating an authority to intervene in the States of the South held by the military or financial institutions constituted by the North and rigorously devoid of the (supranational) legitimacy attributed to them, devoid, in effect, of any sort of "legality" whatsoever. It forms the matrix for a supposedly consensual officialese, a *lingua franca* that operates around the clock. The ideological operator *par excellence* for ultimodernity, it achieves maximal effect when it allows the law to transcend itself as the moral, as was particularly flagrant in the case of Kosovo. The vulgate of ultimodernity, as modern, can only work through the universal: all that is left to imperialism, which can no longer assert civilizing superiority, is the obscure universality of "human rights." What it cannot win on the field of law it tries to win on the field of the "moral" — for which anything goes, since the validation of these affirmations does not require the seal of constitutionality, but only the power of dominant opinion, assured in advance to those with the means to manipulate it.

The term "international civil society" is more pretentious. In effect, it illustrates — at least in the traditional sense of the term, as nowadays it has become an object of subversion[8] — the explicit theme of a (global) civil society without a (global) State, of a "law without a State," the ultimate stage in which the law would realize its own essence, which is to tend toward interactions freed from

The Rule of Imperialism and the Global-State in Gestation

any authoritarian constraints, from any state arbitrariness lording over individual freedom. This thesis would be perfectly justified if the law of the market could pass for a natural law, and the state's authority for an artifice, a temporary historical stage. This implies an idea of the law of the market as "natural law," based on the utilitarian argument of the market as the rational (productive) form *par excellence* of economic interaction, sublimated into an argument for the common good, thus of individual happiness, which would be its ultimate right. It is against this thesis that metastructural theory is directed: against the idea that we can think the law outside of the State, the economy outside of politics. On the ultimate level of the rational understanding, *the market* is never but one possible mode of coordination, always tied in polarity to its "other," which is the *organization* — not only in an alternate relation, but also in an intertwined one. On the foundational level of juridico-political reason, that which concerns the declaration of rights, no one enters into contract with anyone else unless its subject concerns a worldly object to which any third party can aspire as well — barring an agreement among all on the conditions of appropriation and interindividual contractuality. Modern "natural" right — or modern "culture," as it were, inasmuch as it is the rejection of every law of nature — is that through which property is only a pretension to ownership, which can be criticized, i.e., that through which private or public property is never assured, but always open to dispute. It is what keeps the owner from falling asleep. The "(so-called international) law without a State" of the "international civil society," falls in fact under the regime of a dogmatic slumber, the "State (of global class) without law": it is the arbitrariness of capitalist ownership given as a common rule outside a disputable constitution and exercising itself through the secretive power of its global apparatus of private States (see below), and the hegemony exercised by the systemic (imperialist) center on the emerging institutions of global stateness.

The term "ultra-imperialism" has resurfaced in order to designate the stage at which imperialism has arrived today. A certain amount of tension on this subject can be found amongst Marxists. On the one hand there are those who insist on the planetary division into great economico-political spheres, the imperialist "triad" as well as the "continents" open henceforth to political action, while on the other hand there are those who, without underestimating this side of things, emphasize the multilateral aspect of relations of domination within the context of globalized capitalist competition. Odile Castel[9] talks in this sense of "ultra-imperialism." This approach pushes a view that highlights the sprouts of the "global State," "complex" because it bears the mark of systemic hierarchy. The argument we propose, which is not unrelated to this view, only supposes that, questioning the "structural" (class) nature of this stateness, we show the connection to the "metastructural" conditions of that which in modern times is given as belonging to the state: there is no State in the modern sense of the term, including that on a global level, without the presupposition of a power *ostensibly* common to all under the sign of equality and freedom (declaration/denegation). Economic categories cannot suffice here: truly political presuppositions belong to the globalization of social struggles. The power of the critique of neo-liberal globalization can be attributed to the work of respected economists, its weakness to the marginal involvement of political philosophy.

The word "empire" has known a great success through T. Negri and M. Hardt's book, where it is associated with a rich investigation and a series of brilliant intuitions. It is, in my opinion, problematic in the sense that it is sustained by an operative collusion-confusion, which singularly weakens its heuristic aspect and its political reliability, between *systemic* categories, those of the world-system (those of imperialism), and *structural* categories, those of the emerging global-State. In a typical fashion, the "empire," supposed to refer to something like the global *system*, is defined by specific *structural* traits: it would be at the same time a "monarchy" (like the American presidency), "aristocratic" (like the multinationals) and "democratic" (like the workers unions), according to an old typology of "regimes" (which depends precisely on an abstract order of the *structure*, and not of the concrete order of the *system*, in the sense, common today within Marxism, to which I give these terms). This notion of empire thus constitutes an epistemological obstacle in the proper sense of the term, a conceptual double exposure, an initial confusion, which does not allow thinking the essential: the dialectic between two orders (system and structure), the support taken by imperialism from the global form of statification, and the universal stake represented by it even if the book is clearly filled with these questions. It is not that the contradictions are not perceived. They are often put into play even majestically, illustrated with philosophemes from Spinoza, Deleuze and Foucault. What is lacking, in my opinion, are the analytical means of their dialecticization. Hence, the "center" works *at the same time* as both a monopoly on power and the producer of law.[10] This reference to Empire as a machine, "self-validating,

The Rule of Imperialism and the Global-State in Gestation

autopoietic," a mix of Luhmann and Habermas, which validates itself through its communicative process,[11] does not give, it seems to me, a clear take on the dialectical relation between the "multitude" and the institution. As for the Foucauldian category of biopolitics — very innovative within the context of an analysis of the processes of domination fixated solely on ownership over means of production — it is used here without getting to the Marxist critique of capitalism. The latter is structured around the dialectical contradiction between the production of *concrete* riches, *the condition and measure of life*, and the *abstract* finality of profit as the horizon of capital, accumulation of power-over-power at the cost of the *destruction of all life*. However, the usage to which is put the category of "biopolitics" — the idea according to which, alternately, "the production of life has now become an object of power,"[12] and "a process of the multinationals,"[13] destroys, in my opinion, this contradiction, which it nevertheless wants to show. In relation to this, capitalism, in its nearly achieved essence of "global market," would find itself faced "*directly* [emphasis added] with the multitude without mediation."[14] At the heart of this theoretical weakness, based on a liberal presupposition that isolates the category of the market (understood to be the "panopticon of imperial power"[15]) as the general principle of the capitalist economic order, is the idea of the world as a "self-validating" machine that crushes under the weight of conceptual indifference the forms proper to modern (versus natural) social rationality: the bipolarity market/organization (with their presupposed correlates of interindividual/central contract), modes of coordination that are diametrically opposed *and class factors* that are only relatively homologous.[16] As for deterritorialization, its advent occurs in a manner that one can judge premature and *unilateral* if we believe that the category of "intervention" itself[17] presupposes territories and good state subjects that intervene on the ground against rogue-States. Through this collusion between the structural and the systemic, the problematic of "class" as well as that of the nation-State is weakened, and thus local, citizen intervention is weakened as well, to the benefit of symbolic global action, the "snake" against the "mole." The same applies to imperialism, supposed to cede its place to empire, bad "for itself," but better "in itself."[18]

There have been other characterizations of the "global society" undertaken under the sign of "complexity" (notably by Edgar Morin). The outline we have sketched here suggests that such work should be considered within the structure/system grid. The structure of capitalism, included within the Marxist topography, is infinitely complex in its functions and contradictions. Its complexity is interlaced with that of the world-system. In its essence, it is nothing but a social logic of the whole that has come to overdetermine the entire complexity of previous social, familial, religious, and communitarian (etc.) formations, which overdetermine it again in return. It thus appears only as a point of reference within chaos, targeting possible common actions.[19]

Violence and Ultimodern War

These clarifications allow us to interrogate the diverse nature of "ultimodern" violence.

If we start with the classic Humean considerations concerning "the conditions of justice" that relate the peaceful character of social relations to their relative equality, and relate violence, by consequence, either to factual inequality or to the open prospect of absolute victory over the other, we will understand that modern violence occurs largely within the systemic relation (of imperialism) rather than the structural relation (of class). From this perspective, we also observe that the "exponential series of exploitation," namely the series of structure/system/Structure as explained above, acts to further multiply the violence.

As Serfati[20] shows, military violence between large nations, which are more or less equal and can only confront each other militarily under threat of mutual destruction, is currently an occurrence of secondary order. Violence today primarily concerns intra-state conflicts in the South, the object of which is often state construction conducted under the shadow of the dominant States. On the one hand, State construction, far from being obsolete, presents itself like a vertiginous game of power in archaic countries like Afghanistan, for example, where there is a question of which group (ethnic, linguistic, religious, geographic) will succeed in diverting it for its own ends or appropriate it entirely, in all its administrative, socio-economic and cultural elements. The game is generally recognized as such, but its theorization remains weakened by the tendency to think that the only determining relations are those of the market — a tendency due to the difficulty of placing the concept of organization at the same epistemological level. On the other hand, under these conditions it is the dominant States, pushed by their interests to control these zones, that play a crucial role in the disproportion of violence (arms and information supply, logistic and media structure, etc.) — a role that is also due to their predominant position in supranational bodies. As a result, the essential character of these wars is that they already figure as civil wars — in a dual sense, no less: both on the level of the quasi-States of the South and on the level of a vaguely global State. Adversaries are not enemies of the nation, but criminals against humanity. Religious, and thus civil, wars. Private wars, outside of international norms. Mercenary wars, no longer fought by citizens. Police operations. "Ethical" wars…We know what kind of meaning to ascribe to these terms.

If we define "terrorism" as an act of deadly violence exercised on either a specific or random target for political ends within a State of law deemed to possess a monopoly on legitimate violence, we could certainly associate it with "State terror," a government by means of deadly violence outside presumably legitimate norms. But terrorism and terror do not necessarily form corresponding poles of violence. They would be distinguished from war, a supposedly reciprocal form of violence, except for the fact that the latter generally ends in the massacre of prisoners and the civilian population. The terrorism of embargo is closely related — without danger to the party imposing it, it condemns the receiving side to a fuzzy, massive, anonymous, statistical death. As for kamikaze terrorism, it is the mad weapon of those who have been disarmed, those who confront an adversary of zero-death (an adversary who possesses a monopoly on effective violence, the capacity to kill without being killed, and even the capacity to wage war without declaring it). The kamikaze is the one who has no other weapon but his own death. Even so, death does not belong to him. Others send him to his death in their stead and for their own glory, yet end up only disqualifying themselves in advance, having betrayed the code of honor without which a war of liberation would be impossible.

The Politics of Humanity and World Citizenship

It is remarkable that within the "world citizen movement" economists play the key role, while jurists remain in a marginal position. The lack of jurists is all the more regrettable for the fact that the objective of imperialism is, precisely, to obscure the question of law, to make it disappear within a moral problematic

Jacques Bidet

that leaves open the greatest possible means of manipulation. Yet as far as law is concerned, there is at least a body — as undeserving as it may be, it is at least identifiable as such: the United Nations' General Assembly, which is supposedly responsible for interpreting and ruling about the law, if only indirectly, putting it into action in the name of all. Morality, by contrast, is left to individual belief, that is to say to the power, mainly private, of the media, whose immense capacity to persuade relies on a privileged possession of the means to know, to chose what is worth knowing, to make it known and to interpret it. During the Kosovo crisis, the right of nations to self-determination demanded supra-national intervention backed by the power of constraint. Only the UN, whose prerogatives are officially recognized by all nations, was deemed qualified, through the Security Council, to command the necessary process to restore peace including the military means required by the situation. Had it otherwise been impossible, had the law been powerless, the demands of morality, hardly negligible, would have still been felt: under no circumstances could one let the Kosovars be massacred. But such was not the case. Nothing blocked the UN's action: no veto opposed it since Russia itself was prepared from the outset for full involvement. Nevertheless, the "allies" deliberately chose (if we may say it thus) "morality over law," rejecting any action within the framework of the law, i.e., action under the authority and control of the UN. Choosing NATO instead, they refused to be submitted to a global law — in spite of the fact that, under the circumstances, it would have been the sole means equal to the level of the situation. Hence, we can imagine that they had important interests in magnifying the importance of morality over law.

Critical jurists, whether or not they hail from Marxism, remain nonetheless stuck between the disciplinary and professional exigencies of the *realist position* (privileged by legal positivism), which identifies only the norms in effect as law, and those of *modern natural law*, which imposes the idea that the legitimacy of the law can only be rooted in a democratic political community on the basis of shared values — and on a global scale, these should be universal — reformulated as norms and procedures. Given the interference from this dual requisite, they lead a "critique of (existing) law" and a project of juridical order on a world-scale, based on universal values. Yet they have difficulty recognizing, in my opinion, two aspects of the juridical phenomenon. On the one hand, the sole fact of committing oneself through treaties to an objectively irreversible process

The Rule of Imperialism and the Global-State in Gestation

explodes (as far as the point under consideration is concerned) the conceptual framework of the "treaty" itself, transforming a fact formally related to "international law" into a fact of "global law," even though the terms of such law are dictated by the most powerful party. As far as this global law is concerned, we cannot establish the concept outside the consideration (structural/metastructural) of a global State community, which emerges as such like an enigmatic object of investigation (and this is the notion of "global Stateness" that these jurists have a hard time, in my opinion, to grasp). On the other hand, global law, inasmuch as it depends on a global *statist* centricity, bears a perverse relation, exacerbating the asymmetry of international law, to the system of the world, which is marked by *systemic* centricity, the one of "centers" *versus* "peripheries." This is the situation that must, I believe, be fully taken into account in order to tackle the question of law in a real way.

The meta/structural problematic, introduced in *Théorie générale*, would contribute, amongst other things, to dialectically overcoming the antagonism between legal positivism and natural right. *Metastructure* is not natural right understood as transcendental interpellation, it is rather the quintessential modern affirmation (juridico-economico-political) inasmuch as it bears a mode of social ontology (i.e., it is not nothing): on the one hand, it can be traced to its appearance and historical expressions; on the other hand, it introduces effects whose importance lies in the fact that citizens can seize them for their own. The positive conditions of its existence lie within the (social) structure, simultaneously revealing its character to negate what is. The "real fact" of law is thus to be analyzed within the articulation of the metastructural pretension and the structural positivity — a "dialectical" articulation, as shown by political *action-struggle*, which, during its development, constantly rephrases and reformulates structure and metastructure. Within this historical dialectic of modernity, formulated in its most abstract form, the first moment, that of the modern "declaration," is not to be conceived as the foundation for the others, but as a dynamic reference.[21]

Hence, if we admit that a new form of global stateness is emerging, we must also admit, at the same time we recognize the ambiguous and contradictory fact of global law, the concept of a "politics of humanity." Humanity, through infinitely weak bodies like the UN General Assembly whose principles are unimpeachable, declares rights that are the rights of everyone, but in the name of which it claims to be a responsible subject, able to exercise a common power equal for all.

Jacques Bidet

One can recognize the figure of the social contract. Even though it leads most often to all sorts of blunders, there is no other form from which we could at least *start* — those who would do without simply enter into the practice unwittingly.[22] One must above all emphasize against liberalism, which, depending upon its various versions, sees in it either the basis of modern society, the ideal it pursues, or some fable of "origins" that this figure is precisely the only one from which we could conceive[23] the capitalist structure of class at the same time as its critique. This figure appeared, historically, quite prematurely, and it is only with the advent of ultimodernity that it finds coherence. Locke and Kant, as we know, start political discourse by admitting that (if men are free and equal) "the Earth belongs equally to everyone": it is actually the goal of their theories to explain the rules of cooperation while partaking of its use. The social contract can only be understood, thus radically, as a contract among everyone about everything (it is in this sense a theme taken and yet redirected away from T. Negri: ultimodernity no longer knows any "outside"). The treatment of the subject at the level of a particular State is thus an inconsequential ramification, a reflection of the anachronism of a still-dispersed humanity, fragmented in a temporary patchwork of different nation-States, unable to answer on its own. Far from being an erratic extension of the social contract, the global social contract that (already powerful) fiction is the truth, fragile and ambiguous, of the social contract.

That's why the "global-State," in the sense of a minimal jurisdiction (both to which some power should be attributed and that would also be in the form of a State of rights), does not come from a "federation" according to this concept. It is not federal, and this is the absolute novelty in comparison with any existing federation, like the ones through which the United States or the Federal Republic of Germany were created, or those in which the new continental entities agglomerate, like Europe or America. It is no longer a question of a collection of pre-existing entities, each with its territory, yet which accept to delegate a part of their prerogatives to a common central power. In the phenomenal order, everything is happening as if it were a question of heading towards a "global federal power," remaining piously respectful of the autonomy of States that were previously independent on their own territory. This is in effect the kind of renunciation of sovereignty that the WTO formally requires. But these sorts of "renunciations" can only be conducted on the basis of the recognition that the

The Rule of Imperialism and the Global-State in Gestation

"Earth belongs to everyone," or rather that everyone has the same juridical relation to the Earth, in the sense that no right derives from force, *de facto* State, or acquired advantage, but only through free and equal agreement among all. The fact that this agreement effectively realizes itself only through power relations does not prevent it from officially establishing itself only by reference to a position that is not a position of power but the recognition that no one can unilaterally declare himself the legitimate ruler of this or that. The legitimate order comes from an agreement among everyone, and it occurs within a world in which no specific State can still pretend to hold absolute rights over its territory without the others' agreement.[24]

It would not be useless to approach this question in formal terms as a principle of justice.[25] A universal order can only present itself as legitimate from the perspective of those occupying the worst position. It can only advance itself based on the Machiavellian principle of effective struggle by those who have the least. Hence, the precondition for its realization is that they must not be dispossessed of what they have. If the nation, seen from the perspective of the legitimate power of everyone to its territory, becomes thus indefensible, a defense can still be launched from a universalist point of view, like the fragmentary space from which concrete projects of solidarity and life-in-common are launched in opposition to the abstract logic of profit. The "law of the multitudes," according to which the oppressed and the exploited are most often in the majority against a dominating minority, creates a dialectic between the promotion of a politics of humanity and the "people's struggle" against imperialism. Whether or not a democratic power will appear on a global scale must be measured against the capacity for the nations and populations of the South to find in it the means of their own defence, as well as their equal rights to the entire planet, in the form of its concrete transformation through technology and culture, equal rights to dispose of resources and of knowledge, to self-organization where they reside and/or eventually migrate for a better life.

It is not the goal of this essay to suggest concrete programs of action. These projects suggest themselves today within the vast process that we call the World Citizen Movement and of which the forums, from Seattle to Porto Alegre, have become symbols. But this movement has its ordinary course in *every* anti-class and anti-systemic struggle and action throughout the world.

Jacques Bidet

Notes

1. A first version of this text was presented at *Congrès Marx International III*, Paris, 2001. I would like to thank Annie Bidet-Mordrel for her observations and criticisms, as well as Marcelo Kohen for his objections and corrections. The remaining mistakes are my own.

    The analysis given here — on a theme that I have been working on since my 1991 article, "Demain, le Sur-Etat?" [Tomorrow, the Super-State?], *Actuel Marx* No. 10, *Ethique et politique*, PUF, 1991 — is based on a more systematic demonstration found in my book, *Théorie générale*, PUF, 1999, Chapter 6, "Le système du monde [The world system]", pp.233–306. This analysis directly opposes that of M. Hardt and T. Negri as presented in their recent book *Empire* (Cambridge: Harvard University Press, 2000). On the philosophical level, it does recognize the same imperative to think facts and norms together in a relation of immanence. It thus also shares some of their Spinozan presuppositions, now dialectically understood in the constellation joining "metastructure" (the meaning of this term will gradually become clearer), structure (of class) and system (of the world), and social practice.

2. I refer to *Explication et reconstruction du Capital* [Explanation and Reconstruction of Capital], to be published by PUF, which forms, together with *Théorie générale* [General Theory] and *Que faire du Capital?* [What to do about Capital?], PUF, Paris, 2001, a trilogy explaining a new kind of marxism. In *"Topologie d'une alternative* [Topology of an Alternative]*"* the first entry of the *Dictonnaire Marx Contemporain* [Dictionary of Contemporary Marxism] (edited by J. Bidet and E. Kouvélakis, PUF, 1999), I give a general introduction to my ideas.

3. See Christopher May, "Intellectual Property Rights, Capacity Building and Informational Development in Developing Countries," in William Drake and Ernest Wilson III (editors), *Governing Global Electronic Networks, International Perspectives on Power and Policy*.

4. See Monique Chemiller-Gendreau, "Peut-on faire face au capitalisme? [Can One Confront Capitalism?]," in *Le droit dans la mondialisation* [The Law within Globalization], M. Chemiller-Gendreau and Y. Moulier Boutang (editors), Actual Marx Confrontation Collection, PUF, 2000. She wants to show that there is law in the proper sense only through an "articulation between contracts and law," an idea that supposes an implicit common will. It is thus that I have tried to show in Book 1 of my *Théorie générale* that there is no modern law without antagonistic co-implication of inter-individual and central contractuality, according to the matrix of the metastructure of modernity.

5. Marcelo Kohen, "Manifeste pour le droit international du XXI siècle" [A Manifesto for International Law of the 21st Century], in L. Boisson de Chazournes and V. Gowland-Debbas (editors), *The International Legal System in Quest of Equity and Universality*, Kluwer Law International, 2001, p.128.

6. See Robert Charvin, *Relations internationales, droit et mondialisation* [International Relations, Law and Globalization], L'Harmattan, 2000, p. 78.

7. In *Le Monde*, for example, we can often find the term, more or less ambiguous, of the "international financial community".
8. The term "civil society", negatively referring to that which does not arise from State institutions, finds itself effectively put forth both semantically and rhetorically, according to the law of class struggle, to highlight and develop the most antithetical of terms: on the right, there would be private relations, especially economic, while on the left would be relations of free association, solidarity and citizenship.
9. Conference given at *Congrès Marx International III*, Paris, 2001, published in *Le capital et l'humanité* [Capital and Humanity] *(Actuel Marx No. 31)*, PUF, 2002.
10. Michael Hardt and Antonio Negri, *Empire* (Cambridge: Harvard University, 2000), p. 15.
11. *Ibid.*, p. 34.
12. *Ibid.*, p. 24.
13. *Ibid.*, p. 31.
14. *Ibid.*, p. 237.
15. *Ibid.*, p. 190.
16. It is also within this dialectical framework that we should find a place for the foucauldian category, truly dialectical, of "discipline," essential to the critical construction of the concept of organization.
17. Michael Hardt and Antonio Negri, *Empire* (Cambridge: Harvard University, 2000), p. 18.
18. *Ibid.*, p. 43.
19. There exists, of course, other necessary approaches, notably in terms of "space", or the ones that take an interest in regions, networks, information flows, etc. To demonstrate how these categories do not, however, efface the major points of reference deriving from the Marxist tradition is beyond the scope of this paper.
20. Claude Serfati, *La mondialisation armée: le déséquilibre de la terreur* [Armed Globalization: The disequilibrium of terror], Textuel, Paris, 2001.
21. During the French Revolution, for example, the Declaration of 1789 figures as a "metastructural" expression rendered possible by a determined state, occurring at a certain conjuncture, in the social structure. This class "structure" was contradicted by laws against it (a voting system based on the poll tax, grain laws, and martial law), as well as the "system" (of the world), including the attempts by what was already then called "the right" to maintain slavery and to start imperialist war. The politics of liberation, shows by the Jacobinist discourse and the peasants', as well as the slaves', struggles refers constantly to the Declaration — not in order to repeat it, but in the context of an antistructural and antisystemic struggle that transformed it, constantly ascribing to it new meanings at the same time it revolutionized the social order.
22. M. Hardt and T. Negri themselves also call for a "post-modern republicanism" (*Empire*, p.210), and more specifically, at the end of their book (pp. 396–411) a three-fold right to global citizenship, minimum income, and the appropriation of modes of production, information, and communication. Clearly invented, thus perfectly "modern", even ultimodern.

Jacques Bidet

[23] I would re-emphasize that this point concerns a demonstration furnished by Marx in his theory of the reversal (*Verwandlung*) of the market as an alleged social contract under the sign of "natural and citizen rights" (*Capital*, Book 1, chapter VI) under capitalist domination. *Théorie générale* tries to coherently formulate all the various premises and implications behind this kind of dialectical concept of modernity.

[24] Regarding this point, we ought to reconsider the argument proposed by Kelsen concerning whether international law is the foundation for state law, or the opposite (see his *Théorie pure du droit* [Pure Theory of Law], Dalloz, 1962, pp.430–449)? Kelsen concludes the two perspectives are equivalent in the eyes of juridical science. I would say, for the reasons that I provide above and in the name of an interpretation of the principle of contractuality as a principle of "equiglobality" (*Théorie générale*, 622A, 914, 933), that the second perspective is a phenomenal or empirical view of a process that henceforth can only give a reasoned account of itself by resorting to the first perspective.

[25] See the intervention by Alex Callinicos at the *Congrès Marx International III*, available in the collection: *Le capital et l'humanité (Actuel Marx, No. 31)*, PUF, 2002.

CARL SCHMITT AND WAR:
ON *THE NOMOS OF THE EARTH*

YAMADA HIROAKI
—Translated from Japanese by Joshua Young

The Nomos of the Earth, how does one describe this book? Published in 1950, it is seen as Schmitt's representative work from the post-war era. Should we therefore consider this text to be the great compilation of Schmitt's thought extending over several decades? Or should we look at it as a sign of his accommodation to the situation in which it was written, a sign of his new apostasy in what is said to be his repeated changes of thought, or even look at it as a book of self-vindication or self-justification in a scholarly disguise. Whatever answers one gives to these questions, of the following at least we can be certain: *The Nomos of the Earth* contains a great number of ideas that are urgent and necessary for us to take up and re-examine simply because we live in today's world, a world where the Bush administration has attacked Iraq and has realized with overwhelming military force a "victory," though a very tenuous and doubtful victory.

To put it in a single sentence, the theme that runs through *The Nomos of the Earth* from beginning to end is the problem of how to stave off a civil war[1] that is a war of annihilation, a civil war that washes with blood, the blood that flows between "brothers." To follow Schmitt's expressions, staving off means finding a bracketing limit — *Hegung* — to war, placing war into a framework. Limiting war, however, is not the abolition of war itself. As we will see later, for Schmitt that impossibility was self-evident. As Schmitt says, it is precisely the bracketing of war, which is not its abolition, that is "the highest form of order within the scope of human power," and that is "the core issue of all systems of international law." Furthermore, only "war to which a framework is applied" can be the guarantee against "the escalating cycles of revenge," that is, against "the nihilistic acts of revenge and hatred whose meaningless goal lies in mutual annihilation." Or to put it another way, it is the one and only security against raising antagonism to absolute antagonism.

And so, how can we make possible this limitation of war that is presented as perhaps the only hope allowed to the human race — or is this a possibility at all? To understand Schmitt's answer to this problem it is necessary that we first come to understand his thinking on unlimited war.

International Civil War

What Schmitt considered unlimited war was the era of religious civil wars that raged in Europe in the sixteenth and seventeenth centuries. When Schmitt talks of the dark period of the fighting within the corporal body of Christianity, the fighting that happened between Protestant and Catholic that split apart the unity of the Christian community, we sense a feeling that goes beyond just disgust, we sense a feeling close to fear. He calls the religious wars an "international civil war" and a "super-territorial war of annihilation." This combination of attributes, the combination of "international" and "super-territorial," contains a certain anachronism as the civil wars in question predate the establishment of the modern nation-States. On the other hand this anachronism foreshadows his response to the question of what can possibly act as a limiting framework on war. The nation-State put an end to the religious civil wars. In other words, according to Schmitt, the limitation of war — or to put it another way, the rationalization and humanization of war — is nothing other than the creation of the nation in its modern sense. The limiting of war for that reason is above all the limiting of war to war among nation-States: "All progress of the *droit des gens*, everything that mankind has developed thus far in what is called international law, consists of one singular accomplishment: ... the rationalization and humanization of war. This meant that European war was limited to conflicts on European soil, and was conceived of as a relation among states and among armies organized by states" (NE 121/184; NoE 149). [2]

Carl Schmitt and War

However, in order to be able to say that limiting war to war among nation-States is the limiting of war itself, not just any concept of the nation-State will do. Limiting war is premised upon establishing and realizing a particular concept of the nation-State along with a certain concept of sovereignty. This is a conception of a sovereign nation state that is endowed with a territory complete unto itself (a territorially sovereign nation-State that opposes — is in contradistinction to — others of the same kind according to clearly defined territorial borders, and that can be regarded as a homogeneous political unity on the interior of that territory).

As Europe was divided into a number of sovereign nation-States a decisive alteration in the concept of war became possible (we should not forget that for Schmitt the history of international law was nothing other than the history of the concept of war). The results of this alteration appeared as a fundamental overturning of the concept of the just war — *gerechten Krieg*. The concept of the just war was at that time decisively separated from the concept of the legitimate causes of war (*justa causa belli*), concepts that until then were indivisibly linked. In order for the legitimate causes to act as a limit on war, it was necessary for there to be a judge that could decide on the propriety of the legitimate causes, a judge positioned above the participants of the war. If in the European middle ages the concept of a just war had any kind of regulating power on war, the role of the final arbiter was presumed to be played by the authority of the Christian community and the Church of Rome. When that presumptive authority disappeared, the result was the dissolution of the concept of war from the classical doctrine of the just war ("just war is not at all war, it is the administration of justice; at the same time unjust war is not war, it is rebellion" said Johann Oldendorp). Of course, the dissolution of the concept of war does not lead to the dissolution of war itself. On the contrary, what came out of the dissolution of this concept of war was the era of religious civil wars that Schmitt saw as a phenomenon of war without limit. And in order to find refuge from this newly born disaster, it was necessary to renovate the concept of the just war, to rebuild the very concept of war in a new form. Schmitt saw the key to doing that in "formalizing" the concept of the "proper enemy" and in the concept of a just war founded on the concept of a proper enemy.

To follow Schmitt's thinking, at least in terms of the objective of limiting war, the attempt to define the concept of a just war according to "legitimate causes," that is, according to the concrete, actual circumstances, is destined for failure.

This is because, in cases when a higher authority does not exist, the judgment of whether legitimate causes exist or not is entrusted in the final instance to the decision of the participants in the war, and as is to be expected, the participants already see the legitimate causes to be on their own side. Accordingly, in order for the concept of the just war to have any benefit as a regulatory principle, the legitimacy had to be completely separated from the actual contents of the conflict and must be defined purely formally (that is, separated from any subjective judgment). Justice had to be rearranged according to this form. The important matter is that this formalization only came about by replacing the concept of "legitimate causes" with the concept of "the proper enemy." According to Schmitt, it is precisely at this juncture that the sovereign state plays a role. The formalization of the just war with this idea of the proper enemy means that in reality war has become purely a matter of nation-States. This is because only sovereign territorial nation-States can face each other as equal enemies. "Since the end of the middle ages, since the age of nations of the sixteenth to the twentieth centuries, European international law has tried to push aside the doctrine of legitimate causes. The formal foundation for regulating proper wars was not the international authority of the church, but rather the mutually authoritative sovereignty that existed between the nation-States. The situation of international law between nation states came about from the idea of the *justus hostis* instead of from the doctrine of *justa causa belli*, and so all wars amongst nation states, between sovereigns of equal authority, were named legitimate [*rechtma_ig*] wars. For two hundred years this legal formalization succeeded in rationalizing and humanizing war, or to put it another way, it succeeded in limiting [*Hegung*] war" (NE 91/136; NoE 126).[3]

In other words, in the concept of the proper enemy — *justus hostis* — there holds a much higher regulatory power than in the concept of legitimate causes. Schmitt is quite insistent on this point. "The question of the *bellum justum* was distinguished sharply from that of *justa causa belli*. *Justum bellum* is war between *justi hostes*: 'just' in the sense of 'just war' means the same as 'impeccable' [*einwandfrei*] or 'perfect' [*perfekt*] in the sense of 'formal justice' [*formgerecht*], as when one speaks of *justum matrimonium* [law of marriage]" (NE 124/190; NoE 153). "Essentially all war is bound to 'war that has form,' to what is called in French *une guerre en forme*. To the extent that a war "has form," no one, whether participants or neutrals, has any authority to criticize the justice of the war. All

Carl Schmitt and War

'justice' comes back to this 'form'" (NE 138/214; NoE 167)? Schmitt sees the application of form to war as the greatest historical achievement of the sovereign territorial nation-State.

And yet, can we truly call this the limiting of war? That a nation-State has sovereignty means that each of the various nation-States is individual and is seen as the highest form of subjectivity,[4] it means that they do not accept any manner of higher deciding mechanism above them nor any universal principle. In this absolute nature of national sovereignty, theoretically we find the unrestricted nature of the national will. War is therefore the inherent right of the sovereign nation-State, and there cannot be any kind of regulatory basis from the outside that can restrict this right. At the same time however, the sovereign nation-State is equal to others in this unrestricted nature. Accordingly, we see the application of a principle that inhibits discrimination toward the enemy as a criminal and that inhibits the alteration of war into a police action, in short a principle that staves off wars of annihilation. "The removal and avoidance of wars of destruction is possible only when a form for the gauging of forces is found. This is possible only when the opponent is recognized as an enemy on equal grounds — as a *justus hostis*. This is the given foundation for a bracketing of war" (NE 159/250; NoE 187). With regard to this bracketing, or limiting, principle, the objectives of war do not matter, being a part of the absolute nature of the nation state's sovereignty (that a sovereign nation-State is free regardless of the objectives of a war). On the contrary, such lack of distinction is simply the erasure of thinking of the legitimate causes of war, and that, as we have seen, is for Schmitt the starting point for realizing the limiting of war.

However, the concept of the proper enemy presumes a mutual recognition between opponents as proper enemies, and so when this system functions for the first time there must be somewhere a security that the parties will respect each other as enemies of equal sovereignty, a respect based upon the recognition of each other as proper enemies. That this security cannot be found in the self-restraint of the will of the sovereign who is essentially without restriction is pointed out by Schmitt himself when he uses the metaphor "the bonds of the escape artist" — *Selbstbindungen eines Entfesselungskünstlers*. So where resides the effective restraint that leads opponents to respect each other as enemies of equal right? For an answer to this question we must turn to the spatial order that encompasses the sovereign nation-States.

Yamada Hiroaki

The Spatial Order

We have, until now, deliberately ignored the sequence in which *The* Nomos *of the Earth* unfolds, and this has meant that we have consciously driven into the background the central themes of the work. *The* Nomos *of the Earth* opens with the following proclamation. The earth is "the mother of the law"; law is first law in its proper location. When this relationship with place disappears, law loses its efficacy, it morphs into a fictional/empty specter. In other words, law unites the situational order — *Ordnung*— and the established place — *Ortung* — and is fundamentally a geo-attribute (a mechanism of the earth) — *erdhaft*. If we are to locate this idea in Schmitt's intellectual development, it seems natural to look at it as a development of his "thinking the concrete situation" found in his 1934 text "Three Varieties of Legal Thought." The opening of *The Nomos of the Earth* applies the meaning space — *raum* — to the adjective "concrete"; the concrete situation has simply changed terminology to become the spatial order. Of course we can question the historical and political implications of this intellectual development, as any spatial order names a global spatial order, or to be more specific, it must be thought of as one or more individual spheres of regulation, and in such a concept it is impossible to not see the parallel with the idea of a fascist sphere and above all with the idea of the life sphere — *Lebensraum* — promoted by the Nazis. However, we will put aside that issue for now in order to first clarify the role that the idea of spatial order plays in the theme of the limiting of war.

"The restrictive power that the obligation of international law puts on the sovereign nation state cannot exist in the problematic voluntary bonds of the unrestrained sovereign. It can only be based in the common belonging to a single space that is restricted to protective borders, that is, only in the comprehensive operations of the concrete spatial order" (NE 198/310; NoE 227). We have already mentioned that Schmitt emphasizes the territorial character of the sovereign nation-State, but it is decisive that this territorial limitation is not the territorial confirmation that has the potential to freely expand in unlimited space. The territorial limitation is itself limited, and it redraws boundaries, it divides the interior of the territory that was itself drawn with borders. Of course we can question whether that situation occurred historically in that manner. However, from a structural point of view the organization precedes the individual component parts of that system. And so the fact that Europe is demarcated as a single system does not reveal the restricting power of such a system. To repeat, this system is not at all an abstract structure. It is something with a foundation in the land that is bounded; it is an actual contents. "The essential and very effective bond, without which there would have been no international law, lay not in the highly problematic, voluntary ties among the presumably unrestrained wills of equally sovereign persons, but in the binding power of a Eurocentric spatial order encompassing all these sovereigns. The core of this *nomos* lay in the division of European soil into state territories with firm borders" (NE 120/182; NoE 148).

Equilibrium

A particularly important political idea here shows its face. Yes, the idea of "balance." At the same time that Schmitt mobilizes this concept, he also introduces a crucial change to it. In exactly the same way that he took his 1930s key word phrase "thought of the concrete situation" and spatialized it as the *raum* order, he also spatializes the concept of equilibrium. The orderliness of *raum*, or more properly, *raum*'s power to establish order, is grounded in the existence of this spatial balance. "The binding character of a comprehensive spatial order immediately is recognizable if the spatial order is conceived of as a balance. The concept of a political balance is significant only in the sense that it provides a picture of a comprehensive spatial order of European states" (NE 160/252; NoE 188). "[T]he concern is [...] rather with the realization that the concept of an equilibrium expresses spatial viewpoints in a specific sense, and illuminates the idea of a comprehensive spatial order inherent in this balance. Therein, despite all criticism and political mis-use, lies the great practical superiority of the concept of balance, because therein lies its capacity to achieve a bracketing of war" (NE 161/253; NoE 189).

This usage of the concept of equilibrium — that is, how Schmitt gives it a clearly positive and affirmative nuance — probably astounds those who have come to know Schmitt through his works of the 1920s. "Despite all criticism and political mis-use" he says. But at least in the 1920s, the Schmitt who says this was one of the most vehement critics of balance in the political sense. Such statements must surely bring to mind the Schmitt who furiously protested against the parliamentary multi-party nation state and the liberalism that was its undergirding metaphysics. In short, what happened to the Schmitt of *The Crisis of Parliamentary Democracy* (1923)? In that work Schmitt declares that the linkage of parliamentarism and democracy, which hitherto had seemed quite self-evident, was not founded in any necessity, and was furthermore just a creation of historical contingency. The principles on which the two depend are in fact totally different, says Schmitt. Schmitt argues that the principle that founds democracy is "identity" (sameness between the governing and the governed), and the essence of this identity lies in the single point "that all decisions handed down must have validity only in relation to those themselves who decide." On the other hand, the metaphysical foundation of parliamentarism is nothing other than liberalism, and the fundamental principle of liberalism itself is "equilibrium" (whose primary political expression is the separation of powers).

By carrying out this division between parliamentarism and democracy, Schmitt can attack parliamentarism/liberalism as ineffectual, not able to effect necessary decisions in times of need. In that sense we can say that there is a single line of thought that runs through Schmitt's works of the 1920s, from his 1919 *Politische romantic* ("Political Romanticism") to his 1921 *Diktatur* ("Dictator") and 1922 *Politische Theologie; vier Kapitel zur Lehre von der Souveränität* ("Political Theology") to his 1923 *The Crisis of Parliamentary Democracy*; which is to say that the object of Schmitt's attack on Romanticism is above all its escape into "perpetual dialogue," which avoids all responsible decisions. What appears to Schmitt in Romanticism that must be denied is a classical precedent of liberalism's indecisiveness. Romanticism, for Schmitt, is the spiritual ancestor of the citizenry class who engages in useless debate. Schmitt's infamous statement of decisionism, "a sovereign is someone who can make decisions in emergency situations," ("Political Theology") is a judgment against liberalism's concept of equilibrium.

And yet in *The* Nomos *of the Earth* Schmitt calls back the concept of equilibrium to play a decisive role. Could this be part of the heralded conversion in Schmitt's thinking after 1932 from decisionistic thinking to a thinking the concrete situation; could it be a new conclusion in Schmitt's thought? We must see that this so-called conversion is not an actual conversion at all. Which is to say that, despite the outward appearance of resolve, within the decisionist thinking that he put forth there had always already been what he would come later to call the concrete situation. This is clear in the above argument from *The Crisis of Parliamentary Democracy* defining democracy, a book which when looked at from a chronological perspective was written during his most decisionist period.

Carl Schmitt and War

What we cannot overlook in the rigorous distinction that Schmitt makes between parliamentarism and democracy is the particular form that his definition of democracy as identity takes. In this form, democracy is not tied to certain actual systems of representation or of direct election, and as a result, democracy becomes something that can adhere to any kind of system without paradox. What is crucial is that this definition of democracy has an affinity to the formal character exhibited in Schmitt's decisionism. The decisionism he puts forth also is not founded in any system nor preceded by any principles; this decisionism is truly a matter of "decisions from nothing," and is free from all restrictions of content. Through this affinity democracy and decisionism can be neatly linked together. Decisionistic democracy, we know all too well the historical name of this phenomenon. It goes without saying that it is dictatorship. To the extent that it secures the identity between the governing and the governed, dictatorship according to Schmitt's definition would seem to be the most direct and most thorough democratic form of government. This is because the decisions of the dictator are nothing other than the decisions of all the people.

But what in reality is the identity of the governing and the governed? Here we have in Schmitt the key to the conversion from decisionism to a thinking of the actual situation, from a pure formalism to an ontological thinking, or rather the key to understanding the supplementary relationship, the very illicit cohabitation, between decisionism and thinking of the concrete situation, between formalism and ontology. When we look at the reality of it, the aforementioned identity is a completely abstract phenomenon, and not at all something real we can see or grab in our hands. In its actuality this matter of identity comes back to the issue of a "recognition" (*Annerkennung*) of identity, or rather it has political implications only as that issue. As a practical matter such recognition has only two possibilities. In one, in which the recognition of identity becomes the general will of the ruled, the recognition is actively constructed from the side of the rulers (the means for doing so do not enter into the equation here; however, there is no doubt that this is simultaneously a process of "identification," a process that positively fashions the governed as a "subject body"[5]). The second possibility is that identity, with a quite different, aformal, principle, is enfolded in the existing order, and as such the problems of recognition disappear and are substituted by a single actual principle. Schmitt chooses the later route, and the actual principle at work here is homogeneity — *Homogenität*.

While in the first edition of The *Crisis of Parliamentary Democracy* (1923) this principle still only appears surreptitiously, in the preface to the second edition (1926), Schmitt himself unambiguously proclaims what he is thinking of under the name of identity.

> Every actual democracy rests on the principle that not only are equals equal but unequals will not be treated equally. Democracy requires, therefore, first homogeneity and second—if the need arises—elimination or eradication of heterogeneity. [...] A democracy demonstrates its political power by knowing how to refuse or keep at bay something foreign and unequal that threatens its homogeneity. The question of equality is precisely not one of abstract, logical-arithmetical games. It is about the substance of equality. It can be found in certain physical and moral qualities, for example, in civic virtue, in *arete*, the [EXT]classical democracy of *vertus* (*vertu*). [...] Since the nineteenth century it has existed above all in membership in a particular nation, in national homogeneity. (LP 13-14/14-15; CDP 9)

And as though this were not sufficient to emphasize that his premised basis of democratic identity is nothing other than homogeneity, Schmitt pushes the point once again, this time in reference to Rousseau.

> The general will as Rousseau constructs it is in truth homogeneity. That is a really consequential democracy. According to the *Contrat social*, the state therefore rests not on a contract but essentially on homogeneity, in spite of its title and in spite of the dominant contract theory. The democratic identity of governed and governing arises from that. (LP 20/21-22; CDP 14)

Right at this moment when formalism seems to assert itself, an inescapable concrete principle rises from the background, like a twin sibling (or like a specter from the past?). And the exact same thing can be said about Schmitt's argument concerning the limiting of war. At the same moment that he asserts a formalization of the concept of the just war according to the "proper enemy," he claims a concrete principle as the necessary guarantee of this formalization; that is, he insists on the role of the concrete spatial order, the European equilibrium of territorial nation-States. It is not hard to see from this situation that the equilibrium that is at issue has no points in common with the liberal concept of balance. The balance of the liberal sense is an equality between heterogeneous entities. Meanwhile in the equilibrium of the comprehensive spatial order of Europe, there is no room for the entrance of heterogeneous entities. Europe is literally an

Carl Schmitt and War

equilibrium of "homogeneous entities." Though somewhat lengthy, let us here quote a decisive statement from *The Nomos of the Earth*.

> The theory of international law between respective nation states was based in the balanced spatial structure of territorial nation states that were complete unto themselves—these being entities that have confirmed territorial boundaries and unassailable land areas. The isolation of individual sovereigns from each other is merely an external view. In reality equality - *aequalitas* - forced all entities into the following situation. That is, it allowed entities to consider the affairs of all the others, and also allowed them to conduct war in an orderly fashion, instead of as an exercise in mutual destruction, and this culminated in a new balance. Essential for the spatial foundation of the bracketing of war was that thereafter war was confined to the European territorial order and was consistent with its system of balance. Such an order of international law thus was not a lawless chaos of egoistic wills to power. All these egoistic power structures existed side-by-side in the same space of one European order, wherein they mutually recognized each other as sovereigns. Each was the equal of the other, because each constituted a component of the system of equilibrium. Consequently, every important war between or among European states concerned all members of the European community of states. (NE 139/216; NoE 167–168)

Schmitt does not at all try to hide the very limited nature of the real possibility of limiting war. For him, despite some twists and turns, the continental wars that were fought within Europe from the seventeenth century to the end of the nineteenth century are the single era, the single place, that realized a limiting of war. However, in order for Europe to establish and support a land as a single comprehensive territorial order it was absolutely necessary that there continue to exist "a fundamental difference of the land situation" between the land of Europe and non-European land, that is, that there continue to exist a confirmed free space outside of Europe, a gigantic liberated space that the great European powers were allowed to freely acquire. In other words, it was absolutely necessary that Europe continue to secure an overwhelming superiority in relation to the other parts of the globe. At the end of the nineteenth century, with the establishment of the western hemisphere due to the appearance on the geopolitical scene of the United States of America and with the rise of Asia led by Japan, the circumstances disappeared for such a global world order, and with them the possibility for the limiting of war.

What sort of conclusion is this? How can we be content when the possibility of evading annihilatory wars and stopping the escalation of war are really so delicate and only exist with such tenuous provisos. Does Schmitt's limiting of war really only exist to rationalize existing international law, to ratify the imperial expansion in which Europe divides up the world according to that law? For the moment, let us not jump to conclusions.

Sibling Rivalries — War of Brothers

Schmitt's written work for the most part resists being restricted to a single meaning, or rather resists definition as its political meaning. But that is not because he hesitates to make bold declarations. Anyone who is even a little familiar with Schmitt knows how he likes conclusive assertions. He continually sought an explosive argumentative power in his writing. Yet despite this there is always political ambiguity floating about in what he writes. Why is this? It is because every time Schmitt intervenes into the situation — and he almost always intervenes when he writes; that is, he writes to dispute — he conspicuously avoids direct confrontations, especially avoiding clearly indicating an enemy. This could be a result of Schmitt carrying out his interventions under the guise of scholarship, writing in the form of general theses of legal studies and political science. That is certainly the main cause that we simply cannot ignore. However, we must also take issue with the implications of his occasionalism. Which is to say that in most cases Schmitt's analyses come to serve equally two (or perhaps more) completely contrary political aims. We should keep in mind, for example, passages such as the following from *Legalität und Legitimität* ("Legality and Legitimacy," 1932) where he argues for the validity of a method of simple majority rule.

> To the extent that it can be premised on the substantial homogeneity of the whole national people, gauging the popular will according to a recognized simple majority is to be permitted as effective. That is, in such cases minority parties do not get shut out by numbers, and the vote is nothing more than an expression of the will and the unity that is assumed to exist latently. As I've said previously, all forms of democratic rule, because they are founded on the assumption of an indivisible homogeneous and unified national people, in reality as well as in essence, do not exist as democratic governments in any minority parties much less in numerous indefatigable minority parties. To recognize the procedures of majority rule does not

> mean abandoning what is seen as true and proper to relativism or agnosticism — to do so when confronting important and fatal decisions would be suicidal, or only possible in simple, unimportant situations, as Hans Kelsen recognizes "only good in times of relative tranquility." Rather by a unified belonging to a united national people, a democratic rule is based on the premise that the many are the same and fundamentally want to be one. (LL 21/41–44)

If we put aside the surreptitious yet glaring move from *Homogenität* to *Gleichartigkeit*,[6] Schmitt's declarations here, which are directly connected to the recognition spoken of in the preface to the second edition of *The Crisis of Partiamentary Democracy*, have not received any actual revision at all. And yet the performative implications of this text become exactly opposite between the time it came out (1932) and after Hitler's power grab in March of 1933, and especially after Schmitt joins the Nazi party in May of that same year. If we follow Helmut Quaritsch's persuasive argument, Schmitt's plan in 1932 was to prevent Hitler's usurpation of power, and Schmitt sought, in order to reject the Nazis acquisition of power which would have been confirmed by the dissolution of parliament and the holding of new elections in which the majority party's hold would be consolidated, to put an end to the elections with these pronouncements on emergency situations (that is, he emphasized the propriety of that mechanism).[7] The existence of the Nazis itself indicated the non-existence of national homogeneity, and accordingly the simple application of the principle of majority rule was ineffectual, and even dangerous. And yet this was not explicitly written into the text. And for that reason after the Nazification of Germany with Hitler's rise to power, this text did not require any revisions and now fit neatly with the Nazi ideology and even became a justification for the Nazi ideology. The subsequent change of the key term homogeneity from *Gleichartigkeit* to *Artgleichheit* in the 1933 book "The Nation, The Movement, and the People" accomplishes a decisive racialization.

Should we assume from this that the term *Homogenität* used in his 1926 text already has in it racial connotations? Though the temptation to see it so is quite strong, the important point is to understand why Schmitt was so stuck on this idea of "homogeneity indivisible." The issue here is once again the real possibility of civil war.

To ward off civil war; as we have said this is the fundamental theme that runs through *The* Nomos *of the Earth* (even when it is not fore grounded). And Schmitt strongly criticizes the doctrine of the just war as the making absolute of enemy relations, criminalizing the enemy and dehumanizing war by connecting war to morals and ethics. What he finds unforgivable in just war theory is the very ideology of civil war which aggravates antagonism and which leads to the ultimate evil of war of extermination. We can even say that for Schmitt just war and civil war are synonyms. Of course one can take these arguments in *The* Nomos *of the Earth* as Schmitt's self-vindication after having been accused of war crimes in the post-war era, but even if that perspective does include some part of the truth, we must say that it is a rather superficial view. It seems that for Schmitt civil war was rather an object that gives rise to an anxiety over the very existence of the race. Civil war is thus war between brothers, a matter of a sibling rivalry.

War between brothers. This phrase brings up two opposing images. One is in the end a comforting image: the idea of war as a struggle between familiars, a struggle between those who share the same daily existence and the same recollections of their origins; that is, a struggle that opens up to the possibility of reconciliation. The other image, a contrary and most dreadful image, is of an annihilatory war with no reconciliation where blood cleanses blood, a war built on a hatred born of "minute differences" precisely because the parties share so much in common, war built on an endless loop of familiar abhorrence. To repeat, the image that Schmitt adopts is the later. And just because of that the turning of the later into the former carries a decisive importance.

Without a doubt there is a linkage between Schmitt's emphasis on the public character of the enemy (in a political sense) found in his *The Concept of the Political* and this anxiety toward civil war. In that sense recent studies of Schmitt's work are not mistaken to try to see a continuity between *The Concept of the Political*, *The* Nomos *of the Earth*, and "A Partisan Theory," or to put it another way, between "the public enemy" and "the proper enemy." By limiting the politically significant enemy to a public enemy, the intent is to wipe out as much as possible the emotional component of "hatred" from the concept of the enemy. "The enemy in the political sense is not the private adversary whom one hates" — *Den Feind im politischen Sinne braucht man nicht persönlich zu hassen.* The public enemy can be a private friend without issue. Or to turn it around, though one is a private friend, publicly they can be an enemy.

Carl Schmitt and War

However, in *The Concept of the Political*, the restricting of the enemy to the public enemy (for that is the only politically "proper enemy") does not mean that relations toward the enemy are lenient or that enemies should purport a mutual respect. At the same time that Schmitt rejects the separation of the concept of antagonism from ethical, aesthetic, and economic spheres of consideration, he also strongly resists the rarefaction of that concept in symbolic or metaphorical understandings. He says that the concept of the enemy necessarily contains the possibility of real conflict. The concept of the enemy always already includes the real possibility of physically killing the opponent and destroying their existence. "The friend, enemy, and combat concepts receive their real meaning precisely because they refer to the real possibility of physical killing. War follows from enmity. War is the existential negation of the enemy." *Der Kreig folgt aus der Feindschaft, denn diese ist seinsmäßige Negierung eines anderen Seins* (BP 33/26, CoP 33). The strong tension — *Spannung* — that is imposed on people's daily lives by this real possibility of negating existence is what Schmitt sees as the essential nature of politics, and when that disappears, both the concept of the enemy and the concept of politics disappear along with it.

But who after all is this enemy? For what reason can those people become our enemy? Or why can we ourselves become seen as an enemy? Schmitt's thinking on this in *The Concept of the Political* confuses the reader: "the political enemy need not be morally evil or aesthetically ugly; he need not appear as an economic competitor, and it may even be advantageous to engage with him in business transactions. But he is, nevertheless, the other [*der andere*], the stranger [*der Fremde*]; and it is sufficient for his nature that he is, in a specially intense way, existentially something different and alien" (BP 27/15–16; CoP 27). Just what is the meaning of this "sufficient" — *genügt* — in the phrase "it is sufficient for his nature that he is existentially something different"? Does it mean that our others, our strangers, are all latently our enemies? If so, we can say that it is the other side of the Möbius strip of Schmitt's logic where he emphasizes "the indivisible homogeneity" of the national people that is the fundamental condition of democracy.

However, we should probably see this definition of the enemy as a kind of exorcism for Schmitt, a kind of projection. By projecting antagonism onto the other or the stranger, he sets aside the most dangerous antagonism, that is the possibility of antagonism between the same people, between familiars, between brothers. What makes this later antagonism so dangerous in comparison with the antagonism toward the other is that in this the enemy becomes undefined and so the self itself cannot be regulated. And in such a situation the raising of the antagonistic relationship to the absolute antagonistic relationship can no longer be constrained. In a 1947 memorandum Schmitt writes the following.

> Were Franz Kafka to have written a tome called "Enemy", it is clear that it would have been about giving rise to the anxiety of the uncontrolled nature of the enemy (there exists no other anxiety worth calling so. The essence of anxiety is the indication of an enemy whose proper shape is not known.) To use reasoning against this (and thus reasoning means the high level of politics) would be to clearly define the enemy (and this is always at the same time to define oneself). With this act of definition anxiety — *Angst*— would cease, but fear — *Furcht*— would remain. However, if we do not share the same concept, how will we take something from this unrestrictedness? How can we turn it into something bracketed and restricted? Particularly in reference to the situation of civil war — *Bürgerkriegslage*— when the combatants do not hold any concept in common whatsoever, and when all concepts — *Begriff* — become interventions — *Übergriff* — into the enemy camp.[8]

Here lies the decisive importance of the concept for Schmitt. In turning the indefinable to a definable nature, the shape of the enemy becomes apparent (and at the same time one's own shape becomes seen), which plays the trump card against the fundamental anxiety. Accordingly, the limit thought, or the taking to the limit of the concept, that Schmitt faces as though he cannot resist it, at the same time can be seen as constructing its limit (its localization). If we look at them from a different perspective, the surpassing the limits of sovereignty by decisions concerning (within) emergency situations, the surpassing of limits of the concept of the political by determinations of friend and foe, aren't they connected to the matters of sovereignty and political matters pushing their own limits and connected to the matter of staving off the covering over of the whole?

Toward the end of the last chapter of his "Prison diary" (1950), the chapter titled "The Wisdom of Isolation" Schmitt writes, "so just who can be my enemy? I recognize him as an enemy, but I must also recognize that he also recognizes me as an enemy. In this mutual recognition of recognition exists the greatness of what is called the concept. [...] Theologians tend to define the word enemy as that which must be made nothing — *vernichtet*. But I am a legal scholar — a

Jurist — not a theologian" (ECS 89). This last phrase contains a double meaning. The enemy is not to be made nothing of. First of all as a concept, the concept of the enemy is not an empty one and so it exists physically. Yes, the enemy is not to be made nothing of, resisting the "numerous psuedo-theological myths about enemies" of our times. And if political science is theology made vulgar, and if it rests on the real possibility of substantially making nothing of the enemy, then the role of legal studies is to put a stop to the realization of that possibility. We should see this as the final pronouncement of the legal scholar Schmitt, who is not a political scientist. Schmitt's post-war works do not betray this pronouncement. However, the question remains as to whether this kind of staving off can be realized as the universal and abstract norm (system) that is imagined by conventionalism, or whether an actual and real security is necessary.

Once Again into the *Nomos* of the Earth

As we have previously mentioned, with the disappearance at the end of the nineteenth century of the global spatial order in which Europe was the center, the security that was European international law disappeared, as did the security for limiting war. From that phenomenon Schmitt drew two observations. The first is that the world had moved to a new stage of spatial development, and that this stage had still not revealed its final conclusion nor its final order. The primary factor of the development to this stage Schmitt saw in the birth of the spatial order of the western hemisphere created by the United States' combination of an isolationist policy and an interventionist policy founded in the Monroe Doctrine. The birth of this spatial order at the same time was the writing into existence of a great space — *Grossraum* — as a new unit of international law, a unit which surpassed the territory of the sovereign nation state. "The Monroe Doctrine and the Western Hemisphere have been linked together. They define the sphere of the special interests of the United States. They encompass a space far exceeding the boundaries of the state proper — a *Grossraum* in the sense of international law. The traditional American interpretation of the doctrine in international law has been that juridically it constitutes a zone of self-defense. Every true empire around the world has claimed such a sphere of spatial sovereignty beyond its borders" (NE 256/403-404; NoE 281).

To what sort of conclusion does this lead? (We can see from the above quote that the concept of the great space is one with the concept of the hegemonic nation state). Once the concept of the great space is given justification, no one can expect that its expansion of borders will naturally stop at any point. Schmitt expresses this by using the words of a certain American jurisprudence scholar. " [I]n the fall of 1940, the American international law specialist Philip S. Jessup added the following statement to Boggs' treatise: 'Today the dimensions change rapidly, and the interest we had in Cuba in 1860 corresponds to our interest today in Hawaii; perhaps the argument of self-defense will lead the United States one day to pursue war on the Yangtze, the Volga, or the Congo'" (NE 260/408; NoE 284–285). If there is anything that can restrict this great sphere of expansion it can only be another such great sphere. Accordingly, our planet has been brought to one clear, yet still unresolved, dilemma. That is, to use a philosophical vocabulary, the dilemma of universalism and pluralism. This is the dilemma of "whether or not this planet is to perform as a machine of global monopoly for one power, or whether pluralism is to regulate a new international law of the earth in spheres of coexistence that are ordered for and by oneself, in spheres of intervention, and in cultural spheres." Schmitt puts this in the following way. The development of this global space "is compelled either to make the transition to a *Grossraum* and to find its place in a world of other recognized *Grossraum*, or to transform the concept of war contained in traditional international law into a global civil war" (NE 271/427; NoE 296).

In short "the core issue of spatial construction of international law" and "the great antithesis of world politics" takes the following form. A global spatial order of a world ruled unilaterally, or the coexistence of multiple large-scale spaces; a central world governance, or a spatial order equilibrium. Looking back over the first half of the twentieth century Schmitt posited the later schema, realized as the equilibrium between the two world empires of the United States of America and the Soviet Union, and through the dissolution of one, the world moved on toward the definitive form of a unilateral rule. Whether only the creation of truly new (and plural) great spheres could be the principle of resistance to this unilateral rule, or whether even that unhappy conclusion would be ineffective, all that would be left would be the progression of a civil war without the frame of the sovereign nation-State and magnified to a global scope, a world civil war unstoppable until the complete penetration of unilateral rule.

Carl Schmitt and War

One looks in vain for an answer to this issue in either *The Nomos of the Earth* or in the later "Partisan Theory." On the one hand it was at least clear to Schmitt that the United Nations could not act as a third-party source of resistance. He had already written in the 1926 published "The Central Problem of the International League of Nations," "It seems that the British government wishes to use the International League of Nations to legitimate its desire toward the area of Mosul. Yet Britain is one of the great countries, and so when it comes to the British Navy having to fight for some reason, surely they will not look to receive the mandate of an international organization. In the decisive moment, England will continue to be its own judge concerning matters of its own country. This is simply the way of true sovereignty."[9] If one switches America for England, and the United Nations for the League of Nations, this forecast holds true to today's reality. We should probably also add that as the very successor to the maritime empire of Britain that held the *nomos* of the seas, America, when seen from the League of Nations order that was built upon the *nomos* of the continental land mass, was from the beginning on the outside.

The second observation that Schmitt took from the events at the end of the nineteenth century is that there was a decisive revival of the concept of the just war. The primary reason for this revival was the appearance of new means of destruction founded in technological development. In order to make possible the use of the incredible destructive power of modern weapons that are continually refined and made more powerful, it is absolutely necessary to thoroughly discriminate against the enemy, that is, to criminalize, to make a monster of, to make a demon of the enemy. For isn't it true that if the enemy is not such a monster then the ones who use such means of annihilation are themselves monsters? And such discrimination is even more urgent and inevitable when there is an overwhelming difference in the fighting power of the two sides. "If weapons are conspicuously unequal, then the mutual concept of war conceived in terms of an equal plane is lacking. To war on both sides belongs a certain chance, a minimum of possibility of victory. Once that ceases to be the case, the opponent becomes nothing more than an object of violent measures. [...] The victors consider their superiority in weaponry to be an indication of their *justa causa*, and declare the enemy to be a criminal, because it no longer is possible to realize the concept of *Justus hostis*. The discriminatory concept of the enemy as a criminal and the attendant implication of *justa causa* run parallel to the intensification of the means of destruction and the disorientation of theaters of war. Intensification of the technical means of destruction opens the abyss of an equally destructive legal and moral discrimination." (NE 298/469; NoE 320–321)

We might suggest here that the loss of the confirmed place of the theater of war by the rapid refinement of weapons in fact underlies Schmitt's thinking on the "spatial order." The submarine and the airplane had shaken up what had been until then the basis of the world spatial order by adding a perpendicular axis to the spatial order that had been a flat dichotomy of sea and land. In that sense what Schmitt calls space must be understood from beginning to end as first of all the battle field.

The second reason for the revival of the just war is the criminalization of war itself. Starting with the Geneva Convention's attempt in 1924 to make war illegal, and also in the Kellogg-Briand treaty of 1928, we see steps taken to criminalize formally war as the policy measures of nation states. In Schmitt's eyes there was nothing so disgusting as the criminalization of war itself. Which is to say, that to criminalize war was to revive just war in the worst possible form, because it must bring about a monopoly of war. Already in the second edition of *The Concept of the Political* we can read the following most cynical statement. In short he says today's most promising way to approve war is to promote a war founded on pacifism, a war in opposition to war.

> Presently this appears to be a peculiar way of justifying wars. The war is then considered to constitute the absolute last war of humanity. Such a war is necessarily unusually intense and inhuman because, by transcending the limits of the political framework, it simultaneously degrades the enemy into moral and other categories and is forced to make of him a monster that must not only be defeated but also utterly destroyed. In other words, he is an enemy who no longer must be compelled to retreat into his borders only. The feasibility of such war is particularly illustrative of the fact that war as a real possibility is still present today, and this fact is crucial for the friend-and-enemy antithesis and for the recognition of politics. (BP 37/33; CoP 36–37)

Schmitt's understanding of the times, as unfortunate as it is, exceeds the situation of his present moment (and also goes beyond the ulterior motive of pardoning Nazi Germany and of pardoning his own commitment to it); his warning signal continues to burn brightly today. It is clear that one cannot return to the era of European common law that he idealizes. And further, because that era was never more than a system of limiting war for the sake of Europe and within Europe, which first became a possibility in having a giant space that opened up to the free colonization in its own exterior, for the people who exist in that exterior there never was a meaning to the idea of return.

And so now, where is our cause for hope? Schmitt continued to talk of the inevitability of the distinction of friend and foe. However he never talked of the friend in the individual, positive sense, the friend that is not the corollary of the enemy. Does this mean that to the extent there is no enemy there can be no friend? Or rather, the friend that exists at that moment is just a private friend, and that the public friend is nowhere to be found? Friends have to exist in the separate dimensions of love and hate. And further, must we be content to merely talk about the world's final interdependence?

The questions seem to open onto one another without answers. Here we can simply quote once again those "final words" of this person Schmitt who continued to think about the enemy that is not the friend and about antagonism as the basic principle of politics. "Theologians tend to define the enemy as that which should be made nothing — *vernichtet*. But I am a legal scholar — a jurist — not a theologian."

Notes

[1] Translator's note: "civil war" is literally an "internal war" (内戦); in the English translation of *The* Nomos *of the Earth* this term often appears as the Latin *bellum intestinum*.
[2] Quotations of Schmitt's work are cited parenthetically in text in the following manner: the title abbreviation, German original page number/Japanese translation page number; English translation (when available) title abbreviation and page number. Quotations are from the following texts:
   1. The *Nomos* of the Earth: (abbreviated NE; Eng. Trans. NoE)
   Der Nomos der Erde im Vo"lkerrecht des Jus Publicum Europaeum (1950), 4. Aufl., Berlin, Duncker & Humblot, 1997.
   『大地のノモス』新田邦夫訳、福村出版、1976年。
   The Nomos *of the Earth in the International Law of the Jus Publicum Europaeum.* Translated and Annotated by G. L. Ulmen. Telos Press, Ltd. 2003.
   2. The Crisis of Parliamentary Democracy: (abbr. LP; Eng. Trans. CPD)
   Die geistesgeschichtliche Lage des heutigen Parlamentarismus (1923), 8. Aufl., Berlin, Duncker & Humblot, 1996.

『現代議会主義の精神史的地位』稲葉素之訳、みすず書房、1972年。
The Crisis of Parliamentary Democracy. Translated by Ellen Kennedy. Cambridge, Mass.: MIT Press, 1985.
3. Legality and Legitimacy (abbreviated LL)
Legalität and Legitimität (1932), 4. Aufl., Berlin, Duncker & Humblot, 1988.
『合法性と正当性』田中浩　原田武雄　訳、未来社、1983年。
4. The Concept of the Political (abbreviated BP; Eng. Trans. CoP)
Der Begriff des Politischen (1932), 6. Aufl., Berlin, Duncker & Humblot, 1996.
『政治的なものの概念』田中浩　原田武雄　訳、未来社、1970年。
The Concept of the Political. Translated by George Schwab. New Brunswick, N.J.: Rutgers University Press, 1976.
5. Ex Captivitate Salus (abbreviated ECS)
Ex Captivitate Salus (1950), 2. Aufl., Berlin, Duncker & Humblot, 2002.

[3] Schmitt seems to have learned this logical construction from Hobbes. In his 1938 Der Leviathan in der Staatslehre des Thomas Hobbes ("The Leviathan in the state theory of Thomas Hobbes") Schmitt writes "there is no right or wrong in wars between nation states. That is the business of nation states, and as such there is no necessity for it to be right/just." This is principally the same as Hobbes's statement that in the state of nature (struggle of the many against the many) there does not exist right or wrong. For his part, Hobbes in The Leviathan for the most part does not make an issue of the relations between sovereigns. However, in one of the exceptional places he does, at the end of chapter 30, he declares that the law between nation states is the same as natural law ("a sovereign, in order to establish the security of his people, has the same authority as any individual has to secure that individual's own safety."). This is the same as saying that the mutual relations amongst sovereigns is the natural state. We must take note here that Schmitt draws out both Hobbes's conclusion as well as his assumption of the actual equality amongst individuals (an equality of strength) in the state of nature, the state of war of the many against the many. Conversely Schmitt tries to see in this a principle for limiting war. However, the great point of commonality between Schmitt and Hobbes is in their placement of civil war. For both of them civil war is "the great evil of this world" with which all politics must struggle. Compared to this the abuses of authoritarian rule barely register comment. But for Schmitt civil war is even more evil than Hobbes's natural state. This is because, as we will show later, civil war is a war (the discrimination of an enemy) that brings with it a concept of a just war.

[4] Translator's note: shutai (主体) — "subject" in the corporeal agent sense of the word.
[5] "shutai" — see note 4.
[6] Translator's note — three German terms, which all end up as "homogeneity" in English, are translated by Yamada into three separate Japanese character compounds with separate nuances. Gleichartigkeit is translated as dōshitsusei (同質性), which means of the same nature; Artgleichheit is translated as dōshusei (同種性), which means of the same species; and Homogenität is translated as toushitsusei (等質性), which means of a uniform nature. The second term, dōshusei, refers to a racial identity, while the other two terms work with the difference between an identical nature and an equal nature.

7 See the third section, "Grundprägunjen Carl Schmitts", of Helmut Quaritsch's *Positionen und Begriffe Carl Schmitts*. Berlin: Dunker & Humblot, 2. Aufl., 1991. Japanese translation:『カール シュミットの立場と概念』宮本盛太郎　初宿正典　古賀敬太　訳、風行社、1992年。

8 *Glossarium*, Berlin, Duncker & Humbolt, 1991, 36. This passage is quoted in Alexander Garcia Düttmann, *Freunde und Feinde: das Absolute*, 1999. Japanese translation:『友愛と敵対絶対的なものの政治学』大竹弘二　清水一浩訳、月曜社、２００２年、p. 41–42.

9 From *Die Kernfrage des Völkerbundes*, Berlin, 1926, p. 11.

AGAINST THE CLOSURE OF THE WORLD: WHAT IS AT STAKE IN THE NEW "GREAT TRANSFORMATION"

YOSHIHIKO ICHIDA AND YANN MOULIER BOUTANG
— Translated from French by Christine LaMarre

At a time when so many voices cry out against the unbearable openness of globalization, against the dissolution of national boundaries and other totalities, it may seem paradoxical to raise a voice that calls for a struggle against closures. Yet, perhaps paradoxically, we see globalization in terms of its authoritarian rigidity, and it is against the globalization's closures that we feel we must fight.

Insofar as we cannot accept America's nationalist and imperialist mobilization, the outcry against the war seem to us less dangerous than pro-war declarations. Yet it is also less suited to the times: it fails to plan or think on the basis of the actual course of things. It conceals its emptiness under a more or less sophisticated and reassuring rhetoric, which responds point by point to the much less sophisticated war rhetoric. What we fear is that the military operation will already be over before the outcry against the war begins in earnest.

We think it a mistake to repeat the thesis of discontinuity in vogue since September 11. We must think about continuity, about that which prepared the authoritarian turn to war, namely, difficulties in governance and in the invention of new regulations. We must go back to the inflexibility that characterized the European repression during the years 1975–85, as well as Tiananmen.

When it came to deregulating old style capitalism and its double (i.e. real socialism), global capitalism went from success to success. Now, however, one gets the feeling that the machine has rather quickly seized up. The neo-liberal utopia of capitalism began to eat its hat as early as 1982 with the Reagan plan to bail out the S&Ls (American Savings Banks) and the two largest debtor nations in the world (Mexico and Brazil). And after 1989, the absorption of the Second World became a financial nightmare. Out of this growing uncertainty of the liberal dream came the G8 ceremony — summit meetings of the seven most powerful countries in the world, plus Russia. When, at the end of the Gulf War, Bush Senior spoke of the new world order to be put in place, the demise of liberalism was all too clear. Bush had to call for the installation of order precisely because the globalization of democratic aspirations (and of other behaviors) had begun to run counter to the globalization of markets. The constitution of great imperial ensembles like the European Union with its one currency is one attempt to create less turbulent, more orderly zones. In this respect, September 11 is the culmination of events, proving by absurdity that the center of the world economy is fragile. Of course, there were prior demonstrations of its fragility — the greatest financial collapse in human history (the Asian economic crisis of 1997) and the collapse of triumphant "hedge funds" (LTCM). The American government partly averted these crises with commitments that ran counter to its liberal ideology insofar as the United States began to intervene more massively and directly into monetary and financial circulation — much as it had done with the construction of information highways.

But of what does this "seizure" consist of? Our thesis is that, fundamentally, this seizure marks the failure of the first phase of market colonialism within post-Fordism, as realized primarily in the Internet and produced in the new "great transformation." Added to classical contradictions (that is, classical in the Marxist sense: growing economic inequalities between North and South), this failure had led to war and to an authoritarian turn in global politics. War is but the surface manifestation of a crisis in governmentality that expresses a fundamental tendency of globalization. Let us outline some of the essential characteristics of this great transformation in order to elucidate this crisis.

A New Model of Knowledge Production

From the time of Adam Smith, it is common to see knowledge production as somehow different from industrial production. Knowledge production is supposed to involve a cooperative model, rather than a division of labor. Thus art, artistic creation and science have long been considered differently from industrial production — as separate from it. With the internal globalization of capital and its external "worldization" (*mondialisation*), a twofold change occurs. While, one the one hand, the spheres of art, science and knowledge are more and more sway over the market or on the operations that undermine the market (we speak of a quasi-market); on the other hand, the industrial production becomes more and more immaterial and similar to the production of knowledge by means of knowledge. Such changes are not without precedents. In the *Gundrisse*, Karl Marx called analytical attention to the growing ascendancy of the science of industrial capitalism, as embodied in transnational firms. Moreover, Research and Development (R&D) departments go back to the 1920s and 30s, particularly in the pharmaceutical and agricultural industries (such as pesticides). One sees a progressive reduction in the autonomy of science vis-à-vis technological imperatives. Moreover, as the Frankfurt School noted, the presumed independence of the cultural production from production proper is called into question. The full realization of such tendencies required only a further "immaterialization of production" (that is, the rise of service industries), in conjunction with the revolution in New Technologies of Information and Communication (NTIC). Thus the divisive model of industrial production contaminated the cooperative model of knowledge production (research and artistic creation), and vice versa. The result is a major transformation in the overall system of production, a transformation so far-reaching that we feel compelled to speak of a genuine metamorphosis or mutation of industrial capitalism, that is, capitalism of the industrial age (or Fordism, if one resorts to the terminology of the school of regulation). Let us offer a tentative sketch of some of the features of this new "great transformation."

1. With the irresistible rise in the role of information, virtualization has come to characterize today's economy. In its contribution to capital formations, the immaterial economy overtook the material economy around 1995. The subsequent domination of service industries was merely a manifestation of a shift of the center of valorization toward cognitive processes. The production of material goods from other material goods diminished in importance, giving way to the production of knowledge through knowledge. Prospects for growth in developing economies and in emerging countries are now strictly tied to this reorganization of production.

2. Data capture, that is, the processing and storing of data in digital form, has come to play a fundamental role in the production of knowledge. It has also begun to play an important role in production proper through the industrial use of small, decentralized computers (from around 1986), which became linked together in ever more powerful networks, such as the Internet (1995) or the Web. This is the NTIC revolution. The very rapid democratization of personal computers (PC), in conjunction with the accessibility of means of transmission of information, has had a profound impact. In terms of their cost, output and this linkage in the worldwide network, the revolution in PCs is still underway. In the coming decade, the utilization of biological, rather than electrical, media will increase computer memory capacity and lower costs. The use of new electrical conductors will allow information borrowing from already existing networks, and thus to lower cost further. Innovations in biotechnology and life sciences (such as mapping the genome) stimulate NTIC, and vice versa. This does not so much recall the Industrial Revolution as it does the Renaissance and the Copernican Revolution. In these respects, it is possible to speak of a new paradigm or socio-technical model.
3. Innovation has assumed a fundamental and endogenous role in economic growth. This innovation builds primarily on interactive cognitive processes of social cooperation. This happens because previously tacit knowledge, once digitalized, becomes readily available to companies, the market and public sector. Technical progress is no longer exogenous to industrial production and social interaction. NTIC are thus characteristic of a "socio-technical system." During the development of industrial capital, forms of knowledge and sciences had remained distinct from industrial capital even as industrial capital incorporated them. Now, however, they become its hegemonic site, the *leading part* of the system. This is what is meant by the term *knowledge-based economy*.
4. Adam Smith provided the model based on the division of labor, which became indispensable in modeling pin manufacture, and which Taylorism perfected. This model is now invalid at three levels. First, at the level of specialization of activities, growth in productivity is no longer determined by the reduction of complex tasks into simpler ones, or by separation of intellectual conception from manual execution in order to diminish the delays incurred when providing specialized training for workers. Second, the size of the market

loses its pertinence in a world geared toward production in small units and an "economy of variety" (as R. Boyer calls it) that is subject to sudden changes in demand. Third, with respect to the coordination of complex processes, the Smithian and Taylorist division of labor is no match for innovation. Gains in productivity no longer result in economies of scale designed to compensate for diminishing returns. These three factors no longer constitute the ironclad law of economics.

5. In post-Smithian forms of the division of labor, which some recent studies refer to as a new *cognitive division of labor*, economies of training come to play the leading role in differentiating markets and determining intercapitalist competition. Autonomy and intelligence (defined as the faculty of providing a satisfactory response to an environmental modification, to an unexpected and unscheduled change in context) become major sources of value, because the uncertainty of demand gives rise to market complexity. In the political economy of second stage (that is, industrial) capitalism, the factory and industrial production dominated the system, and such matters as circulation, consumption, redistribution and reproduction remained subjugated to them. As the commodity form (represented in Smith or Richard by the monetary exchange of manufactured goods) shifts toward the productive consumption of labor itself, it comes to subordinate the valorization of capital as money. Today, value is no longer produced in the factory via the Smithian division of labor. Rather, it derives from a cognitive division of labor in which the autonomy of agents and the formation of collectivities ceases to contradict productivity, for it accords with the new modifiable and modified processes ever at play in production to allow for continual adjustment to environmental changes.

6. This enlarged notion of the production of value had already appeared within Fordism in the forms of financial functions that became necessary in dealing with uncertainty and risk. Where such financial functions saw risk largely as linear and stochastic processes (as in the so-called technology of finance), sudden shifts in production sequences have an impact on the peaks and valleys of the moment of production itself, due to the use of digital data and the high-speed processing available through NTIC. Consumption now becomes coproduction within this "production in flux," for consumption produces that which has already been sold. The market then precedes

production, and production must integrate itself into the market ever more tightly. Consumption comes to provide the information necessary for the regulation of material production, which is supposed to respond in "real time," instantaneously. What political economy was formerly considered *output* becomes *input*, and *input* plays a crucial role in reducing the risk of not selling all the goods. The multiplication of *feedback loops* makes for a general condition of reversibility (flexible production) and for combinations of production and consumption that are at once indivisible and unstable. With respect to knowledge production, this model is especially pertinent because it can account for production–consumption sequences that were unheard of within the order of material production inseparable from rigid temporal sequences.

7. As the concept of directly productive labor loses its hold, reliance on individual performance within the company becomes less pertinent, as does factory performance (productivity indices, for instance). What is more, under conditions of globalization, performance that spreads over a productive territory (and sometimes over the entire economy of a country) loses its hold, while an individual's creativity or cognitive inventiveness takes the form of a multiplicity of affects and information. In sum, creation and invention function under a permanent regime of *overdetermination*, insofar as they become the site for the condensation of multiple factors. It is imperative to resist causal explanation of production that rely on an Aristotelian model (with final, formal, efficient and material causes), for there is no longer any difference between economic, artistic and political activities. A political activist finds or invents actions to take in a given situation, a painter determines which strokes to apply to her canvas, and a human worker imagines a new product. Is this not a sort of synesthetic effect like that announced in Rimbaud's poem *Voyelles*? Such a poem produces neither a sexual symbolism (for Jungian analysis to decipher) nor a children's book of ABCs. One might speak of a "materialism of encounter" like that imagined by Althusser, like the Chinese characters gleaned randomly from packets of tea for Pound's *Cantos*. Some mathematicians admit that the idea for a new theorem comes more easily to them in the cafeteria than in their offices with a blank sheet of paper in front of them. Insofar as the homogeneity of input is no longer a given, it becomes more and more difficult to determine which elements are the efficient ones

vis-à-vis economy performance on micro- and macro-economic scales. The question is not the traditional one of the irreducibility of complex labor to simple labor. Rather it is one of the irreducible plurality of input as a whole, as well as of the dissolution of the traditional division between labor and capital. This is surely what encouraged R. Nelson and P. Romer to generate the ternary distinction between *hardware* (material-machine), *software* (programs) and *wetware* (brain activity), instead of the binary distinction of capital and labor. To their tripartite distinction, we would insist on a fourth dimension that is now essential everywhere, that of the productivity of networks. Basically, it makes no sense to introduce an absolute separation between the two major kinds of input, especially in the case of advanced capitalism. Even at the stage where capital subsumes labor, it is not possible to treat the activity of living labor as simple labor, as simple muscular energy expended to transform materials. If this view is not satisfactory, it is because abstract labor in Marx's theory is not a biological invariant. Still, one might object that, even if labor is complex, living labor, as a labor process, can nonetheless be reduced to the operation of sophisticated machinery or to objectified knowledge. In response, we must insist on the two-fold nature of living labor. On the one hand, it is an expense of energy that will be partly consumed and partly crystallized within the new mechanisms of a subsequent cycle. On the other hand, living labor persists as a means of production throughout the cycle. It cannot be entirely objectified or reified. It remains as an intermediary form of consumption. As it is used as energy, it becomes a way of producing labor from labor. It then emerges in the form of competence, as a form of knowledge that resists its complete reduction or objectification into nothing more than human capital.

8. If one wished to identify the single trait that best characterized third-stage capitalism, one would have to address the relentless growth in importance of a fourth component that emerges in models of social and productive cooperation. One would have to stress the vital role played by the *network* or *netware* as a *tertium quid* between the market and hierarchy. Computing makes network society possible, through digitalization, programming, the spread of PCs, and emergence of the internet. Network society overturns the conditions for the production, exchange, and innovation of knowledge. It thus transforms the possibilities for firms to capture value. Network society

(re)materializes what Marx called *general intellect*, strengthening its *democratic* nature. In the network, every point becomes a center of the whole by dint of its virtual productivity. The network resists hierarchical divisions, making cause/effect, material/means/product, and consumption/production interchangeable. It is this paradoxical situation that best characterizes the network.

9. Four inputs are absolutely necessary for the production of knowledge-goods, namely, *hardware, software, wetware* and *netware*. These imply a central labor for labor as a living activity that is not entirely consumed or reduced to dead labor via mechanization. They also rely on implicit or contextual knowledge. Such contextual knowledge expresses the level of development of productive forces within a society. Yet it is not reducible to mechanization, to objective or scientific knowledge, or to standardization as human capital.

10. The information commodity continues to replace material goods. Consequently, the paradigm used to describe labor power under industrial capitalism proves less and less appropriate in describing the capitalism's mobilization of human activity. Nor is it suitable in describing the human cooperation indispensable to capitalism; for the old paradigm drew on theories of energy and entropy, treating labor power as a quantum of energy alternately consumed or reconstituted. The information commodity, however, refers to language and sign production. The *living* activity of the brain and the *interconnection of brains* have become the major source for development, and so the idea of separating labor power from the laborer and his or her affective capacity becomes a rather inoperative fiction. Similarly, it is no longer possible to separate educational training from the productive consumption that is now part and parcel of labor activity.

11. From a macroeconomic point of view, a crisis in the instruments of national accounting characterizes the age of cognitive capitalism, which calls into question the supposedly immutable laws that economic doctrine had erected. As invisibility and interactivity become more and more common, economic analysis cannot reject externalities operating on the margins of the capitalist system. Externalities, both positive and negative constitute the general conditions for positive growth, for investment, for the distribution of revenues. A paradoxical situation acerbates the "market norm" — transfer prices are not commensurable with market prices, and transaction costs are infinite.

Against the Closure of the World

The complexity and multiplicity of interactions incurred for a single operation have economic implications, generating ripples of positive and negative effects. Such ripple effects defy systematic measurement, for measures of the market rely on calculations of an increasingly incoherent labor time, on marginal utility, or scarcity, or on the proven needs of an individual in isolation. Evaluating externalities becomes indispensable in understanding the real economy. Yet, at the same time, it raises greater and greater difficulties within the framework of market allocation of goods and services, because the cost of the cognitive transaction becomes infinite. The globalization of economic calculus has two motifs. First, operations are exceedingly complex. Second, it is prohibitively expensive to determine a price through market mechanisms. As a result of such changes, growing or constant returns provide a more plausible hypothesis than decreasing returns, if one is to account for innovations within companies, for the adoption of new technologies, and for economies outside the network.

12. With respect to its use, depreciation, appreciation, and its non-exclusive character, the specificity of the new information commodity raises two types of problem for both the neoclassical and critical models of the political economy. The first type of problem, already discussed in relation to the American "new economy," is that of pertinence of global laws to the theory of costs in the case of knowledge-goods. These are close in nature to public goods, and rarity is no longer the fundamental factor. The *net economy* allows one to store information about consumers with *cookies*, for instance. And it costs little or nothing to reproduce such knowledge-goods and information-goods. Such features call into question the principle of unitary prices as well as the ability of the market to re-equilibrate. In the classical economy, only monopolistic companies could consistently monopolize through price discrimination. This is no longer true.

13. The second type of problem involves the nature and the specification of assets that enter into market exchange. The increasingly public nature of knowledge-goods calls into question the possibility of producing them via the market system. Moreover, NTIC removes obstacles to the reproduction of immaterial goods and allows for almost infinite storage of them, which makes the establishment of proprietary rights for such goods very difficult. Knowledge-goods cost a great deal to produce, yet these costs are not

recuperable (sunken costs), because the digitalization of knowledge contents makes them reproducible at little to no cost. The only cost is that of support and transport, which makes it ever more difficult to enforce proprietary rights. This raises the problem of *new closures.* There are the cases concerning copyrights on music being downloaded on the Internet, for example. Another example is the problem of patenting software. The commodification of biotechnologies provides a third example.

The Crisis in Governmentality in the World Economy

Simply put, the new "great transformation" makes it increasingly difficult to realize and appropriate the surplus produced by capital. Because it was founded on the objective, calculable cost, the prior criterion of dividing surplus from net no longer proves functional in the production of knowledge by means of knowledge, affect by affect. Nor does the modern system of proprietary rights work within the network arising form the interconnection of brains, as *general intellect.* The immediate outcome is a severe crisis in the governmentality proper to second-stage capitalism.

If we go back only a few years to the NASDAQ fall, the crisis is readily evident in the disillusion with start-ups, and in the failure to bring the world of intellectual cooperation under the umbrella of market relations. This failure is tied to the emergent space of the Internet and new technologies, which enabled a space free of market relations, or at least a space of loosened market constraints.

The first wave of commodification and closures in the fourteenth and fifteenth centuries unfurled its attack against the human and collective dimension of traditional community (the communal lands of the English villages or the Russian Mir, beloved of the later Marx). It attacked with progress, with technical instruments, and with a formidable growth in productivity. Reuniting and centralizing the three components of propriety (*usus, fructus, abusus*) fashioned private property on the model of Roman law for the ownership of things. It became the basic unit and primary support for theories of natural right and contractual relations. This movement coincided with, or went in the same direction as, the production of goods and value. There was considerable synergy and coherence between them.

Against the Closure of the World

Things no longer work in the same way today. The unity and centralization of property rights crumble with the emergence of NTIC and the displacement of sources of value toward the sphere of production of living by means of living, knowledge by means of knowledge. Ownership of immaterial goods deposes the hegemony of ownership of material goods. Because immaterial goods can no longer be defined by the possession of capital or of goods, access and relationships now command the production of new knowledge and living. As a consequence, classical property, characterized by the hegemony of the right of *abusus* (total alienability) over *usus* and *fructus*, becomes an obstacle. Marx would have spoken of the unbearable heaviness of the organic composition of capital, whence the current obsession with *weightless economy* (*Dan Qha*) and with lightness (*lean production*). There is thus a crisis in ownership, in defining it. Ownership is no longer ownership of a good, a thing, of its definitive sale. Rather, it entails control over a relation and especially over the system that permits one to capture, reproduce and relate life experiences. In short, it entails control over networks and especially the network of network, the Internet. In his book, *The Age of Access*, J. Rifkin nicely described this transformation in ownership, and the ever more strategic importance of the use of information and access to use it. The customer for a given good subscribes to a relation. This relation does not promise enjoyment of predefined goods but proposes an interactive co-production of short-lived products, not only services but also life experiences, affects, flows of virtual images, and memory-processing devices. In sum, *usus* and *fructus* become far more important than *abusus* or alienability.

This is only half the story, however. To make *usus* and *fructus* (*usufruit*) appropriable (that is, to define and enforce property rights), goods and relations must themselves be divisible and exclusive, and certain intrinsic characteristics safeguard this status, such as the difficulty in producing them (manufacturing secrets) or the authority to reproduce them (patents and copyrights). It is here that contradictions appear with the new economies. As capitalism relies more producing knowledge from knowledge, living labor retains its status as living labor, relations of exchange and interaction become more difficult to encode and recode within the market process and within enforceable property rights. There are two major reasons for this.

First, when knowledge or its application is digitalized, knowledge is not reduced to simple labor but to information that can be copied at little to no cost.

Consequently, the network cannot be closed like some old boys' club. The network is open and expansive by design (its form) and by contents (digital information). It is no longer legitimate to close or limit access on the basis of knowledge or risk (the principle of precaution). In his articles in the *Reinische Zeitung*, Marx showed that, although theft of wood was as difficult to repress as poaching, a ban could be enforced. It is harder to repress the theft of knowledge and likewise material processes that are now produced from software or software programs. In other words, in order to make a profit within this new configuration of production, that is, in order to appropriate the fruits of the production of knowledge from knowledge, capital must resort to forms of naked violence whose efficiency is ever more in doubt. Insofar as the productivity of the network depends on it being open and expansive, it becomes more productive when less controllable by the system of property rights and law enforcement.

Second, the wage form went hand in hand with proletarianism. The more the production of material goods mobilized an accumulation of capital to the deprivation of the proletariat, the easier it was to impose a wage labor contract as the dominant form of productive relation. The proletariat abandoned all right over the product that he did not himself make. Only the reunion of capital and the labor force was productive. In the *Gundrisse*, Marx is very clear about this, as P. Straffa and C. Napoleoni demonstrate. Marx consistently denounced the Prudhommian stance that the wage earner might claim his "labour right" over the product. The wage contract made this labor right the exclusive property of the employer. In the new "great transformation," however, a deproletarianization occurs. Whether funded by a public research foundation or by Bill Gates at Redmount, a programmer who develops new software knows that he has created something; he feels himself to be as much an author as any artistic creator. Significantly, American lobbying groups recently led an offensive against European legislation that rejects the industrial patenting of software. They protested that software producers paid with public sector funds had falsely claimed ownership of their software by disseminating it free of charge, as an *open source* or GPL (General Public License), a *copyleft*. They argued that, on the contrary, the public bodies that funded software research own the results exclusively, just as in the private sector. The classical analysis of radical Marxism simply saw an attempt to divide wage earners. In reality, however, this movement begins the disintegration of the coherence of the wage earner as a condition for the exclusion of the

Against the Closure of the World

proletariat from ownership of the product within the capitalist division of labor.

Given that this is the way things are with the new great transformation, we should add that the regime of war occurs essentially as *backlash* (reaction) with respect to the intrinsic contradiction that eats away at the transformation. Of course, especially after September 11, the regime of war might well be called a strange sort of peace in which two states are no longer discernable, whether war occurs or not. In any case, this is the contradiction: to pull out of recession, should one push further toward openness (disclosure) or toward new closures? In its backlash, the United States counts on an authoritarian stance toward other countries. In a stance that is in effect complicit with the "terrorists," who are at heart their double, the United States strive to introduce or to invent binary distinctions amid the multitudes. Inevitably, war tends to hierarchize countries and to discourage immigration. It is also an attempt to outrun the contradiction itself. Its partisans justify American "unilateralism" (apparently symptomatic of a return to the old imperialism) as a lone rational act in the midst of uncertainty, much as quantum physics tries to sustain its rationality, even if only in Prigogine's vulgarized version (see Alain Joxe, *L'empire du chaos*). In relation to the current great change, unilateral policy is more advanced and more faithful to reality than nostalgic republicanism or defensive sovereignty. In fact, George Bush's national security advisor, Condoleeza Rice, clearly stated, "The international community does not exist." Evidently, she refers to the system of sovereign nation-States. If all long-term forecasts are in vain, if the effect of a policy is all the more uncertain when carried out long term, then in fact short-term unilateral policy proves rational for a State. What *I* want now is more *certain* than the acts of *others* tomorrow. Needless to say, however, only the fragility of the process can justify this rationality. If we trust physics, the two characters are reciprocal and inseparable. Can policy that counts on fragility do anything other than to flee in advance? It opts for flight because it adheres only to the superficial aspect of the fundamental transformation, and it does so in advance because the recognition of its own fragility anticipates the coming failure.

PART 4

THE MULTITUDE AND THE FOREIGNERS

THE SO-CALLED/SELF-SAYING PEOPLE

JEAN-LUC NANCY
— *Translated from French by Richard Calichman*

The social contract, and the sovereignty that it produces or creates, provides the solution to the insolvable problem (it therefore does not provide the solution…) of a self-presence that the multitude retains outside of any presentable and *sui*-presentable self. The people can only say *self* to itself as a *so-called/self-saying* [*soi-disant*] *people*. The subject of enunciation enunciates itself as subject of the enunciated (of the *declaration*, as this will thenceforth be the case for all the "rights of man"), but its real presence is attendant upon the execution of the content of the enunciated: the people will appear when the principles of the constitution take effect, since it is the constitution that constitutes the people. Yet the constitution only constitutes them as subject of its enunciated, leaving them missing as subject of the enunciation. The instituted people lack the instituting people, unless it be the reverse.

In all ways, sovereignty as self-institution or self-declaration exceeds or lacks itself. The "sovereign people" are therefore nothing less than the exemplary form of the subject as excess and/or lack of self. But the knowledge of this lacking excess properly creates the people as subject. Not being themselves, the people make themselves into law (they make themselves into law or remain silent). The fantasmatic *self* (the self of the one and only God) makes itself the symbolic and actual *law*. The "we" knows itself as a population of *equals* without regard for the collective or individual *ego*. Thus the *contract* which establishes sovereignty

Jean-Luc Nancy

as *nothing* (to use Bataille's word), that is to say, as the *res* of the people, the *res publica* as *person/nobody* [*personne*] in both senses of this word — this contract represents the assumption of contact without any transgression of the gap. That is why equals are not sons of a father, but *brothers* in the precise sense that the Greek *phrater* never was a blood brother (*adelphos*) but rather a member of a clan-like and religious brotherhood.

One objects to the sovereign people when either they are ineffective or in the throes of totalitarianism. In fact, they are suspended between nothing and everything. But to oppose them, as is done today by a certain left — the multitude being formed in mobile and short-lived councils, in soviets that remain outside of power — is to send them at once toward nothing and everything. The contract as an *unrelieved responsibility for contact* consists in making the people *something*. This is what the Third Estate first demanded. But now as then, this phrase must not be understood with resignation or qualification. The people demand to be neither nothing nor everything, but *something*, that is to say, the *real* of being-with, the real of "us" which precedes every *I* without making itself any *I*, and which thus opens the space of the public *thing* that no identity supports, neither national nor sovereign, being the only real tension of the people toward itself insofar as this tension constitutes its being, undiscoverable as presence or entity.

The oxymorons of the concept(s) of the people represent the *concreteness* of their reality (contact and contract are the forms of this concreteness). The people cannot be founded or proved; they exist, the factuality of contact attests to this while the ideality of the contract constitutes its truth, which is given precisely in the non-resolution of contact in interiority, naturality or figurality, as well as the non-resolution of the contract in any founding origin.

This can be shown by the *name* or *noun* "people." For if "people" here implies an undiscoverable concept, this is because this common noun should, according to the expectation modeled upon theocracy, be resolved in a proper noun. When Rousseau says, "If there were a people of God, they would be governed democratically. A government so perfect does not suit men,"[1] he says two things at once: on the one hand, government as self-regulation (which for that matter is no longer "government," as he says) is not possible for men, but on the other hand, God is not a people (Rousseau sums up everything here by writing *Dieux*, with capitals and in the plural). Indeed, this is why "secularization" is a vain

The So-Called/Self-Saying People

notion: one does not transpose theological attributes without changing the entire scene. If the one and only God indicates anything, it is not within the order of the people as such, but rather within the order of the proper noun. For this name, which exists "at the edge of the language and on the tip of the tongue" [*au bord de la langue*],[2] is that in relation to which a subject *contracts* an infinite debt, and this contract represents, as Derrida shows, the general possibility of the contract, or the "contract form of the contract."[3]

A violent tension toward the Name (e.g., "Frenchman," "Corsican," "Kosovarian," "Quebecois") emerges within the contraction of the contract which, because it is contracting and contractual, that is to say, *not* generative, foundational or identifying, but enunciative, leaves the name of the people on the edge of language, devoid of propriety and consequently designating the *one* of the people as non-one, neither unique nor unitary — untranslatable, therefore, but opening upon an indefinite translation within the people, who do not cease being unnamed.

In this sense, the name of a people must be each time merely the common noun "people," without ever becoming proper — as if, in German, just as in other languages, one would focus on the discontinuity rather than continuity in the etymological chain that links *Deutsch* to *Volk*. Here the same holds true for the name of God when this name is the common noun "god," devoid of all propriety other than the absence of name and presence. In a theocracy, the proper nouns "god," "prince" and "people" comprise a single configuration, appropriating and exclusive. Whereas in a democracy, far removed from "political theology," politics *as* atheology is put into action.

Now if the people's name is unnamable, each person nevertheless receives his name from the people — from the people as populace, with their customs, and from the people as public, through "the state" of the same name. My name is given to me by the people and binds me to them as to myself through the contract existing at the edge of language, that is to say, at once the contract of contact and that of an alterity that the people do not reduce but *confirm*.

The people confirm alterity (the multitude, the double law of contact, foreignness within the people, within the self and between peoples), that is to say, in short, they insure it, guarantee it (which comes down to guaranteeing the excess over all guarantees that always constitute the multitude and foreignness) — and at the same time, therefore, in an oxymoronic or paradoxical fashion, they hold together and separate the one from the other (individuals, groups, networks).

Jean-Luc Nancy

Contract, commerce, concrete, contact, confirmation: such is the declension of *cum*, of the *with* that the people put together and cut up. In this sense, one might understand anew the expression according to which the people would be a "community of destiny." For as soon as destiny is announced as transcending the people, in a task of domination or civilization (of civilization *as* domination), or else as immanent within them, in the production of their integrated, integrating and integral organic body (these two tasks being perfectly able to work in conjunction with one another), then this ominous expression can receive another meaning within the logic and topology of being-with. This is perhaps what would explain the fact that this same expression, extremely equivocal when we read it today in the 1927 book titled *Being and Time*, can also be found in a 1921 text by Martin Buber, which is devoted to clearly distinguishing the people from the nation and nationalism.[4] The other meaning of "community of destiny" would be this latter, where the people's destiny is the people themselves, neither within the immanence of their self-production nor the transcendence of their civilizing or imperial mission, but within the being-people itself, in the contact, contract and commerce *with themselves*, and *therefore* with other peoples as existential or *transcendental factuality* of being-with, which is itself in turn the existential factuality of being as a whole or of being-there in the sense of *Dasein* and *Mitdasein*. The "community of destiny" is merely the destiny of being-with, and this destiny is the concreteness of *ex*-isting in every sense of this concept (from the *ex nihilo* of birth to the *in nihilum* of death, which are the two extreme modalities of *with* and *peopling*).

Destiny or fate, contingency and sharing, the common lot of being-in-common and the banal fate of the absolute ordinary, conjoining *us* all together where *we* separate from ourselves, whether to be born or to die, to love or hate, to regroup or disperse. A union of what by definition proceeds from the deposition and nullification of the one, and which thus defines the fact and the right of the *so-called/self-saying people*.

But in order for this necessary contingency to be recognized or recognize *itself* and function (which is here one and the same), in order that it be recognized and function as a "self-saying without self" — saying self and saying that it is without self, the contract stating that it accepts contact while contact refutes the contract, the instituting people missing within the instituted people — in order that there be something which cannot be self-consciousness, then, there must be self-confidence.

The So-Called/Self-Saying People

Confidence will be the final necessary element in the declension of *cum*. As Valéry notes, "Society is a fiduciary mechanism — it requires a creed and credit."⁵ Society's *creed* is neither the belief in an authority above it nor in a hypostasis of itself, no more than credit rests on the interest discounted by the creditor without also and first of all requiring a confidence whose most formidable instruments for debt recovery cannot nullify the moment when knowledge and certitude are overshadowed. (Once again, it is the profound history and structure of commerce that must be examined, and therefore the history and structure of capital and *value* in general, of *fiduciary* value as the supposed — or *believed* — representation of real value, whether this latter be thought in terms of use or productive labor, in terms of thing or man).

In effect, the *creed*, considered not as adherence to a fantastic knowledge but as affirmation of that firmness where all knowledge is lacking, is the *act* (and not the representation) of that which Hegel names *politische Gesinnung*, "political disposition," which consists of "a confidence (*das Zutrauen*), i.e., consciousness that my substantive and particular interest is contained and preserved in the interest and end of another."⁶ But consciousness as confidence is a consciousness that puts the very moment of the self within the other (in Hegel, the definition of love is not far off, but of course what is again in question here is the definition of love, friendship, brotherhood and solidarity). Such consciousness contains a moment of unconsciousness: certitude in the other, that is, outside of all certitude. Is this not the occasion to recall that, if the people exist somewhere in Freud — between the masses, authority and identification — they do so not simply "within the unconscious," but *as* this latter? We should say: "The unconscious is structured like a people — as a peopling, population and populace."

Confidence belongs to contact, as what one would call its "affective" condition: but affect is nothing other than the capacity to be affected, that is, touched or "contacted." If, as Freud remarks,⁷ "being in contact" — touching in both the narrow and broad sense (metaphoric or rather, precisely, metonymic) — constitutes the "central prohibition" of the taboo (and the proper name of the initiated can be, as Freud notes, one of these untouchables), then this is because contact is dangerous. It is dangerous because it exposes — it exposes the skin [*expeause la peau*], the limit, to an overflow of or in the other, to death or *jouissance* of or for the other. What is given with the people — their factuality as existential given — and what the people give, therefore give to *themselves* while being given, is the proximity and threat of the other, the two together and one within the other, for these are two sides of the same (which, moreover, must first of all not be limited to people in the sense of man, for we *also* comprise the people with those that populate the world *with* us). Sameness is the "self" of the people in their sovereign *nothingness*, which consequently is just as dangerous as it is necessary, just as absent as it is present, and just as fictitious as it is real. *Commerce*, in all its forms (market, sexual, one's company or conversation with others), always harbors this ambivalence: the equivalence of the same within the incommensurability of the other. *Value*, as absolute or in itself, is suspended between these two also as *nothing* (valorous sovereignty and the distinctive value of the sovereign are endlessly exchanged *as nothing, res communis*).

The relation to value thus understood is confidence. Confidence is intrinsically heteronomic, as Derrida underlines,[8] for it is in and of the other, and I would add: it pertains to the other within the other, that is to say, to the value in him (in her). Not what he/she is worth (by what measure? in which market?), but in the sense that he/she *is* (rather than *has*) absolute value *as other and same*.

Confidence in this sense is also given, within an existential factuality. For if I did not have trust in the absolute value of the other-same (which, once again, can also be non-human, as it to a great extent is in certain cultures, but in any case value is *not human*, it is the unhumanizable within man, the unidentifiable, the actual infinity of meaning), then I would not even have a relation with the other, and therefore neither one with the same.

Now confidence is faith — faith and fidelity. There can be no people without fidelity and faith. Faith is not belief, if "belief" is understood as the fragile knowledge of an uncertain representation. Rather it is the entire thought of monotheism in its opposition to the idols, in the Israelite alliance with God or the Islamic return to Him, as based upon what Luther calls "confidence in the sole fidelity of God."[9] To deconstruct this thought is to suspend the name of God as object of belief. To deconstruct is to put one's faith in a faith without God. That is to say, in a firmness that is strengthened from and in the other. It is the Hebrew *amen*, which has passed through the Arab *imen* and the language of the Christian faith, as formed from a verb which speaks of strengthening and holding — in being held and strengthened within the other. Faith does not consist in relying upon the other (as that which would have the strength for such holding), but rather in holding on to that where nothing provides a strength that I could

The So-Called/Self-Saying People

appropriate to myself. Faith is the firmness of impropriety, and is therefore that without which, outside of any *assured* appropriation, we would hold dear neither life, language nor meaning.

Confidence is therefore, paradoxically, self-confidence to the extent that the other holds both in me and for me the place of insurance (insurance for value and meaning, of sovereignty). Confidence is confidence in the other to the extent that the other represents or exposes me, the unrepresentability of the *self* which, being *to itself*, would no longer instill confidence. Thus confidence is confidence in the very confidence of the *so-called/self-saying*, which opens and closes contact and contract.

Confidence in confidence, or this fidelity that the multitude itself implies — for fear of not being the multitude, but a swarm, mob or herd — and which opens the unassignable place of the people within the multitudes themselves: this fidelity is the senseless promise of sense or meaning (or of value). It fulfills no need, demand or expectation. It does not base the *with* on interest, but on itself: on the proximity (*apud hoc*) of the other whose exorbitant intimacy makes us share both death and *jouissance*, that is, makes us share the absolutely unshareable — which perhaps, in the final analysis, itself consists in nothing other than the *co-existential factuality* of the *with*.

Given this factuality, the people are the *so-called/self-saying*. They say this factuality and they say themselves, as they must, through a voice rather than a representation. The proposition that the people are a voice, or a literature, which amounts to the same thing, would bring together Heidegger (the Heidegger of *Contributions to Philosophy: From Enowning*) and Deleuze.

A voice, the trace of a meaning, not meaning *properly speaking*, but its trace or promise. A voice by which the people call themselves, saying themselves. The voice of the people, the voice of God, that is, the declarative voice, resonant and renaming, the *phémé* which, as Hesiod declared, was widely believed to never disappear since it was itself a divinity. Or the *vox populi*, which from at least Alcuin to us reveals the strength rather than the modulation of this voice, the power of the necessity and resistance of the people's concreteness.

Or again, this time echoing Heidegger and Deleuze as well as Blanchot, singular voices, spaced and isolated, even solitary, the solitude of the voices by which the muted rumbling, which runs "below the world like everyday words" and the "pleas of tired and unhappy men,"[10] finds a distinct voice that is opposed to the shout of dictators who wish to capture for themselves the enunciation of the people.

NOTES

1. Jean-Jacques Rousseau, III, 4, fin.
2. Jacques Derrida, "Des Tours de Babel," trans. Joseph F. Graham, in *Difference in Translation*, ed. Joseph F. Graham (Ithaca, NY: Cornell University Press, 1985), p. 185. [Graham translates this phrase only as "at the edge of the language"].
3. *Ibid.*, p. 186.
4. Martin Buber, "Nationalism," in *The Writings of Martin Buber*, ed. Will Herberg (New York: Meridian Books, 1956), pp. 277–280.
5. Paul Valéry, *Cahiers* (Paris: Gallimard, 1973), vol. 2, p. 918.
6. G. W. F. Hegel, *Philosophy of Right*, trans. S.W. Dyde (Amherst, NY: Prometheus Books, 1996), p. 255. (To be sure, I am slightly overinterpreting this passage, whose "patriotism" I do not take up). [Translation slightly modified].
7. Sigmund Freud, *Totem and Taboo: Some Points of Agreement between the Mental Lives of Savages and Neurotics*, trans. James Strachey (New York: W.W. Norton, 1950), pp. 18–35.
8. Jacques Derrida, *Politics of Friendship*, trans. George Collins (London: Verso, 1997), p. 196, where he adds, "the heteronomic disproportion of sovereign friendship."
9. Martin Luther, "Sermon sur les Rogations," in *Œuvres*, trans. Matthieu Arnold (Paris: Gallimard, 1999), vol. 1, p. 245.
10. Maurice Blanchot, *The Book to Come*, trans. Charlotte Mandell (Stanford: Stanford University Press, 2003.)

ANTHROPOS AND HUMANITAS:
TWO WESTERN CONCEPTS OF "HUMAN BEING"[1]

NISHITANI OSAMU
— Translated from Japanese by Trent Maxey

There exist two families of terms that signify "human being" within European languages. The first is "human" or "humanity" in English and *"humain"* or *"humanité"* in French. The second is "anthropos" as it is employed in "anthropologie." The former stems from the Latin word signifying human being (*homo, humanus*), and the later also signifies human being in Greek. Of course, the latter is not used by itself within modern European languages, but is used as a root (anthropo-) to form mostly academic terms (for example, *"anthropoïde," "anthropomorphisme," "anthropométrie"*, and *"anthropophage"*). Still, considering *"anthropologie,"* the term for all-encompassing knowledge of human being (or the human race), contains this root, it carries plenty of weight in contemporary language.[2]

Research regarding human being is referred to as *"anthropologie"* under many circumstances,[3] but this term is not used to refer to "human being" or "the human race" in general. In those circumstances, terms such as "human being" or *"humanité"* are used. Although some difference exists between languages in regards to how the terms are used, these terms — "humanity," *"humanité,"* or *"Humanität"* — are invariably used to designate "human being" or "human nature" as a general concept. The source of this usage can be located in the Latin word *"humanitas,"* employed by Renaissance period intellectuals, and which then came into wide use following the expansion of the modern world. *"Anthropologie,"* on the other hand, appears to have been used to some extent in contrast to "*théologie*" during the Renaissance period. During the secularized formation of knowledge in the nineteenth century, however, it came to designate a discipline that studies "human being" in an entirely different manner.

"*Anthropos*" and "*humanitas*," to be certain, are not distinguished between in academic and general usage for practical reasons alone. People (in this case "European humans") know how to employ the distinction between these two without being taught. For example, humans who possess "civilization" are "*humanitas*," never "*anthropos*." These two designations, moreover, are not selected according to the differing contexts of the same object, nor do they create a simple oppositional binary within a genre called human being. Rather, there exists an inextricable and fundamentally asymmetrical relation between the two. That asymmetry performs a systemic function related to the regime of modern "knowledge" itself (for that very reason, this distinction is made automatically whenever people speak "knowledgably"), a function that constitutes the "double standard" of modern human, or humanistic, knowledge. In other words, "*anthropos*" cannot escape the status of being the object of anthropological knowledge, while "*humanitas*" is never defined from without but rather expresses itself as the subject of all knowledge.

What is the asymmetrical nature of this relation?

"*Anthropologie*" denotes "the study of human being." As is well known, however, the domain of the object of "*anthropologie*" is not so general. What we typically understand by this term — represented by the names Malinowski and Lévi-Strauss — is the study of the life, practices, and customs of a given human group; that is to say, it is the study of society and culture (there is, of course, also "*anthropologie physique*," but more on that later). The emergence and development of this type of scholarship is well known. Although its establishment as an academic discipline came much later (late nineteenth and early twentieth centuries), the motif of its knowledge reaches back to Columbus' time. That motif was born from Westerners' travels into the unknown world and their encounters with human beings of different types. Westerners discovered the "New World," conquered it, colonized it. As soon as the land and its inhabitants ceased to be a threat, Westerners began to take an interest in the strange customs and lives of the conquered, thus beginning to observe and record their "ecology." This intellectual activity took place not only in the New World, but in Africa and the

Anthropos and Humanitas

Asia-Pacific region as well, and it is this form of knowledge that has been generally referred to as "*anthropologie.*" In other words, the varieties of non-Western "human species" that came into the view of Westerners during the course of the modern period became an object of study referred to as "*anthropos.*"

For this reason, "*anthropologie*" does not concern itself with Western human beings in most cases. Westerners, particularly contemporary Europeans, have in general not become objects of "*anthropologie*" (this state of affairs has changed in recent years with attempts at the anthropology of the city and the anthropology of organizations).[4] What does become the object of anthropological study is "ancient society," as studied by Frazer and Reagan. Frazer's timeless study, *The Golden Bough*, attempts to illuminate ancient agricultural society by determining the significance of a mysterious episode in ancient Roman mythology. What this indicates is that Western society can become the object of "*anthropologie,*" but only in "antiquity," i.e., before the West became the West; it can then appear as the "Other" to the gaze of modern knowledge. Put differently, "*anthropologie*" has always dealt with human beings that were the "Other" to European modernity. "*Anthropologie,*" in other words, made its object of study, first of all, the various mutations of humans Europe discovered outside of itself, and, second of all, what could be called the already lost self of modern Europeans located in the ancient past.

In sum, there are two categories of humans that serve as objects for "*anthropologie.*" One category includes extra-European humans and another includes ante-European humans. How, then, can these two categories both become the object of "*anthropologie*"? From what perspective can these two statuses — extra-European and ante-European — be deemed to be in common?

Since Columbus, Westerners have viewed novel "varieties of people" as "children" incapable of understanding Western social codes or norms. These are the "primitives," and they cannot come to understand "civilization," or if they can, they are "immature people" who must be "civilized." In this manner, the difference between self and other is captured in terms of "backwardness" of realizing human "civilization." The difference that became apparent in the geographic event called "encounter" — difference, of which there must have been alternative forms of acknowledgment — was taken into the perspective of historical time and translated into temporal terms.

The inhabitants in and around the land named "America"[5] were initially interpreted according to the point of reference available at that time: the Greek code of "barbarian." That interpretation was not historicist from the beginning, but the added layer of Christian interpretation — its perspective of salvation history — prepared the way for historicizing the position of the "barbarian." Later, this interpretation was replaced by the "progress of civilization," a vision of secular history that inaugurated the age of "Enlightenment." The inhabitants were thus positioned as "those who are not yet civilized," over and against the "civilized man" represented by Europeans. That is to say, they were relegated to the status of those who are "behind" on the ladder of "progress." This historical vision of progress, moreover, was reinforced, and it gained "scientific" confirmation with Darwin's theory of evolution.

What is referred to as "modernity," which began with this "discovery" of difference, is not merely a historical time period but also a form of consciousness. It is a consciousness that positions itself as "new" while at the same time historicizing the "Other." It possesses the ability to translate spatial difference into temporal difference. Thus, encountered difference is often interpreted as "backwardness" or "progress" according to a temporal measurement, and subsumed within a historical vision deemed universal. Under this regime of knowledge, difference encountered within the temporal order and difference encountered within the spatial order become commensurable. For this reason, the two "Others" — extra-Europe and ante-Europe — constitute the domain of knowledge called *"anthropologie"* wherein they can both be treated as *"anthropos."* This academic discipline is shaped within the limitations imposed by the regime of modern knowledge.

"Anthropologie," as mentioned above, is not restricted to the social or cultural domains alone. What is called *"anthropologie physique"* (what in Japanese is called *keishitsu jinruigaku*, i.e. the anthropology of the body) studies the physical, morphological characteristics of human beings. This field is sometimes considered a branch of ethnologie in the broad sense, but its character is closer to "natural sciences" such as morphologie, physionomie, and phrenologie. Its interests and approach to the studied objects resembles *histoire naturelle* of the eighteenth century, i.e. the taxonomical study of flora and fauna. This type of *"anthropologie"* (*anthropologie physique*) has provided indexes with which the age of human bones exhumed by anthropologies can be determined. When biology came to

Anthropos and Humanitas

be socially applied in the late nineteenth century, this anthropology also came to be used to connect bodily or facial features to specific personalities (applied in criminology), or to determine the law-like identity of human beings. It belongs to the discipline of anthropometry.[6]

These two "anthropologies" which are now captured under the rubric of ethnology were, in fact, formed within different contexts. One (*anthropologie*) was produced out of the interest and curiosity Westerners developed towards those with customs and habits entirely different from their own, those who were "of the same kind," but remained clearly "different." The other (*anthropologie physique*), however, emerged from the taxonomical interest in observing and recording the physical conditions of individual human beings within Western society. Its knowledge, therefore, did not develop in response to the distinction between the "inside and outside" of the West, but rather in response to the other distinction between "self and other" within West: the distinction between "spirit and body." In this sense, *anthropologie physique* developed by observing the human body as matter in nature, as in the cases of physiology and anatomy. Still, these two "*anthropologique*" gazes do overlap. The Westerner, confronting the "*anthropos*," treats the object just as a naturalist would treat a specimen of natural history. The customs of the human beings in the field are for the anthropologist, the flora and fauna of the naturalist. "*Physionomie*," moreover, helps physically determine the difference of the "Other." In this manner, the two branches of "*anthropologie*" — regardless of what they originally pursued — can be harmonized without conflict to the extent that they maintain the scholarly posture of framing the "Other" as an object of cognition. Physical dimensions as well as cultural and social dimensions, supplement each other in forming the object of anthropological knowledge.

Both forms of *anthropologie* — cultural and physical — place human beings, be they individuals or groups, within the observable category of "*anthropos.*" Moreover, the self-evident fact remains (so self-evident, in fact, that it attracts no attention) that this cognition is always Western. The cognition of the world (or human beings) is neither objective nor universal. This is so because this cognition is oriented, in principle, from the perspective of the West (*l'Occident*). Within the European languages, the word to orient (*orienter*) overlaps with the word for the East (*Orient*). To orient also means to "direct," and, like a vector sign, a function of power is contained in that act. Knowledge that is now generalized is "directed" from the universalizing West to the rest. I will avoid wading too deeply into this "directional determination" of the awareness we have of the world, and the accompanying problem of the centralization of the West, problems that today have seriously lost their bearings.

Who, then, establishes "anthropos" as the object of cognition? Who, in this situation, occupies the space of subject? How can we categorize this subject of cognition? And to whom does this cognition belong? The answer is none other than *"humanitas"* in the dual sense of the word. Dual, in the sense that the word points to human beings themselves as well as the knowledge they possess. Signifying "human nature" as opposed to *"divinitas,"* this word came to designate classicism, the study of Greco-Roman texts that propelled the Renaissance from the fourteenth century onwards. Why was this form of scholarship called *"humanitas"*? Because this study was the pursuit of human knowledge by humans, no longer relying on God or religion (Christianity).

Ancient Greece became an exemplar because the Greeks did not rely on a mythical explanation of the world, but attempted to rationally explain human beings and the world they live in by employing human intellect and understanding. As is often repeated, they sought to make human beings the measure of all things. Later, however, this consistent principle of explanation was subsumed by the will of the single God who created the world, and Christianity monopolized the framework through which a wide array of people explained the world for over a millennium. Against this regime of knowledge which was based upon scripture and centered upon theology, the people of the Renaissance discovered an example of free knowledge in antiquity. For this reason, there existed in Classicism a will towards a knowledge centered on human being. The pursuit of knowledge guided by human reason was, at the same time, the pursuit of human possibility and of human essence itself. In a sense, it was an adventure to search for what human beings were and could become, an expression of the will to illustrate human nature through knowledge. All of this is condensed within the word *"humanitas." "Humanitas"* possesses the dual meaning of the independent pursuit of knowledge by human beings released from religious restraints and human nature expressed through that pursuit.

"Humanitas" (humanism) thus studies *"humanitas"* (human being). *"Humanitas"* can therefore also be the object of knowledge. However, in this

case the object of knowledge is not natural or physical human being, but rather the knowing subject itself.

In other words, "*humanitas*" is the knowledge of the knowing subject, and in that sense is knowledge based on the subject's self-reflection; that which knows and that which is known are both the subject. This human being as subject observes what itself is and how itself acts, moving from self to self, achieving expression of itself for itself. In sum, "*humanitas*" is the self-understanding of human being as a subject. This self-referential form of knowledge clearly expresses the character of human cognition called "*humanitas,*" especially its independence and self-sufficiency released from the authority of God and the explanatory logic founded upon God.

In this manner, "*humanitas*" gains significance as an intellectual activity in pursuit of the universal essence of that which is human. It is the answer to a single question: "what is a human being?" And the pursuit itself of that answer takes place as the creation of that which is essentially human. If human beings are knowing beings, "*humanitas*" is the pursuit and realization of "*humanitas*" by "*humanitas.*" The coincidence of the subject that gives birth to knowledge, the object of that knowledge, and the knowledge given birth to, cannot but evoke the expression "Trinitarian" in spite of the escape from divine authority. This Trinitarian coincidence achieves complete expression, following the age of Enlightenment thought, in Hegel's philosophy.

Hegel's philosophy, specifically its concept of absolute knowledge, is composed around "self-awareness (self-knowledge)." Hegel, who struggled to unify knowledge and existence, subject and object, theorized this unity through the dialectical logic of the subject that realizes itself fully in the positing of empirical knowledge. For this reason, he stresses the subjective formation of knowledge. In other words, knowledge is the act of knowing and, at the same time, what is produced by the act, the substance of knowledge. This latter form of knowledge is not merely some unchanging wisdom, but is made concrete in discourse; it is conceptually grasped reality (existence). Reality carries no meaning unless it is conceptually grasped in this manner, and the only reality worth pondering is that which is posited by knowledge. This is what is expressed in the formula "what is real is rational, what is rational is real."

Hegel understood this knowledge as the self-formation or self-realization of *Geist*. He first characterizes consciousness in terms of its "negativity."

Consciousness, which emerges from the darkness of nature, confronts the world as nothingness, and in confronting it, negates it. By negating the world, consciousness turns it into an object to be assimilated into understanding and expressed as knowledge. At the same time, consciousness realizes itself within this knowledge, knowledge that is at once subjective and objective. Through this process, the essence of human being that was at first only "negativity," comes to be realized through empirical knowledge. At the end of numerous repetitions of this process, negativity shows itself as a fully realized *Geist*. This *Geist* is none other than the spirit of the world realized by the labors of human consciousness. Furthermore, what is expressing itself in this *Geist* is a totally humanized world that is grasped by human beings and enfolded into their possibilities. In this way the trinity of knowledge — subject, object, and self-awareness — completes its circuit.

In creating an immanent totality, this philosophy no longer requires transcendent judgment or an outside. For this very reason, whether this philosophy was atheistic or not became the subject of great debate. Feuerbach, Hegel's disciple, was able to describe this philosophy as the expression of a human spirit that no longer required God as its basis; he called it the study of human being: "*anthropologie*." Here too, "*anthropologie*" appears. Within the context of philosophy, however, it remains set against "*theologie*," and in spite of Feuerbach's unintentional declaration, spirit (knowledge) as the realization of human essence by human beings is, in fact, the essential characteristic of "*humanitas*" under consideration here.

The foregoing are the two separate concepts Western knowledge employs concerning human being. The difference between "*humanitas*" and "*anthropos*" is not merely of categories, but rather corresponds to their differing relations within the operation of knowledge. Put simply, people are "*humanitas*" so long as they relate to knowledge subjectively, while those who remain the object of that knowledge are "*anthropos*." "*Humanitas*" produces knowledge and enriches itself by possessing that knowledge. "*Anthropos*," therefore, designates the position of the object that is absorbed into the domain of knowledge produced by "*humanitas*."

This relationship does not pertain to the operation of knowledge alone, however. Or rather, knowledge operates beyond the level of cognition. To "know," as Hegel's use of the term "*Herrschaft*" clearly indicates, is to establish

Anthropos and Humanitas

the relationship between subject and object. Grasping and defining something as an object is, literally, to capture it and, furthermore, to gain the ability to manipulate it. It is already an operation of power. Within this relationship, the subject is active while the object can only passively accept that activity. Moreover, to grant something the status of object is to assimilate it into the subject's world of cognition, granting it the right to exist there. Things can exist if they are left alone, but in order for them to be recognized as actually existing, they must gain the position of object within the subject's gaze. Otherwise, they cannot exist meaningfully within the "human world" defined by "*humanitas*." "*Anthropos*" is precisely this existence that is only recognized as an object within "*humanitas*" or its domain of knowledge.

For Western knowledge, i.e., for "*humanitas*," the "varieties of people" it encounters unavoidably appear as "*anthropos*." That relationship remains unchanged from the time when Europeans first encountered the inhabitants of the discovered new world. Europeans came to call that land "America" in memory of an explorer's "accomplishment," but what the original inhabitants called the land was of no significance to them.[7] Ignoring such names, they named the land "America" and took possession of that vast land and its surrounding regions. They described and managed the world according to their conventions alone. In other words, a "new world" was defined, and along with it a discourse to describe it; the world that preceded it was relegated to the realm of "nonexistence" by this act of definition. Ever since, the world can only speak of this place as "America." This is how unknown worlds, alien worlds are assimilated into the domain of "*humanitas*." What was accomplished with the naming of "America" may thus be called the prototype of "*humanitas'*" ever-expanding act of self-definition.

The debate that took place in mid-sixteenth century in Valladolid, Spain between the Dominican missionary Las Casas and the renowned Aristotelian of the day, Sepúlveda indicates that the definition of "*humanitas*" did indeed take place at this time. Westerners, as the subject of knowledge, debated seriously at this time whether or not the "humanity" of the "red skinned" beings they encountered should be recognized. In other words, they debated whether they would be "*humanitas*" or not. What was actually debated under the authority of Pope was whether or not these beings could become Christians, whether they could understand the gospel. Given the absence of biological and racial conceptions of humanity at the time, it amounts to the same difference. As is well known, Las Casas is considered a forerunner of moral "humanism,"[8] and Sepúlveda was also a first rate classicist, i.e. a "humanist" of his day. In any case, members of *"humanitas"* argued over its boundaries, as the owner and judge of knowledge concerning itself. In that space, the "red skinned" people were placed beneath even the *"barbaroi,"* those who do not possess words with which to speak of themselves.

They were bestowed the status of "primitives." Ever since, the relationship has been formalized between humans who possess knowledge and humans who receive the determination of that knowledge and are captured within its rule. This asymmetrical relation between *"humanitas"* and *"anthropos"* is being continually reproduced: the former as the owner of knowledge, the latter as the owned object of knowledge and as a manipulated object to be folded into the domain of knowledge. True, it is not as though *"anthropos"* did not retain its own records, its own knowledge. The Mayans and Aztecs who survived the conquest have recorded the faint traces of their survival, their myths, legends, and customs in several written texts. They did not, however, preserve them in their own language. The texts are written in the Spanish language they were taught by the Spanish missionaries along with Christianity. In essence, the traces of their survival are communicated in the language of *"humanitas."* The *"anthropos"* were able to preserve their "knowledge" because they learned the language of *"humanitas."* In other words, they had to become *"humanitas"* to some extent in order to leave a trace in the domain of knowledge. The knowledge that is produced in this manner is preserved as yet another possession of *"humanitas."*

This structure remains basically unchanged to this day. In general, to gain knowledge (scientific, academic) in the various non-Western regions means, above all else, to study Western knowledge and its methods. Of course, "knowledge" exists anywhere, but that kind of "knowledge" only speaks regionally. Put another way, it cannot be "universal" because the form of knowledge operative in the world today has, basically, spread from the West. The modern education system itself, along with the content it teaches, was imported from the West. The disciplines that constitute the university are formed within frameworks developed in the West during the nineteenth century. To put on knowledge said to be universal, to make it one's own, or to assimilate into that knowledge, therefore,

Anthropos and Humanitas

signifies "*anthropos*" approaching "*humanitas*" and assimilating itself. It means moving from a mere receiver of knowledge to a possessor of universal knowledge, and even a producer.

Modern knowledge has accumulated in this manner. Of course, we can all receive this knowledge in principle, non-Westerners included. However, in what fashion? For example, those who are fortunate in former colonies study Western languages at their former colonizer, thus forming themselves as subjects of knowledge. That means escaping the station of "*anthropos*" and becoming a subject who possesses and produces knowledge, i.e. "*humanitas*." We might call this process "humanization." Those "*anthropos*" who become "*humanitas*" through this process, however, no longer behave as "*anthropos*." Those who were "humanized" in this fashion under colonial rule were often the most loyal servants of the colonial regime; a common point made by Franz Fanon and Aimé Césaire.

In any case, "*humanitas*" is neither closed nor exclusionary; it is rather gracious and open, capable of encompassing all. Because of this, all human beings can approach the types of knowledge designated "*humanitas*." And for this very reason, as "*humanitas*" became "universal" knowledge in conjunction with the globalization of West, it was established as the "standard" of global knowledge. Now, all scholarly knowledge is basically the embodiment of "*humanitas*," and as the general knowledge concerning human being and its world, "*humanitas*" functions as the standard in all domains.

The "universality" of that knowledge is guaranteed, however, only so long as "*anthropos*" accepts it and transforms itself into "*humanitas*." Only by doing so does the "semi-*humanitas*" expand and this knowledge become a form of knowledge applicable to and acceptable by all human beings. If, however, the natural consequence of "civilization" is for all "*anthropos*" to become "*humanitas*," and to do so is deemed the liberation of "*anthropos*" from a passive position to become a yielder of universal knowledge, then the effect of "*humanitas*" upon "*anthropos*" will always contain a one-sided "self-righteousness." This will be the case so long as "humanisation" is assumed to be the "natural" result of civilization. The problem of people who were oppressed and whose languages were robbed as a result of the dominating desire of knowledge arises from this fact. This is also where the question of "whether the subaltern can speak," discussed in historical research and anthropology in recent years, arises.[9]

In today's world, where the movement of Western globalization has been completed, those who were once only "*anthropos*," whether they like it or not, must now become "*humanitas*" to a greater or lesser extent (we might call it "humanization") if they are to speak of the world or of human being. The "humanized" former "*anthropos*," however, do not constitute a self-identical "*humanitas*" that chose to define itself. Intended or not, they introduce non-identity into the world of "*humanitas*." This does not indicate a flaw in "*humanitas*," but rather is a change of "*humanitas*" itself brought about by its globalization. The now global "knowledge of human being" universally contains within itself this non-identity. Only the self-identical "*humanitas*" refuses to acknowledge this. The self-identity of "*humanity*" is something that is formed, and this process of formation itself, it is believed, must be maintained; this self-identity cannot stop the movement of subsuming difference and totalizing itself.

What is necessary for knowledge today is not for all to become "*humanitas*" through and through and expand the recognition of "*humanitas*" as the self-evident horizon of "universal knowledge." What is called for instead is rendering "*humanitas*," which insists upon its "universality," an object of "*anthropologique*" consideration as one version of "*anthropos*." We will be unable to liberate knowledge regarding human being from its unilateral and oppressive structure unless we clarify the kinds of structures and restraints it places upon our "knowledge."

The unilateral relationship between "*humanitas*" and "*anthropos*" determines not only the general regime of knowledge, but also, the deeper way in which those Westerners who unquestioningly identify themselves with "*humanitas*" view the world. The discourse of "liberation" or "democratization" advocated by the political leaders of the United States of America today is perhaps the most extreme example. "Freedom" and "democracy" are indeed concepts that have developed to express the most important values within the discourse of "*humanitas*." Does that mean, however, that people must first enter the domain of "*humanitas*" in order to approach those ideals? If "*humanitas*" is a regime of "universal" knowledge, and if "*humanitas*" ostensibly encompasses all human beings, discourses that seek to forcibly "liberate" and "democratize" people would not emerge. As the "Council of Valladolid" clearly indicates, "*humanitas*" distinguishes between what is "*humanitas*" and what is not, and by nullifying the excluded half, the regime of "*humanitas*" establishes itself upon that "*nothingness*." Put

Anthropos and Humanitas

differently, "*humanitas*" is itself an idea, but it also functions as a regime that is a subject and activity that realizes that idea. It functions, in other words, as a ceaseless "humanization." Moreover, only what this "*humanitas*" brings about is deemed true "freedom" and "democracy."

For those who are "humanized" by this "liberty," however, they can only be "free" with the accompanying theft of language and the oppression or erasure of self, just as the Aztec survivors could only leave behind records in Spanish. But for "*humanitas*," what is being erased is precisely the source of "unhappiness" for these people, the negative circumstances of the "*anthropos*" that must be given up and overcome in order to become more like "*humanitas*." They therefore insist that it is the natural "right" and "duty" of "*humanitas*" to "liberate" these people, even by force.

I will not rehearse here what is daily taking place in Afghanistan and Iraq. Yet, the "Council of Valladolid" which once debated the principles of creating and administering an "American world" is clearly taking place again today, including the fact that the rights and interests of the colonizers are involved. The original representatives of "*humanitas*," the "human race" of "old Europe," have learned through the difficult experience of dealing with the end of colonial rule (i.e., anti-colonial conflicts and their aftermath, along with the colony-less reorganization of domestic affairs) that the relationship between "*humanitas*" and "*anthropos*" cannot be simply one-sided. That experience underlies the so-called "oldness" of Europe. But, so long as the "new" *humanitas* that settled the "virginal land" affirms the regime called "America" that it created, this "new" *humanitas* will pursue the nullification and "humanization" of "*anthropos*" as the natural task appointed to itself. "*Humanitas*" gave the name "America" to the "New World"; it now behaves as though it believes without a shadow of doubt that "America" is the name for the "New World" that must be remade. It thus seeks to place the entire world beneath this name.

Those who do not doubt that they are "*humanitas*," the "universal human beings," view themselves as the possessors of civilization, justice, of universal values. They believe that they possess the right to spread their own "justice" and "arbitrariness" the world over. To be more specific, they do not "believe" this; if "rights" are produced by "power" alone, as a question of sheer "power" beyond all questions of thought and conviction, they employ that "power." They label those who do not submit to that power "rogues," and "evil ones," using the threat of "evil" as an excuse to further strengthen and demonstrate that "power." Therefore, even nuclear weapons are used because although they are the flowers of civilization for *"humanitas,"* once in the hands of *"anthropos"* they become "evil weapons of destruction" that threaten civilization. If nuclear weapons are to be used, however, as they once did, to "liberate" and "democratize" *"anthropos,"* they will demonstrate their essence as "tools of civilization." Effective bombing employing the best of technology does not kill human beings, it destroys the cages of *"anthropos,"* bestowing upon them the virtuous accomplishments of humanitas. In this way, the forcible rule of a *"humanitas"* infused with "power" is established. That rule of "power" (or more clearly, that rule of "terror"), however, may be a space of "freedom" so long as one assimilates the etiquette decorum of *"humanitas,"* just as the *"anthropos"* who assimilated themselves to *"humanitas"* under colonial rule.

This "rule of terror," or the "terror of freedom," is merely an absurd nightmare today. Unless we seriously question the knowledge and self-sufficient existence of *"humanitas,"* it will become the reality of tomorrow. What will help us dismantle this self-sufficiency is not *"humanitas"* or *"divinitas,"* but rather, as already mentioned, an *"anthropologique"* gaze that will closely observe *"humanitas"* as one version of *"anthropos." "Anthropos"* is not a candidate for promotion to *"humanitas"*; it is the term for human beings placed under the gaze or relationship of reciprocity. We must now mirror the position of *"anthropos"* back to *"humanitas."* In spite of *"humanitas"* establishing itself with *"anthropos"* as its mirror, its current representatives have forgotten this, idealizing a world without "mirrors," and thus seek to destroy all "mirrors." Who cannot see the madness of such behavior?

Notes

[1] This essay is a revised version of a talk given on 10 March 2003 at the Maison des Sciences de l'Homme — Ange Guepin in Nantes, France. That talk was based upon an essay entitled "European "Human Being" and "Human Race": Anthropos and Humanitas" [*Yôroppateki 'ningen' to 'jinrui' — antoroposu to fumanitasu*] in *Definitions of the Twentieth Century*, vol. 4 *The Century of Border Crossings and Refugees* [*Nijjusseiki no teigi 4 ekkyô to nanmin no seiki*] (Tokyo: Iwanami shoten, 2001), 35–38.

[2] For purposes of convenience, all subsequent references to Western terms of *"humanité"* and *"anthropologie"* will be in French.

Anthropos and Humanitas

[3] Morphological studies of human being, customs and life forms of various human groups, or studies of the human study of god and the cosmos.

[4] As seen in the recent work of Marc Auger in France (anthropology of the city), there are attempts to apply anthropological methods to contemporary society and civilization.

[5] This name was ostensibly first used by the German cartographer Waldseemüller in his *Cosmographiae introductio* (1507), when he credited the Italian explorer Amerigo Vespucci with confirming that the newly discovered land was indeed a continent. In any case, it is a name determined by Europeans.

[6] The newest version of this *"anthropométrie"* (although little different from the original except for the use of computers) has been introduced to the world as "biometrics," and was used in the recent confirmation of Saddam Hussein's identity. Instead of such "serious" applications, the inspiration "anthropometrie" provided to the painter Yves Klein has produced far more fruitful results.

[7] It is worth remembering that it was the black slaves who were brought to this land by the Europeans that paid attention to the "radical erasure" caused by naming, and resurrected a name from "before the conquest" when they established the Republic of Haiti.

[8] The concept of "humanism" as we know it today does not necessarily arise from the *"humanitas"* or *"humanismo"* of the Renaissance. It does, however, relate to the human-centered value ascribed to *"humanitas"* within Western tradition.

[9] See, for example, Gayatari Chakravorty Spivak, "Can the Subaltern Speak?," in Cary Nelson, Laurence Grossberg, eds., *Marxism and the Interpretation of Culture* (Urbana: University of Illinois Press, 1988).

ECOCENTRIC MOVIES:
BISEXUAL AND ITALIAN TRANSCULTURATIONS IN TURN-OF-THE-MILLENNIUM CINEMA

SERENA ANDERLINI-D'ONOFRIO

Introduction

In ecological discourse, indigenous cultures are often seen as sources of sustainable knowledge; communion with nature is reflected in one's bond with the land.[1] By reflection, immigrants and transcultural persons turn out to be constructed as speckles of a generalized "pollution," "foreigners" suspended from, and not knowledgeable about, the territory. I will argue that there is a specific sustainability in migrant and transcultural consciousness. This consciousness, I claim, privileges the global over the local, and is as important as indigenous consciousness. Due to the specificities of my position as a bisexual of Italian origin, this consciousness is especially visible in the two transcultural modes produced by affiliations with bisexual and Italian identities.[2] As a signifier, bisexuality destabilizes the gay/straight binary, and points to a "polymorphously perverse" primitivism that blurs the distinctions between humans and nature. Italy, on the other hand, signifies the destabilization of binaries like West/East, North/South, and colonizer/colonized, for in the transition between antiquity and modernity it has changed positions with respect to all of them, only to reacquire its former status in the Cold-War and Post Cold-War eras. As destabilizers of cultural binaries, both "Italy" and "bisexuality" point to the mutability of all such constructs. The spaces of transculturation they produce are analogous: respectively, they transfer social and erotic energies between overdeveloped and maldeveloped social orders and between the straight and the gay world. My argument moves in favor of certain changes in perspective: a theoretical shift from identity to epistemic politics; a reinterpretation of eroticism as a healthy, teachable art that enhances one's sense of holism; and a reappraisal of slavery as the mistake of treating "others" as mere resources, a mistake often repeated today any time a plant, animal, or human is not respected as a being per se.

The proposed analysis of three contemporary movies, *The Loss of Sexual Innocence*, *Besieged*, and *Summer of Sam*, further deploys my argument. In *Loss*, *Besieged*, and *Sam*, bisexuality and Italy are deployed as transcultural modes that delineate specific ecological perspectives. In *Loss* and *Besieged* they intersect to produce ecological awareness at the global level. In *Sam*, they evoke symbiotic, orgiastic forms of erotic expression that provide access to premodern epistemic modes where the binary self/other dissolves. In all three films, Italian and bisexual characters appear against settings that are critical to their self-understanding: North Africa, Central Italy, and the Italian section of the Bronx, in New York City.

Bisexuality and Italy: Two Modes/Spaces of Transculturation

Geographically, Italy occupies a transcultural space between Northern Europe and Africa; historically between antiquity and modernity, East and West, the colonizer and the colonized.[3] As a result of Italy's inclusion into the Post-World-War II block to the West of the Iron Curtain, in the late 1980s, the number of immigrants to Italy became larger than the number of Italians who emigrated abroad (Carrara 143–145; Pankiewicz 1999). The vast majority came from countries that were neither affiliated with the European Union nor part of the paltry colonial legacy of modern Italy.[4] As opposed to the Post-World-War II Italy that I grew up in, in today's Italy it is typical to find Philipino engineers working as household help, Nigerian women caught up in prostitution rackets, and Mexican nuns employed as hospital nurses. Many immigrants also come from countries of the former Eastern block. While this flux might have started as a transition, with immigrants passing through Italy to reach their North European destinations in traditional host countries like Germany and France, it soon became apparent that many intended to stay. Since 1989, as the media has often proclaimed, the country has been transformed from a *paese di fuga*, a country of flight, to a *paese ospite*, a host country. In film, both in Italy and abroad, this transformation has encouraged a reflection on how the new situation affects Italian discursive and ecological spaces.

The cultural imagination of Italy evokes times when awareness of nature's agency was widespread. Both in pre-imperial antiquity and in the early modern era, the region hosted centers of cultural development respectively based in Tuscany, Lazio, Campania, Calabria, and Sicily, and in independent city-states like Florence, Venice, Genoa, Rome, and Amalfi. Before the onset of Empire in Ancient Rome, and of modern rationalism respectively, both classical and early-modern cultures were organized in rather sustainable ways. Harmony and moderation were held in high respect. Love was considered an art, and the sacred dimension of eroticism was acknowledged.[5] Classical polytheism and Renaissance holism anthropomorphized nature and attributed various forms of agency to it. Humans were aware of their participation in nature, a revered global force object of their imitation.[6] They represented the human figure in its wholeness and its natural, nude state.[7] The Italian landscapes of today are studded with these diachronic legacies. In contemplating the porous stones of classical ruins host to stray cats and unkempt shrubbery; the historic aqueducts, fountains, and sewers still in use today; the patrician villas on the ridge of volcanic lakes; the public display of marbled bodies of both genders typical of Renaissance sculpture and painting; the curvaceous designs of Baroque architecture and other sites of entwinement between human and natural legacies, an observer wonders about what those more sustainable relationships with nature might have been, and becomes aware of nature's ability to host their memories today. In this transcultural space, nature comes across as a force that one must second rather than dominate, perhaps ambiguous in its intent, but certainly not simple matter devoid of agency. Just like Italian transculturations produce modes of knowledge, so do bisexual ones.

In the 1990s bisexuality was a movement that grew out of the uncomfortable position bisexuals came to occupy in the gay and lesbian liberation movement, whose focus on identity politics had become somewhat narrow. Its bases were the metropolitan areas with a significant gay presence. The AIDS scare only made the position of bi men more awkward, since they were often blamed for being promiscuous and therefore spreading infections. Bisexuals were the "fence sitters" and the "cop-outs" who wanted the benefits of gay liberation but were not prepared to participate in its struggles. Bi women did not suffer from the same stigma. At this time, most bi women activists had formed themselves in the feminist movement. They were expert collaborators, communicators, and organizers. As feminists, these leaders articulated a position that countered the negative stereotyping. Their sense of community and equality gave bisexuality a forthright, inclusive character. Women were its ideological protagonists and they were also at the forefront in the safer-sex education campaigns that made sex-positive standpoints possible in those difficult times.[8]

By and large, bisexuals contributed to queer cultural discourse a fluid and hybrid sense of identity and an in-flux notion of sexual orientation that takes into account genetic and environmental factors, as well as individual and group choices. A binary construction of sexual orientation has so far prevailed in affluent, high tech, and industrialized societies. This binary, which constructs homosexual and heterosexual eroticism as incompatible, has often too readily been accepted by gay and lesbian cultures, sometimes as a bargain for acceptance by the larger society. In the 1990s, bisexuals shook up the ground on which this binary construction rested, to point to the reality of bisexual experiences and practices, both within and outside of gay communities, and to the need to develop a thought that would reflect this reality.[9]

Bisexual epistemology points to ways in which an insider's experience in both discursive arenas can lead to modes of knowledge conducive of more sustainable belief systems. According to bisexual theorist Merl Storr, in a sustainably developed world, "the homo/hetero divide" might prove useless. In her view, this culturally constructed binary "organizes the understanding of sexuality in the overindustrialized world" (p. 8), but does not serve the best interests of sexual players. Vandana Shiva, an ecofeminist based in India, warns that when pre-modern cultural arenas import models of development from overindustrialized regions, "maldevelopment" often ensues, suggesting that bisexual interpretations of the erotic can be more conducive of, and congenial to, a sustainable, ecocentric future.

"Overindustrialized" and "maldeveloped" spaces are coeval in Italy, which, for all its *miracolo economico* of the 1960s, is a recently industrialized nation that barely made it into the European Union. (Italy met the economic parameters of the Maastricht Treaty thanks to the strict fiscal responsibility of the 1992 progressive administration). At the center of the Mediterranean, the country is positioned like a bridge between Africa and Northern Europe. Africa has paid the highest price of modernity, its lands, waters, plants, animals, and people having often been reduced to mere resources, and its ecological crisis has only worsened since the end of the Cold-War Era. Northern Europe has formalized modern scientific rationalism as a philosophy, engendering its attendant concepts of sexuality, colonialism, and the nation-state. Despite the Vatican's continuing anti-birth control politics, Italy has one of the world's lowest birth rates, which of course makes room for immigrants (Carrara, 129). The Vatican, with its global tentacles in cultures with a Catholic colonial legacy, serves those willing to bargain their right to be sexual against legality and education, and the dignity they confer. Lay(wo)men or clergy, all immigrants not from the European Union are tagged *extracomunitari*. Most Italians attribute raising crime rates to them, even as they are known to be necessary for the economy (Bellu, 12; Bianconi, 3; Galluzzo, 3; Rumiz, 13). Many Italians are in favor of granting immigrants citizenship, even though there is no formal naturalization system, and, when an amnesty opens the doors to naturalization, the years spent as an illegal count towards residency (Bellu, 12; Parrenas, 367). This system produces a hybrid of modern functionalism and pre-modern holism. At best, it results in a vague assimilationism that does not resolve the cultural-diversity issue. At the worst, it plays right into the hands of the fascistic xenophobia that has enabled the Berlusconi regime.

Likewise, bisexuals camouflage well in maldeveloped societies where being out is not a realistic option. For example, in Mexico, men who have male and female lovers consider themselves straight as long as they don't "take" (Carrier, in Storr 1999). In South Africa, male lovers of married men are called "boy wives" (Stobie, in Anderlini-D'Onofrio 2003). And in Australia, women married to openly bi men are an integral part of local queer communities (Pallotta-Chiarolli, in Anderlini-D'Onofrio 2003). Even though the recent acronym GLBT positions us as legitimate members of the queer community, we are still constructed as proverbial "fence-sitters" in conventional gay and lesbian rhetoric. Bisexual and Italian communities are thus positioned "on the fence" between modernity's winners and losers. Since a more equitable and sustainable mode of development is needed, the questions is, are Italian and bisexual transculturations part of the problem or part of the solution?

Serena Anderlini-D'Onofrio

An Overview of *Loss, Besieged,* and *Sam*

While *The Loss of Sexual Innocence* and *Besieged* argue about the question of Italian and bisexual transculturations, *Summer of Sam* presents concrete images of it. *Loss* by Mike Figgis and *Besieged* by Bernardo Bertolucci are two European co-productions released in the summer of 1999. *Summer of Sam* is a Touchstone production by African-American director Spike Lee. The films present transcultural spaces between binaries as areas of mediation with respect to conflicts between people of African and those of North-European origin. The films are not *about* Italians or Italy, but all three present Italians and Italy as important elements in the global post-modern landscape. Figgis's film has a long Roman sequence, with two characters connoted as Italian carrying on into the last segment of the movie. *Besieged* uses Rome's historical center as a conducive décor for its interracial romance. *Summer of Sam* uses the Bronx as the setting for a productive crisis in the life of the local Italian-American community.

The diegesis emphasizes the agency of the environment and downplays human agency. The movies have no heroes. Their characters are part of in-flux communities. They represent isolated persons in powerful landscapes and cityscapes and group members seeking integration in the larger whole. A viewer gets to know them visually, in a contrast of close-ups and wide-frame takes. In *Loss* several central characters are nameless, while in *Besieged* many central scenes are wordless, in accordance with the films' ecocentric design.

Loss has been aptly described as an "autobiographical epic" (Ritter, 1999). The central character, played by Julian Sands, is a British youth who grew up in Kenya and came to cinema from avant-garde theater and music. The settings include Kenya in the 1950s; the British city of Newcastle in the 1960s; Rome, Italy, and its vicinities as well as Tunisia, today. Saffron Burrows plays the enigmatic double role of a pair of female twins separated at birth. One grows up to be a British woman, the other is the bisexual woman from Italy whose acts posit the epistemic question in the film's diegesis. There is also a hyperreal tropical landscape, could be Congo or Nigeria, which represents a pre-Lapsarian Garden of Eden in the film's diegesis. Adam is a young African actor from Nigeria; Eve a Scandinavian-looking young woman. As they play naked in the rainforest and its lakes, they gradually discover each other's erotic potential.

Ecocentric Movies

Besieged, the work of a consummate master of Italian cinema, presents the interracial romance of British pianist Mr. Kinsky and Shandurai, his cleaning-lady from Kenya. The film's settings are Nairobi's vicinities, in Kenya, and the Spanish Steps or the *Piazza di Spagna* area in the historical center of Rome. The film stars the light-skinned African-American actress Thandie Newton, and the very white actor from Britain, David Thewlis. The Italian actor Claudio Santamaria plays the gay student who befriends the African refugee.

Summer of Sam's African-American director is also famous for controversial portraits of Italian-Americans in *Jungle Fever* (1991) and *Crooklyn* (1994). This 1999 pastiche successfully combines grotesque, dramatic, comical, and mystery elements to portray Italian-American life and sexual activities in the Bronx, during the heyday of the serial killer David Berkowitz, also known as Son of Sam, in the exceedingly hot New York summer of 1977. The film stars John Laguizamo as Vinnie and Mira Sorvino as Dionna, the main couple in the diegesis.

These atypical films would fit in a queer course on Italian cinema, not in a straight one. Each presents bisexual eros as an important cognitive moment in the diegesis. The Italian twin in *Loss* is smart and sensual. First presented in her bed, with one hand she holds her cellular phone to answer her boyfriend's call, with the other she strokes the hair of her female lover lying next to her. This woman, aware of her bisexuality and in control of her eroticism, later helps a blind elderly woman cross the piazza of a small Italian village when a conflict arises between her dog and the stray dogs that populate the piazza. She shows compassion when all others are indifferent. At the airport, in a face to face with her lost British twin, her warmth wins over her sterner, unresponsive sister.

The epistemological question, "are indigenous people part of 'civilization' or part of that pool of natural resources 'civilized' people believe to be at their disposal?" guides the films' diegesis. The bisexual Italian twin treats the natives with the respect they deserve, even at the price of her own life. Her awareness can be attributed to her transcultural access to mutually exclusive epistemic positions. In *Besieged*, the ghosts of colonialism, primitivism, and sadomasochism play in the field of erotic energy between the independently wealthy Englishman and the female refugee from Kenya. A gay Italian man provides the ground connection for the two foreigners to relate. He takes Shandurai out to gay bars where he dances with male African immigrants, and claims she's the only woman for whom he'd give up his gay life. In *Sam*, a double standard about monogamy organizes the Italian-American community. Men cheat on women and feel guilty about it. Women worry about being sexy enough to keep them interested. Vinnie cheats on Dionna and she ignores her own pleasure to seduce him. But since the serial killer is known to target brunettes, Italian women wear blonde wigs for protection. Dionna's white drag excites Vinnie and she follows him to a group-sex event where she begins to enjoy the attention of other partners, male and female. This turning point in their relationship opens new possibilities the two are not quite prepared to deal with.

Ecocriticism and Ecofeminism

Ecocriticism and ecofeminism are two complementary analytical methods useful in discussing these films. While ecocriticism considers settings and landscapes as active participants in a narrative's diegesis, ecofeminism focuses on the mediating position of women and the feminine in an epistemological system that constructs "man" and "nature" as separate/separable entities, the latter controlled by the former. Ecocritic Lawrence Buell points to the need for a new epistemological perspective: "western metaphysics and ethics need revision before we can address today's environmental problems," because the "environmental crisis involves a crisis of the imagination the amelioration of which depends on finding better ways of imagining nature and humanity's relation to it" (2). Ecofeminists like Carolyn Merchant, Val Plumwood, Greta Gaard, and Shamara Shantu Riley elaborate this vision.

In *Ecology*, Carolyn Merchant salutes ecology as "the critical theory of the environment and natural world," and traces current ecological concerns back to Horkheimer and Adorno's negative views of modernity (5). Based on the philosophical implications of the well-known Gaia Hypothesis, Val Plumwood offers a new paradigm for the relationship between humans and nature. If the Earth is a sentient, live organism — she explains in *Feminism and the Mastery of Nature* — then "non-human" nature is not just a set of material resources modern science and development can exploit and control. Her suggestions as to just what the epistemological changes anticipated by Buell might be are very clear: "Once nature is reconceived as capable of agency and intentionality . . . the great gulf which Cartesian thought established between the conscious, mindful human sphere and the mindless, clockwork natural one disappears" (5). For

Plumwood, self and other must become symbiotic: overcoming this dualism "means acknowledging the other as neither alien to and discountinuous from the self nor assimilated to or an extension of the self" (6). She concludes that the "way of relating to the other that is especially associated with women . . . contains the seeds of a different human relationship to the earth and . . . of human survival on it and with it" (7).

The African-American and queer perspectives of Shamara Shantu Riley and Greta Gaard bring ecofeminist discourse depth of field. Shantu Riley points to slavery as condition in which humans are reduced to mere resources, treated like cattle who can be sold and bred against their will. Humiliating as it is, this experience shows what happens when beings with their own agency and intentionality are not recognized for what they are. As a descendent of slaves, Shantu Riley advocates the ecowomanist project of reconfiguring "everyone's relationship to nature" (194) to one in which there are no "mere resources."

In "Toward a Queer Ecofeminism," Gaard further explains this new way of relating to others emotionally, erotically, and sexually. Historically, all forms of erotic expression have been present in nature, including cannibalistic, transgender, hedonistic, homosexual, and bisexual ones. The "difference" of their legacy is seldom emphasized but not quite suppressed. Heresy, primitivism, witchcraft, and other non-normative forms of erotic expression, Gaard concludes, look "unnatural" only in an epistemic perspective deluded enough to reduce nature to matter the human mind can easily control (119).

My position is between Buell and Plumwood, with special attention to the depth of field provided by Shantu Riley's ecowomanist and Gaard's queer perspectives. I focus on Italy as a space of transculturation between Africa and Northern Europe and on Italians who, both within, but mostly outside of Italy, demonstrate the kind of relatedness to both fellow humans and the earth that might model the survival strategy Plumwood advocates. These spaces of transculturation, I claim, are epistemically bisexual.

More About *Loss*, *Besieged*, and *Sam*

The interpersonal dynamics represented in *Loss* and *Besieged* are traversed by erotic energies that cannot be easily categorized as either straight or gay. The films also present vast ecological systems as entities with an agency of their own, which places their narratives in the wider context of Gaian theory — the belief that the Earth is a being with its own intelligence and volition. In each film the female character aware of the bisexual eros at play also envisages ways to integrate human agency with the agency of the ecological systems that host it.

Buell's ecocritical perspective points to the strong presence of Italy as a bioregon in all three discussed films. In the first two, Italy is a bioregon in action. In *Besieged,* the Spanish Steps area, in Rome's historical center, evokes renaissance holism with its terra colors, marble trim, and baroque design. The curvaceous backdrop is completed by the wide spiral shape of the staircase that organizes the interactions between the African immigrant and her British employer in the historical building owned by Kinsky. The moldy interiors repeat these impression, with their wrought iron, baroque tapestries weaved in gold and purple, abstract paintings, coda piano, and dusty marble nudes. This décor is so sensual that it almost indecorously panders to Shandurai and Mr. Kinsky's spiritual and erotic union, whose primary language is music. As in the popular song, "*Roma nun fa la stupida stasera,*" the singer anthropomorphizes the eternal city by asking her to "act smart tonight" and hold the candle to his idyll; so in *Besieged,* Rome is like a third character who makes the impossible thinkable. In *Loss* too, the Roman sequence is the segment in which the Italian twin is visualized against her less sensual British sister, and where the Julian Sands character meets her and is wrapped in the charming authenticity of her erotic aura.

In the third movie, *Sam,* the absence of Italy shapes the identity of the Italian-American community. Here, the memory of Italy is the symbolic space where the transculturation occurs. The Italian section of the Bronx is one of many "Little Italy's" where Italian immigrants settle and form communities. These Italians are not the ones who, in the 1990s, benefit from the cheap labor of the new, *extracomunitari* immigrants. Italian-Americans are descendents of the rejects of an unevenly developed Europe; the agricultural laborers who, at the turn of the century, fled a depleted Southern Italian region, attracted by the myth of an industrial revolution that would turn them into the cheap labor of the North-American affluent society in which they sought entry.

Second and third generation Italian-Americans still struggle to fit in. They are as grotesque, marginalized, and "different" as Shandurai's grandchildren may someday be in Italy. As Greta Gaard has suggested, for oppressed people identity is shaped through relationships to place, to people, to animals, to the Earth.

Ecocentric Movies

Displaced persons feel "separated from the Earth" (1996, 163), and this separation also often involves a "loss of language." For the 1970s Southern Italians in the Bronx, transculturation means they can neither speak the oral dialects of their ancestors, nor access standard Italian; yet the overtones, accents, and rhythms of their English can be traced back to Italy. The smell and taste of food, the marked facial traits and olive skin, the coded gestures and idioms, the names of these transcultural people trace them back to their lost bioregion; so do their own, self-defensive institutions: the mafia and the vigilantes. Their uprooting is perhaps not as radical and complete as that of Africans brought through the slave trade, but it is not completely different from it either. The industrial revolution, a speck of whose dream they sought to capture, has captured them instead, reducing them to mere appendages in a production system they have no respite from or purchase in.

In her analysis of the location of African-Americans in ecofeminist discourse, Shamara Shantu Riley argues that during slavery, women and men of African origin were displayed "on auction blocks as masters described their productive body parts as humans do cattle" (193). In Lee's film, Italian-American women are similarly reduced to body parts and flesh by the serial killer obsessed with them. This experience turns them into apish creatures constructed as part of that "nature" whose intentionality and agency are denied by the very system they sought to buy in. It is Lee's ability to visually capture this in his grotesque images that marks the authenticity of his contribution to Italian-American culture, pace insiders and their fury. Despite the sense of place provided by the human presence, the ecological degradation of the ethnic neighborhood results in the well-known insularity and bigotry Lee so vehemently critiques.[10] This situation points to what is shared in the condition of Italian-Americans and African-Americans in today's New York City and its vicinities. But it is this primitive, almost subhuman quality that provides Italian-American women with the source for a consciousness that humans who believe nature to have no agency have long-since lost.

In all three examples, either Italy or Italians are positioned in the transcultural space between maldevelopment and overdevelopment, signified literally and metaphorically by Africa and Northern Europe. This space is traversed by a stream of erotic energy that invests players regardless of their gender and is therefore bisexual. For those who are aware of it, this bisexual energy opens avenues of knowledge crucial to a symbiotic understanding of otherness, and the awareness of ecocentrism and sustainability that ensues. The central question of my article at this point then is whether this transcultural space — connoted as Italian and bisexual — reinforces constructed binaries or dissolves them. My sense is that the subject positioned in the transcultural space can dissolve the binaries that block access to a more sustainable future, but a positive understanding of transculturalism is necessary to actualize this potential.

The three bioregions of Africa, Italy, and Northern Europe are coeval. In the Old-World perspective of *Loss* and *Besieged*, Italy is a signifier for the space of transculturation located in the Mediterranean region. In the New-World perspective of *Sam*, it signifies the memory of a depleted bioregion fled by the rejects of the industrial revolution. My ecocritical claim is that this bridge between a technologized, ecologically correct Northern Europe, and Africa's deprecated ecosystems — ravaged beyond repair and beyond belief — constructs these two systems as coterminous and more interconnected than "civilized" Northern Europe cares to admit. My ecofeminist claim is that its transcultural function redefines ecological balance according to its own history. In Italy, ecological conservationism protects not just "wild nature" but also ruins, vestiges of prior ages when depredations were less thorough and efficient. In a way, Italy's historical legacy is a sort of primitivism that equips it to be hostess to the imagination of an ecologically sustainable future.

In both *Besieged* and *The Loss of Sexual Innocence*, Africa is a space of devastation, violence, and terror. The opening sequence of *Besieged*, before the titles, has parallel cuts from three scenes: the streets of a Kenyan village whose walls are being plastered by the military with posters of the dictator who has won the latest coup; the hospice for disabled children where Shandurai works, a sad display of abandonment and hopeless grief; and the immense oak tree home to the tribal singer. The sequence ends with the kidnapping of Shandurai's husband by the military while he is teaching grade school, as she watches and wets herself in terror. This troubled memory is framed as a nightmare dream, as we jump cut to her waking up in Rome, in her maid's room. The tribal singer's voice is symbolic of a lost pre-colonial coherence. The man and the song reappear every time Shandurai tries to reach out for the memory of a Pan-African purity that probably never existed, and is voiced in a tribal language she seems to no longer understand. The opening scene of *Loss* presents another complex image of colonial sexual exploitation. At the edge between the tropical forest and a coffee plantation of the 1950s, a cabin serves as the school where an elderly white man trains an adolescent female *mestiza* in reading. Laid back on a lounge chair, his gaze is on the garters and bra that incongruously wreath her prepubescent body, as she stands up — her face buried in the book — for the purpose of being on display for him. The protagonist, now a little boy, peeps in from the openings that air the room. The colonial planter concedes that "the natives" can become literate, but the price is that they turn themselves into sexual commodities. The young *mestiza* does not have a desire of her own. Her sexuality is prostituted to the Western gaze — a boy's and an old man's. In the final sequence of *Loss* a heterosexist rivalry between two white men — one Italian and one British — causes the accident in which an African boy is killed. The group is crossing the desert in a jeep to look for the right site to shoot a movie. It includes a Westernized African man, the bi Italian twin her Italian fiancé, and the Julian Sands character. He desires the twin, she is aware of it, but there has been no pass between the two. Her fiancé senses the thing, and provokes Sands, who is at the wheel and accidentally hits a Berber boy walking on the road side. Burrows's concern for the boy makes the others stop at the accident's scene, after some hesitation. One wonders if they are really sorry or just afraid, and one realizes that their epistemic perspective might hide from them the fact that agency and intentionality are characteristics of the creature they have killed. After the accident, she offers to stay as a hostage with the Berber people while the others seek help. She trusts she will be less threatening to them as a woman. But her trust is unwarranted, for they begin to stab her and the Julian Sands character barely manages to rescue her body. Her sacrifice mediates the transculturations of Africa and Northern Europe.

The Western gaze projects an epistemic appropriation that reduces others to resources for its own use. But Italy and some of its people are presented as spaces of mediation where opposites can meet and the possibility of a dialog begins. In *Besieged*, Italy is hospitable to Shandurai, with its accessible higher-education system and generous high-bourgeois eccentricities. The house where she works and lives looks like a run-down museum that — even in its semi-decadent state — speaks of its own history. Shandurai does not know how lucky she is, being spared the infested ghettoes where other *extracomunitari* live, often with no plumbing or sewers. One can presume that her partial integration is a result of her lighter skin color, her youth, her modest and somewhat exotic beauty, her hard work, intelligence, and studiousness. She is the "new blood" Italy needs to feed its multiculturalizing society and production system. Her subdued exultation at her success as a medical student provides a glimpse of her possible upwardly mobile future. To respond to the advances of her British suitor, she demands that he get her African husband released. Kinsky sells all his possessions and bribes the local African priests to obtain this. The ending sequence shows parallel cuts of Shandurai perched on Kinsky's bed, and her husband's black finger pressing the bell of Kinsky's building. Shandurai has now a choice between two men, yet is not free to choose not to be with a man.

As a bridge between the technologized, ecologically sustainable North and the ravaged African ecosystem, Italy shows that the higher sustainability of Northern Europe is based on the colonial exploitation of Africa, and the resulting environmental disaster therein. But what is the role of Italy in this binary? Does it support it or undermine it? The bridge is accessible, and generously lends its support to users. But its ecological balance is delicate, and it may collapse if overcharged. Like Italy, Shandurai and the twin are suspended between maldevelopment and overdevelopment. In *Besieged*, Rome mediates between a Briton and a Kenyan. In *Loss*, the death of the Italian twin is an allegory of the bridge's fragility. Their female bodies occupy the transcultural space between the two bioregions and the straight and gay communities. For the female African immigrant this space is a source of inner conflict and ambiguity. She does not want to choose between her African husband and her British lover, yet she cannot afford not to choose because she is an immigrant. For the bi twin from Italy, transculturalism is more consciously and freely chosen. She is an active bisexual, and she is the only female member in the movie team that is working in Africa. Her sacrifice symbolizes the price of the negative constructions of transculturalism that surround and precede her. For both, bisexuality and Italy are epistemic modes that provide access to the imagination of a more symbiotic system where sustainable forms of development are equitably distributed.

Summer of Sam

Summer of Sam provides images of this symbiotic system. Vinnie and Dionna's excursion into the orgiastic represents a return to the polymorphous perversity Freud condemned as childish or primitive. It recuperates a space of erotic

Ecocentric Movies

expression where both women and men unlearn cultural inhibitions and relearn the multiple forms of pleasure humans can experience. This founds new relational modes that reconfigure nature and use the erotic as a vehicle to reach out to the sacredness that agency and intentionality grant all creatures.

The latest serial killer in New York City is fixated with brunettes with marked facial traits and a shade of olive skin. He kills them as they are having sex in their sweethearts' cars. This destabilizes the fragile equilibrium of the Italian-American community. But ironically, under his threat, parking-lot sexual activity becomes even more widespread and frequent. Parents are aware of where their kids make out, even as they pretend ignorance of it, and they recommend that their daughters wear blonde wigs hoping to fool Berkowitz.

The transcultural "Little Italy" presented in this movie is a mini bioregion that has been captured by, and enslaved to, the Western epistemological system, and is, therefore, destroying itself. Italians are looking for the serial killer among themselves, and they find him and beat him up, even though, as it turns out, the guy they blame is only an innocent victim. The "boys" are on the alert, as usual. The pack meets at the street corner marked as "dead end," site of the ordinary small drug dealing, bragging, and scoring. They yell at each other while in very close proximity, they gesticulate, wiggle, and smirk, as if words alone were not sufficiently meaningful. The sense of insularity and defensiveness that pervades their community emphasizes their animal qualities.

His previous work about Italian-Americans warrants Lee's harsh treatment of his lighter-skinned neighbors. In *Sam*, the Dagos and Guineas of *Jungle Fever* and *Crooklyn* become the vehicles for a statement about environmental health and sickness. In drag as one of her paler, North-European sisters, Dionna performs the sexy blonde for her husband Vinnie. She is turned on by this just like he is. Both have been co-opted by the colonizer's gaze, just like the young female African reader in *Loss* who only desired to please her master. Yet, it is this drag that empowers them to transgress the boundaries of conventional erotic expression and join the group-sex party at the proto New Age joint Plato's Retreat.

The scene opens with a pan on nude bodies made soft by the waters in the pool and Jacuzzi. It cuts to two women kissing, as the camera pans on Dionna and Vinnie who sit next to them and begin their sexual play. In this new setting, we briefly see the couple enjoy each other more melodiously than elsewhere in the film; their impulses no longer controlled by the monotheistic Catholic-guilt system. Lee's representation of the orgy glances at a form of erotic expression that does away with the epistemic imperative to appropriate non-human nature, women, and the so-called "inferior." The orgiastic bridges the "homo/hetero divide" that, in Storr's view, organizes erotic expression in overdeveloped social orders. Straight and gay erotic modes merge in this transcultural space traversed by bisexual energies. Dionna and Vinnie's orgiastic experience reconnect them with the polytheistic and the primitive. In this symbolic return to a pre-slavery system, distinctions between "humans" and "nature" do not exist, and erotic ecstasy expresses the sacred energy of all living creatures. For Dionna, this is both new and familiar. She's finally finding her own *jouissance* and is not preoccupied with pleasing Vinnie.[11] However, quickly enough a male sexual player enters the game. A medium shot shows Dionna enjoying, but predictably, neither is prepared for this breakthrough. A close-up on Vinnie, as he is fucking her with the other man in close proximity, shows that he can't stand the competition, nor his wife's pleasure in the symbiotic eroticism. The scene quickly ends with a cut to the street where the two have a fight. They eventually break up, for Dionna's pride is wounded when she discovers he has a mistress.

Conclusion

Deployed as transcultural discursive modes in turn-of-the-millennium cinema, both bisexuality and Italy delineate specific ecological perspectives within sustainability discourse. In films like *Loss* and *Besieged*, bisexuality transfers erotic energy between gay and straight modes of erotic expression; Italy transfers social energy between overdeveloped and maldeveloped social orders.

The films present circulations of erotic energies that bypass gender and point to a transcultural bisexual eros. Italy tweaks the conflation of nature and "wild nature" that governs mainstream North American ecological discourse. It participates in both Africa and Northern Europe and belongs in neither. This bridge across the Mediterranean is host to and produces bisexual women who understand that there are no mere resources. Shandurai and the Italian twin occupy the transcultural space where a symbiosis of binaries is possible and enable erotic energies to circulate therein. Their bisexual epistemic position contributes to gay and straight erotic modes and is contained by neither. It is a prelude to the orgiastic and the primitive, where the boundaries between sexual players dissolve, where women's pre-Oedipal *jouissance* is possible, and where gender does not block a lovers' spiritual and erotic communions.

In *Sam*, Italy becomes a signifier of the signification process produced by the bridge between Africa and Northern Europe. The film moves past western epistemology and taps into a cosmic sense of the erotic bisexuality it helps to access. In the heyday of sexual maniac Sam Berkowitz, the Italian Bronx is conducive of erotic experiments that temporarily dissolve binaries and access epistemic modes that construct nature and humans are equals. The orgiastic experience of Dionna and Vinnie does not resolve their marital problems. Yet it opens a new perspective on the divide that organizes sexuality in the "overindustrialized" world. Monogamous Dionna begins to enjoy the orgy's symbiotic eros, while adulterous Vinnie has problems with it. Her symbiosis sheds a new light on the "polymorphous perversity" Freud dismissed as childish and primitive. The orgy scene is a consensual erotic performance in which each individual's sexual energy dissolves into the energy of his/her fellow beings. This mode of erotic expression acknowledges the other as "neither alien to and discountinuous from the self nor assimilated to or an extension of the self" (6), which is exactly what Val Plumwood's ecofeminist project envisages. Bisexual and Italian transculturations in these three films reconfigure the orgiastic, often dismissed as pre-Oedipal and primitive, as an ecofeminist mode of erotic expression whose symbiosis is conducive of global ecological awareness.

Works Cited

Anderlini-D'Onofrio, Serena, ed. "Women and Bisexuality: A Global Perspective." *The Journal of Bisexuality* 3: 1 (forthcoming in June 2003).

Barolini, Helen. *Umbertina*. Salem, New Hampshire: Ayer, 1989.

Bellu, Giovanni. "Tre italiani su quattro con l'incubo degli immigrati." *La Repubblica* (July 21, 2000): 12.

Bertolucci, Bernardo. *Besieged*. Screenplay by Bertolucci, Bernardo and Clare Peploe. Produced by Massimo Cortesi. Fiction & Navert Films with Mediaset, 1998.

Bi Academic Intervention. *The Bisexual Imaginary: Representations, Identity, and Desire*. London: Cassell, 1997.

Bianconi, Giovanni. "Nelle grandi città oltre la metà dei furti commessi dagli stranieri." *Corriere della Sera* (July 21, 2000): 3.

Buell, Lawrence. *The Environmental Imagination*. Harvard University Press, 1995.

Carrara, Antonio, Nancy Levy-Konesky, and Karen Dagett. *Rivista*. Fort Worth, Texas: Holt, Reinhart and Winston, 1994.

Casanova, Giacomo. *The History of My Life, Vols. 1–12*. Johns Hopkins University Press, 1997.
Cixous, Hélène. "Aller à la mer." *Le Monde* (April 28, 1977): 1029: 19.
_____. "L'Essort de Plusje." *L'Arc* (1973): 54: 4652. (Issue on Derrida.)
De Marco Torgovnick, Marianna. *Crossing Ocean Parkway: Readings by an Italian American Daughter*. The University of Chicago Press, 1994.
Dodd, Elizabeth. "Forum on Literatures and the Environment." *PMLA*: 114: 5 (October 1999): 1094–1095.
Figgis, Mike. *The Loss of Sexual Innocence*. Screenplay by Mike Figgis. Produced by Patrick Wachsberg and Barney Reisz. Red Mullet, Summit Entertainment, and Newmarket Capital Club, 1999.
Gaard, Greta. "Hiking Without a Map: Reflections on Teaching Ecofemnist Literary Criticism." *ISLE*: 3: 1 (Summer 1996): 155–182.
_____"Toward a Queer Ecofeminism." *Hypatia* 12: 1 (Winter 1997): 114–137).
Galluzzo, Marco. "'Troppi immigrati, reati in aumento': Sodaggio Censis sulle paure degli italiani: ma gli extracomunitari servono all'economia." *Corriere della Sera* (July 21, 2000): 3.
Garber, Marjorie. Vice *Versa: Bisexuality and the Eroticism of Everyday Life*. New York: Simon and Schuster, 1995.
Garzanti. *Il grande dizionario della lingua italiana*. Milan: Garzanti, 1987.
_____ . *La nuova enciclopedia universale*. Milan, Garzanti: 1985.
Horatius Flaccus. *The Collected Works of Horace*. Biblio Distribution Center, 1961.
Irigaray, Luce. *This Sex which is Not One*. Tr. Catherine Porter. Ithaca, NY: Cornell University Press, 1985.
Kaahumanu, Lani and Lorain Hutchis, eds. *Bi Any Other Name: Bisexual People Speak Out*. Boston: Alyson ,1991.
Kraniauskas, John. "Translation and the Work of Transculturation." *Traces* 1: 1: 95–109.
Lacan, Jacques. *Ecrits*. Tr. Alan Sheridan. New York: Norton, 1982.
Lee, Spike. *Summer of Sam*. Screenplay by Lee, Spike, Victor Colicchio, and Michael Imperioli. Touchstone, 1999.
Librairie Larousse. *Petit Larousse Illustré*. Paris: Librairie Larousse, 1985.
Lovelock, James. *Gaia: A New Look at Life on Earth*. Oxford University Press, 1979.
Merchant, Carolyn ed. *Ecology*. Atlantic Highlands, N.J.: Humanities Press, 1994.
Pallotta-Chiarolli, Maria and Sara Lubowitz. "'Outside Belonging': Multi-Sexual Relationships as Border Existence." In *Women and Bisexuality: A Global Perspective*. Forthcoming as The *Journal of Bisexuality*: 3: 1, ed. Serena Anderlini D'Onofrio.
Pankiewicz, Flavia. "The Problem of Immigration in Italy." In *Differentia: Review of Italian Thought*: 8–9 (Spring/Autumn 1999): 47–56.
Parrenas, Rhacel Salazar. "Mothering from a Distance: Emotions, Gender, and Inter-Generation Relations in Filipino Transnational Families." *Feminist Studies* 27: 2 (Summer 2001): 361–390.
Plumwood. Val. *Feminism and the Mastery of Nature*. London: Routledge, 1993.
Pramaggiore, Maria and Donald E. Hull, eds. *Representing Bisexualities: Subjects and Cultures of Fluid Desire*. New York University Press, 1996.

Pratt, Mary Louise. *Imperial Eyes: Travel Writing and Transculturation.* London and New York: Routledge, 1992.
Ritter, Peter. "Pride Goeth Before the Fall." *Minneapolis City Pages*: 20: 970: (July 7, 1999).
Rumiz, Paolo. "E nel Veneto ultra cattolico oggi il diavolo è l'uomo nero." *La Repubblica* (July 21, 2000): 13.
Shantu Riley, Shamara. "The Politics of Emergent Afrocenric Ecowomanism." Carol Adams ed. *Ecofeminism and the Sacred.* New York: Continuum, 1993.
Shiva, Vandana. *Staying Alive: Women, Ecology and Development.* London: Zed Books, 1989.
Starhawk. *Webs of Power: Notes from the Global Uprising."* Gabriola Island, Canada: New Society Publishers, 2002.
Stobie, Cheryl. "Reading Bisexualities From A South African Perspective." In *Women and Bisexuality: A Global Perspective.* Forthcoming as *The Journal of Bisexuality*: 3: 1. Serena Anderlini D'Onofrio ed.
Storr, Merl. *Bisexuality: A Critical Reader.* London: Routledge, 1999.
"*The Treaty of Maastricht.*" http://www.uni-mannheim.de/users/ddz/edz/doku/vertrag/engl/m_engl.html
Tucker, Naomi. *Bisexual Politics: Theories, Queries, and Visions.* New York: Harington Park Press, 1995.

Notes

[1] Ecological discourse often emphasizes a sense of place and the bonds between a culture and its physical space. In *Webs of Power* and especially in the chapter "Our Place in Nature" (160–168), indigenous cultures are presented as models for alternative forms of globalization and the new social order the global movement wishes to create. Starhawk claims that "developing bonds to place" (163–166) is essential to reverse the process of corporate globalization. As she explains, "The whole system we call 'globalization' is predicated on the destruction of this bond [to place]"(165). While these voices may not intend to construct transcultural persons as less ecologically aware than indigenous persons, their rhetoric tends to marginalize transcultural subjects from ecological discourse.

[2] I propose to view affiliations with bisexual and Italian identities as social spaces that enable certain transcultural modes. They are post-modern versions of what Pratt calls "contact zones," the areas where groups from cultures unknown to each other met and interacted during the modern colonization processes (1–15, also in Kraniauskas, 1970. In these social spaces, Italy and bisexuality exists neither as signifieds nor as signifiers per se, but rather as symbols of a Lacanian order, stages in an ongoing process of semiosis that transfers the unit signifier/signified to a new symbolic level.

[3] In the course of antiquity Italy became the center of the Roman empire, which encompassed most known areas in classical cultures. But in modernity it became the prey of European colonial powers such as Spain, Austria, and to a lesser extent, France.

Spain dominated southern Italy for several centuries (1559–1713 and beyond; Garzanti 1985, 1323). In Spanish colonial parlance the region came to be know as *las Indias para aca*, the Indies on *this* side (namely to the East of Spain, as opposed to the West Indies).

4 In late modernity Italy established some form of colonial dominion over Somalia, and Eritrea (1896), and later, with Mussolini, Albania (Garzanti 1985, 734).

5 In antiquity, the Latin poet Horace was a major voice that viewed eroticism as a learnable form of artistic expression; in modernity the Italian memoir writer and adventurer Giacomo Casanova speaks in a similar perspective (Horatius Flaccus 1961; Casanova 1997).

6 The concept of mimesis, from Aristotle's *Poetics*, pervaded early-modern Italian thinking about aesthetics. The Italian school systems still values imitation as a mode of learning. For example, in teaching writing, the imitation of models for style and elegance is still widely practiced today.

7 In an Italian Renaissance painting, the frame never cuts off a human body part. Even as some coverage of genital areas was encouraged, frontal nudity was not connoted as pornographic. But chopping of a human figure would be disrespectful of its integrity, and therefore prostituted, which is the meaning of the Greek root "pornē" (Garzanti, 1987, 1448; Larousse 791).

8 More on the bisexual movement and women's participation in it in *Women and Bisexuality: A Global Perspective*, ed. Serena Anderlini-D'Onofrio; *Bi Any Other Name: Bisexual People Speak Out*, Lani Kaahumanu and Loraine Hutchins eds.; and *Bisexuality: A Critical Reader*, Merl Storr ed.

9 The numerous books on bisexuality of the 1990 that reflect this movement include: *Representing Bisexualities: Subjects and Cultures of Fluid Desire*, ed. Maria Pramaggiore and Donald E. Hall; *Bisexual Politics: Theories, Queries, and Visions*, Naomi Tucker ed.; The *Bisexual Imaginary: Representations, Identity, and Desire*, ed. Bi Academic Intervention ed; and *Vice Versa: Bisexuality and the Eroticism of Everyday Life*, by Marjorie Garber.

10 For an insider's critique of this insularity and provincialism, see De Marco Torgovnick 1994, 6–7 and ff.)

11 My use of the word *jouissance* is related to Lacanian theory but does not quite coincide with it. On the one hand, Lacan theorized female *jouissance* as erotic ecstasy based on mysticism. On the other, he conflated the clitoris with the penis as signifieds to which the phallus refers. (*Ecrits*, essays on "The Signification of the Phallus" and "Jouissance.") But the clitoris, unlike the penis, is purely an organ of pleasure, having no reproductive function. My *jouissance* is both physical and spiritual, and is related to women's ability to "be" more than one, theorized by Irigaray in *This Sex which is Not One*, and to imagine the pre-Oedipal as an amniotic immersion into the other, as in Cixous's "L'Essort the Plusje."

BODIES AND TONGUES:
ALTERNATIVE MODES OF TRANSLATION IN FRANCOPHONE AFRICAN LITERATURE

TOBIAS WARNER

> ce que vous appelleriez barbarie est le mouvement inépuisable des scintillations de langues, qui charroie scories et inventions, dominations et accords, silences mortels et explosions irrépressibles
> — Édouard Glissant

Translation is often seen as a key component of what is called world literature, which to many readers is a promising venue for cultural dialogue. But is translation a way of communicating across the frontiers of language, or is it the very act of translation that defines where one language begins and another ends? While it is certainly a powerful tool, in order to understand the nature and potential of translation, we must come to terms with its role in the ideologies of the empires that carved the current geocultural globe and the nation states that have followed. In this paper, I seek to establish the genealogy of European theories of translation and demonstrate their complicity with imperialist ideologies. In contrast to this tainted legacy, I examine how two francophone African authors developed alternative modes of translation, using the borders of languages and literatures as sites of survival and resistance.

Underwriting my current study is Naoki Sakai's claim that translation is not a bridge between languages, but rather what divides them. This inversion stems from the deduction that only in translating can one actually claim to deal with two distinct languages. What we commonly conceive of as "translation," then, is a strategy for defining and managing the difference between languages. This most common representation of translation is complicit with diverse strategies of domination and subjectification: because it territorializes linguistic communities, translation elides the fundamental discontinuity that precedes it, manufacturing manageable species difference out of the singularity and incommensurability of languages. In his *Translation and Subjectivity*, Sakai shows how "Japan" as a nation became thinkable only when a group of eighteenth-century scholars translated texts from Chinese into Japanese, a non-distinct language their work performed into existence. The implications of this way of thinking about translation are more than conceptual. Each territorialized, unitary language is paired off against another commensurable unity — a move that in turn enables the representation of larger unities, such as "the nation" or "the West."

Translation's discursive power regulated linguistic and literary flow through the borders of emerging cultural provinces of the European nation-states. In the imperialist era, translation was subsumed into a machine that processed otherness, driving the project of knowledge that accompanied and legitimated European colonization.

Yet this is only one mode of translation. In this study, I propose that postcolonial African writers deployed alternative modes of translation. Alternative modes of translation are forms of linguistic relation and composition that resurrect the Babel which conventional translation elides. In 1968, two francophone African writers, Yambo Ouologuem and Ahmadou Kourouma, published their first novels — *Le Devoir de violence* (*Bound to Violence*) and *Le Soleil des indépendances* (*The Suns of Independence*), respectively. In these works, alternative modes of translation are a means of resistance within the constraining linguistic and cultural politics of post-independence Africa. Both authors were writing in French in the wake of two powerful discourses on "Africa" in that language: the European projects of knowledge (including the exoticist, travel and ethnographic traditions) and the resistance movements of indigenous intellectuals. The means and ends of these discourses differed greatly but they shared a schematic framework: Europe and Africa as bodies against each other. To contend with these coercive figures, Ouologuem and Kourouma employ modes of composition that oscillate inside-outside languages. In alternative translation, the joining of languages occurs as the relation of multiple singularities and discursive fields, not as a supposedly reciprocal communication between two separate language communities. The usual representation of translation subsists on metaphor and originality; a translation is necessarily a reference to an original creation. The modes of translation in this study subvert such a relationship. The sites of alternative translation are spaces of appropriation and metamorphosis. These practices draw languages and literary canons into a mutual becoming.

Yambo Ouologuem's novel remains controversial because of its many plagiarisms. These supposed crimes form the crux of my argument: that Ouologuem used plagiarism as translation to corrupt the integrity of cultural bodies. The novel's infamous myriad of borrowings contests the "belonging" of language — both the speaker's possession of language and anyone's belonging "in" a language — instead producing an assemblage of stolen discourses and languages that mimics European engagement with Africa.

Ahmadou Kourouma's *Les Soleils des indépendances* is a multilingual composition that makes translation a site of resistance and survival by speaking in a hybrid tongue. Much of style of *Soleils* is drawn from Malinké, the author's first language, and grafted onto literary French. The text bristles with so many Malinké idioms that one can no longer properly call it French. Against the grain of African fiction, which often sought the "way out" through didactic stories and metaphor, Kourouma chose the metamorphosis of language itself.

Translations of Empire

Translation in its imperial form serves as a mechanism for the self-representation of the state and the border control of cultural empires. This particular discursive strategy does have an extensive genealogy. Its use is traceable at least to Marcus Cicero, who is the first recorded author to describe translation in its modern form — as the communication of cultural currency between two communities, not merely the utilitarian endeavor of an interpreter. The Roman orator translated Greek speeches into Latin and praised the benefits the practice had on his own rhetoric. "By giving a Latin form to the text I had read," he wrote in *De Oratore*, "I could not only make use of the best expressions in common usage with us, but I could also coin new expressions, analogous to those used in Greek, and they were no less well received by our people as long as they seemed appropriate."[1] For Cicero, translation imported a foreign element into a linguistic community, to the gain of that community. Translating Greek speeches enriched Latin oratory, and by extension the Romans themselves.

The genealogy of European translation is inextricably linked to the evolution of European nationalism. Skipping quite precipitously forward, the schema remains the same: in nineteenth-century Europe, the benefits of translation are still reaped by the recipient (now national) culture. In this period, one is either translating the ancient Greeks and Romans into the national language or one is translating from another European language into one's own. Translation imports and reaffirms the nation's connection and place in the unbroken lineage of Western civilization, while simultaneously managing the frontiers with other national cultures. One could say it is a way of recollecting origins and mediating difference. Thus it intervenes at a critical juncture in national culture, when the nationalist must make sense of the fundamental discontinuity between humanism and nationalism.

The German philologist and nationalist Wilhelm von Humboldt praised translation "because it increases the significance and expressiveness of one's own language." For Humboldt, the genius of language is universal, but the form it inhabits is national. "It is a marvelous feature of languages," he wrote in the preface to his translation of Aeschylus, "that they all first reach into the usual habits of life, after which they can be improved on *ad infinitum* into something nobler and more complex by the spirit of the nation that shapes them."[2] The European nation was forever improving itself and its language through the translation and imitation of the ancient Greeks. Humboldt could point to no greater step in the refinement of German national character than Johann Voss' translations of the Greek and Latin classics.

The translation of other European literatures also benefited the national culture. This dynamic was often figured along the lines of economic exchange. Johann Wolfgang von Goethe, Humboldt's contemporary, likened the translator to a merchant in the "general spiritual commerce" of the world, the free market of self-interested nationalist literatures.[3] But as a mediator (or enforcer) of cultural difference, the translator was also a potential traitor. While translation could benefit the national literature through a trace amount of the Other, the nation also ran the risk of infection. "When you offer a translation to a nation," wrote Victor Hugo, "that nation will almost always look on the translation as an act of violence against itself."[4] This is the stuff of bourgeois hysteria, a nation's fear of "infusing the substance of another people into its own very life-blood." Hugo, consummate anti-bourgeois that he was, believed that a certain "forced introduction of the cosmopolitan into local taste" was necessary for the health of the nation. But despite his irony and satire, the basic viability and distinctiveness of national culture was not in question. As in Humboldt's writings, a trace amount of foreignness will improve the national culture. Though violent, translations are beneficial only insofar as they add to national literatures.

The representation of translation as the transference of the spirit of one civilization into another played an even more important role in the ideology of empire, from the Holy Roman Empire to the European imperialism of the nineteenth and twentieth centuries. In his seminal study of European-American imperialism in the New World, Eric Cheyfitz identified a crucial component of the poetics of imperialism: the *translatio studii et imperii*. "*Translatio*" is a form of cultural metempsychosis in which learning and empire pass from one body to another.[5] The germ of the *translatio* was Ecclesiastes 10:8 — "Because of unrighteous dealings, injuries, and riches got by deceit, the kingdom is transferred from one people to another" — which medieval historians used to make sense of the fall of Rome and the ensuing mobility of Christendom.[6] When the Roman Empire fell, a new empire could rise and become legitimate by translating the old empire and its learning into itself. Empire had to be re-translated in order to be renewed. The idea outlasted the Middle Ages; a variant of the *translatio* ideology is at work in the nineteenth-century discourse cited above. The Greeks again had to be translated, in order to improve and legitimate the cultural project. And when the European nation-states expanded into imperial powers, the *translatio* turned outward. The ancients were not merely translated into the national culture; the national culture had to be translated outside of itself onto uncivilized peoples. In *The Poetics of Imperialism*, Cheyftiz shows that the terms of empire were terms of translation: proper and literal versus savage and figurative. Only in this schema could the native become a barbarian, and thereby be dehumanized and dispossessed. In the imperialist *translatio*, the native was translated into the terms of empire (the proper), only to be excluded from it as a barbarian or a savage (the figurative).[7]

> The European process of translation...displaced or attempted to displace...Native Americans into the realm of the proper, into that place where the relation between *property* and *identity* is inviolable, not so these Americans could possess the proper but so that having been translated into it they could be dispossessed of it (of what, that is, they never possessed) and relegated to the territory of the figurative.[8]

It might seem reductive, or at least hasty, to assume that the same formula of *translatio* is at work in multiple European colonization projects. Therefore permit me to briefly invoke the remarks of Otto Van Bismarck, in Protocol No. 1 of the 1884–5 Berlin West African Conference, when Africa was partitioned among imperial powers of Europe.

> In convoking the Conference, the Imperial Government was guided by the conviction that all the Governments invited share the wish to *bring the natives of Africa within the pale of civilization by opening up the interior of that continent to commerce, by giving its inhabitants the means of instructing themselves, by encouraging missions and enterprises calculated to spread useful knowledge*, and by preparing the way for the suppression of slavery. [9]

Translatio brings the learning of the empire to the natives while it dispossesses them of their property. The legal and performative power of the Berlin conference was effectively translational: by extending the limits of the civilized world, the natives no longer existed outside it; what they never owned as such became property, to which they then had no right, since they were savages. [10]

The transubstantiation of civilization always leaves a residue. The passing of European colonialism and capitalist expansion into other forms of domination was no different. In the decade immediately following independence, a specter was haunting the former West African colonies. Since the *translatio* operated through the figure of translation, this haunting was linguistic. French decolonization left an amorphous structure called *francophonie* in its wake. *Francophonie* is a theory of the post-colonial French-speaking space based on the idea of shared language: former colonies can share in the universal, humanistic fruits of French civilization through their access to the French language. *Francophonie* is arguably a form of *translatio* ideology that has outlasted the empire itself. France is both at the center of *francophonie* as the locus of universal humanist values, and continually exporting itself. It is theoretically open to the changes it will undergo in francophone mouths, and indeed combinations of French and local languages are the vernacular all over urban West Africa. Yet, as Christopher Miller has pointed out, the space of *francophonie* admits no such changes to the French language in its literary form. The prominence of *francophonie* in the cultural life of newly independent West Africa foreclosed certain linguistic possibilities. Writers within its field could not absolutely reject the *studii*, or learning of empire. This is partly why *francophone* authors developed

Bodies and Tongues

alternative modes of translation while continuing to write in French, while anglophone writers broke more readily with imperial languages.[11]

As well as these linguistic constraints, the two novelists in this study had to contend with the place of Africa in French-language discourse. Francophone African literature in the 1960s was caught between what are referred to as the Africanist and Nativist discourses — thoroughly unpacked by Christopher Miller and Anthony Appiah, respectively. The Africanist tradition in French literature figured Africa as a blank slate, without history, but available to Europeans as a shadowy figure of savagery or origin — purely primitive raw material.[12] The Nativist movements, most notably Negritude, sought to valorize and make present what "Africa" was missing in European discourse (culture, history, philosophy, literature). By and large this meant a retreat into an idealized, pre-colonial past or a broadly essentialist pan-African vision.[13] The Nativist response was both the admission and celebration of monolithic difference. Leopold Senghor's essentialist formulation of the Negritude project typified this strategy of reverse discourse, and was widely influential among African intellectuals at the time of independence. In its attempt to revivify African culture and reconnect it with the glories of its vanished empires, Negritude employed its own version of the *translatio studii et imperii*. Artists could "resuscitate" African culture by translating the essence of African-ness into French.

"Orientalism," writes Edward Said, "[is] a Western style for dominating, restructuring, and having authority over the Orient.... ."[14] Africanist discourse operated along similar lines, but the status of "Africa" was considerably different. In contrast to the "Orient," Africa offers itself as a blank in Western discourse, an absolute zero, the absence of history and rationality. In this sense, Christopher Miller argues, it is the opposite of the overdetermined Orient: "Africa is the Other's other, the Orient's orient."[15] "Africa" represents the failure of the European discourses of knowing that constructed the Orient. Africanist discourse was always wary of the knowledge it offered about Africa, for the continent was a giant dark spot, an unknowable darkness. "Darkness," Miller writes, "can be known only by shedding light on it; that is, it cannot be "known" as such."[16] Thus "Africa" is a negation, an absent third entity in the cultural hierarchy of the Orient and West that gives both intelligibility. The *translatio* helped construct "Africa," because an absence can only receive culture from outside itself.[17] Africanist discourse was a dangerous project of knowledge, however: in "Africa" the *translatio* encounters its own foundational negation — the complete absence of culture as such. The hysteria this produces is precisely where Yambo Ouologuem's *Le Devoir de violence* seizes the reigns of translation.

The Bodies of Yambo Ouologuem

> *But what shall I say about those who really deserve to be called traitors, rather than translators, since they betray the authors they try to make known, robbing them of their glory and, at the same time, seducing ignorant readers by showing them black instead of white?*
> — Joachim Du Bellay

The Malian Yambo Ouologuem emerged onto the French literary scene as something of a prodigy. A graduate of L'Ecole Normale Superieure, his first novel, *Le Devoir de violence,* was published by Les Éditions du Seuil. It became the first novel by an African to be awarded the Prix Renaudot. In 1972, however, Ouologuem's success turned sour and he was accused of plagiarism. Critics began identifying a staggering number and variety of borrowings from sources as diverse as Graham Greene, André Schwartz-Bart, Shakespeare, African epics and the work of early anthropologists. The scandal reached its height when the *Times Literary Supplement* published a passage from Ouologuem's novel alongside a passage from Graham Greene's *It's a Battlefield*. The two were nearly identical. Greene quietly expressed his wishes to Ouologuem's publishers and, after a brief controversy in the French literary press, *Le Devoir de violence* was withdrawn from circulation. Ouologuem has since abandoned writing in French.[18]

The book was controversial even before its borrowings were discovered, because of Ouologuem's portrayal of an African past overflowing with the exploitation and enslavement of the masses by the ruling elite. The narrative constantly revels in scene after scene of extraordinarily sadistic violence. If text is an intervention in Africanist and Nativist discourses, it does not intervene from outside. Ouologuem recycles the "savage continent" tropes of the Africanists and proceeds to ruthlessly satirize the reliance of Nativist projects on the ancient African empires for their legitimacy. With dizzying intertextuality and blistering omni-criticism, Ouologuem inserts these discourses into each other and himself in the middle, making everything inseparable — mutually destructive *and* constitutive. This move undermines both discursive strategies from an ambiguous and thoroughly compromised position. Ouologuem somehow succeeds at using pornography, sadism and sensationalism to lure in the European reader while presenting a satire of nationalism and its mythmaking to the African reader. All of this in borrowed language — or language that *could be borrowed*, for the presence of these fragments of adaptation throws the authenticity of the whole text into question. After the bloody orgy of *Le Devoir de violence*, it is no longer possible to ascertain what belongs to whom. This is as true of Ouologuem's borrowings as it is of his characters, but it is especially devastating with regard to putative totalities of cultures and languages. By performing the inversion that links Africanism to Nativism, Ouologuem makes it impossible to say where "Europe" ends and where "Africa" begins.

Most of the critical rehabilitation of Ouologuem's work in recent years has focused on his European borrowings, casting him as a sort of post-structuralist African saboteur. This approach produced many of the most astute readings of the novel,[19] but it has overlooked the wealth of African sources — oral and written — in the novel. In a promising study, Thomas Hale identifies the *Tarîkh es-Soudan* and the *Tarîkh el-Fettâch* (the chronicles of Askia Mohammad, the sixteenth-century conqueror who expanded and islamicized the Songhay empire) as a source for Ouologuem's poetics and a target of his polemics.[20] Hale demonstrates how Ouologuem adapts the chronicles into his portrayal of the Saïfs, who rule the fictional kingdom of Nakem in the novel. The Saïfs are portrayed as cruel and decadent rulers, and though there is a basis for this in the chronicles, Ouologuem greatly exaggerates it. Hale argues that Ouologuem mines the medieval epics for their salacious and gory bits, hyperbolizing them as a lure for European readers. Ouologuem's narrator also piles doubt on the chronicles' reliability, distances them from his own account and questions their role in perpetuating the social order.

Ouologuem's novel reinterprets the Songhay rulers to trap European readers with sensationalism, and critique the way in which the Songhay past informs the social hierarchy of the Sahel to this day. Hale reads the novel's sympathies as lying with *négraille*, the oppressed masses, since Ouologuem himself is Dogon, a traditionally animist ethnic group who resisted islamicization by the Songhay conquerors during the sixteenth century. As a result of another Islamic conquest in the nineteenth century, this time by El Hadj Umar Tall, a small number of Dogon were converted and this Muslim elite continues to be politically dominant. Thus the castigation of Muslim rulers comes into clearer focus for Hale: "for those of his readers who see Sahelian history from a Dogon perspective, the demystifying portrayals of the powerful Songhay rulers must generate smiles of recognition."[21]

The only problem with this account is Ouologuem's own polyvalent identity. He is Dogon *and* from an elite Muslim family. His family was likely among the Dogon who converted to Tijaniya Islam during El Hadj Umar Tall's *jihad*. The Tall family is still powerful in Bandiagara — Ouologuem's birthplace — and the Dogon who converted, joined a privileged Tidjaniya Muslim elite. Based on his explorations of Ouologuem's background in Bandiagara, Christopher Wise suggests the Talls as a possible fit for the Saïfs.[22] He describes the Dogon sentiment towards the Talls as ranging from ambivalence to resentment. So perhaps it is possible to read *Le Devoir de violence* as self-critique: Ouologuem's background as torn between the ruling aristocracy (of the Saïfs) and the *négraille* (in which he includes the "N'Dogos," an anagram of "Dogons"). Indeed, the way Ouologuem's own cross-identifications informed *Le Devoir de violence* has gone largely unnoticed by Euro-American critics.

As close as this angle comes to dubious authorial criticism, it opens a new approach to Ouologuem's intertextuality. Throughout the scandal and even the recent rehabilitation, critics have taken for granted that Ouologuem was reacting against the classic Western concept of originality. While Ouologuem obviously was chafing at the West's fetishism of originality and doubtless knew how his borrowings would be received, there remains another potential source for his poetics. As I mentioned, Ouologuem is a Tijiane Muslim. The Tijaniyya are one of the major Sufi Muslim brotherhoods that dominate Islam in West Africa. Bandiagara, Ouologuem's birthplace, holds special significance for the Tijaniyya. El Hadj Umar Tall, the nineteenth-century conqueror who spread the brotherhood's influence across the Sahel perished in a nearby cave. Bandiagara was also at the center of certain key doctrinal upheavals. The feature of the Tijaniyya that has special importance for Ouologuem's poetics is the brotherhood's affection for book learning and the minutiae of Arabic scholarship. In West Africa, I often heard the Tijaniyya referred to as *"la confrèrie du livre,"* the brotherhood of the book. In their orientation they are distinctly arabophile. Growing up in a Tijiane family, Ouologuem almost certainly enjoyed as thorough a religious and cultural immersion in Arab learning as he did in Western culture at the École Normale Supérieure. And it is in Arab literary criticism that we find a different notion of plagiarism.[23] The conventions of classical Arabic poetry drastically limited what the poet could write about and how he could do so. Perhaps for a European author a limited range of themes and treatments seems stifling, but as Gustav Von Grunebaum notes, this was not the case.

> The comparatively small number of motives admitted to literary treatment by the conventions of Arabic poetry has, in nearly all periods, compelled the individual poet to make his contribution within a strictly drawn circle of accepted subject matter. Such restriction of the poet's freedom ... of necessity makes for repetitiousness and a certain lack of invention. To the modern reader, indeed, this stifling rule of convention would seem to eliminate even the possibility of originality.[24]

The response was the development of techniques of improvisation and reference within these constraints. Both poet and audience developed tastes for "modifications and embellishments of the traditional treatment."[25] A poem's worth derived from the esthetic strength of its reworkings and reference to tradition, not from its providential "genius." "The Arabic concept of originality," Grunebaum writes, "and hence the concept of plagiarism as well, do not coincide with those that have been current in the West for the last three or four centuries."[26]

The term for such borrowings was *sariqat*. In his examination of the collections of *sariqat* compiled by Arab scholars, Wolfhart Heinrichs expands considerably on Grunebaum's study. Heinrichs identifies several different forms of borrowing. The general notion of *sariqat* holds that a poet developed his right to his borrowings through the improvements he made. "The common denominator of 'good' *sariqa*," Heinrichs writes, "is that it endows one's poem with a quality of intertextuality which for the connoisseur enriches it beyond what its mere words say."[27] Even at their most literal, Ouologuem's many borrowings always have an added angle or two for the reader who tracks down their source.

This is especially true of his most famous "plagiarisms," in which we find alternative translation at work. Two borrowings in particular led to the scandal that ruined him. In 1972, two separate discoveries blew the case wide open. Eric Sellin noted the similarities of certain passages to Schwartz-Bart's *Le Dernier des justes* in an article in *Research in African Literatures*.[28] Legally, however, it was not the Schwartz-Bart borrowings that triggered the backlash. The most infamous borrowing of all comes from Graham Greene's *It's a Battlefield*. As the story goes, a researcher in Australia first discovered the borrowings and informed Greene. On May 5, 1972, the London *Times* published two articles concerning the burgeoning scandal: a front page news report discussing the withdrawal of the novel from various markets, and a sensational piece in the *Literary Supplement* (TLS) that placed passages from *Le devoir de violence* and *It's a Battlefield* side by side, with a short commentary underneath. Here is my reproduction of their schema:

« J'habite ici tout seul, fit-il d'un air triste et un peu guindé, ma femme est morte. (Il craqua une allumette, introduisait la flamme dans une lampe a pétrole, et des murs blancs montèrent autour d'eux.) Prenez des oranges pendant que j'allume les autres lampes. » Il s'agenouilla auprès de quatre autres appareils, et les douces flammes crépitèrent au bout de son allumette, avec un sifflement. « C'est pas mal chez vous, susurra effrontément Awa. Ce que vous en avez, des livres ! — Ce sont tous ceux que j'ai écrits, mentit l'administrateur. — Ce doit être merveilleux d'écrire. — On tente de dire quelque chose. Euh… Aimeriez-vous visiter la maison ? Elle est d'excellent goût, n'est-ce pas ? Naturellement, ajouta Chevalier baissant la voix, il y manque le cachet féminin.»	"I live all alone here," Mr Surrogate said, a little stiffly and sadly, "my wife is dead." He switched on a light and the white walls rose around him. "have a nut while I light the fire?" He knelt and the gentle hissing flames sprang from his match end. "It's lovely here," Kay Rimmer said, "What a lot of books you have." "Those are my own," Mr Surrogate said. "It must be wonderful to write." "One tries to exert an influence. Would you like to see the flat? It's small, but choice, I think. Of course," Mr Surrogate added with a lowered respectful tone, "it lacks the female touch. A man's den." But the word den was a shocking misnomer; Mr Surrogate went from room to room switching on the lights, and everywhere he went white paneling, cream walls, pale jade walls sprang, like sentries to attention. […]

Puis, évoluant de pièce en pièce, l'administrateur alluma les lampes; et partout où il entrait, surgissait — sentinelles au gardes-à-vous : panneaux blancs, peintures sur verre, murs crème, plafonds de jade pâle.
[...]
L'homme poursuivait son chemin à pas menus, ne signalant rien à l'attention de Awa, comme s'il eût désiré faire de cette femme, l'humble gardienne de ses trésors. Sa tête se penchait, comme pour murmurer le désir qu'il avait de garder pour lui la courtisane, si belle, et l'orgueil que lui causait la perfection do son propre goût.

« Ma chambre à coucher », dit-il, s'éclipsant devant une porte rose, et promenant une lampe.

Awa eut le souffle coupé par le plaisir que provoquèrent en elle les tentures roses, le lit en demi-cercle, la courtepointe en soie, que l'on eût juré jonchée de pétales de roses.

— Oh! dit-elle, apercevant une glace aux reflets profonds, qui la flattait mieux que tout hommes aux paroles douceureuses. Aôôh! gloussa-t-elle, à la vue du seul tableau accroché au mur. Comme elle est jolie! Qui est-ce ?

— Ma femme, répondit Chevalier, sans la regarder.
Le portrait était juste au lit. C'était le premier visage qui le frappait au réveil. Ce visage lui disait bonjour le matin, lui

Mr Surrogate padded ahead, switching on the lights; he drew attention to nothing; with his smooth blond head deprecatingly bent he might have been the humble custodian of his treasures; no one could have guessed the fierce smothered pride which bowed his head in recognition of his perfect taste.

"My bedroom," he said a little drily, opening a pink door, turning on several lights. Kay Rimmer gave a gasp of pleasure at the rose hangings, the semi-circular bed, the silk bedspread like a waste of fallen petals.

"Oh," she said, catching sight of the great mirror with its deep reflections, which flattered her more than a soft-spoken man. "Oh," she said again at the sight of the only picture on the walls, "how lovely, Who's that?"

Mr Surrogate answered without looking: "My wife." It faced the bed. It was the first face he saw in the morning. It greeted him, before Davis, with its beauty and its malice and its integrity.

"How you must have loved her," Kay Rimmer said softly, under the spell of that face, and for a moment Mr Surrogate longed to tell the truth, that it was hung there as an atonement to his dislike, as a satisfaction for his humility, because of its reminder of the one woman who had never failed to see through him. "Let me show you the kitchen," he said quickly.

faisant don de sa beauté, de sa malignité, de sa vertu.

« Comme vous avez dû l'aimer! hasarda Awa, fasciné par ce visage. » Et pendant un moment, Chevalier eut envie de lui crier la vérité: que sa femme était là non parce qu'il l'adorait, mais parce que le tableau ne pouvait être ailleurs, parce qu'il lui rappelait l'unique créature qui avait lu clair en lui.

« Venez, que je vous montre la cuisine », se dépêcha-t-il d'éluder.

La cuisine évoquait un paysage de rêve, avec ses fenêtres blanches, son buffet blanc, son ensemble blanc, son four à charbon émaillé, ses murs et son plafond bleu pastel.

Par l'écartement des rideaux, Awa aperçut, dans la maison voisine, qui se brossait les cheveux, une splendide négresse, nue devant un miroir: un vaste lit à deux personnes attendait ses abonnés. Une ordonnance mettait la table pour le petit déjeuner du lendemain ; ailleurs, le capitaine Vandame écrivait, devant un caporal au garde-à-vous.

« Ils font tous quelque chose de différent », murmura-t-elle, cependant que son regard reyenait au grand lit, et ses pensées vers la courte pointe rose, dans la chambre de Chevalier, puis vers Saif.[29]

The kitchen was like a snowdrift with its white casement and white dresser and white table and enameled gas stove and its deep blue walls and ceiling.
[…]
Through the chink of the curtains on a top floor she saw a woman brushing her hair; a great double bed waited for its inhabitants; a maid laid breakfast; a man wrote letters; a chauffeur lent from the window of a little flat above a garage and smoked his last pipe.
[…]
"Everyone doing something different," she said, her eyes going back to the double bed, and her thoughts on the pink bedspread in the other room and Jules and a half a loaf is better than no bread and the lovely dead indifferent woman on the wall.

Bodies and Tongues

The curious thing about these passages is just how *un*-sensational they appear. In both, a man shows a ladyfriend the contents of his home with disingenuous modesty. Why did Ouologuem bother with this description? And why did this one invoke censorship? Other borrowings have much more provocative content.[30] Ouologuem uses sweeping, grand-narrative passages from *Le dernier des justes* for the epic narration of his opening chapter. He mines ethnographies and historical studies for especially graphic accounts of suffering. A selection from Maupassant's *Boule de Suif* describing the corpse of a German soldier is seamlessly integrated into the section on World War I — as a deft, indirect commentary on the entanglement of individuals in the ruins of war. As I already mentioned, the adaptations of the Askia Mohammed chronicles evoke and satirize the mythic African past. How, then, did such an apparently innocuous passage, that reads quite like a real estate tour, become the focus of the scandal? Of course, there were other excerpts from Greene, and the author's request for the novel's suppression did not stem from any special sanctity he attached to this particular passage. Nonetheless, this borrowing became the evidence, so to speak.

Ouologuem made subversive modifications to the appropriated passage. Both Mr. Surrogate and Chevalier are Europeans putting the material culture inside their homes on display. The women they are trying to seduce pay particular attention to the Europeans' collections of books. In Ouologuem's version, Chevalier lies and tells Awa that they are all the books he has written. Of his library, Green's Mr. Surrogate says, "One tries to exert an influence"; "On tente de dire quelque chose," says Chevalier with mock humility. Ouologuem turns the library into a fiction, a lie. In each home there is also the dead wife's portrait, which the uncultured women recognize while almost confusing it with a mirror. The dead wife is the organizing logic of the wealthy home. Only through her absence is the European's cultural wealth intelligible. One can detect the play of absence and non-culture inherent in Europe's othering hierarchies. The man seduces the woman in both Greene and Ouologuem, but to greatly different effects. In *Le Devoir de violence*, Awa is a spy sent by the devious local ruler, Saif. Though Chevalier subjects Awa to awful perversions, she nonetheless succeeds in *"lui delier la langue."*[31] The exhibition of cultural wealth becomes an opportunity to steal it, to "undo the tongue" of the European.

Insidious as these alterations may be, they only illustrate the manner in which Ouologuem plays with content inside his constraints. The *éclat* of this particular theft lies elsewhere. The real culprit was Ouologuem's use of an alternative mode of translation, in this case, plagiarism-as-translation. This was a crime of possibility that the censorship response sought to contain.

The schema in which the TLS presented the passages is noteworthy. Under a headline "Something *New* Out of Africa?" the two texts are boxed off side by side. We are faced immediately with a schema of equivalence-difference. The two texts are set off as bodies against each other, exactly as one would represent a translation. Their boundaries are literally inscribed by the borders enclosing them. Yet this gesture is itself undermined when the TLS describes the relationship between them as one of plagiarism. If one text is a copy, or a "loose but stylish version [elsewhere: translation],"[32] of the other, then it is precisely their difference that is in question. Looking at the page, one is supposed to conclude that these are different texts, but through reading them and the TLS's own commentary, we are supposed to understand them as nearly identical — though one should remain a mere copy. Such a play of identity is the additional complication plagiarism-as-translation introduces. The act invokes the traditional schema of translation by moving a text from one language to another. In order for a text to move between languages, the languages themselves must be distinguished. Thus at first plagiarism-as-translation seems to reify the distinction between authors, literatures, and languages. Yet the practice also draws out the unspoken relations of force and theft that construct and separate canonical literatures.

To understand how this is possible, let us consider the component parts of plagiarism-as-translation. Plagiarism is a form of textuality (stolen text) that calls into question the ownership of a text. Translation is a form of textuality (linguistically transferred text) that separates languages while purporting to link them. The "common sensical" views of these phenomena treat the interdependent relationship between difference, originality and worth as self-evident. Naturally, the plagiarism and the translation are both different from (and inferior to) the original. Ouologuem's poetics realizes the radical potential for a synthesis of these forms of textuality. Plagiarism-as-translation coordinates the iterability of translation with the subversive designs of plagiarism into an attack on the privileged nature of the original. It breaks the hierarchy in two directions: the bodies of languages (kept apart to keep one above the other) are opened onto each other, and the privileged rights of the author (the West's dearest myth, the *translatio* of European genius through the ages) is violated.

Bodies and Tongues

It was *Le devoir de violence*'s combined attack that made it intolerable to Western literary sensibilities. The Graham Greene passages ignited the controversy and censorship because they were an incident of plagiarism-as-translation. A novel that only plagiarized French authors could never have achieved the same level of scandal. Nowhere is this clearer than in the London *Times* article, which compares selections from three texts instead of two: *It's a battlefield*, *Le devoir de violence* and *Bound to violence* (RalphManheim's English translation).

> Greene (It's a Battlefield): "I live all alone here," Mr Surrogate said, a little stiffly and sadly, "my wife is dead."
>
> Ouologuem (*Le Devoir de Violence*): "J'habite ici tout seul, fit-il d'un air triste et un peu guindé, ma femme est morte."
>
> Manheim (*Bound to Violence*): "I live all alone here," he said sadly and a trifle stiffly. "My wife is dead."[33]

The comparison does not reaffirm the primacy of the original as the *Times* seems to think it does. Notice how the texts are voiced, given the identity of their "authors." If the passage is indeed plagiarized, then both Ouologuem *and* his translator become Greene. If the passage is a translation, then Ouologuem "turns" Greene and Manheim seems to be either Ouologuem or Greene, depending on whether one privileges translation or plagiarism as the primary mode of identity. To say Ouologuem's crime is plagiarism is to miss the point: the passage that tripped him up was a translation of a translation. Plagiarism-as-translation allows one to violate Walter Benjamin's dictum that there can be no translation of a translation.[34] Putting a plagiarized text into a system of translation makes the unwitting translator repeat the original plagiarist's crime, passing on the shock waves in language after language. Censorship was the last ditch attempt to halt the text on its line of escape. The borrowing from Greene's novel was the main source of hysteria because it demonstrated that plagiarism-as-translation made it possible to translate a stolen translation, to repeat the action until "my language" and "my text" lose their meaning. The radical proposal of plagiarism-as-translation is this: what has been stolen once can be stolen again. All the riches of European culture, all the wealth of the ancient, imperial Askias, all the spoils of the current crop of African dictators — all of it stolen or built on suffering. Ouologuem's poetics literalize these relations of force and theft, while at the same time suggesting a way out, if only the performance could be repeated an infinite number of times.

Ending-for-Sure: *Langue* and Metamorphosis

> *Imagine a man lost in the wilderness at night. He must find his way back to his people at any cost...So what can he do?... he resorts to a procedure that for all its strangeness was actually used: he begins to bark...As he walks along, the traveler produces random barking noises. If there are any dogs in the vicinity, they will bark back, thus revealing the location of human settlements...To find the way home, the traveler must bark. To become a man (again), he must first transform himself into a dog.*
> — Abdelfattah Kilito

In *The Author and His Doubles*, a collection of essays on classical Arabic culture, Abdelfattah Kilito discusses the many ways Arabic authors played with identities. His topics range from the notion of "orphaned" or "fathered" poetic ideas and the *sariqat* borrowings, to famous authors who purposefully misattribute their writings to shield themselves from critics. Properly speaking, Kilito belongs to the previous mode of translation, but like many things relating to Ouologuem, he is out of place. In the final chapter of his book, Kilito relates a parable of a man who becomes a dog, from which I have taken my epigraph.[35] Kilito's anecdote unfurls into the condition of languages in Ahmadou Kourouma's *Les Soleils des indépendances*. The parable concerns a real strategy used by the ancient Arabs to find their way home at night. The lost traveler would bark like a dog, in the hope that real dogs will bark back and lead him home. But the man who barks must confront the dangers of metamorphosis. Once you start barking, Kilito shows, there are many more possibilities than a happy ending. The man could forget his own language and only be able to bark. Or the dogs he thinks he hears could be false dogs — other men in the same predicament. Indeed his whole tribe could be barking to find him; they too could have forgotten how to speak, or else they could have wandered off in search of him. If this has happened, the man could find another tribe of strangers in their place, among whom he is as good as an animal, an ape, because he cannot speak their language. In trying to speak the language of dogs the threat is that one will become a dog, and never find one's own language again. In speaking the language of animals, one becomes animal.[36]

As one sends out language in search of the Other, where it goes, who returns it, and even what one is at its return are all subject to the power of metamorphosis. For Walter Benjamin, translation is such a call in the dark.

> Unlike a work of literature, translation does not find itself in the center of the language forest but on the outside facing the wooded ridge; it calls into it without entering, aiming at the single spot where the echo is able to give, in its own language, the reverberation of the work in the alien one.[37]

The alternative mode of translation Ahmadou Kourouma practices is a form of linguistic metamorphosis. "La métamorphose," Deleuze and Guattari write, "est le contraire de la métaphore. Il n'y a plus sens propre ni sens figuré, mais distribution d'états dans l'éventail du mot. La chose et les autres choses ne sont plus que des intensités parcourues par les sons ou les mots déterritorialisés suivant leur ligne de fuite."[38]

This tension between metaphor and metamorphosis is crucial to the European genealogy of translation that I discussed earlier. Indeed, the common representation of translation operates metaphorically: one language references another, allowing one to perceive likeness and difference at the same time — the very function of metaphor. The *translatio* of the *translatio studii et imperii* is rooted in this same device, since it allows the spirit of the empire to survive in a new body, by referencing the continuity of the imperial project of knowledge. Metamorphosis is closely related to Deleuze's idea of *devenir*, "becoming." In Kourouma's metamorphic form of translation, languages do not reference each other while remaining the same; instead, they are made other to themselves. Languages are thrown into a process of constant becoming.

My reading dreams of apprehending *Les Soleils des indépendances* at the points of Malinké–French interconnection. For this illusive understanding it relies on the readings of others. As I do not speak nor understand more than a few words of Malinké, I am obliged by contingency to look elsewhere, to rely, in a sense, on translators. For a detailed consideration I turn to Makhily Gassama's *La langue d'Ahmadou Kourouma*.[39] Gassama examined the many forms of Kourouma's *langue* that resemble Malinké idiom, cataloguing the many instances, linguistic inventions, transference and replacement.

In reading *Les Soleils des indépendances*, the first conflict one encounters is how to talk about language with regard to the text. As Gassama notes, *Soleils* opposes *langue* to *langage*, not *parole* (parole remains silent; it is the unspoken oral dimension of Kourouma's reworking).[40] The single Malinké term kumaña — "means of expressing oneself" — collides with the French *langue/langage*.[41] Western readers are far more familiar with the *langue/parole* opposition. Here *langue* and *langage* — already a murky distinction — are drawn into each other through *kumaña*.

Wary of this opposition, I approach the English "translations" of these terms with caution. *Langage* will be translated as language. *Langue* is the more slippery term. I will use it untranslated except when its modifier makes an interesting point. This is partly to avoid a conflation for the simple convenience of the Anglophone reader. I am also attempting to preserve some of the opacity of the French terms, and most especially the confusion created among them by *Soleils*. Yet *langue* and *langage* are often interchangeable, and almost always rendered as "language" in English. Why then this preference for *langue*? According to *Le Robert*, *langage* means a "fonction d'expression de la pensée et de communication entre les hommes, mise en oeuvre par les organes de la phonation (parole) ou par une notation au moyen de signes matériels (écriture)." It also can mean one's "façon de s'exprimer." *Langue*, by contrast, is first the literal tongue, next a "système d'expression du mentale et de communication, commun à un groupe sociale (communauté linguistique)" and also, like *langage*, the "façon de s'exprimer" of an individual, but more at one's style.[42]

Langue is more of a system of expression, and *langage* more a function of expression — but not much of an opposition seems tenable between them. Why promote one then, especially *langue*, the system? Even Gassama writes that Kourouma "asservit la *langue française*, qu'il interprète en malinké, pour rendre le *langage malinké*, en supprimant toute frontière linguistique".[43]

I am really after the ancillary meanings of *langue*, not its (non)opposition with *langage* as system-function. Refraining from translating *langue* is my refusal to assign it a single meaning: *langue* connotes personal style of expression, language co-extensive with a community, and also the organ of speech itself.

Refusing to translate *langue* tends toward an association with the particular, the personal, and the minor, while at the same time associating the word with the *langue* of a people, the Malinké in this case. Of all the meanings of *langue*

Bodies and Tongues

(language, style, tongue), my reasons for choosing the last possibility are most in need of clarification. I use *langue* in part to provoke an unstable, bodily dimension that anticipates certain pitfalls of Kourouma's mode of translation. By using *langue*, the idea of language is (re)inscribed into the body. Clearly, this involves an immediate reterritorialization, a bodily one. Language becomes a tongue. Perhaps, though, this is merely a contingent re-territorialization, an ephemeral embodiment of language. Deleuze and Guattari distinguish two territories of language-*langue*:

> Riche ou pauvre, un langage quelconque implique toujours une déterritorialisation de la bouche, de la langue et des dents. La bouche, la langue et les dents trouvent leur territorialité primitive dans les aliments. En se consacrant à l'articulation des sons, la bouche, la langue et les dents se déterritorialisent...D'ordinaire, en effet, la langue compense sa déterritorialisation par une reterritorialisation dans le sens. Cessant d'être organe d'un sens, elle devient instrument du Sens.[44]

In preferring the bodily dimension, do I not give *langue* over to the territorialization of the body? Why revert to this primitive territoriality? Precisely to evade the re-territorialization of a certain representation of languages as bodies unto themselves (also the encroachment of filiation, paternity and maternity upon language). The *langue* is suspended between the claims of possession of the speaker, the collectivity and itself. To whom does a *langue* belong? As a *langue*, expression escapes possession as a constitutive part of totalized "languages." A *langue* is not implicitly possessed by its user; a claim of possession would encounter Derrida's monolinguistic dilemma.[45] Instead, the *langue* is the process of the speaker, the author; the translator as subject-in-process.

Up until this point I have been relying blindly on Gassama's reading of Kourouma. Yet Gassama was engaged, like any one who claims to "translate" in the usual sense, in the maintenance of a certain schema of cofiguration. In order to proceed, I must take this schema into account. My reading desires to draw out the connections (not all of them evident) made available by Gassama's translations, while simultaneously resisting his representation of translation. This is, of course, impossible. But in the spirit of Glissant's poetics of Relation, I humbly suggest that only in working toward an impossible totality can one reveal the latent possibilities of such an unstable composition.

Gassama's book is invaluable for its discussion of the Malinké–French interaction from the position of a Malinké reader, though its analysis is somewhat marred by persistent essentialism. Gassama's favorite of Kourouma's techniques is the way he makes French words mean differently. Gassama describes a three step process: "l'auteur désémantise le mot en le vidant de sa substance, de ses valeurs traditionelles...l'auteur charge le mot de nouvelles valeurs...l'auteur replace le lecteur dans son univers linguistique habituel et celui-ci prend conaissance des nouvelles valeurs que véhicule le mot."[46]

A word is emptied of its meaning, invested with new (Malinké) meaning, and replaced in its context. Gassama makes extensive use of packaging and gastronomic metaphors: after losing its traditional signification, the word "devient un 'emballage perdu' qu'Ahmadou Kourouma récupère et rembourse."[47] There is also talk of serving up Malinké in a French porcelain platter.[48] Later, Kourouma is said to have "vidé les mots de France de leur contenu gaulois pour les charges, comme les colporteurs malinké, de nouvelles marchandises, proposées à la consommation du francophone."[49] This image is a mixture of commerce and consumption. The author empties a word of (French) signification, fills it with Malinké (food) and sells it on the francophone market. In Gassama's representational schemata, *francophonie* ensures that Kourouma's *langue* can never be an instrument of deterritorialization; *francophonie* necessarily implies the persistence of certain economies, both linguistic and monetary, in which the text can challenge expectations but is ultimately obliged to deliver a product for consumption.

Returning to words: *vidé, jugé* and *viandée* share a common register. Most of Kourouma's neologisms are in some way denunciatory, as Gassama points out.[50] Kourouma stretches the words to accommodate the sense of betrayal, emptiness and frustration his characters are left with under the suns of the independences. Gassama, however, is very keen on extending Kourouma's poetics to a betrayal of the French language itself.

What happens when a word becomes *un vidé*? Gassama suggests that the alteration of a word makes the it other to itself, further extrapolating that Kourouma does violence to the French language. Gassama writes that Kourouma "brutalizes and betrays the French language."[51] Has he betrayed French? Or a French word? Or simply a word? What is the object(ive) of this linguistic violence? Is it plausible to assume that *un vidé* acts upon *the* French language? From Gassama's contention that *vider* has become other to itself, it does not follow that Kourouma's *langue* makes French other to itself. What is at issue here is an implicitly metonymic representation of the process of translation. Word for word becomes one language for another. When the word speaks, in a discussion of language, in a translation, it is never for itself — it speaks for the entirety of a language unity. It is made to speak, to represent totality.

Language-Word is in many ways similar to *langue-parole*. The Word is a particular instance of the language, and when it is translated, we say we are translating from French into English, or Malinké into French. Thus the translation-act dismisses the particular instance of the Word, while simultaneously relying upon it for its claim of exchange between totalities.

"Si le roman de Kourouma," Gassama writes, "était traduit en malinké ou dans *toutes autres langues africaines*, son peuple s'y fût retrouvé, comme il se retrouve dans les poussières de l'harmattan."[52] The equivalence and interchangeability that Gassama assigns to African languages is stunning. His appeal to the harmattan is a familiar gesture that literally "grounds" cultural essence in the physical landscape. Jean-Pierre Makouta-M'Boukou performs a similar equation when he writes of Kourouma: "il glisse d'un ordre considéré comme la norme par excellence, par l'Occident et par les aliénés, à un des ordres 'marginaux' humains, l'ordre *malinké*, mais cet ordre malinké, c'est aussi déjà l'ordre négro-africain, en général."[53] He too places the Mandé in metonymic relation to Africa. In "naming" the instances of Malinké influence in Kourouma's style, Makouta and Gassama seek to connect it to "Negro-African" style and expression more broadly.

In his most detailed reading, Gassama compares the tenses available to the verb "to finish" in French and Malinké. *Finir* makes its appearance in the first sentence of the novel: "Il y avait une semaine qu'*avait fini* dans la capitale Koné Ibrahima, de race malinké, ou disons-le en malinké: il n'avait pas soutenu un petite rhume...."[54] *Avoir fini* here is intended to convey "to have died." In French, however, *Etre fini* should have been the obvious choice. Gassama tries to account for the decision to use *avoir*.

> Nous avons dit que la langue malinké est une langue *agglutinante*. Le mot peut connaître des mutations multiples, qui modifient son sens ou sa fonction.; il suffit, pour cela, de lui ajoindre des éléments affixaux: dans le verbe malinké *abāna* (il est fini: il est mort), le préfixe *a* constitute, en fait, le pronom-sujet, qui varie non par genre, mais par le nombre, la personne et le temps du verbe...*a* signifie donc: *il* ou *elle*. Et *bāna*? Celui-ci n'introduit

> aucune notion de temps...Ne commandant aucun verbe auxhiliare, ne contenant aucune notion temporelle, le mot malinké *abāna* n'est donc rien de moins qu'un radicale, un infinitif: "finir". Seul le sens contextuel du mot guidera l'allocutaire...Donc le morphème *abāna* pourrait être littéralement traduit: *il-finir* et l'on notera que chaque élément a conservé sa pleine autonomie dans la phrase, sans la moindre modification morphologique.[55]

Rendering *il-finir* in French forces a choice between *avoir fini* and *être fini*. Even in this explanation, Gassama cannot discern a reason for the choice of *avoir fini*, except to say that Kourouma wishes to point out the absurdity of French auxiliary verbs. In order to find a more conclusive answer, Gassama explores precisely which form of *abāna* Kourouma is approximating with *avoir fini*. He breaks down the six main temporal forms of *bāna* grammatically. The verb is "conjugated" by the addition (agglutination) of particles that denote person and time to the verb root *bāna* (sometimes *bā* only). *Adibā*, for instance, is a future form (he will finish) composed of the root (*bā*) plus the particles *di* (tense) and *a* (person).[56] The present form, *ayebākā*, seems to be the most likely source of the derivation *avoir fini*, but this is not an uncomplicated present tense:

> *ayebākā* signifie littérlalement — et l'image et à retenir — : *il-mourir-sur*! Le suffixe *kā*, dans les langues *mandé*: malinké, mandingue, diakhanké, bambara, etc., toutes juxtaposantes, signifie *sur*; en fait, *kā* conserve sa valeur de préposition marquant la "position en haut" ou "en dehors", donc introduit la notion de distance, d'éloignement dans l'espace aussi bein que dans le temps...*être sur*, c'est en quelque sorte ne plus être là où on était, donc "avancer" en même temps que l'objet concret ou abstrait qui nous "porte"; il y a, à travers ce mot, la notion de simulatnéité, de mouvements synchroniques. Le suffixe *kā*, en malinké, grâce à ses alliances dans le mot, est chargé d'une valeur bien supérieure à celle de la préposition française *sur*, qui ne laisse transparaître aucune notion de temps.[57]

Kourouma tries to convey the inevitability of *il-mourir-sur* (he-die-for sure) by *avoir fini* (to have finished): he was *sure* to die, he has *finally* died. Clearly, *être fini* (to be finished) is insufficient; *avoir* has more of an implication of process. "Ibrahima Koné a fini" (Ibrahima Koné has finished–died)[58] comes as close as one can to deploying (in the past tense) the certainty of *il-mourir-sur*, itself an approximation of *ayebākā*.

Bodies and Tongues

The hunt for *avoir fini* brings up more questions than it answers. The importance of Gassama's discussion of *abāna* does not lie in establishing a source for Kourouma's poetics, but rather in his interrogation of the verb itself. What breach is there between *finir* and *abāna*? How can one "end" in French and in Malinké, and where do these languages "end"?

The attempt to temporalize French in the manner of Malinké expression draws out a divergence in the present tense. *Ayebākā*, the present form of *abāna*, is not a simple present, as we have seen. The particle *kā* imparts not only a sense of progressive, inevitable action, but also a sort of distance in time and space (because it retains its prepositional connotations — on top of, outside of). This produces estrangement in the heart of the present, a notion of no longer being where we were. The present, Gassama writes, is a

> division arbitraire du temps vu de façon absolue... nous avons vu que son expression, en malinké: *ayebākā*, ne pourrait être rendue en français par: *il finit*, mais par la périphrase: *il est en train de finir*, notionellement plus juste puisque la forme: *il finit*, n'est rien de moins qu'une simple convention.[59]

The present in Malinké is different from the present in French, Gassama says. It differs in its ending. The present tense in French is more rigid, though this is a convention, existing only through intention. The "fuzzy contours" of the present are more richly colored in agglutinating languages. The present is always ending, but its endings in French and Malinké are incommensurable.[60]

Then what happens to the "endings" of these languages when Kourouma writes in a *langue* that calls French verbs into metamorphosis, creating an assemblage that accommodates qualities of the Malinké present tense? I am suggesting that these languages defer, not differ, in their "endings." What Gassama presents as the difference of "ending" between two languages is really the quality of ending within language. What does it mean "to end" in a language? How does one language end differently from another? What does it mean to say it-ends-for-sure in a language? To say this of language? To say of language: ayebākā, il-finir-sur, its-ends-for-sure. The present of a language is promised like ayebākā: its-ends-for-sure. Language promises and threatens itself, and this is its present. Language never ends (is boundless), and language ends-for-sure, because this is the condition of its being. It must promise its ending.

Throughout *Soleils,* Kourouma finds solutions to West African social ills in neither the secular, self-interested state, nor in the withered epic past. The charge of unhelpful negativity continues to be leveled at *Soleils,* and it is indeed (like *Devoir*), a bitter, vituperative book. Yet both novels offer ways out; the mistake is to look for solutions in explicit social critiques. It is best to forget narrated content, and look to the becoming of language. Kourouma wrote in a new tongue, a metamorphic *langue.* His *langue* is his answer — a collective assemblage that gives voice to Malinké people, not through a regime of translation but a rather transformative engagement with "French."

In reconsidering Ouologuem's work, we must similarly brush aside the searing polemics he directed at all sides, and — as we have done with Kourouma — look to his treatment of language. Ouologuem's attacks were aimed at destroying the bodily integrity of literatures, and realizing the mutually destructive and constitutive nature of cultural relations.

But to what end? To answer, it might help to turn to Ouologuem's two other published books, which were mostly ignored. The first was *Lettre à la france nègre,* a book of sarcastic essays. He also wrote a collection of pornographic stories, *Les milles et une bibles du sexe,* which he published under the pseudonym Utto Rudolph (though he graced the preface with his own name). In the most infamous essay in the *Lettre,* Ouologuem elaborates a plan for mass-producing the detective novel, which many critics have taken as a blueprint for *Devoir. Bibles* concerns an orgy/parlor game in which participants wager stories of their sexual exploits in order to enslave one another. It is no accident that Ouologuem picks two of the most formulaic conventions of Western culture: pornography and the detective novel. The operation and continued consumption of these genres is based on their potential for endless repetition. Ouologuem discerns that this is due to their reliance on formulae and recognizable codes. Therein lies the only "constructive" component of Ouologuem's poetics. He invests his hopes in the possibility that an African might gain control of the codes, for once, manipulating them off into infinity — so the arbiters of culture never catch up. Yet catch up they did, for he violated the most sacred fiction of all: the myth of the author.

While Ouologuem disintegrated literary bodies, Kourouma employed a metamorphic tongue. The alternative modes of translation they used were possible and necessary in the wake of colonialism, in order to defend and extend their marginalized and hybridized subject positions. Both texts exploit the fact that languages, literatures and cultures are themselves fictions; their autonomous existence is only conceivable after we have posited the difference between them, in part through a process we call translation. The hope of my work is to promote ways of translating otherwise, of putting into play linguistic relations that lay bare the ways communities are historically and culturally intertwined, inseparable from each other after centuries of contact. Alternative modes of translation contest the totality of languages and cultures, and allow one to dream of other forms of community, based on relation instead of dominion.

Notes

1. Cicero, from *De oratore*, 55 BCE. Quoted in "Translation/History/Culture: A Sourcebook." André Lefevere, ed. London: Routledge, 1992. p. 46–7
2. Humboldt, from the preface to his translation of *Agamemnon*, 1816. Quoted in Lefevere, 136–7.
3. Goethe, from *Schriften zur Literatur*, 1824. Quoted in Lefevere, p. 24–25.
4. From his preface to his son's translations of Shakespeare, 1865. Quoted in Lefevere, p. 18.
5. See Eric Cheyfitz, *The Poetics of Imperialism: Translation and Colonization from The Tempest to Tarzan*. Philadelphia: Univ. Pennsylvania Press, 1991.
6. See Ernst Robert Curtius, *European Literature and the Latin Middle Ages*. (Princeton: Princeton University Press, 1953, p. 29.
7. Thus translation allows the mobility of the kingdom of heaven. One of the first definitions of translation, of course, is "to convey unto heaven". In *translatio*, heaven is itself conveyed. As religion was replaced by humanism in the Enlightenment, the kingdom of Man (its humanistic values and hierarchies) was transubstantiated through the magic of the *translatio*. Alternative modes of translation, on the other hand, are post-human, speaking in appropriated and (dis)assembled tongues rather than in any one language.
8. Cheyfitz, p.59.
9. Otto Van Bismarck, Protocol No. 1, quoted in *The Scramble for Africa*. R. J. Gavin and J. A. Betley, eds. (Ibadan: Ibadan Univ. Press, 1973, p. 129). Naturally, the powers paid lip-service to abolishing the slave trade, and effectively did nothing to end it.
10. The decline in sovereignty described by Michael Hardt and Antonio Negri in *Empire* begins (for Africa) at this Berlin conference table. Not, as might be assumed, in the agreements that divvied up the continent itself, but rather in the strategies the powers used to arbitrate their own conflicts of interest. The European empires managed to postpone their first civil war for another thirty years by agreeing on ground rules for colonization, and, crucially, by resolving the fate of the disputed Congo. The most novel, prophetic, and ominous aspect of the Berlin treaty, however, was the creation of the Free Trade Zone of the Congo, to be administered by the International Association of The Congo. The Association was the brainchild and diplomatic proxy of Leopold II

of Belgium. Most importantly, the Association was a *corporation*, not a state. The Congo basin was ceded to its control, with the intent that the Association would manage the area for all the European powers. This required certain gymnastics of international law; namely, France and Germany and finally all the nations involved recognized the *sovereignty* of the Association. Thus a corporation sat as an equal at the most important imperial conference of the nineteenth century. The echoes of this moment still resound today in Africa. The Congo under Leopold's control became one the worst human rights disasters of African colonialism. Diamond mining juntas have infested the Congo ever since, supported by the foreign corporations that crave their product. The future model of European engagement with Africa was the Association, not the waning imperial nation-states.

[11] Take for example, the Kenyan Ngugi Wa'Thiongo, who in 1977 ceased to write creatively in English, choosing instead his first language, Gikuyu. Ngugi's refusal forced his readership to follow him *in translation*. But, since there is no "anglophony," the strategies and ideologies of English language hegemony are less theorized and ultimately more insidious. Ngugi, with all the best intentions, could only repeat the nationalist use of translation, appealing to absolute difference (and cofiguration) to safeguard community.

[12] Cf. Christopher Miller, *Blank Darkness : Africanist Discourse in French* (Chicago: University of Chicago, 1985).

[13] Cf. Kwame Anthony Appiah, *In My Father's House: Africa in the Philosophy of Culture* (New York : Oxford University Press, 1992).

[14] Edward Said, *Orientalism* (Vintage Books: New York. 1979, p. 3).

[15] Miller, 16.

[16] Miller, 19.

[17] "Black Africa is reduced to a noncivilization, receiving life only from the outside." Miller, 18.

[18] *Le Devoir de violence* was republished by Le Serpent à plumes in April, 2003, ending more than thirty years of censorship. Ouologuem himself has also resurfaced, making several noisy public appearances.

[19] Cf. Miller and Appiah.

[20] Thomas Hale, *Scribe, Griot, and Novelist: Narrative Interpreters of the Songhay Empire* (Gainesville: University of Florida Press, 1990, p.140–160).

[21] Hale, 148.

[22] Christopher Wise, "Qur'anic Hermeneutics, Sufism and *Le Devoir de violence*: Yambo Ouologuem as Marabout Novelist," in *Yambo Ouologuem: Postcolonial Writer, Islamic Militant*, Christopher Wise, ed. (Boulder: Lynne Reiner, 1999) p. 222.

[23] I am deeply grateful to Shawkat Toorawa for pointing me toward these references.

[24] Gustav von Grunebaum, "The Concept of Plagiarism in Arabic Theory" in *Journal of Near Eastern Studies*, vol. 13, July 1955, no. 3, p. 234.

[25] Ibid.

[26] Ibid.

[27] Wolfhart, Heinrichs. "An Evaluation of *Sariqa*" in *Quaderni di Studi Arabi*, vol. 5–6, 1987–88, p. 360.

28 I suspect that like all of Sellin's rather vituperative denunciations over the years, the initial whistle-blowing probably had more to do with stung pride than a sense of justice — he has ceaselessly tried to disown his own exaggerated praise of the novel when it first appeared.
29 *Times Literary Supplement*, 5 May 1972: p. 525. The passages from *Le Devoir de violence* are from pages 68–69. The passages from *It's a Battlefield* are from pages 56–58.
30 See Christiane Chaulet-Auchour's "Writing as Exploratory Surgery " in Wise's *Yambo Ouloguem* for an extensive passage-for-passage comparison of LDV with its various inter-related texts.
31 Yambo Ouologuem, *Le devoir de violence* (Seuil: Paris, 1968, p. 71).
32 Tim Devlin, "Echoes of Graham Greene halt prizewinning book." *The Times* (London), May 5, 1972.
33 Devlin, p. 2.
34 "because meaning attaches so loosely to them." "The Task of the Translator" in *Illuminations*, Trans. Harry Zohn (New York: Schocken Books, 1968, p.81).
35 See Abdelfattah Kilito, *The Author and His Doubles*, tr. Michael Cooperson, Syracuse: Syracuse Univ. Press, 2001, p. 100–110.
36 This concept is derived from the "1914: One or Several Wolves?" section of *A Thousand Plateaus.*— Deleuze and Guattari's counter-reading of Freud's famous Wolf-Man case. Rather than a becoming-animal, my study is concerned with the "becoming-Malinké" of French.
37 Benjamin, 76.
38 Gilles Deleuze and Félix Guattari, *Kafka: pour une littérature mineure*. (Paris: Editions de minuit, 1975, p. 40). "Metamorphosis is the contrary of metaphor. There is no longer any proper sense or figurative sense, but only a distribution of states that is part of the range of the word. The thing and other things are no longer anything but intensities overrun by deterritorialized sound or words that are following their line of escape." Translation by Dana Polan.
39 Cf. the section on Kourouma in Jean-Pierre Makouta-M'Boukou's *Introduction à l'étude du roman négro-africain de langue française*. Makouta divides Kourouma's style into three levels, based on the distance a given utterance from Malinké.
40 Makhily Gassama, *La langue d'Ahmadou Kourouma, ou le français sous le soleil d'Afrique*. Paris: ACCT-Karthala, 1995, p. 22.
41 *Ibid*., 23.
42 Translations to phrases in this paragraph: "function of the expression of thought and communication between people, made manifest by the organs of phonation (speech) or through notation by material signs (writing)"; "manner ofself-expression"; "system of the expression of thought and communication, common to a social group (linguistic community)".
43 *Ibid*., 23.
44 Deleuze and Guattari, *Kafka*, p. 35. "Rich or poor, each language always implies a deterritorialization of the mouth, the tongue, and the teeth. The mouth, tongue, and

teeth find their primitive territoriality in food. In giving themselves over to the articulation of sounds, the mouth, tongue, and teeth deterritorialize...Ordinarily, in fact, language compensates for its deterritorialization by a reterritorialization in sense. Ceasing to be the organ of one of the senses, it becomes an instrument of Sense." Translation by Dana Polan.

45 "Il faut déja savoir dans quelle langue *je* se dit, je *me* dis...De tous les points de vue, qui ne sont pas seulement grammaticaux, logiques, philosophiques, on sait bien que le *je* de l'anamnèse dite autobiographique, le *je-me* du *je me rappelle* se produit et se profère différemment selon les langues. Il ne les précède jamais, il n'est donc pas indépendant de la langue en général." (Jacques Derrida, *Le Monolonguisme de l'autre*, Paris: Galilée, 1996, p. 54). "I" cannot say myself outside a language. There is nowhere for my ownership of language except inside the language of which "I" am a consequence. Language is always intended for and directed at the Other, and thus the subject cannot claim to possess even her own speech, making her loss of language total. (Cf. also Frantz Fanon: "Étant entendu que parler, c'est exister absolumennt pour l'autre").

46 "the author desemanticizes the word by emptying it of its substance, its traditional values...the author fills the word with new values...the author puts the reader back into his habitual linguistic universe, where [s]he takes notice of the new values the word carries." [Translation mine] Gassama, 25–26.

47 "becomes a lost package, that Ahmadou Kourouma recovers and re-packs" *Ibid.*, 44.

48 *Ibid.*, 27

49 "emptied France's words of their Gallic content to fill them, like Malinké merchants, with new goods for the consumption of the francophone" *Ibid.*, 118.

50 *Ibid.*, 51.

51 *Ibid.*, 25.

52 "If Kourouma's novel were translated into Malinké or into *all other African languages*, its people would find themselves [in it], as they do in the dusts of the harmattan." *Ibid.*, 118, emphasis mine.

53 "he slides from an order considered the norm *par excellence*, by the West and the alienated, to one of the "marginal" orders of humanity, the *Malinké* order, but this Malinké order is also already the Negro-African order, in general." Makouta, 303.

54 Ahmadou Kourouma, *Les soleils des independances* (Paris: Seuil, 1968, p. 1).

55 "We have said that Malinké is an agglutinating *langue*. The word can undergo many mutations, that modify its meaning or function; all it takes are attaching particles: in the Malinké verb *abāna* (he is finished; he is dead), the prefix *a* constitutes the subject pronoun, which varies not by gender but by number, person and verb tense...*a* thus means: *he* or *she*. And *bāna*? This introduces no notion of time... commanding no verb auxiliary, containing no notion of time, the Malinké word *abāna* is nothing less than a radical, an infinitive: "to end [finish]". Only the contextual meaning of the word will guide the speaker...Thus the morpheme *abāna* could be literally translated: *he-die* and one should note that each element has conserved its autonomy in the phrase, without the least morphological modification." Gassama, 28–9.

56 Gassama, 38.

Bodies and Tongues

[57] "*ayebāka* literally means — and the image is worth retaining — : he-die-for-sure! The suffix *kā* in the Mandekan languages: Malinké, Mandingue, Diakhanké, Bambara, etc. all juxtaposing languages, means *sur* [on and sure]; in fact, *kā* conserves its prepositional status marking the 'higher position' or 'outside of', therefore introducing the notion of distance, of estrangement in space as well as in time...*être sur* [to be on, sure], is in some sense to no longer be were one was, to 'advance' at the same time as the concrete or abstract object that 'carries' us; there is, through this word, the notion of simultaneity, of synchronized movements. In Malinké, the suffix *kā*, due to its alliances within the word, is filled with a value far superior to the French preposition *sur* that allows no notion of time to shine through." Gassama, 39, original emphases.

[58] Kourouma, p. 1.

[59] "an arbitrary division of time, in absolute terms... we have seen that its expression, in Malinké, *ayebāka*, could not be rendered in French by: *il finit* [he finishes], but by the paraphrase: *il est en train de finir* [he is finishing], conceptually more accurate since the form: *il finit* is nothing but a simple convention." Gassama, 40.

[60] Gassama, 41.

A Rift in Empire?
The Multitudes in the Face of War

Brian Holmes

The February 15 antiwar demonstrations proved it: the self-organization of free singularities is possible on a planetary scale. And that was an event, despite all that followed. In a manifesto-text written just after those demonstrations, I used the language of Negri and Hardt to say that the multitudes could create a rift in Empire. In a context where the Aristocracy (the great transnational companies) had been weakened by a string of financial disasters, where the Monarchy (the political and military command of the earth) had fallen apart in serious dissension, I wanted to encourage the democratic action of the Plebe, against the scorn of the American, British, Spanish and Italian leaders. It was a moment that had multiplied the world's political stages, overflowing the traditional mechanisms of representation.

This overflow of the multitudes had the surprising character of any real event. Yet it wasn't unexpected. We had just crossed another threshold in the constitution of the networked resistance that became visible with the movements against neoliberal globalization. And now everyone can see how many other thresholds remain. After the war in Iraq, I still think the multitudes can produce a rift in Empire. But that rift must be *produced*, in Europe and throughout the world. How to seize the opportunity of refusal that revealed itself during the war? How to go much further? Here I'll look into the meaning of these words, *multitudes*, *rift* and *Empire* — in hopes that some work with words might help prolong the movements against war.

Brian Holmes

The multitude is a figure of political philosophy. But it is inseparable from the actual pathways of the multitudes, as a set of singularities that comes into being through productive activity. What's new is the intersection of thinking and production. Labor — the simple activity of earning a living — is no longer an object of politics, but its departure point, its language or its very principle.

It is known that contemporary labor involves linguistic creativity, the expression of affects, spontaneous cooperation. These are the sources of innovation, indispensable for cognitive capitalism. But no boss can command creativity, expressivity, cooperation — these things cannot be submitted to any disciplinary regime. On the contrary, a certain kind of insubordination must be actively encouraged, in the very interest of productivity. And the possibilities of cooperation must be extended, so that everyone can cross the geographic, cultural and economic distances that separate the participants in a contemporary work group. Modern managerial technique consists in establishing a flexible framework for productive relations. Clearly, the paradigmatic framework for contemporary labor is the Internet. The advantage of such networked systems, for contemporary managers, is to isolate the individuals they link. Yet the ties of optical fiber are real, like the cooperation they encourage. And the establishment of this productive framework took networkers by surprise, because it allowed so much freedom. Now we see that this freedom is always associated with highly personalized control of the employees, via advanced techniques of surveillance. Everything that happens in the productive framework will also be surveilled, and the ideas, expressions and collective behaviors that prove harmful to the business will be repressed.

Between insubordination and surveillance, creativity and control, you have one of the internal contradictions of the new production regime. The fact that it puts thought to work guarantees the extension of the contradiction beyond the limits of salaried activity. As André Gorz writes in his recent book, *L'immatériel*: "The more work calls on talent, virtuosity, the production of the self... the more these capabilities tend to overflow their limited application to any determinant task." Therefore the worker "will locate his dignity in the free exercise of his capacities, outside of the working context: journalists writing books, ad designers creating artworks, computer programmers demonstrating their virtuosity as hackers and developers of free software, etc." One might feel tempted to laugh at this image of "ad designers creating artworks." The results have been mixed, to say

A Rift in Empire?

the least. We have seen an outpouring of collective narcissism, a facile idealization of expressivity and interactivity — particularly in the magazine–gallery–museum world, where "ad designers creating artworks" had their day in the sun, throughout the 1990s. But something seems to have changed since then.

The immaterial laborer who thinks, speaks and creates on the job, then finally leaves that job behind to practice a form of creative expression, very soon feels the fragility of her position. Nothing permits her to survive while doing what she had nonetheless been consistently encouraged to do. Reflecting on her own predicament, she can meet all kinds of people: similar individuals marginalized by the effects of the same contradiction, then many others who have never been fully integrated into the productive system. By making the comparison between one's own situation and those of others, one attains a broader understanding of contemporary social relations, with their hierarchies of inclusion/exclusion extending across the earth. A personal experience of marginality, of precarious labor conditions, can encourage all kinds of solidarities, near or far. This moment of politicization implies at least a partial exit from the productive framework imposed by capitalist management. What then becomes interesting is to continue putting thought to work. With this difference, that the work has become autonomous: it consists in weaving alternative networks, in view of solidarities and dissenting expressions.

It is at this point that the concept of the multitude can become doubly useful for the multitudes: as an ontological concept, and as a concept of class. As an ontological concept, the multitude indicates a plane of immanence where human singularities discover their fragile potential — that is, the possibility of developing their own individuation through cooperation with others. But as a class concept, the multitude points to everything that stands in the way of this development. That obstacle is Empire: i.e. the sum total of control techniques forged by the corporations and states. These control techniques come to bear on our flesh as *biopower*: the capacity to manage, channel and parasitically exploit the creative power of cooperating singularities. Today, biopower increasingly takes on the explicitly repressive forms of surveillance and the police. Not only will workers be surveilled on the job; but the entire population will also be surveilled, while moving through the open systems of transport, exchange and communication. And surveillance is necessarily followed by the police. For the multitudes of the movements against capitalist globalization, Imperial power has taken on the perfectly standardized face of the "robocops" who carried out the repression in Seattle, Nice, Gothenborg, Genoa, etc. But through the visor of the robocop, what we see — in addition to their eyes — is an organizational mutation that gives rise to the Imperial state.

Here I refer to the book by Bob Jessop, *The Future of the Capitalist State*. Jessop analyzes the paradigmatic shift from a Keynesian national welfare state, to a postnational Schumpeterian workfare state. What do these words mean? The contemporary state no longer cares about the "effective demand" of the workers, nor about any kind of Keynesian social insurance; its preoccupation is with encouraging entrepreneurial innovation, which for Schumpeter was a major source of surplus value. But this kind of innovation, necessary for competition, is done by a fairly small part of the population, marked by a strong tendency toward exit. They tend to leave the constraints of the productive system. As soon as people quit working, the state's problem is no longer that of their welfare; on the contrary, they must be pushed back into the most servile and exploited positions, by way of the coercive programs that Tony Blair calls workfare. The state takes on the role of a collective manager for the flexible labor force — an imperative role under the transnational regime of networked competition. Thus it becomes postnational, adapting to the extended frameworks of capitalist productivity. Yet like the economy it serves, this Imperial form of the state is not stable, or even viable. It is shot through with grotesque contradictions, whereby technical and organizational innovation, the new mainspring of capitalist competition, leads to the political rationality of unlimited war.

Here, to my mind, lies one of the greatest ironies of the current period. The multitudes, as Toni Negri has never ceased to explain, are incommensurable: their immaterial expressions and cooperative innovations are irreducible to the measure of labor time, and therefore to the hourly wage. This disproportion of the multitudes can be understood from several different angles. On the one hand, it translates the enormous creative potential of scientific knowledge, particularly as it accumulates in the form of technology: and how shall we evaluate the "productivity" of the finger that activates a machine? On the other hand, it brings the indeterminacy of esthetic experience into play at the very heart of social relations: and how shall we judge the "value" of different expressions? Thus work is uncoupled from wages, and tends to become autonomous. But throughout the 1990s, this uncoupling, this absence of any viable measure, acted in favor of

A Rift in Empire?

financial speculation, encouraging the most exaggerated valuations of certain sectors, notably where high technology is the vehicle of human expression. The irony lies here. The crash of the new economy in spring 2000 was followed by a general slowdown throughout the world, putting an end to the "roaring nineties." Shortly thereafter, in the face both of an inevitable recession and intense criticism over the conditions of his election, G. W. Bush took the September 11 terrorism and the state of exception it justifies as the ideal means to consolidate his shaky presidency — and more broadly, to realize the disciplinary vision of the American neoconservatives. For it is war, and no doubt war alone, that allows the state to impose its discipline on an autonomous labor force, after it has been mobilized and deceived by the untenable promises of a contradictory production regime.

So we come to the question: What is to be done? As soon as the US took the warpath toward the Iraqis and their oil, the multitudes reacted, overflowing all the bounds of political consensus, and infiltrating all the networks. In Europe the mobilizations were particularly strong: because people remember the 1930s, and they recognize the state of exception, the attempt to impose a new discipline. Great Britain saw the largest demonstration of its history; Italy and Spain were shaken by repeated mobilizations and direct actions; and France, Germany and Belgium translated public opinion into political opposition, within the arenas of the UN, NATO and the European Union. These dissensions at the heart of the political and military command are new: they mark a first step, a fragile chance to be seized. But can one really speak of a rift in Empire?

First, look at the reality: since the early 1990s, the European Union has increasingly become a distorted mirror of the United States. That is to say, a regional free-trade bloc built up according to the rules of Imperial competition. This neoliberal turn may be cloaked in social charters, but at this point, they count for very little. And the risk that appears with each bout of European chauvinism, whatever its pacifist or anti-American overtones, is that under its cover, countries like France, Germany and Belgium will form a falsely social-democratic center, constructed around a core of protected industries, armament above all — while living in reality off the exploitation of peripheries, internal or external. The danger is that the political class will use familiar hegemonic formulas to reinstate the existing hierarchies of inclusion/exclusion, but on a continental scale. These hierarchies, forged according to the old Fordist model, are protected at gunpoint today. And so France, Germany, Belgium and Luxembourg held meetings on April 29, 2003, to speak about founding a common military force. In the newspaper *Le Monde* of that same day, a text appeared under the title: "European Defense: Time to Take Action!" The authors were four CEOs from the European defense lobby — our familiar representatives.

Life is elsewhere. The politics of the multitudes consists in opposing the techniques of control, in escaping them — but in such a way that the production of this exodus is itself linguistic, cooperative, affective. What's interesting in the networked demonstrations is exactly that: what André Gorz called the "free exercise" of each one's creative faculties. But this self-organization is just a foretaste of deeper resistance. A real rift in Empire will require a transformation of the specific forms of redistribution and coercion put into operation by the state, and the creation of more viable frameworks for productive existence. We must dissolve the Schumpetarian postnational workfare state, which upholds unlimited competition and war. And that means carrying out political struggles on the measured ground of representative democracy, without forgetting that the power of the multitudes overflows all the borders. The challenge of the twenty-first century, in Europe and elsewhere, is to construct social infrastructure that can sustain the incommensurable — outside any technique of capture and control.

REFERENCES

"We Plebians," posted to the list-serves nettime and multitudes-infos, 19 February 2003.
Negri, Toni. "Pour une définition ontologique de la multitude," *Multitudes* 9, 2002.
Gorz, André. *L'immatériel: connaisssance, valeur et capital*, Paris, Galilée, 2003.
Virno, Paolo. *Grammaire de la multitude*, Paris, l'Eclat, 2002.
Jessop, Bob. *The Future of the Capitalist State*, Cambridge, Polity Press, 2002.

Appendix
Sovereign Police, Global Complicity:
Addressing the Multitude of Foreigners

Proposed by Naoki Sakai and Jon Solomon

The co-editors of this volume of *Traces* seek contributions that deal with the new political and cultural forms of complicity with constituted power occurring in the globally unified, statist space of today. "Sovereign Police, Global Complicity" aims to renovate the models of structure and system, class and center-periphery, and expose new metastructural forms adequate to the social practice of the multitudes (who are foreigners by definition, regardless of national-state identification) rejecting the gradual identification of Humanity with stateness in the age of global Empire.

We would like especially, but not exclusively, to call for contributions by authors who are not writing in their native language and furthermore not in English, yet who would write the text with regard to the problems of translation into both central and peripheral languages. Naturally, contributions in any of *Traces'* languages may be accepted.

The topics of this issue should focus on the political implication of new types of organization that exceed the boundaries of the national and the international, or detail the way in which nationalisms in different countries aid and abet each other. Topics eagerly sought for this issue include: inter-state police cooperation; international crime/illegal immigrant organizations; transnational courts of commercial law; conflicts of interpretation and juridical sovereignty; the role of U.N. organizations and their relation to individual states; the relation between

U.S. nationalism and global security; and finally the ways in which crude U.S. nationalism works in complicity with other forms of nationalism around the world.

It may assist authors to know that we pose the problem thus:

As sovereign power moves from an international order of class struggles within nation-states competing for territorial appropriation to a new kind of super "stateness" that lacks both a central republican body and the antagonisms of class or national interests resisting the unilateral logic of the market, we are faced with more and more institutions, for instance, those that deal with international commercial law, that are neither national nor international. This transnational stateness, motivated by a transnational, private, commercial understanding (as opposed to law, which must refer to a social body), pretends to produce a global civil society that would be a reign of law without the State. Since, however, there is no articulation of inter-individual to central contractuality, the reality is actually quite the opposite: a State without law. In this global state-without-law, the nature of sovereignty in its relation to the movements of the multitudes follows a logic of the police. Henceforth, the systemic struggle between center and periphery itself is aligned, or shall we say, complicitous, with the emergence of a super-state, or, quite simply, the identification of Humanity in general with Stateness. Indeed, today's wars, now launched in the name of Humanity, signal the coming of an age in which the meaning of Humanity itself has started to gradually coincide with Stateness.

The Gulf War set the precedent for global complicity with the order of sovereign police, now consolidated by the war in Afghanistan, in which the two figures of modern central order, imperialist and statist, converged. Although the U.N. arrogated to itself the ultimate right, that of war and legitimate violence, which had formerly exclusively defined the power of the sovereign state, it immediately divested itself of this power by granting the conduct of the war to a private force, that of the United States and its allies, which appropriated the power of the police, placing itself beyond jurisdiction.

Needless to say, the object of police operations is not an enemy, but an outlaw. Sovereign Police and the Foreign Outlaw: these are the fundamental figures of the political relation today. Our knowledge of this relation, however, instantly implies a third, equally crucial if less well understood, figure: Knowledgeable Bodies.

Appendix

It is well known that knowledge in the Human Sciences has been deeply intertwined with national sovereignty and language in the modern period. Hence, it is not enough simply to speak of structural complicity (such as that among elite classes who give extorted consent to the U.S. sovereign police while using anti-americanism as a tool to achieve their own ends) and systemic complicities (between national states and imperial organizations), but it is also necessary to speak of the kind of complicity found in the subjective technology of translation.

Translation is precisely the point of suture between the structural and the systemic in a world formally organized around the contradictory principles of market and sovereignty. If the revolutionary response to class struggle has been the proposition of equality-plus-liberty, the parallel response to the systemic struggle of inter-state competition must be the notion of human multitudes, the multitude of foreigners that I am.

Among the multitudes, however, one does not find a practice of address adequate to the multitude of foreigners that I am. Without such means, every discourse tends to fall back in the systemic logic of national translation, which aims to make every enunciation comprehensible on the basis of its presumed destination.

The co-editors of this special issue of *Traces* envisage making it into a social space where the multitudes can practice types of address alternative to those institutionalized by various disciplines in the Human Sciences and various communicational media in the world. Hence, our emphasis on the complicity of knowledgeable bodies takes the form of a call for manuscripts not written in my national language for my national audience.

What we are calling for in this proposed journal issue is neither a final accounting of nor a final solution to the problems of complicity. Approaches of this sort always bring us back to the aporetic imbrication between technology and ethics. Instead, we would rather choose to pose the problem of complicity in terms of an effect of sovereignty in the conjunctural moment when the essence of sovereignty has been revealed and the possibility of democratic thinking in terms of non-sovereignty has irrevocably opened. Understood as an effect of sovereign power, in which the excluded (and not the enemy) is the matrix of the political, complicity can be seen as an event, something that takes place — neither simply an atemporal ethical problem nor a challenge to economic administration, but a crisis inherent in the human appropriation of terrestrial space.

Submission Guidelines

Traces is published in Chinese, English, Japanese, and Korean. Each article accepted for publication is translated into all the languages of the series. In addition to the languages of *Traces* publication, submissions in French, German, Italian and Spanish are particularly encouraged.

All manuscript contributors for publication consideration should be submitted in triplicate to: *Traces: A multilingual series of cultural theory & translation*, 388 Rockefeller Hall, Cornell University, Ithaca, New York, USA 14853–2502, A manuscript for submission should be prepared, in the first instance, with endnotes and not footnotes. The entire manuscript should be *double-spaced* throughout, including endnotes and block quotations. The author's name, address and email should appear only on a detachable cover page and not anywhere else on the manuscript. This applies to endnote matters where reference may identify the author. A disk version of the manuscript must be provided in the appropriate software format upon acceptance for publication.

English language submissions should conform to the reference system set out in the *14th edition of The Chicago Manual of Style*, following the guidelines for endnotes and not footnotes. Examples of the preferred style may be consulted throughout this issue of the journal.

Submissions in languages other than English, please provide the following references in the order listed:

Books: Author's full name/Complete title of the book/Editor, compiler, or translator, if any/Series, if any, and volume or number in the series/Edition, if not the original/Number of volumes/Facts of publication — city where published, publisher, date of publication/Volume number, if any/Page number(s) of the particular citation.

Submission Guidelines

Chapter in a Book: Author's full name/title of the article/Title of the book/Full name of the editor(s)/Inclusive page numbers of the chapter in the book [follow the above guideline for Books, for the rest].

Article in a Periodical: Author's full name/Title of the article/Name of the periodical/Volume (and number) of the periodical/Date of the volume or of the issue/Page number(s) of the particular citation.

Unpublished Material: Title of the document, if any, and date/Folio number or other identifying number/Name of collection/Depository, and city where it is located.

Public Documents: Country, state, city, county, or other government division issuing the document/Legislative body, executive department, court, bureau, board, commission, or committee; Subsidiary divisions, regional offices, etc./ Title, if any, of the document or collection/Individual author (editor, compiler) if given/Report number or any other identification necessary or useful in finding the specific document/Publisher, if different from the issuing body/Date.

For all subsequent references to already cited reference: Author's last name/ short-title form/Page number.

Submission of an article implies that it has not been simultaneously submitted or previously published elsewhere. Authors are responsible for obtaining permission to publish any material under copyright. Contributors will be asked to assign their own copyright, on certain conditions, to *Traces*. For further guidelines, please contact the *Traces* office: <Traces@cornell.edu>.

Acknowledgment: Traces is receiving support from Hitotsubashi University, Japan Foundation, New York University, and the Dean of the College of Arts and Sciences, Asian Studies Department, and the East Asia Program at Cornell University.

TRACES PUBLISHERS

Traces Editorial Office
350 Rockefeller Hall
Cornell Univeristy
Ithaca, NY 14853-2502
USA
traces@cornell.edu
fax: +1.607.255.1345

Chinese:
Jiangsu Education Publishing House
31, Ma Jia Jie
Nanjing 210009
P.R.China
traces@1088.com.cn
tel: +86.25.3303497
fax: +86.25.3303457

English:
Hong Kong University Press
14/F Hing Wai Centre
7 Tin Wan Praya Road
Aberdeen, Tin Wan
Hong Kong
China
hkupress@hkucc.hku.hk
http://www.hkup.org
tel: +852.2550.2703
fax: +852.2875.0734

Traces Publishers

Japanese:
Iwanami Shoten
2-5-5 Hitotsubashi
Chiyoda-ku, Tokyo
Japan
tel: +81.3.5210.4000
fax: +82.3.5210.4039

Korean:
Moonhwa Kwahaksa
5–15 Chungjung-ro 2-ga,
Seodaemun-ku, Seoul
Korea
transics@chollian.net
tel: +82.2.335.0461
fax: +82.2.335.1239

www.ingramcontent.com/pod-product-compliance
Lightning Source LLC
Chambersburg PA
CBHW052044220426
43663CB00012B/2438